Other Books and Series by Jeff Bowen

Cherokee Intermarried White 1906 Volume I thru X

Applications for Enrollment of Creek Newborn Act of 1905 Volumes I thru XIV

Applications for Enrollment of Choctaw Newborn Act of 1905 Volumes I thru XX

Choctaw By Blood Enrollment Cards 1898-1914 Volumes I thru XX

Oglala Sioux Indians Pine Ridge Reservation 1932 Census Book I
Oglala Sioux Indians Pine Ridge Reservation Birth and Death Rolls 1924-1932 Book II

Census of the Sioux and Cheyenne Indians of Pine Ridge Agency 1896 - 1897 Book I
Census of the Sioux and Cheyenne Indians of Pine Ridge Agency 1898 - 1899 Book II

Northern Cheyenne Tongue River, Montana 1904 - 1932 Census 1904-1916 Volume I

Northern Cheyenne Tongue River, Montana 1904 - 1932 Census 1917-1926 Volume II

Identified Mississippi Choctaw Enrollment Cards 1902-1909 Volumes I, II & III

Sac & Fox - Shawnee Estates 1885-1910 (Under Sac & Fox Agency) Volumes I-VIII
Sac & Fox - Shawnee Estates 1920-1924 (Under The Sac & Fox Agency, Oklahoma) & Wills 1889-1924 Volume IX
Sac & Fox - Shawnee Deaths, Cemetery, Births, & Marriage Cards (Under The Sac & Fox Agency, Oklahoma) 1853-1933 Volume X

Visit our website at **www.nativestudy.com** to learn more about these and other books and series by Jeff Bowen

Portrait of Tecumseh from Lossing's
The Pictorial Field-Book of the War of 1812
is a pencil sketch drawn by Pierre Le Dru,
a young French trader at Vincennes, circa 1808.

Other Books and Series by Jeff Bowen

Compilation of History of the Cherokee Indians and Early History of the Cherokees by Emmet Starr with Combined Full Name Index
(Hardbound & Softbound)

1901-1907 Native American Census Seneca, Eastern Shawnee, Miami, Modoc, Ottawa, Peoria, Quapaw, and Wyandotte Indians (Under Seneca School, Indian Territory)

1932 Census of The Standing Rock Sioux Reservation with Births And Deaths 1924-1932

Census of The Blackfeet, Montana, 1897- 1901 Expanded Edition

Eastern Cherokee by Blood, 1906-1910, Volumes I thru *XIII*

Choctaw of Mississippi Indian Census 1929-1932 with Births and Deaths 1924-1931 Volume I
Choctaw of Mississippi Indian Census 1933, 1934 & 1937, Supplemental Rolls to 1934 & 1935 with Births and Deaths 1932-1938, and Marriages 1936-1938 Volume II

Eastern Cherokee Census Cherokee, North Carolina 1930-1939 Census 1930-1931 with Births And Deaths 1924-1931 Taken By Agent L. W. Page Volume I
Eastern Cherokee Census Cherokee, North Carolina 1930-1939 Census 1932-1933 with Births And Deaths 1930-1932 Taken By Agent R. L. Spalsbury Volume II
Eastern Cherokee Census Cherokee, North Carolina 1930-1939 Census 1934-1937 with Births and Deaths 1925-1938 and Marriages 1936 & 1938 Taken by Agents R. L. Spalsbury And Harold W. Foght Volume III

Seminole of Florida Indian Census, 1930-1940 with Birth and Death Records, 1930-1938

Texas Cherokees 1820-1839 A Document For Litigation 1921

Starr Roll 1894 (Cherokee Payment Rolls) Districts: Canadian, Cooweescoowee, and Delaware Volume One
Starr Roll 1894 (Cherokee Payment Rolls) Districts: Flint, Going Snake, and Illinois Volume Two
Starr Roll 1894 (Cherokee Payment Rolls) Districts: Saline, Sequoyah, and Tahlequah; Including Orphan Roll Volume Three

Cherokee Intruder Cases Dockets of Hearings 1901-1909 Volumes I & II

Indian Wills, 1911-1921 Records of the Bureau of Indian Affairs Books One thru *Seven*

Other Books and Series by Jeff Bowen

Native American Wills & Probate Records 1911-1921

Turtle Mountain Reservation Chippewa Indians 1932 Census with Births & Deaths, 1924-1932

Chickasaw By Blood Enrollment Cards 1898-1914 Volume I thru V

Cherokee Descendants East An Index to the Guion Miller Applications Volume I
Cherokee Descendants West An Index to the Guion Miller Applications Volume II (A-M)
Cherokee Descendants West An Index to the Guion Miller Applications Volume III (N-Z)

Applications for Enrollment of Seminole Newborn Freedmen, Act of 1905

Eastern Cherokee Census, Cherokee, North Carolina, 1915-1922, Taken by Agent James E. Henderson
    Volume I (1915-1916)
    Volume II (1917-1918)
    Volume III (1919-1920)
    Volume IV (1921-1922)

Complete Delaware Roll of 1898

Eastern Cherokee Census, Cherokee, North Carolina, 1923-1929, Taken by Agent James E. Henderson
    Volume I (1923-1924)
    Volume II (1925-1926)
    Volume III (1927-1929)

Applications for Enrollment of Seminole Newborn Act of 1905 Volumes I & II

North Carolina Eastern Cherokee Indian Census 1898-1899, 1904, 1906, 1909-1912, 1914 Revised and Expanded Edition

1932 Hopi and Navajo Native American Census with Birth & Death Rolls (1925-1931) Volume 1 - Hopi
1932 Hopi and Navajo Native American Census with Birth & Death Rolls (1930-1932) Volume 2 - Navajo

Western Navajo Reservation Navajo, Hopi and Paiute 1933 Census with Birth & Death Rolls 1925-1933

Cherokee Citizenship Commission Dockets 1880-1884 and 1887-1889 Volumes I thru V

Applications for Enrollment of Chickasaw Newborn Act of 1905 Volumes I thru VII

SAC & FOX - SHAWNEE MARRIAGES, DIVORCES, ESTATES LOG BOOKS VOLS. 1 & 2, LOG BOOKS BIRTHS & DEATHS

(UNDER THE SAC & FOX AGENCY, OKLAHOMA)

1846 - 1924
VOLUME XI

TRANSCRIBED BY
JEFF BOWEN
NATIVE STUDY
Gallipolis, Ohio
USA

Copyright © 2022
by Jeff Bowen

ALL RIGHTS RESERVED
No part of this publication can be reproduced
in any form or manner whatsoever
without previous written permission from the
Copyright holder or Publisher.

Originally published:
Santa Maria, California
2019

Reprinted by:

Native Study LLC
Gallipolis, OH
www.nativestudy.com

Library of Congress Control Number: 2022900261

ISBN: 978-1-64968-140-9

Made in the United States of America.

This series is dedicated to
Tanner Tackett
the Constant Gardner
and Friend
and
In memory of
Raina Mae Fulks.

Ab·sen·tee

noun: **absentee**; plural noun: **absentees**
>1. a person who is expected or required to be present at a place or event but is not.

>(According to Webster)

Shawnee

noun, plural Shaw-nees, (especially collectively) Shaw-nee.
>1. a member of an Algonquian-speaking tribe formerly in the east-central U.S., now in Oklahoma.

>(According to Dictionary.com)

Shawnee Teaching

"Tagi nsi walr mvci-lutvwi mr-pvyaci-grlahkv, xvga mytv inv gi mvci-lutvwv, gi mvci-ludr-geiv. Walv uwas-panvsi inv, wa-ciganv-hi gi gol-utvwv u kvgesakv-namv manwi-lanvwawewa yasi golutv-mvni geyrgi.

"Tagi bemi-lutvwi walr segalami mr-pvyaci-grlahkv, xvga mvtv inv gi bemi-lutvwv, gi bemi-ludr-geiv gelv. Wakv vhqalami inv, xvga nahfrpi Moneto ut vhqalamrli nili yasi vhqalamahgi gelv!"

Translation:

"Do not kill or injure your neighbor, for it is not him that you injure, you injure yourself. But do good to him, therefore add to his days of happiness as you add to your own.

"Do not wrong or hate your neighbor, for it is not him that you wrong, you wrong yourself. But love him, for Moneto loves him also as He loves you!"

Thomas Wildcat Alford
circa 1936

Special Note

You will notice throughout these volumes the author has attempted to duplicate from the original documents places on the page that were destroyed due to water damage. Whole sections of a page could be missing or torn into multiple pieces. In order to duplicate the damage you will find various shapes with a white format to try to represent the damage and the loss of the ability to completely transcribe many of the pages.

TABLE OF CONTENTS

Introduction	ix
MARRIAGES	3
DIVORCES	59
ESTATES LOG BOOK VOLUME 1-INDEX	67
ESTATES LOG BOOK VOLUME 1	71
ESTATES LOG BOOK VOLUME 2-INDEX	115
ESTATES LOG BOOK VOLUME 2	119
LOG BOOK RECORDS OF	
BIRTHS & DEATHS-INDEX	241
LOG BOOK RECORDS OF BIRTHS	247
LOG BOOK RECORDS OF DEATHS	287
INDEX	301

INTRODUCTION

The history of the Shawnee is fascinating. Naturally the most famous Shawnee known would be Tecumseh, born circa. 1768, after four other siblings before him. His father was Puckeshinwa, a Shawnee war chief from Ohio. Puckeshinwa crossed the Ohio close to what is now Gallipolis with his fourteen year son Chiksika by his side. As they followed the lead of Chief Cornstalk during the fall of 1774. Tecumseh's famous father was mortally wounded during the fight they would soon encounter. The Shawnees were unexpectedly discovered by a couple of early morning turkey hunters from the settlement called Point Pleasant. These hunters ran as fast as possible back to where the Ohio and Kanawha Rivers meet and sounded the alarm that the Shawnees were coming, the fight lasted most of the day but not without loss to both sides. The Shawnees were badly outnumbered. Pucheshinwa was carried back across the Ohio or as the Shawnees called it the *Spaylaywitheepi*, with the intention to take him back to his village. He must have known his time was short as he laid there telling Chiksika to make sure he devoted his time not only to Tecumseh's but also his younger brothers training in becoming warriors. Pucheshinwa succumbed to his wounds shortly after that request and was secretly buried deep in the forest that day. Chiksika saw his father mortally wounded while defending their home. He had a reverence for his father as a great warrior. He wanted to follow his father's path and not die an average death. In his heart, it had to be on the battlefield as a warrior. Tecumseh followed his brother's every step and planned to die defending his land as his father and brother had. There was no surrendering or giving in to the Americans.

There are several descriptions out there of Tecumseh from his contemporaries, but David Edmunds found one during his research that seems to be the most commanding of any found. "Captain John B. Glegg, Brock's aide-de-camp, who was present at the meetings between Brock and Tecumseh, recorded one of the most vivid descriptions of the Shawnee. According to Glegg, in August 1812 Tecumseh still was in the prime of his life, giving the impression of a man ten years younger. Tecumseh's appearance was very prepossessing; his figure light and finely proportioned; his age I imagined to be about five and thirty [he actually was forty four]; in height, five feet nine or ten inches; his complexion, light copper; countenance, oval, with bright hazle eyes, beaming cheerfulness, energy, and decision. Three small silver crowns, or coronets were suspended from the lower cartilage of his aquiline nose; and a large silver medallion of George the Third, which I believe his ancestor had received from Lord Dorchester, when governor-general of Canada, was attached to a mixed coloured wampum string, and hung around his neck. His dress consisted of a plain, neat uniform, tanned deer-skin jacket, with long trousers of the same material, the seams of both being covered with neatly cut fringe; and he had on his feet leather moccasins, much ornamented with work made from the dyed quills of the porcupine."[1]

There were approximately 39 years that passed between Tecumseh's and his father's deaths.

It is hard to believe that the Shawnee's history being as extensive as it was during the early stages of the United States that their descendants' records were so closely guarded under the care of a vegetable bind in an leaky attic. Not only the Shawnee's but also the Sac & Fox, the Pottawatomie and the Kickapoo. There are also many other tribal affiliates to be found in this series, not to mention someone like Jim Thorpe and his family members of the Sac and Fox tribe. Not only was he a gold metal Olympian and multiple sport competitor, but at the time one of America's favorite sons. Thank goodness someone was finally conscious of the situation. The description in the next paragraph explains the neglect of these important documents as given by the Oklahoma Historical Societies Microfilm Catalog.

"In 1933 a survey of Indian tribal records in Oklahoma revealed that the files of the Shawnee and the old Sac and Fox agencies had been sadly neglected, and the lack of space for storing them properly had resulted in much loss. Charles Eggers, Superintendent of the Shawnee Agency, reported that most of the non-current records of his agency were boxed in a storehouse. The papers of the old Sac and Fox Agency were in the loft of a warehouse which was also used for storing vegetables. The roof of the building leaked and the papers were in danger of destruction from moisture. Following the passage of the Congressional Act of March 27, 1934 (H.R. 5631 Public No. 133) which placed the tribal records in the custody of the Oklahoma Historical Society."

As described above the history of the Shawnee people isn't an ordinary history but an extraordinary time in all of our ancestors' lives. Reading Allen W. Eckert's extensive studies taken from what is known as the Draper Papers, a historical record meticulously documented beginning circa 1830. Though Draper covered an approximate time between the 1740's to the 1810's, his collection covered documents and transcriptions concerning Boone, Kenton, Rogers Clark and Joseph Brant, not to mention a considerable amount of Shawnee history from the entirety of the Ohio and Mississippi Valley's. Other authors such as Colin G. Calloway and R. David Edmunds provide an in depth study of the Shawnee people as well as Tecumseh and his life leaving no rock unturned in their research.

As you read different references you find diverse opinions on Tecumseh's mother as to what tribe she came from. Eckert through Draper's work says, "This was

---

[1] Tecumseh, R. David Edmunds Pg. 162-163, Para. 3-4

when Pucksinwah, then twenty-six, led the war party against the Cherokees that had resulted in the capture of Methotasa."[2] Indicating Tecumseh's mother might have been Cherokee. Yet, R. David Edmunds writes, "In 1768, while the Iroquois were selling Shawnee lands at the Treaty of Fort Stanwix, a Creek woman married to a Shawnee man gave birth to a son at Old Piqua, a Shawnee village on the Mad River in Western Ohio. The woman had a difficult labor before giving birth in the small lodge especially constructed for that purpose, some distance from the family's wigwam. The mother, Methoataske (Turtle Laying Its Eggs), had grown up among the Creek villages in Alabama and had met her husband when some of the Shawnee sought refuge among the Creeks during the 1750s. The father Puckeshinwa, remained with his wife's people until about 1760, when the family left Alabama and migrated to Ohio."[3]

You also will find different opinions on how they dressed back then or wore their hair. In Edmunds' book *Tecumseh*, his brother the Prophet Tenskwatawa states, "Warriors should again shave their heads and wear the scalp locks worn by their ancestors." And yet in Thomas Wildcat Alford's *Civilization*, he says, "We boys wore our hair short, very much as the girls of today wear their hair bobbed. This is the way Shawnee men always have worn their hair. Never did they braid it, as some other tribes do."

Alford's book *Civilization* out of the many resources read was likely one of the most informative and enjoyable references in the study. Thomas Wildcat Alford was born in 1860 and belonged to the Absentee Shawnee tribe. He states that he was a descendant of Tecumseh. He spoke about when his family slept under the stars each night and that he never had an English name until his father had him go to school at a Quaker mission. Mr. Alford also talks about two things with real clarity. Alford educates us about clans in the sixth chapter, expounding upon the active history of the Shawnees and the different responsibilities of each as well as divisions among the clans that created tribal changes. These dissensions were nothing new. Anyone that has read extensively about the Shawnee will realize that Alford understood his people and their history. When he wrote about tribal clashes or divisions during the early days, he managed to translate on paper their strength and character. He showed for generations they literally believed they were given an ability to make themselves self-reliant when it came to survival. They traveled far and wide following their own path while installing their own way of life that made them powerful adversaries whether it be against the British, the French or the Americans moving west. Other tribes found them to be awful enemies or potent allies. Then he compares their tribal government

---

[2] A Sorrow in Our Heart, Allen W. Eckert Pg. 22, Para. 3
[3] Tecumseh, R. David Edmunds, Pg. 17 Para. 1

and the clan leaders to being quite similar to the U.S. Presidency and the different government entities. Alford also brings up business committees for the tribe.

He starts with a concise description of the clans, "Originally there were five clans composing the Shawnee tribe, including the two principle clans, Tha-we-gi-la and Cha-lah-kaw-tha, from one of which came the national or principal chief. The remaining three, the Pec-ku-we, the Kis-pu-go, and the May-ku-jay, each had its own chief who was subordinate to the principal chief in national matters, but independent in matters pertaining to the duties of his clan. Each clan had a certain duty to perform for the whole tribe. For instance the Pec-ku-we clan, or its chief, had charge of the maintenance of order and looked after the celebration of things pertaining to religion or faith; the Kis-pu-go clan had charge of matters pertaining to war and the preparation and training of warriors; the May-ku-jay clan had charge of things relating to health and medicine and food for the whole tribe. But the two powerful clans, the Tha-we-gi-la and the Cha-lah-kaw-tha, had charge of political affairs and all matters that affected the tribe as a whole. Indeed, the tribal government may be likened to the government of the United States, in which each state (clan), with it governor (chief), is sovereign in local matters, but subordinate to the president of the United States (principal chief) in national matters. The difference is that the president of the United States must be elected, and may be changed with each election, while the principal chief came to his office by heritage and held it for life, or during good behavior.

At the time of which I write the Shawnee tribe had been divided for many years, and only the Tha-we-gi-la, the Pec-ku-we, and the Kis-pu-go clans were represented in the Absentee Shawnee band. These three clans always had been closely related, while the Cha-lah-kaw-tha and the May-ku-jay had always stood together, and were represented in the group that I have mentioned as living in Kansas at the time of the Civil War."[4]

As referenced earlier Thomas Wildcat Alford brought up their present Indian agent, Thomas, on September 13, 1893, wanting him to present a list of prominent men in their tribe to hold positions on a business committee. This presented a whole new world for the tribe with new pressures through white change so to speak. The government was instilling in their world the destruction of their heritage in tribal customs and culture all to control Indian land through allotment. When he was being told to help form this committee, he was actually being told, what we are doing is we are wiping out your way of life forever. The Congress of the United States was presenting the abolition of all tribal governments so the land could be manipulated through the Curtis Act of 1898. They said, we are splitting the land up. They were allotting so many acres to each tribal member. How much they got depended on

---

[4] Civilization, Alford; Pg. 44, Para. 1-2

whether they planned to farm or raise cattle. If they were building herds they were given double the land for grazing. Alford said, "It was on the thirteenth day of September, 1893 that Agent Thomas informed the Shawnees that he had been directed by the Commissioner of Indian Affairs to submit for approval the names of seven of the most prominent men of the tribe who would constitute a Business Committee to supersede the chiefs and councilors of the old tribal government. The Business Committee was to represent the Absentee Shawnees as a tribe in all dealings with the United States and to act in an advisory capacity to the individual members of the tribe. They were to certify to the identity of grantors of sales of land and to act for the tribe in other matters.[5]

During the study it was noticed that the Curtis Act being enacted on June 28, 1898 and Alford's mentioning its initiation during 1893 became a point of interest or at least premature. It was found that Congress had actually started working in this area of seizure approximately five years prior to the agent's notification, "In 1893 Congress began a special allotment process for the Five Tribes, enacting a number of laws that affect the governmental powers of the tribes. Some of these laws, like the 1889 and 1890 Acts, extended certain Arkansas laws over Indian Territory and expanded federal court jurisdiction; they are relevant today only insofar as they may indirectly affect tribal judicial powers."[6]

Their mention of these laws only being relevant today, though actually not spoken, plead plausible deniability while coinciding with the Indian Reorganization Act of 1934. The government was on a mission. Land and control. The allotment had to take place. They were wanting statehood. They were wanting the Native people to be under one umbrella with everyone else. Tribes were nations. Just like a foreign nation, they were their own government. Originally our constitution was modeled after the Iroquois model, had to start somewhere? So what we did was split up the land among the people that already owned it. Then we took what was left, approximately 90 million acres and sold it at a profit. Who got the money? Only the politicians at the time know? But years after taking the chiefs and councils away there was likely mass chaos like a town hall today. So the government likely was wanting out of the tribal control business. At least enough that they could just control it without being in the bullseye so to speak. Congress and the state had already achieved its goals. So this act was written with the statement that it was a model to make all think we do this for you. "The IRA was intended to provide a mechanism for the tribe as a governmental unit to interact with and adapt to a modern society, rather than to force the assimilation of individual Indians.

---

[5] Civilization, Alford; Pg. 161, Para. 2
[6] Federal Indian Law, Cohen; Pg. 781, Para. 3

The IRA was also an attempt to improve the economic situation of Indians. The Act was intended to stop the alienation of tribal land needed to support Indians, and to provide for acquisition of additional acreage for tribes. Tribes were encouraged to organize along the lines of modern business corporations; a system of financial credit was included to reach this economic objective."[7] Interestingly enough Cohen and Alford both mention this same organizational technique, only one as law and another as a tribal member.

It is disconcerting just in reading a reference from Senator Charles Curtis as he mentioned in his biography that by the time Congress finished rewriting the bill he had submitted he hardly recognized it. "Officially titled the "Act for the Protection of the People of Indian Territory", the Act is named for Charles Curtis, congressman from Kansas and its author. He was of mixed Native American and European descent: on his mother's side -Kansa, Osage, Potawatomi, and French; and on his father's - three ethnic lines of British Isles ancestry. Curtis was raised in part on the Kaw Reservation of his maternal grandparents, but also lived with his paternal grandparents and attended Topeka High School. He read law, became an attorney, and later was elected to the United States House of Representatives and Senate. He served as Vice-President under Herbert Hoover. In the usual fashion, by the time the bill HR 8581 had gone through five revisions in committees in both the House of Representatives and the Senate, there was little left of Curtis' original draft. In his hand-written autobiography, Curtis noted having been unhappy with the final version of the Curtis Act. He believed that the Five Civilized Tribes needed to make changes. He thought that the way ahead for Native Americans was through education and use of both their and the majority cultures, but he also had hoped to give more support to Native American transitions."[8]

The records within this series concern The Absentee Shawnee as well as many other people with different tribal affiliations. Also within these pages are closely related tribes that were under the same agency (The Sac & Fox Agency, Oklahoma) for many years like the Sac & Fox, the Pottawatomie and the Kickapoo. There are likely state recognized Shawnee tribes in the United States, but, "The Absentee Shawnee Tribe of Indians of Oklahoma (or Absentee Shawnee) is one of three federally recognized tribes of Shawnee people. Historically residing in the Eastern United States, the original Shawnee lived in the areas that are now Ohio, Indiana, Illinois, Kentucky, Tennessee, Pennsylvania, and other neighboring states. It is documented that they occupied and traveled through lands from Canada to Florida, from the Mississippi River to the eastern continental coast. In contemporary times, the Absentee Shawnee Tribe headquarters in Shawnee, Oklahoma; its tribal jurisdiction

---

[7] Federal Indian Law, Cohen; Pg. 147 Para. 1-2
[8] Curtis Act of 1898, Wikipedia

area includes land properties in Oklahoma in both Cleveland County and Pottawatomie County." [Today] "There are approximately 3,050 enrolled Absentee Shawnee tribal members, 2,315 of whom live in Oklahoma. Tribal membership follows blood quantum criteria, with applicants requiring a minimum of one eighth (1/8) documented Absentee-Shawnee blood to be placed on its membership rolls, as set forth by the tribal constitution. Though it is not a formal division, there is a social separation within its current tribal membership between the traditionalist Big Jim Band, which kept cultural traditions and ceremonies and has its primary populace in the Little Axe, Norman area, and the assimilationist White Turkey Band, which adopted European ways of the European majority, with many families based in the Shawnee area. Regardless of historical viewpoints, the bands cooperate for the future of the tribe."[9]

When this study was first pursued an old Xerox copy of a catalog that sat on the shelf for twenty five years was the first place searched for a viable source. It was titled, "Catalog of Microfilm Holdings in the Archives & Manuscripts Div. Oklahoma Historical Society 1976-1989". As mentioned in the description from this catalog's Introduction for the Sac and Fox Indian Agencies, it states, "In 1901 the Sac and Fox Agency was divided. The Sac and Fox Agency itself remained at the old site near Stroud with jurisdiction over the Sac and Fox and the Iowa. The Shawnee, Potawatomi and Kickapoo Agency (sometimes simply called the Shawnee Agency) was established about two miles south of Shawnee, Oklahoma. The agencies continued their separate existence until 1919 when they were merged becoming the Shawnee Agency.

Of course today in 2018, everything is digital and on the computer. You have to be thankful for having an old catalog and books on a shelf. There is nothing like the feel of holding a book in your hand. You can pick it up when you want and let your eyes travel to anywhere or any time in history. It has solid print that nobody can manipulate or change. It's just yours to wrap yourself up in without any glowing distractions as Native Americans call them, "Talking Leaves".

Jeff Bowen
Gallipolis, Ohio
NativeStudy.com

---

[9] Absentee-Shawnee Tribe of Indians Wikipedia

Sac and Fox-Shawnee – MARRIAGES
Undated and 1901 – 1922

Sac & Fox – Shawnee
1846-1924   Volume XI

DEPARTMENT OF THE INTERIOR

UNITED STATES INDIAN SERVICE

Seneca School, Quapaw Agency,
Wyandotte, Okla., May 4, 1914.

Mr. W. A. Eaheart,
   Clerk in Charge,
      Shawnee Indian School,
         Shawnee, Oklahoma.

My Dear Mr Eaheart:

    This is to acknowledge the receipt of your letter of the 29th ultimo making inquiry concerning Mary S. Zane.

    I have been informed that one Irven[sic] P. Zane, an Absentee Wyandot Indian of Kansas City, Kansas,.[sic]   Married a Pottawatomi Indian I am of the opinion Mary S. Zane was at one time his wife or possibly a daughter.

    I have written Mr. Zane, asking about this matter and as soon as I get a reply will inform you.

                  Very respectfully,
                  Ira C Deaver
                    Superintendent.

****

DEPARTMENT OF THE INTERIOR

UNITED STATES INDIAN SERVICE

Seneca School, Quapaw Agency,
Wyandotte, Okla., May 10, 1914

Supt. John A. Buntin,
    Shawnee Indian School,
        Shawnee, Oklahoma.

Dear Sir:

    There is enclosed herewith a letter from Mr. Irvin P. Zane of 1504 North 27th Street, Kansas City, Kansas, in answer to one

Sac & Fox – Shawnee
1846-1924 Volume XI

written to him concerning the location of Mary S. Zane, which is self explanatory.

I have made inquiry from a number of the old Wyandotte Indians but they do of know anyone by this name. There are a great many Zanes in the Wyandotte tribe but none of this name. Mr. Irvin P. Zane is an Absentee Wyandotte.

If this is not the Zane woman you are trying to find, I do not beleive[sic] that any of the Indians here know her.

Very respectfully,

Ira C Deaver

Superintendent.

****

[The letter below typed as given]

1914

Kansas City, Kan May 7th

Mr Ira C Deavers

Dear Friend

Your favor of May th 4st 1914 received   In which you enquire in regard to one Mary S. Zane from Shannee Oak. I dont know of any Mary S Zane   I do know one Sophia May Zane who was a member of the Citizin band of Pottowatomiy who was my former wife to which I am seperated for the past 23 years I have [illegible] children by her in which I have raised to womenhood and both married and are mothers their names are as fowlows Maud B Zane & Jennie M Zane. as to the whareabouts of their Mother it is impossible for me to say   the last time I hurd of her she was living with a man name of Sanderson at Okla City Okla as above stated she has had many allieses

Respectfuly yours

I. P. Zane

1504 North 27th St

K C K

Sac & Fox – Shawnee
1846-1924   Volume XI

CONGREGATIONAL INDIAN MISSION,
Darlington, Oklahoma,
R. H. HARPER, MISSIONARY.

Col. Geo. W. H. Stouch

Darlington.

Returns of Marriage.

DEPARTMENT OF THE INTERIOR
OFFICE OF INDIAN AFFAIRS
WASHINGTON, D. C., April 3, 1901.

To United States Indian Agents
and School Superintendents in Charge of Agencies

As is well known, an Indian who receives an allotment becomes thereby a citizen of the United States and his real estate descends to his heirs according to the laws of the State or Territory in which he resides. This, as well as other considerations, make it imperative that a reliable and permanent record of Indian family relations should be kept t every agency, and especially at agencies where the lands of the Indians have been or are soon to be allotted.

The following instructions are, therefore, promulgated:

1. On and after June 1, 1901, it shall be the duty of each Indian agent to keep a permanent register of every marriage which takes place among the Indians under his charge, said register to record the name of the husband and of the wife, both the Indian and the English name, if both names exist, and in the case of an allotted Indian the name by which said Indian is designated on the allotment roll; also the age, tribe, blood, nationality, or citizenship of both parties, the date of the marriage and the name of the person who solemnized it; or, if the marriage is by declaration before witnesses, the names of the witnesses. The record shall also include the names of the parents of both husband and wife.

2. Before marriage an Indian must obtain a license to marry, either of an agent or of the proper authorities, in compliance with the laws of the State or Territory in which such Indian resides.

3. United States Indian agents are hereby authorized to issue to Indians licenses to marry, which shall be issued without charge, and, so far as practicable, shall conform to the laws of the State or Territory in which the license was issued, and the license shall permit the parties to be married by a clergyman, or by a civil officer, or by declaring before witnesses their intent to live permanently together as sole husband and sole wife: *Provided*, That no Indian shall be permitted to marry a person of any other race except in the manner prescribed by the laws of the State or Territory in which such Indian resides. Each marriage license thus issued shall be entered in a permanent record kept at the agency where it is issued. And when an Indian, allotted or unallotted, receives a license to marry from a civil magistrate it shall be the duty of such Indian immediately to report such license to the agent for permanent record.

4. It shall be the duty of the one who solemnizes the marriage to send to the agency from which the license was issued a certificate giving the names of the persons married, the date of the ceremony, and the name and position of the one who performed the ceremony; or, if the marriage is by declaration, the certificate shall be signed by two witnesses, one of whom shall immediately return it to the agent.

5. No license to marry shall be given to an Indian who has a wife or a husband living from whom such Indian has not been divorced, and the taking by a married man or more than one wife or by a married woman of more than one husband shall not be allowed.

6. If an Indian shall be married on a reservation where such Indian has no tribal rights the agent for that reservation shall transmit to the agent for the reservation in which the Indian has tribal rights a copy of the license and certificate of the marriage of such Indian, and the agent receiving such copies, if he finds that the Indian designated therein has tribal rights at the agency under his charge, shall record the marriage in the register of marriages kept by him; otherwise he will return the copy to the sender with a statement of the facts.

7. It shall be the duty of each Indian agent to make a permanent record by families of all Indians under his charge. The record shall give the name of the husband and of the wife, both Indian and English, and the name of each on the allotment roll, with the date (approximately) of the marriage, and whether the ceremony was performed by a clergyman, civil magistrate, or by Indian custom; also, the names of their unmarried children, whether the fruit of exiting or former marriage. It shall also give, as to both parents and children, the age, tribe, blood, nationality, or citizenship, names of the father and mother (so far as they can be ascertained), and the relationship in the family as husband, wife, son, daughter, stepson, stepdaughter, or other relation. A widow or widower

with one or more unmarried children shall be recorder as a distinct family, and widows and widowers without unmarried children, all unmarried adults, and all minor orphans shall be recorded with the families with which they live, or by themselves if the live alone. If an Indian is living as husband with more than one woman the record shall give the name of each and the order of time in which he professes to have married them. If an Indian has been transferred from, or has tribal rights in another reservation, that fact shall be recorded.

8. Rations may be withheld from Indians who refuse to obtain proper marriage licenses or to give truthfully the information needed for the proposed records.

9. The purport of this circular should be explained to the Indians, and copies should be distributed among the clergymen and others in the vicinity of the reservation who are authorized by law to solemnize marriages.

10. A bonded superintendent of a school while in charge of an agency, and others who are duly authorized by the office, shall have the same authority and shall perform the same duties in regard to marriage records and licenses and the registration of Indians as are herein provided for duly appointed Indian agents.

It is the intention of this office to endeavor to obtain legislation which shall extend over Indian reservations the marriage laws of the State or Territory within which the reservation is located; but whether such legislation shall be immediately secured or not the records, etc., above provided for should be opened at once and kept up to date with the greatest care, since they will be most valuable if only for the purpose of determining the heirs to allotted lands. Agents should familiarize themselves with the marriage laws of the State or Territory and should endeavor to make the Indian familiar with these laws by conforming to them as nearly as practicable in carrying out these instructions.

As soon as they can be prepared, the following books and blanks will be sent to agencies:

1. Registers of licenses and marriages after June 1, 1901.
2. A register of all families.
3. Blanks for marriage licenses issued by the agent.
4. Blanks for certificates of marriage returnable to agent.
5. Blanks for certificates of marriage to be given to persons married.
6. Blanks for certificates of marriage to frame and hang in the home.

Any suggestions which you may wish to offer as to putting into operation the above-described system of registration of Indians and of issuing licenses and recording marriages will be welcomed by the office if submitted *immediately*, and will be carefully considered.

Sac & Fox – Shawnee
1846-1924   Volume XI

Respectfully,

W A. JONES,
Commissioner.

Approved:
E. A. HITCHCOCK,
Secretary.

L   D   M
Land-
Sales.
F I P

Circular #662.

DEPARTMENT OF THE INTERIOR
OFFICE OF INDIAN AFFAIRS
WASHINGTON

July 26, 1912.

Indian custom
marriages, etc.

To Superintendents:

In connection with the consideration of testimony in heirship matters, it becomes important to the Office to have some reliable basis on which to determine whether the alleged marriage, divorce, or adoption was according to the Indian custom of the tribe or tribes to which the parties belonged.

You are therefore requested to call together a few of the older representative members of the tribe or tribes and bands under your charge (preferably the full-blood Indian men and women), and obtain from them their version of what constituted the essentials of an Indian custom marriage between persons in the different social ranks of their tribe or band; also what forms, if any could be dispensed with without rendering the marriage invalid.

Similar information should be obtained concerning Indian custom divorces, the adoption of children and their inheritance rights after adoption, and such other observances as governed their social and family affairs up to the time when they became generally cognizant of their amenability to the civil laws of the State.

It is desirable also to have a statement showing what relation the Indians intend to express by the terms, "father," "mother," "brother," "sister," "son," and "daughter," and whether there are in there language any terms corresponding[sic] to our designation of the relationship of uncle and aunt, or cousin. It appears that in some tribes it was usual for a man to speak of his brothers' children as his own "sons" or "daughters" and for the children to address them as "father" and to speak of them thus. The failure of witnesses to distinguish, in their testimony, whether the relationship was the lineal one of parent and child, or the collateral one, termed in our language "uncle" and "nephew" or "neice[sic]," has frequently been a source of confusion.

To avoid errors in conclusions which the Office must form on the testimony submitted in inheritance cases, it is suggested that witnesses be required to set out plainly in what sense the terms "father," "son," etc., are used.

It appears that in some tribes the eldest daughter is known as Winona or He-nu-kaw, meaning "first born daughter" and the eldest son as "O-hi-ye-sa" or "He-nu-nic-kaw," etc. The second daughter and second son, and the third daughter and third son likewise have names which indicate the order of their births. Other names are given only to children of a chief. It has been of advantage in some instances to know the significance of the given names. You will therefore please interrogate the Indians on this point.

Each subject should be taken up separately and the different observances, as related by the Indians, should be briefly but plainly set out in your answer to this report. It is suggested that this be done by the 1st of September if practicable. If for any reason you should be unable to submit a report by that time, you will then so notify the Office and thereafter have the matter attended to as promptly as possible.

Respectfully,

C F Hauke

7-RFP-10

Second Assistant Commissioner.

Refer in reply to the following: L
33585 - 1886

Department of the Interior.

OFFICE OF INDIAN AFFAIRS,

Washington, January 12, 1887.

Moses Neal, Esq.,
    U.S. Indian Agent,
        Sac and Fox Agency, I.T.

Sir:-

Sac & Fox – Shawnee
1846-1924 Volume XI

Referring to your communication, dated December 14, 1886, relative to the case of E.A. Wiggins, an Oneida Indian, who is said to have married a Sac and Fox woman, but not in accordance with their laws, you are directed to inform Mr. Wiggins that unless he complies with the Sac and Fox laws as to marriage (which he can do by a re-marriage) he must remove from the reservation within a reasonable time. In case he refuses or neglects to comply with this order you will effect his removal.

Very respectfully,

J D C Atkins

Commissioner.

(Allen)

****

Washington

January 12 - 87

J.D.C. Atkins

Commr-

States that unless Wiggins marries according to the States laws put him off the Reserv.

****

Sac & Fox – Shawnee
1846-1924 Volume XI

Sac and Fox Agency, Ind. Ter., April 18th 18 90

Rev. Wm Hurr,
Sac & Fox Agency, I.T.

This certifys[sic] that one Pah-sha-shah-she Having complied according to provisions of the Sac and Fox Laws [Relation to Marriage the Sac and Fox Nation grants said Pah-sha-shah-she a "<u>License</u>" to marry one Waw-maw co in accordance to <u>Laws</u> of said Nation

Walter Battice
Secretary.

Apr 1 - 1876

<u>Know all men by their presents, that;</u> <u>John Gokey</u> and <u>Emma Keokuk</u>, both of Sac and Fox Agency, Indian Territory, did personally appear in an assembly of the people at the Sac and Fox Agency, and while standing, took each other by the hand, and the said, <u>John Gokey</u> acknowledged that he took the said <u>Emma Keokuk</u> to be his lawful and wedded wife, to be unto her a loving and faithful husband, until death: And she, the said <u>Emma Keokuk</u>, did in like manner, take the said <u>John Gokey</u> to be her lawful and wedded husband, to be unto him, a loving and faithful wife until death: whereunto they did, on the<u>, 2nd day of April, A.D. 1876,</u> sign their names: She, as is customary, adopting the name of her husband,.

John Gokey
Emma K. Gokey

And, we whose names are hereunto affixed, were present, and witnessed, the solemnization of the marriage of <u>John Gokey</u> and <u>Emma Keokuk</u>, as above set forth.

****

Sac & Fox – Shawnee
1846-1924   Volume XI

Know all men by their presents, that; John Gokey and Emma Keokuk, both of Sac and Fox Agency, Indian Territory, did personally appear in an assembly of the people at the Sac and Fox Agency, and while standing, took each other by the hand, and the said, John Gokey acknowledged that he took the said Emma Keokuk to be his lawful and wedded wife, to be unto her a loving and faithful husband, until death: And she, the said Emma Keokuk, did in like manner, take the said John Gokey to be her lawful and wedded husband, to be unto him, a loving and faithful wife until death: whereunto they did, on the, 2nd day of April, A.D. 1876, sign their names: She, as is customary, adopting the name of her husband,.

               John Gokey
               Emma K. Gokey

   And, we whose names are hereunto affixed, were present, and witnessed, the solemnization of the marriage of John Gokey and Emma Keokuk, as above set forth.

I hereby certify that the above marriage of John Gokey and Emma Keokuk was solemnized in my presence, this the 2 nd day of April, A. D. 1876.

               Levi Woodard
               U.S. Indian Agent.

****

<u>Marriage Certificate</u>

of

<u>John Gokey and Emma K. Gokey</u>.

Sac & Fox – Shawnee
1846-1924 Volume XI

1.

RECORD OF INDIANS IN LINCOLN COUNTY, OKLAHOMA, WHO HAVE BEEN MARRIED ACCORDING TO THE PROVISIONS OF ARTICLE 2, CHAPTER 23, LAWS OF 1897.

SAC & FOX INDIANS.

HUSBAND'S NAME.	WIFE'S NAME.	ALLOTMENT Subdivision.		DATE RECORD.		
Jack Bear, (Mishewalk)	Sarah Bear (Shequeme)	No. 2,	No. 3.	Aug. 24, 1897.		
Henry Jones, Sr.	Mellissa Jones,	" 6,	" 7.	"	"	"
Henry Jones, Jr.	Emma Jones,	No 9,	" -	"	"	"
Andrew Barker (Kechkoka)	Nora Barker (Kawhuck)	" 42,	" 43.	"	"	"
George Gokey,	Lizzie Gokey,	" 57,	" -	"	"	"
Samuel Brown (Wawasica)	Sissie Brown,	" 60,	" -	"	"	"
Isaac McCoy,	Mary McCoy,(Mahenahkah)	" "	" 72.	"	"	"
David Duncan (Kennotippe)	Lettie Duncan(Ahnakwenguah)	" 135,	" 136.	"	"	"
Leo Whistler (Athatwesknino)	Maude Whistler,	" -	" -	"	"	"
Isaac Goodell (Kishko)	Mary Goodell,	" 83,	" 81.	"	"	"
Thomas [?] Miles, M. D.,	Rhoda Miles,	" -	" 74.	"	"	"
Ulysis S. Grant (Makchepukqua)	Lydia Grant (Kopewequa)	" 180,	" 428.	"	"	"
Moses Keokuk,	Mary A. Keokuk,	" 260,	" 542.	"	"	"
Robert Falls (Kisholonkak)	Emma Falls (Wawkawpe)	" 269,	" 270	"	"	"
Jefferson Davis (Nishkahat)	Rachael Davis (Kekawsoque)	" 347,	" 348	"	"	"
Wm. Parkinson (Shawpallawke)	Maggie Parkinson(Kosequa)	" 329,	" 440	"	"	"
Webster Smith (Wawpeckohoe)	Martha Smith (Kewahawkoque)	-- ,	" 32.	"	"	"
Milton Carter (Chacakahtokehal)	Ella Carter (Wakhenlaw)	" 316,	" 317.	"	"	"
Samuel Johnson (Kahteywah)	Emily Johnson (Nawcawes)	" 234,	"235.	"	"	"
Frank Carter (Quahquakcheoth)	Louise Carter (PeElthew)	" 322,	" 323.	"	"	"
Henry Miller (Kahkayyah)	Mackkohequah Miller,	" 325,	" -	"	"	"
John A. Logan (Kewawtuk)	Hattie Logan (Mawnawquay)	" 330,	" 331	"	"	"
Alex Jefferson (Puckpounah)	Irene Jefferson,	" 403,	" 279	"	"	"
Joshua Givens (Wawsekahanah)	Gertrude Givens (Sawpequaw)	" 431,	" 432.	"	"	"
Tolbert White,	Roxie White,	" 541,	" -	"	"	"
Alex Conally[sic],	Liza Connally,	" 161,	" 266.	"	"	"

Sac & Fox – Shawnee
1846-1924 Volume XI

3.

RECORD OF INDIANS IN LINCOLN COUNTY, OKLAHOMA, WHO HAVE BEEN MARRIED ACCORDING TO THE PROVISIONS OF ARTICLE 2, CHAPTER 23, LAWS OF 1897.

IOWAS.

HUSBAND'S NAME.	WIFE'S NAME.	Allotment Subdivision.		Date of record.		
David Tohee,	Mary Tohee,	No. 44,	No.10.	Aug. 24, 1897.		
John Grant (Kathemenaw)	Mary Grant,	" 22,	" 23.	"	"	"
Benjamin Hollowell,	Nannie Hollowell,	" 38	" 39	"	"	"
Eliza White Kebolt (Pahthehuo-aheme)	Charles Kebolt,	" -,	" 54.	"	"	"
Victor Dupee,	Mary Dupee,	" 72,	" 73.	"	"	"
Frank Kent (Nawanoway)	Emma Kent (Nawanoway)	" 82,	" -	"	"	"
Abe Lincoln,	Maggie Lincoln,	" 84	" 85.	"	"	"

5

RECORD OF INDIANS IN LINCOLN COUNTY, OKLAHOMA, WHO HAVE BEEN MARRIED ACCORDING TO THE PROVISIONS OF ARTICLE 2, CHAPTER 23, LAWS OF 1897.

KICKAPOOS.

HUSBAND'S NAME.	WIFE'S NAME.	Allotment Subdivision.	Date of Record.
Noten,	Kuahquaquah,	No. 112, No. 113.	Aug. 24, 1897.

I, Darwin Filtsch do hereby certify that the foregoing is a true, full and correct copy of pages 1, 3 and 5, of the Indian Marriage Record, of Lincoln County, Oklahoma, which pages contain all the entries in said Record, now on record in my office.

Witness, this 9th day of May, 1914.   Darwin Filtsch
                                               Clerk of the County Court.

Sac & Fox – Shawnee
1846-1924 Volume XI

St. Mary's Kans.   March 6   1899

Contract of Marriage

On the 10th day Sept. 1871 I received the mutual consent of marriage between Joseph Asmidt and Teresa Fortier; before the witnesses John Lane and Joanna Pemami

M. Gailland SJ

The above is a faithful translation of the marriage record of Joseph Asmidt and Teresa Fortier as kept in the archives of the Immaculate Conception Church, St Marys, Kansas.

In witness thereof we affix our signature and append our seal

J.P. [Illegible] SJ

Refer in reply to the following:
Land
43717-1899

Department of the Interior.

OFFICE OF INDIAN AFFAIRS

WASHINGTON,   Jan. 8, 1900.

Lee Patrick, Esq.,

   U. S. Indian Agent,

      Sac and Fox Agency, Okla.

Sir:

~~At the suggestion of Special Agent Taggart in his report of September 9, 1899~~, your attention is invited to the act of the legislature of Oklahoma Territory of March 12, 1897, respecting Indian marriages and divorce, and to the matter of the business committees of the

Sac & Fox – Shawnee
1846-1924 Volume XI

Pottawatomie and Absentee Shawnee Indians, certifying as to wives and husbands. You are instructed as members of each committee, hereafter, to incorporate in your certificates, accompanying deeds of conveyance, whether or not the vendor is a <u>lawfully</u> married person, and if so, whether married by Indian custom or otherwise, and when so married; and whether or not said vendor had another wife living at the time of the execution of such deed of conveyance, and whether said vendor was separated by Indian custom or by legal divorce proceedings, and when; and when married to present wife and whether by Indian custom, or otherwise, <u>giving dates in every case</u>.

These business committees should be impressed with the necessity of at once preparing and completing a perfect record of all the families in their tribe, showing names and ages of husband and wife, dates of marriage, how and by whom married, names and dates of birth of all children and of their parents, and dates of death where any have died, in fact as complete a record of family affairs as it is possible for them to make and keep up.

The importance of these Indians being regularly married and of keeping a record of same, and of getting divorces in the courts when separating, is fully set forth in the act of 1897, and should be enforced upon them and by them.

Very respectfully,
WA Jones
Commissioner.

R. F. T. (B)

Sac & Fox – Shawnee
1846-1924   Volume XI

THE PROBATE COURT,
LINCOLN COUNTY.

REGULAR TERMS BEGIN ON THE FIRST MONDAY
IN JANUARY, MARCH, MAY, JULY, SEPTEMBER,
AND NOVEMBER.

W. L. HARVEY, Judge.

Concurrent Jurisdiction with the District
Court in civil matters to the extent of $1,000.

CHANDLER, Okla.,   July 26, 1900.

Hon. W^m R Gulick
   Actg US Ind. Agent
      Sac & Fox Agency, Okla.
Dear Sir:

    In the matter of the charge against Jackson Ellis for seduction. Complaint having been filed and defendant appearing in Court. The suit was settled and an order authorizing the marriage of Jackson Ellis and Ruth Grayeyes issued.

Parties were married by me today and certificate of marriage delivered to said Jackson Ellis.

               Yours Truly
                 WL Harvey
                    Probate Judge

[Transcription of Marriage License on page 18]
Duplicate
MARRIAGE LICENSE.

	MAN.	WOMAN.
ENGLISH NAME	Alex Jefferson	Sarah Harrison
NAME ON ALLOTMENT ROLL	"	Sarah Carter
AGE	26	24
RELATIONSHIP TO EACH OTHER	none	none
BLOOD OR NATIONALITY	Sac & Fox	Sac & Fox
TRIBE OR CITIZENSHIP	"	"

THEY WISH TO BE MARRIED

1. By a clergyman / civil magistrate in accordance with the laws of this State or Territory

2. By declaring (in the presence of adult witnesses, who shall sign the certificate) their intention to live together permanently as husband and wife.

WITNESS MY HAND, this 6th day of October, 1902.

        Name, S. A. Cordell
        Official designation, Judge of Probate Court

Sac & Fox – Shawnee
1846-1924   Volume XI

No. of License _____   RETURN OF MARRIAGE.

I, We, hereby certify, That _____ Alex Jefferson _____ and _____ Sarah Harrison _____, known by me/us to be the persons described in the above license, were married by me in our presence on the __1st__ day of __November__, A.D. 190 2, at __Sac & Fox Agency__, in the State/Territory of __Oklahoma__ in compliance with the laws of said State or Territory. by declaring in our presence their intention to live together permanently as husband and wife.

WITNESSES: Name _____ William Hurr _____
_____ W R Gulick _____ Official designation _____ Minister _____
_____ Joshua Herron _____ Address _____ Sac & Fox Agency O.T. _____

****
[Copy of original Marriage License]

Department of the Interior.

BOARD OF INDIAN COMMISSIONERS.

Washington, D.C., November 18, 1902

Ross Griffin
   Sac and Fox Agency
      Oklahoma Territory.

Dear Sir:

      Let me thank you for your full and interesting reply to our recent letter of inquiry as to the condition of allotted Indians, etc., at the agency under your care. I note with especial interest the emphasis you put (in what you write,) upon family life, and marriage among the Indians. Can you, without too much trouble, send to me a copy of the statute of your territory approved March 12, 1897, which legalizes marriage and divorce by Indian custom prior to that date, and further provides for the descendants of Indians who have been thus married:

      Yours very truly,

      Merrill E. Gates

****

Department of the Interior.

BOARD OF INDIAN COMMISSIONERS.

Washington, D.C., November 28, 1902

Ross Griffin
   U. S. Indian Agent

Dear Sir:

      Your letter of the 22nd is before me. I wish to thank you for sending the statute regarding Indian marriages.

      Yours very truly,

      Merrill E. Gates
        Secretary.

Sac & Fox – Shawnee
1846-1924   Volume XI

(TO BE GIVEN TO APPLICANTS FOR LICENSE TO MARRY.)

MARRIAGE LICENSE.

No. _____

Sac & Fox _____ Agency.

Okla _____ State or Territory.

License is hereby issued for the marriage of the following persons:

	MAN.	WOMAN.
INDIAN NAME		
ENGLISH NAME	Harry Hall	Jennie Bigwalker
NAME ON ALLOTMENT ROLL	"	"
AGE	37	24
RELATIONSHIP TO EACH OTHER	none	none
BLOOD OR NATIONALITY	Sac & Fox	Sac & Fox
TRIBE OR CITIZENSHIP	"	"
NAME OF FATHER		John N. Bigwalker
NAME OF MOTHER		Sarah Bigwalker
PREVIOUS MARRIAGE		

THEY WISH TO BE MARRIED

1. By a ~~civil magistrate~~ clergyman in accordance with the laws of this ~~State~~ or Territory

2. By declaring (in the presence of adult witnesses, who shall sign the certificate) their intention to live together permanently as husband and wife.

WITNESS MY HAND, this __10th__ day of __March__, 190 3

Name, __S. A. Cordell__

Official designation, __Probate Judge__

No. of License _____

RETURN OF MARRIAGE.

~~I,~~ We, hereby certify, That __Harry Hall__ and __Jennie Bigwalker__, known by ~~me~~ us to be the persons described in the above license, were married ~~in our presence~~ by me on the __10th__ day of __March__, A.D. 190 3, at __Sac & Fox Agency__, in the ~~State~~ Territory of __Oklahoma__ in compliance with the laws of said State or Territory. by declaring in our presence their intention to live together permanently as husband and wife.

WITNESSES:

__W R Gulick__

__Mary Antoine__

Name __William Hurr__

Official designation __Minister__

Address __Sac & Fox Agency__

Okla.

****

Sac & Fox – Shawnee
1846-1924   Volume XI

No. of License _____   **CERTIFICATE OF MARRIAGE.**

I hereby certify, That on this __10th__ day of __March__, 190 3, at __Sac & Fox Agency OT__, the following persons were ~~before us~~ by me united in marriage:

__Harry Hall_____, also known as _____

of the _____Sac & Fox_____ tribe _____Sac & Fox_____ agency,

AND

__Jennie Bigwalker_____, also known as _____

of the _____Sac & Fox_____ tribe _____Sac & Fox_____ agency,

in accordance with license No. _____, issued by __Judge S.A. Cordell__

The Marriage was witnessed by-   *Name* __Rev. Wᵐ Hurr__

__W R Gulick__   *Official designation,* __Minister__

__Mary Antoine__   *Address* _____

(TO BE DELIVERED TO THE PERSONS MARRIED.)

(TO BE GIVEN TO APPLICANTS FOR LICENSE TO MARRY.)

No. _____   MARRIAGE LICENSE.

_____Sac & Fox_____ *Agency.*

_____Okla_____ *State or Territory.*

License is hereby issued for the marriage of the following persons:

	MAN.	WOMAN.
INDIAN NAME		
ENGLISH NAME	George W Pattock	Eunice Hawk
NAME ON ALLOTMENT ROLL		
AGE	44	64
RELATIONSHIP TO EACH OTHER	none	none
BLOOD OR NATIONALITY	Sac & Fox	Sac & Fox
TRIBE OR CITIZENSHIP	"	"
NAME OF FATHER		
NAME OF MOTHER		
PREVIOUS MARRIAGE	none	widow

THEY WISH TO BE MARRIED

1. By a clergyman / ~~civil magistrate~~ in accordance with the laws of this State / ~~Territory~~

2. By declaring (in the presence of adult witnesses, who shall sign the certificate) their intention to live together permanently as husband and wife.

Sac & Fox – Shawnee
1846-1924   Volume XI

WITNESS MY HAND, this **4th** day of **April**, 190 **3**

Name, **William Hurr**
Official designation, **Minister of the Gospel**

No. of License _____   **RETURN OF MARRIAGE.**

I, ~~We~~, hereby certify, That **George W. Pattock** and **Eunice Hawk**, known by ~~us~~ me to be the persons described in the above license, were married ~~in our presence~~ by me on the **4 th** day of **April**, A.D. 190 **3**, at **Sac & Fox Agency**, in the ~~State~~ Territory of **Oklahoma** in compliance with the laws of said State or Territory.

by declaring in our presence their intention to live together permanently as husband and wife.

WITNESSES: Name **William Hurr**

W R Gulick   Official designation **Minister of the Gospel**

Mary Antoine   Address **Sac & Fox Agency**

                                                          O.T.

****

No. of License _____   **CERTIFICATE OF MARRIAGE.**

I hereby certify, That on this **4th** day of **April**, 190 **3**, at **Sac & Fox Agency OT**, the following persons were by me before us united in marriage:

George W Pattock, also known as _____,

of the **Sac & Fox** tribe _____ agency,

A N D

Eunice Hawk, also known as _____,

of the **Sac & Fox** tribe _____ agency,

in accordance with license No. _____, issued by **S.A. Cordell Probate Judge**

The Marriage was witnessed by-   Name **William Hurr**

W R Gulick   Official designation, **Minister of the Gospel**

Mary Antoine   Address **Sac & Fox Agency**

                                                          O.T.

(TO BE DELIVERED TO THE PERSONS MARRIED.)

Sac & Fox – Shawnee
1846-1924   Volume XI

[The following letter is badly smudged and is typed as given.]

Sugar Grove, Ark

[Illegible] 1904

Mr. W.C. Kohlenberg

[Illegible]

I read your letter [illegible...] will say and make [illegible...] right. I could send [illegible] our Marriage Certificate and I guess it is not necessary. We was married at the Court House at Stillwatter, Okla [illegible...] We both lived in Payne Co. We was married by R. J. Basel. Witnesses John S. Hale   O.W. Annis
on the 24 March 1897,
Now if that is not satisfactory let me know at once and I will send papers to you   I dont want to get our Certificate soiled and please see about my mothers lease money and divid it amongst us all. They had ought to be [illegible] of it

Yours truly
Julia [Illegible]
&
G. G. [Illegible]

F. W. MILLER
JUDGE OF PROBATE
COWLEY COUNTY, KANSAS

RECEIVED FRED KEITHLY
SEP 11 1906 CLERK
SAC & FOX AGENCY,
OKLAHOMA.

WINFIELD, KANSAS_____September 10,_____190 6.

Sup't. A. Spl. Disb. Agt.,

Sac and Fox Agency, Oklahoma.

Dear Sir:

We cannot find any record in this Court showing the marriage of Carl Eaves and Lillie Carter (nee Greyeyes). I have looked this over carefully once before for some person. If the license was procured from this Curt, there has never been any record made of it.

The records of the office were not very well kept at that time and they may have failed to ever put it on record. We went back and checked to see if it might be they failed to index but can find nothing of it.

Yours respectfully,

F. W. Miller
Probate Judge.

DEPARTMENT OF THE INTERIOR

UNITED STATES INDIAN SERVICE

Sac and Fox Agency, Oklahoma,

December 1, 1906.

Hon. Sam Smith,

    Probate Judge,

        Payne County,

            Stillwater, Oklahoma.

Dear sir:

    I am advised that Jake Dole and Millie Tohee (alias Amelia Falk, Amelia Tohee, etc) were recently married at your office. Both are Iowa Indians, and Jake now requests that he be given the management of his estate on account of having been married. Will you kindly advise me if it is a fact that they were married, and oblige me. Envelope for reply is inclosed.

Very respectfully,
W.C. Kohlenberg
Supt. & Spl. Disb. Agt.

Encl. Env.

12/5   06

We have issued no license for the parties names.

Samuel Smith,
Probate Judge

Sac & Fox – Shawnee
1846-1924   Volume XI

[The following two letters typed as given]

| U.S. INDIAN AGENCY |
| RECEIVED |
| DEC 19 1907 |
| Ans Mch Vol 11 p 153 |
| SHAWNEE, OKLA. |

The Indian Matrimonial Agency
      Tecumseh Okla

I see your ad in regards of Indian maidens wishing to find suitable husbands in white men. As I am not thourghly acquainted in this matter I desire very much to have you write me giving the parcictlars be. I stand ready to give the very best of references hopeing to hear from you in a pivit letter I beg to remain yours
                                    Resp
      add- T.J. Cloud
        #128 West 3rd St
            Oklahoma City
                Okla

****

Oklahoma City, Okla,   12 - 21 - 1907

| U.S. INDIAN AGENCY |
| RECEIVED |
| DEC 23 1907 |
| Ans Mch Vol 11 p 193 |
| SHAWNEE, OKLA. |

            U.S. Indian Agency
              Shawnee Okla.

Mr. Frank A. Thackery
                  Dear Sir

Your letter just rec- in answer to my letter of recent date - add- to the Indian Matrimonial age- Tecumseh Okla. and in answer to your letter I beg to acknowledge the receipt of same and I thankfully accept the information it imparts. at the same time I beg the privilege of asking for some information on the subject. in the first place I only answered the advertisement as requested to do so feeling ashoured that it was an honorable advertisement and was carried on in a legitment way and now I ask of you if there does exist an honorable agency of that kind if so I would be glad to be informed of sutch for this reason only. if there should appear again an advertisement of that kind I would know how to treat it. I ashoure you I am an honest sober and a hard working man. I am a cabinet maker by trade and I am never without work have all ways found plenty to do. I can and will give you the very best of reference in regards of my entegrity hope to hear from you soon. I beg to remain yours Resp.
            128 W. 3rd St.   T. J. Cloud
            Oklahoma City
                Okla.

Sac & Fox – Shawnee
1846-1924 Volume XI

Ex-Judge Fifth Judicial District of Nebraska

ROBERT WHEELER,
Attorney and Counselor

Telephone { Office, No.2 / Residence, No.119

RECEIVED
JAN 6 1909
SAC & FOX AGENCY,
OKLAHOMA

Tecumseh, Okla. Jan. 4/09.

Hon. W. C. Kohlenberg,

Sac and Fox Agency, Okla.

Dear Sir:-

Can you give me the date, or about the date when Tecumseh Sherman and Dollie Sherman were married under the indian[sic] custom. I suppose some of your records will show this, or show when she first drew money as Dollie Sherman.

I would like this information before Saturday the 9, inst. as there is a matter pending in court here, and to come up for hearing on that date in which this information is very important.

Yours very truly,

Robert Wheeler.

State of Oklahoma,
        ss.
County of Lincoln.

RECEIVED
MAR 1 1909
SAC & FOX AGENCY,
OKLAHOMA

A F F A D A V I T.

Pansy Jones, being first duly sworn, upon her oath states that she is the lawfully wedded wife of Arthur Clarke Jones; that she and the said Arthur Clarke Jones were legally married and have not been divorced; hat the said Arthur Clarke Jones, her husband, has deserted her; That her said husband has for a long time past wholly failed and refused and still fails and refuses to live with or support this affiant; That on the <u>27th</u> day of February, 1909, this affiant gave birth to an infant girl, the lawful issue of the said Arthur Clarke Jones; That this affiant has named the said infant "Naoma Mildred Jones" That this affiant is wholly without means to support the said infant at this time.

Sac & Fox – Shawnee
1846-1924 Volume XI

Mrs Pansy Jones
Affiant.

Subscribed and sworn to before me this 27th day of February, 1909.

[Name Illegible]
Notary Public.

Commission expires the _7_ day of __May__, 19_12_.

[The letter below typed as given]

Shawnee Okla.
Oct 12 - 09

Mr Frank Thackery
Sir

I am sorry that I could not bring Gertrude over to work for you Aaron had her before I knew. They was going to get married She didnt let me know any thing about it I havn't seen her since last Thursday I think that Aaron Wilson aught not do that Some thing aught to be done to him Nellie is coming over to see you about this

Yours Respt   James

DEPARTMENT OF THE INTERIOR
UNITED STATES INDIAN SERVICE

RECEIVED
NOV 3 1909
SAC & FOX AGENCY,
OKLAHOMA.

Otoe, Okla., Oct. 30, 1909.

W. C. Kohlenberg,
    Supt. Sac & Fox School,
        Sac & Fox Agency, Okla.
My dear Mr. Kohlenberg:-

        Can you furnish me with a record of the marriage of Jennie Roubideaux to Tom Lincoln or advise me as to whether such is procurable and if so where. If you can advise me in any way as to the present status of such union it will be much appreciated.

Yours very respectfully,
Ralph P. Stanion
Supt. & S.D.A.

Sac & Fox – Shawnee
1846-1924   Volume XI

JENNIE PICKERING
COUNTY STENOGRAPHER

P. D. MITCHELL, JUDGE

RECEIVED
NOV 23 1910
SAC & FOX AGENCY,
OKLAHOMA.

LULU M REGNIER, CLERK

County Court
Payne County

Stillwater, Okla.   Nov. 14, 1910

Mr. W. C. Kohlenberg
   Sac & Fox Agency, Okla

    Dear Sir:- I am sending you a copy of marriage license and certificate of Henry Hall and Sarah Harris you call for Harry Hall's marriage but I think possible that Henry and Harry Hall are the same.

    I should have answered sooner but the clerk failed to find the record and I wanted to go through[sic] there myself

                Yours truly

                    P.D. Mitchell

****

R. C. GREEN, CLERK

GEO. E. SMITH, STENOGRAPHER

RECEIVED
NOV 14 1910
SAC & FOX AGENCY,
OKLAHOMA.

REGULAR TERM BEGINS ON THE FIRST MONDAY IN JANUARY, APRIL, JULY AND OCTOBER

Pottawatomie County Court

E. D. REASOR, JUDGE

CONCURRENT JURISDICTON[sic] WITH THE DISTRICT COURT IN CIVIL MATTERS TO THE EXTENT OF $1,000.
IN ALL CRIMINAL OTHER THAN CRIMES INFAMOUS.

             Tecumseh, Oklahoma.   11/11/10.

Mr. W. O. Kholenberg[sic],
Sac and Fox Agency, Oklahoma,
Dear Sir:--

    Replying to yours of the 7th inst. I desire to say that after a perusal of the Marriage Records of this office I find that the same fail to show the issuance of a license to Harry Hall (Ne-paw-ko-nah-whah) and Sarah Harris back as far as 1907.

    Hoping this will be satisfactory, I am yours,

                Respectfully,

                    <u>Felix J. Saxon</u>
                    Exo. Clerk Co. Court.

          ****

Sac & Fox – Shawnee
1846-1924   Volume XI

[The letter below typed as given]

RECEIVED JAN 13 1911
SAC & FOX AGENCY, OKLAHOMA.

Cushing Okla
Jan. 10, 1911

Mr. W. C. Kohlanberg

Dear agent

have you bin able to find out when and where Sarah Harris & Harry Hall was married or whether they was ever married atall acording to Law.. and have you heard any thing more from that Deed we are thinking of protesting that Deed if it is not here soon what do you think a bout that. would you or note we aim to be fore long. we will see right a way.   Yours truly
let me have your advice.   G. T. Brown

DEPARTMENT OF THE INTERIOR

RECEIVED JUL 26 1911
SAC & FOX AGENCY, OKLAHOMA.

UNITED STATES INDIAN FIELD SERVICE

Otoe Agency, Otoe, Okla., July 24, 1911.

W. C. Kohlenberg, Supt. & S.D.A.

Sac & Fox Agency, Okla.

Dear Sir:-

Will you kindly advise me as to what the record of your office show in reference to the death of Mary Squirrel, the date of the marriages between such decedent and Thomas Lincoln and Robert Small and the dates of the births of Jack Lincoln and Edward Small. If you can will you advise me as to the dates of the marriages and divorces of the decedent & greatly oblige.

Very respectfully,
Ralph P. Stanion
Supt. & S.D.A.

Mary Small nee Squirrell[sic] died Jan 4, 1904
Jack Lincoln   July 4, 1895
Edward Small March 8, 1898

Sac & Fox – Shawnee
1846-1924   Volume XI

[The affidavit below typed as given.]

Shawnee, Okla.

AFFIDAVIT.

RECEIVED
AUG 15 1911
SAC & FOX AGENCY,
OKLAHOMA.

STATE OF OKLAHOMA) ss
COUNTY OF POTTAWATOMIE.

Mrs Irene Wright, being first duly sworn by me, ulon oath says that she was never married to John Hutchinson, that she was ingaged to be married to him and found out he had a living wife.

She also further states upon oath that she is now legaly married to Earnest Wright, was married at Seminole City Seminole County on the Eleventh (11) Day of November 1910.

Also liveing one mile south of main street on Harrison ave- Shawnee oklahoma. My husband buisness is Farming. We are living by our selves

Were married by a preacher in Seminole, did not ask him his name.

Subscribed and sworn to before me this the
Fourteenth day of August 1911.

_____Irene Wright_____

My commision expires January 18th 1913.

_____[Name Illegible]_____
Notary Public.

I will state for her benefit that her Mother came before me and gave her consent for her to marry Earnest Wright, on November 10th 1910.

_____[Name Illegible]_____

Dallas, Texas
10 – 6 – 11

Hon J A Buntin
  U.S. Indian Agent,
    Shawnee, Okla
My friend:-

Just wanted to inform you of my marriage to Miss Beulah Terry of Hugo, Okla which took place at Paris, Tex, some few days ago. We are visiting here.

We are going to make our house at Hugo, Okla in the near future

Sac & Fox – Shawnee
1846-1924   Volume XI

  I would like to have you call the attention to the Department in regard to the removal of the restriction from the remainder of my land as I want to improve it and live on it.
  In regard to the lease made with Lewis Wantland of Purcell, will say I want it cancelled.
    Trusting to hear from you soon, I am, respectfully,
          C.W. Bradley
  Address
    2219 Five Oak St
    Dallas, Tex.

W. B. CROSSAN   D. REPLOGLE

CROSSAN & REPLOGLE
ATTORNEYS-AT-LAW
OFFICE IN OKEMAH BANK BLDG.

        OKEMAH, OKLA., Nov. 22, 1911.

W. C. Kohlenberg Esq.,
  Stroude[sic], Okla.
Dear Sir:-
  About 1895 a pottawatomie[sic] Indian died at the Sac and Fox agency By the name of Joseph Bennett. His allotment near Shawnee was sold and conveyed by Marry Bennett as his widow and only heir, which deed was approved by the Depertment[sic] of the Interior.
  There is now some question raised as to whether she was in fact his wife.
  Will you kindly inform me if your records there show any thing concerning Joseph Bennett, and especially as to whether Mary Bennett was his wife. He died living very near an old ministers by the name of Wm. Herr and some of the indians[sic] here think he married them. If he has left any record will you please examine it.
  Any information you can give me in this matter will be highly appreciated and if there is any charge send me your bill.

         Very truly yours.
              W.B. Crossan

RECEIVED
NOV 22 1911
SAC & FOX AGENCY,
OKLAHOMA.

Sac & Fox – Shawnee
1846-1924   Volume XI

United States Post Office

Arkansas City, Kan

Dec. 20 1911

Dear Mrs Pleas-

I am returning your letter and am sorry that I cannot give you any information concerning Lillie Grey Eyes and her husband Carl Eaves. I do believe I had not come to Chiloco[sic] or had gone before this marriage took place. I wrote to Mrs. Wind whose parents were Sac and Fox Indians. I mean her step mother and father were, and I enclose her letter. I wish I could find out for you the particulars.

Lillie was the daughter of one of the Sac and Fox chiefs and pretty high strung, this I remember. Her brother Willie got a herd of ponies as his portion of his father's wealth and like some white youth went through with it all in a very short time. I am sending with this one of Annie's books, as you see they are stories for children. Yes come and see me and remember me to Bill and Ida Roberts if you should visit soon, and also to all of my Indian boy & girls, not forgetting ther[sic] good parents.

Your friend

Emma Dek Sluth

****

Otoe Agency   Dec 7, 1911

Dear Mrs. Sluth

I am sending you a letter which explains itself. I can not recall the circumstance but am sure you will know. Please write me if you can give any information desired. I am coming to see you some day- Am enjoying my work here. Am very very busy just now.

In haste with love

Very truly

Mrs. M. J. Pleas

****

Sac & Fox – Shawnee
1846-1924 Volume XI

Dear Mrs. Wind-

Do you know if Lily Grey Eyes married Carl Eaves &c.

Please return all papers and get any information you can in regard to the marriage of Carl Eaves and Lily –

Your friend

Emma Dek-

****

DEPARTMENT OF THE INTERIOR
UNITED STATES INDIAN SERVICE

Sac & Fox Indian Agency,

Stroud, Okla. RFD#2.

November 22, 1911.

Mrs. M. J. Pleas,

Otoe Agency,

Otoe, Okla.

Dear Mrs. Pleas:-

I write you at the request of Mrs. Lillie G. Carter formerly Lillie Greyeyes, a student at Chilocco, Okla., Mrs. Carter whose maiden name was Greyeyes claims that while she was a student at Chilocco she became acquainted with Carl Eaves a Pawnee and that they were married at the Chilocco School on the closing day, June 16th or 17th, 1890; that at this time you were a matron at said school and that you will probably recall the event.

Mrs. Carter has an action in the United States Circuit Court at Guthrie against the United States and certain Pawnee Indians, adverse claimants in the allotment of Carl Eaves.

The outcome of the case hinges largely upon the fact as to whether Lillie Greyeyes and Carl Eaves were ever married; if they were married the form of ceremony.

Sac & Fox – Shawnee
1846-1924   Volume XI

She claims that the minister who performed the ceremony came from Arkansas City, but she has forgotten his name. She also states that they failed to give her a certificate at the time, but informed her that she secure this from Wichita or Newton, or some place in Kansas at any time in the future.

Thinking that you might have some recollection of the event or that you might be able to give some enlightenment, she requested that I write you. She did not know of your whereabouts, but when she mentioned your name I informed her of the fact.

Thanking you for any information you may be able to give us, I am with best wishes,

      Very respectfully,

      WC Kohlenberg
      Supt. & Spl. Disb. Agt.

WCK/WMH

H. M. JARRETT   CLAUDE McLAUGHLIN   GEO. F. CLARK
JUDGE   STENOGRAPHER AND DEPUTY CLERK   CLERK

OFFICE OF

COUNTY COURT OF LINCOLN COUNTY

CHANDLER, OKLAHOMA

      Feb. 2 – 1912

W. C. Kohlenberg
 Stroud, Okla
  Dear Sir:-

    Complying with your request of 1-31-12 am enclosing Certified Copy of Marriage License of the case here in contained.

     Very Sincerely

      Geo. F. Clark

Sac & Fox – Shawnee
1846-1924   Volume XI

[The following two letters typed as given]

Otoe Okla 12/22, 1911

Dear Mr Kohlenberg & Mrs.

I have been [illegible] time answering with reference to the inclosed but just got returns in yesterdays mail. I think Mrs Carter is correct in her statements but can not recall circumstances

The Supt evidently did not "give the bride away" or some of us would remember I think will always remember such occasions under Supt Campbell

Your letter of last year was forwarded to me from here. I certainly appreciated your kind invitation to visit you and hope to do so sometime Supt Stanion enjoyed his visit and certainly thinks Mrs. knows how to manage her and of the line – Is Mrs Dickens with you I heard so, if so remember me to her

I was disappointed in not meeting you at Okla City

Oh how I would like to see you and have an old fashion visit. Cant you come up or over which,

They are waiting on me to go to [illegible] must go.

Merry Christmas & Happy New Year

With love to both

M.J. Pleas

****

Chilocco
Dec 18th 1911

Dear Friend

I am sorry that I can not find out any thing about Lillies marrage the had written to Mr Allen about it and he sent them the addres of some of the employees that were here at that time. All that I know about it is that we heard that Lillie had married a pawnee and i was a Sac and Fox when they come down to her home and it was Carl Eaves and they told me that they were married at school that is all I know about it and I dont believe that Lillie would live with out being married I am going to write you a long letter some time soon but am very buisy just now with love your friend

---

H. B. SEARS
Abstracts, Loans, Insurance
119 N. Broadway
SHAWNEE, OKLAHOMA

Shawnee, Okla., Feb., 20, 1912,

Mr. J. A. Buntin, Supt. Ind. Agency,
    Shawnee, Okla.

Dear Sir.

    I enclose herewith statement of facts to be filled out on Davis Hardin, which I wish you would give me at your convenience.

    We are making a loan on this property and it is very necessary that I have this to complete our loan.

    Thanking you in advance for your usual promptness, I remain,

                  Yours truly,
                        H.B. Sears

H. B. SEARS
Abstracts, Loans, Insurance
119 N. Broadway
SHAWNEE, OKLAHOMA

Shawnee, Okla., Feb., 20, 1912,

Mr. J. Buntin,
Indian Agency,
Shawnee, Okla.,
Dear Sir:-

Sac & Fox – Shawnee
1846-1924   Volume XI

    We are making a loan on a piece of land that makes it necessary for us to have a statement of facts on Ma-tin-a-ya and I enclose herewith a blank form and will thank you to return same to me as soon as convenient.

        Thanking you for your usual prompt attention I am,

            Yours truly,

              H B Sears

Hbs/s

H. B. SEARS
Abstracts, Loans, Insurance
119 N. Broadway
SHAWNEE, OKLAHOMA

            September 21, 1912.

Mr. J. A. Buntin,
  c/o Indian Agency,
    Shawnee, Okla.,
Dear Sir:

    I am working up an abstract on the North Half (N.1/2) of the South East Quarter (SE.1/4) of Section Twenty Four (Sec. 24), Township Ten (10) North, Range Four (4) East, and it will be necessary for me to have a statement of facts on Po-ka-tah-kum, and I inclose herewith a blank and would thank you to let me have same as soon as convenient, and oblige,

            Yours truly,

              HB Sears

HBS/BP

Sac & Fox – Shawnee
1846-1924 Volume XI

H. B. SEARS
Abstracts, Loans, Insurance
119 N. Broadway
SHAWNEE, OKLAHOMA

October 5, 1912.

Mr. J. A. Buntin,

C/o Indian Agency,

Shawnee, Okla.,

Dear Sir:

I enclose herewith the Nah-she-pe-oth Patent which I received from your office this morning. I have made a copy of same which will serve our purpose, and I wish to thank you for your kindness in this matter.

Yours truly,

H.B. Sears

HBS/EF.

RECEIVED OCT 11 1912 SAC & FOX AGENCY, OKLAHOMA.

Cushing Okla
Oct 17 1912

Mr. Horace J. Johnson,

Dear Sir

This is to verify that Nellie R. Hall was married at Chandler Okla on Sept 20, 1912 by C. W. Cameron Christian minister to Robert T Pate

| Witness | Claud McLaughlin |
| and | Geo T. Clark |

Very Respt

Arza B. Collins
Addl. Farmer

Sac & Fox – Shawnee
1846-1924 Volume XI

Re Common Law
Marriages in
Oklahoma.

Sac and Fox Indian School,
Stroud, Okla., Nov. 25, 1912.

Hon. Commissioner of Indian Affairs,
    Washington, D. C.

Sir:

    Under date of November 12, last, I requested information from the U. S. Attorney, concerning the validity of common law marriages in Oklahoma, to which he replied under date of November 16. The reply is not entirely satisfactory and does not give as definite information as I should like in the matter. In his reply, he also suggested that it was a matter which my Department would probably like to pass upon at once, and that it should be submitted thereto. I inclose herewith a copy of my letter to the U. S. Attorney, together with his answer thereto, and have to ask what your Office holds with reference to the validity of common law marriages, particularly amongst Indians since the passage of the Act approved March 12, 1897. It seems to me that Section 3501 would render common law marriages amongst Indians illegal, even if they are not so among white people; however, it does not seem as though the U. S. Attorney would have overlooked this paragraph, if the paragraph is to be construed as it seems to me it should.

    I have written another letter of even date herewith, concerning plural Indian marriages, prior to Act of March 12, 1897, which I have asked to be made special, and I shall be pleased if this can also be made special and considered in connection therewith.

    Please return my letter to the U. S. Attorney and his answer thereto, for the files of this office.

                Very respectfully,

                Supt. & S. D. A.

HJJ/WS
Incls.

****

Sac & Fox – Shawnee
1846-1924   Volume XI

Re Common Law
Marriages in
Oklahoma.

Sac and Fox Indian School,
Stroud, Okla., December 26, 1912.

Commissioner of Indian Affairs,
Washington, D. C.
Sir:-

I have the honor to ask your attention to a communication from this Office under date of November 25th., last, in which I asked the Office to advise me what it would hold with reference to common law marriages of Indians in Oklahoma subsequent to the Act approved March 12, 1897.

A great many of the marriages among the Indians under this jurisdiction, both Sac and Fox and Iowas, and subsequent to March 12, 1897, have been only by Indian custom, which I assume to be about equivelant[sic] to a common law marriage, and in the matter of determining heirs of various deceased Indians who have contracted marriages in this manner, I am unable to complete reports of hearings for the reason that I do not know whether or not a common law marriage is to be recognized.

If it is recognized one set of persons may inherit in an estate ands if it is not recognized an entirely different set may inherit.

I have several case held up now waiting for more light on this subject of common law marriages, and I shall be obliged if the matter can be made EXTRA SPECIAL, and the desired information given me.

Very respectfully,

HJJ/WMH.   Supt. & S. D. A.,

****

[The following letter typed as given]

I have the humble honor of answering yours Aug 30, 1912 in which the Indian Office desires to know of some reliable basis on which they could determine whether they allowed marriage divorce or adoption was according to Indian custom & etc:

Sac & Fox – Shawnee
1846-1924   Volume XI

And what particular custom constituates nothing more that Natures' dictates or which common law marriage has had existed among the whites. (Lee decicion of Missouri grass widow by Supreme Court)

It depends in answer to you second paragraph to the truthful answer of both parties altho the deep thoughtful Business Committee since 1861 had lacd precidents under Wolcotts case v.s. James Acton.

James Acton was a whiteman living with two woman of our tribe. Acton was by his marriage and faithfulness to the custom of our tribe was adopted but question arose in Mr Walcotts mind gave Mr Acton three altarnatives:

First under treaty 1861, he (Acton) could get 160 acres as "head of a family" but having two wives he either had to quit living with both or to consider himself a batshelor to ~~grab~~ to make a white man grab to be entitled to same number of acres.

Jimmy had got old but chosed to live with Angeline (now more)

We did grant a good looking woman who was anxious to get married a cancellation ~~of~~ and licesne prumrable and solemnized under Kansas law. We notified the Kansas husband by publication under Kansas law. Ours was Indian under Indian Territory The womans petition said her husband had left her, abused her had to support her kids eats. Under circumstances husband, not appearing, we granted the good looking woman who dwell [illegible] in her habits and wanted to conform to law – a decree of divorce and she soon married another.

The big Statute Book of the First Legislature of Oklahoma reconizes all marriage [illegible] Indian people

In March 12, 1907 Some decendants of the Puritans and prohibitioners got jealous of Quannah Parker and some Indians of the plains who had some (one or more good looking woman as wives) These fanatics only had the legislature of Oklahoma to legalize Indian marriages up to date but forbid other Natures laws as to Indians until coplied under the Puritan laws or custom of white men.

If she patched his leggings and smoothed his moccasins and he in turn took his bow and arrow to slay game for her support or had taken hatchet to defends their home and he got killed or she, may before or afterward died – Cohabitation in this case constitutes marriage.

If depends on the conduct of either whether cohabitation or living together – if after seperating one or the other picks up another husband or woman it would be declared a to be dessulation or under Puritanic law – a divorce

In the case of Osmit the Business Committee was aware that he had a wife married before a [illegible] at St Marys in the [illegible] She had not followed her husband to the then Territory but took up with another man. Osmit took up with another woman and from such union produced children. Osmit died and left his allotment intestate

Sac & Fox – Shawnee
1846-1924   Volume XI

In May 2 1901 (See your statute relating to Indian Affairs) Congress not only for [illegible...] & etc but in general terms declared all Indian unions legal as if done under Puritanical made.

You asked if there are any Indians living together as husband and wife under Indian custom or if I know of any man having two or three wifes. Go! ask the birds or animals.

If the Department should choose to be soft and mealy mouth let it apprise Mr. Buntin to submit each case to our Business Committee and from the evidence or known facts the Committee will either (following examples of Probate Courts) will decide the proper heirship

Casesa have arisen under this agency to back some grafters but when your humble servant called the Departments attention to these matters one of these matters was about the Mazhe's allotment which has been envolved in courts and not yet settled. About an 80 acres sold by a resident to A.B. Jones also other errors the Indian Office then instructed Thackery to get me off the Committee. I got off but so long as I live I will [illegible] to loan companies who are strict the true status on each case only seven years ago an Indian woman asked me to write to the Indian Office her heirship to [illegible] allotment. The Indian Office submited my letter to Geo E Williams and told Williams to have me in the investigation hearing and wrote Mr Williams a good letter. I was Number 1. My good woman could not prove in altho Mr Williams
Mr A.C. Scott and other good men had the real sympathy to help the woman for an heirship right in which the allottee (according to Hoyle and the Irish) just died two years ago.

Joe Moose

| H. M. JARRETT
JUDGE | CLAUDE McLAUGHLIN
STENOGRAPHER AND DEPUTY CLERK | GEO. F. CLARK
CLERK |

OFFICE OF
COUNTY COURT OF LINCOLN COUNTY
CHANDLER, OKLAHOMA

Feb 3^d 1914

Mr. Horace J Johnson, Supt.

Stroud, Okla

Dear Sir:-

I hereby acknowledge receipt of checks No. 603, 604 & 607 in payment for certified copies of marriage license & etc previously made.

Sac & Fox – Shawnee
1846-1924 Volume XI

Thanks for you remittance.

                    Yours truly

                        Geo. F. Clark

W. H. WILCOX, JUDGE.   J. O. SNOWDEN, CLERK

OFFICE OF
CLERK OF THE COUNTY COURT
STILLWATER, OKLAHOMA

RECEIVED
MAY 21 1914
SAC AND FOX INDIAN SCHOOL, OKLA.

May 20th, 1914.

Mr. Horace J. Johnson,
    Stroud, Oklahoma.

Dear Sir:

    I am in receipt of yours of the 18th regarding Section 3506 of Wilson's Revised and Annotated Statutes of Oklahoma of 1903, and in reply will say that our marriage records do not give the Indians holding allotted lands. As a matter of fact, there are very few Indian marriages on record in this county.

    If you have in mind the name of any Indian whose record you wish, I might, with some additional information, be able to give you the desired data.

                    Very truly yours,

                    J. O. Snowden
                    Clerk of the County Court.

ROY HOFFMAN   EMERY A. FOSTER
HOFFMAN & FOSTER
ATTORNEYS AND COUNSELORS AT LAW.
CHANDLER, OKLA.

PERSONAL

RECEIVED
JUN 5 1914
SAC AND FOX INDIAN SCHOOL, OKLA.

June 4, 1914.

Hon. Horace J. Johnson,
Sac and Fox Agency
Oklahoma.

Sac & Fox – Shawnee
1846-1924   Volume XI

Dear Mr. Johnson:-

What did your question involve about the Brown-Givens marriage. Were any property rights involved. If so, I might be interested and would be glad to be advised confidentially.

Very truly

Roy Hoffman

MEMORANDUM.

VOUCHER FOR MISCELLANEOUS EXPENSES, SUCH AS RENT OF BUILDINGS, TELEPHONE SERVICE, GAS, ELECTRIC LIGHT, AND WATER SUPPLY. ETC.

THE UNITED STATES, June 22, 1914 19

To   Darwin Filtsch (Clerk County Court, ,   Dr.
Lincoln County, Okla.)
(Give post-office address.)   Chandler, Oklahoma

DATE 1914	ENTER BELOW THE SUBJECT MATTER OF THE CLAIM, SHOWING OF WHAT IT CONSISTS.	AMOUNT.
June 22	To Certified copy of Indian Marriage Record of Lincoln county[sic], Oklahoma................................	85
	FOR AGENCY PURPOSES.	
	Paid from "Determining Heirs of Deceased Indian Allottees, 1914".	
	TOTAL................................ $	85

Only eighty-five cents.

THE ABOVE IS A TRUE COPY OF ORIGINAL VOUCHER, EXCEPT AS TO CERTIFICATES.
PAID IN CASH, UNLESS OTHERWISE NOTED AT THE BOTTOM HEREOF.

Services procured under authority dated #53774, May 29 , 1914, attached to original or ~~to~~ voucher No.   64   to account for   4th   Quarter, 1914 , and in accordance with sections ---------- and   4B   of the methods stated on original.
        Letter)   (Number)

Dated   June 22   , 1914

Paid by Check No.   792 , dated   June 22, 1914.   , 1914, for $ .85 .

on   Treas. of the U. S.   , to order of claimant.

****

MEMORANDUM.

CASH

Voucher No. 64 , 4th Quarter, 1914

FOR

MISCELLANEOUS EXPENSES.

IN FAVOR OR
Darwin Filtich[sic], Clerk County
Court, Lincoln County, Okla.

For $ 85/100

Paid by Horace J. Johnson,

Supt. & S. D. A.
(Official title.)

Sac and Fox School, Okla.
(Agency or School.)

Any disbursing or other officer of the United States or other person who shall knowingly present, or cause to be presented, any voucher, account, or claim to any officer of the United States for approval or payment, or for the purpose of securing a credit in any account with the United States, relating to any matter pertaining to the Indian Service, which shall contain any material misrepresentation of fact in regard to the amount due or paid, the name or character of the article furnished or received, or of the service rendered, or to the date of purchase, delivery, or performance of service, or in any other particular, shall not be entitled to payment or credit for any part of said voucher, account, or claim; and if any such credit shall be given or received, or payment made, the United States may recharge the same to the officer or person receiving the credit or payment and recover the amount from either or both, in the same manner as other debts due the United States are collected; PROVIDED, That where an account contains more than one voucher the foregoing shall apply only to such vouchers as contain the misrepresentation; AND PROVIDED FURTHER, That the officers and persons by and between whom the business is transacted shall be presumed to know the facts in relation to the matter set forth in the voucher, account, or claim; AND PROVIDED FURTHER, That the foregoing shall be in addition to the penalties now prescribed by law, and in no way to affect proceedings under existing law for like offenses. That, where practicable, this section shall be printed on the blank forms of vouchers provided for general use. (Act March 1, 1883 § 8, 22 Stat, 451; Ace July 4, 1884, § 8; Cir. 113 Ind. O.)

****

Sac & Fox – Shawnee
1846-1924 Volume XI

5/11/14 **DEPARTMENT OF THE INTERIOR**
OFFICE OF INDIAN AFFAIRS
WASHINGTON

Authority is hereby granted for you to expend, during the fiscal year 1914,
from

(1)	Determining Heirs of Deceased Indian Allottees, 1914.	$	85
(2)		$	
(3)		$	
(4)		$	

for the following:

OBJECT.	UNIT PRICE.	AMOUNT.
FOR AGENCY PURPOSES. To pay the Clerk of the County Court for a certified copy of the Indian Marriage Record of Lincoln county [sic], Oklahoma..		85
The Indian marriage record of the County Court of Lincoln county, Oklahoma contains the names of 68 Indians, the most of whom were allotted under this jurisdiction. This record is desired for the use of this office in securing testimony to be used in determining the heirs of deceased Indian allottees, and will be of inestimable value for the data therein contained in establishing the married relationship of many of the allottees. As this is an immediate need the Office is requested to make this special, and advise me of its action thereon at the earliest possible date. This is a statutory record prepared in accordance with the provisions of Section 3506 of the Revised and Annotated statutes of Oklahoma of 1903.		
	TOTAL.	85

TO:
The Superintendent,
(Title or name.)

Sac and Fox Indian School
(School.)

Stroud, Oklahoma.
(Post Office.)

MAY 29 1914

COPY.—To be filed by the disbursing officer with proper voucher in his copy of memorandum account.

Sac & Fox – Shawnee
1846-1924   Volume XI

****

DEPARTMENT OF THE INTERIOR

Certified copy of Record.

UNITED STATES INDIAN SERVICE

APR 30 A.M.

SAC & FOX AGENCY, OKLAHOMA.

Sac & Fox Indian School,
Stroud, Okla., Apr. 27, 1914.

H. M. Jarrett,
   County Judge,
      Lincoln County,
         Chandler, Okla.,

Sir:-

    Kindly advise me if the provisions of Section 3506 of the Revised and Annotated Statutes of Oklahoma of 1903 were ever complied with. If they were complied with is it possible for you to procure for me a certified copy of the result? We will pay the regular fee for such certified copy.

    Your early attention to this matter will be appreciated.

    A penalty envelope is enclosed for reply which requires no stamp.

                Very respectfully,

                Horace J Johnson

WMH.
                Supt. & S. D. A.,

Enclos:
   Penalty Envelope.

Dear sir:-

    We have what I presume is a very incomplete record of Indian marriages. It does not have to exceed 40 names in it of the most prominent Indians and their wives. It does not show any case where an Indian had more than one wife of making a selection from among them. Judge S.A. Cordell was judge at that time and he tells me he made a trip to the Agency but was unable to make a very complete record in the time he had to devote to the matter. If you desire a certified copy of the record we have kindly advice & will make it and sent to you.

                Very truly,

                HM Jarrett
                County Judge

Sac & Fox – Shawnee
1846-1924 Volume XI

****

Certified
copy of
Record.

Sac & Fox Indian School,
Stroud, Okla., Apr. 27, 1914.

H. M. Jarrett,
    County Judge,
        Lincoln County,
            Chandler, Okla.,
  Sir:-

        Kindly advise me if the provisions of Section 3506 of the Revised and Annotated Statutes of Oklahoma of 1903 were ever complied with. If they were complied with is it possible for you to procure for me a certified copy of the result? We will pay the regular fee for such certified copy.

        Your early attention to this matter will be appreciated.

        A penalty envelope is enclosed for reply which requires no stamp.

                Very respectfully,

                Horace J Johnson

WMH.   Supt. & S. D. A.,

Enclos:
  Penalty Envelope.

****

Certified
copy of
Record.

Sac & Fox Indian School,
Stroud, Okla., May 6, 1914.

H. M/[sic] Jarrett,
    County Judge,
        Lincoln County,
            Chandler, Okla.,
  Sir:-

        Referring to my letter of the 27th. ultimo requesting information as to whether or not the provisions of Section 3506 of the Revised and Annotated Statutes of Oklahoma of 1903 were ever complied with, and your reply thereto, I have to request that you furnish me with a certified copy of

Sac & Fox – Shawnee
1846-1924 Volume XI

the result as shown by the records of your office. We will pay the regular fee for such certified copy.

    A penalty envelope is enclosed for reply which requires no stamp.

    Very respectfully,

        Horace J Johnson

WMH.   Supt. & S. D. A.,

Enclos:
Penalty Envelope.

Pay for
cert copy
Indian mar-
riage record.

    Sac and Fox Indian School,
    Stroud, Okla., June 25, 1914.

RECEIVED
JUL 15 1918
SAC AND FOX INDIAN SCHOOL, OKLA.

Mr. Darwin Filtich,
  Clerk, County Court,
    Lincoln County,
      Chandler, Okla.

Dear Sir,-

    As settlement for the certified copy of the Indian marriage record of your office furnished this office sometime since please find inclosed herewith U. S. Treasury check No. 792, drawn in your favor for 85¢.

    Very respectfully,

TPM   Supt. & S. D. A.
Inc. Check No. 792.

    ****

H. M. JARRETT   CARLAND D. LITTLE   GEO. F. CLARK
JUDGE   STENOGRAPHER AND DEPUTY CLERK   CLERK

OFFICE OF
COUNTY COURT OF LINCOLN COUNTY
CHANDLER, OKLAHOMA

RECEIVED
MAY 11 1914
SAC AND FOX INDIAN SCHOOL, OKLA.

May 9, 1914.

Sac & Fox – Shawnee
1846-1924   Volume XI

Horace J. Johnson,
Stroud, Okla, Rfd. 2.

Sir:-

    Enclosed you will find a certified copy of the Indian Marriage Record, of Lincoln County, as per your request.

    The fee for making copy and certifying same is 85¢, which you may remit to Clerk of County Court.

Yours truly,

Garland D. Little
Dep. Clerk County Court.

CERTIFICATE OF MARRIAGE.

I Hereby Certify, That on the __1st__ day of __May__ A D. 1916 at __Chandler__ in the County of __Lincoln__ in the State of Oklahoma, according to law and by authority

I Duly Joined in Marriage

Mr. __James Scott__ of __Avery, Okla.__
and M __Martha Baker__ of __Avery, Okla.__
in pre sence[sic] of __William Foster__ of __Avery, Okla.__
and __Jesse Carter__ of __Avery, Okla.__

Given under my hand this __1st__ day of __May__ A. D. 19__16__

(S) I.[sic] M. Jarrett
Official Title __County Judge__

(SEAL)

Copied by LGG.
Sac and Fox Indian School.
   Stroud, Okla., May 1, 1916.

Sac & Fox – Shawnee
1846-1924 Volume XI

Births,
deaths &
marriages.

Sac and Fox Indian School,
Stroud, Okla. Mar. 22, 1917.

Mr. A. B. Collins,
 Cushing, Oklahoma.

Dear Mr. Collins:

It is about time to consider the annuity roll for the payment this year and I wish that you would report any births, deaths or marriages which have occured[sic] in your district and which you have not reported heretofore. I find that we do not have either the date of birth or the death of the child born to Harding Franklin's family nor what name was given to the child. There is no name on record for the last child born to the Silas Grass Family here and I wish you would look this up too. The date of the death of Jessie Smith, Ben Smith's wife, is not known and if you can look up your files and find this date I wish that you would report it.

The date of the marriage of Grover Morris, to whom married, legally or otherwise, is not known and there may be others about which I am not informed and I shall be pleased to have you sign the receipt on the duplicate of this letter and return it to this office. if you will furnish this data as soon as you can before we make up the annuity roll.

Saginaw Grant was in the office the other day and report-[sic] the death of his children and the dates thereof also the facts of his marriage.

Very Respectfully,

[end of letter]

Sac & Fox – Shawnee
1846-1924   Volume XI

[The letter below typed as given]

DEPARTMENT OF THE INTERIOR

UNITED STATES INDIAN SERVICE

RECEIVED
APR 3 1917
SAC AND FOX INDIAN SCHOOL, OKLA.

Cushing, Okla.

April 2, 1917.

Mr. Horace J. Johnson.
                  Stroud Okla.
Dear Sir.
        Inclosed find report of Marriages.
Grover Morris to Clara Falls Sept. 5, 1916. at Stillwater okla.
        Pearl Murry to Raymond, Gawhegs Sept 22, 1916. at Guthrie Okla.
Saginaw Grant to Fannie Tyner. Recently I think you have the exact date.

                            Very. Respectfully.

                            Arza B Collins

                         Shawnee Indian Agency,
                         Shawnee, Oklahoma.
                          March 26, 1918.

Mr. Chas. W. Edmister,

    U. S. Farmer,
        Tecumseh, Oklahoma.

Dear Sir:-

        I have before me your letter of March 12th discussing the marriage of the Anadarko girl, Lena Thomas, and one of the Indians out there by the name of Bill Johnson, and note your opinion that these people are probably legally married even tho' they never have secured a license and in other ways never complied with the State laws, since it appears that they both were eligible to marriage and have publicly claimed each other as man and wife under the common law arrangement.

        I expect your opinions in this matter are well founded as I know that in the heirship matters which have been up for years such marriages have been recognized as parties are not debarred from entering into marriage relations by some previous conditions. At the same time this information should not be given out at all and I expect you thoroughly understand that and are already working along that line, but these people should be urged in every way possible to conform to the laws governing the marriage relation and you should press these matters as far as is consistent with reasonable tact in connection with your work and to advise the Indians in that locality to conform especially to the laws under which they must necessiarly[sic] live.

                Very Respectfully,

                              Superintendent.

G-L

****

Lena Thomas-
Marriage.

DEPARTMENT OF THE INTERIOR

UNITED STATES INDIAN SERVICE

                R-2, Tecumseh, Oklahoma,
                March 12, 1918.

Supt. O.J. Green,
    Shawnee, Oklahoma.

Dear Mr Green:
    Your letter of yesterday regarding the Anadarko girl, Lena Thomas who has been married to Bill Johnson in the Indian way, and hoping that some way may be found out to cause them to be married in a legal way. I note the inquiry of Mr Stinchecum about what we know and can do about this matter.

    It is true they have been living together for several years and have one child, Ruby, who was two years old the 1st day of this month. But as to the legality of their marriage, I have been working under the impression for over three years that Indian Custom marriages are legal, that is if they properly let it be known by living together for some time or in other way. The State law says that they have to have a License, but I am informed that the Court rulings reverse this and upheld common law marriages both among whites and Indians. Of course if I am surely mistaken in this, as a man can so easily be then it makes a very different case. But I feel certain that the above is the fact.

    Now if their relation is legal, then nothing can be did except moral suasion, and with Bill Johnson that would be like putting gold filling in a hogs teeth. Some of them I can influence that way but not him. MR[sic] Stinchecum could do more in influencing the woman in an hour than could be did with the man in a life time. However I will have a talk with the woman myself about this.

Even though common law marriages are legal and place the participants within the protection of the law, it is never the less a very bad policy, especially with the women, as those matters should be publickly[sic] recorded, to avoid complications in estates if nothing more.

Bill Johnson was eligible to marriage with this girl, but I do not know about the girl. That is another quite prominent point. This does not hinge on their going to Mexico. In fact their being rigidly agitated about going to school last fall is the only thing that has been influenced by that calculation since I have been here.

Let me hear from you.

Very truly yours,
Chas W Edmister
Farmer.

DEPARTMENT OF THE INTERIOR

UNITED STATES INDIAN SERVICE

Potawatomi Indian Agency
Mayetta, Kansas
November 17, 1920.

Supt. Ira C. Deaver,
Shawnee Indian Agency,
Shawnee, Oklahoma.

Dear Mr. Deaver:

I would be please to have you obtain a certified copy of the marriage of Sacto Chip ko quah and one Bessie Hale, whom it was alleged, were married by the Probate Judge in your County. Also obtain a certificate showing by whom they were married, when and how.

Please obtain this information for me at as early a date as possible and forward the expense bill to me for payment.

Very truly yours,

   A.R. Snyder
Superintendent. A.W.
ARS:AW

Sac & Fox – Shawnee
1846-1924   Volume XI

****

Shawnee Indian Agency,
Shawnee, Okla., Nov. 20, 1920.

Mr. A.R. Snyder,
Supt. Pottawatomi and Kickapoo Agency,
Mayetta, Kansas.

My dear Mr. Snyder:
Enclosed herewith is certified copy of the marriage license issued to Theodore Sacquot of Netawaka, (Netawaka) Kansas, and Bessie Hale of McLoud, Oklahoma.

This is not the name of the man given by you in your letter; but thinking perhaps he had another name, and that this was one and the same person, we secured a copy of the license for you. The cost of the certified copy was seventy five cents.

Yours truly,

Ira C. Deaver,
ICD.   Superintendent.
EVS.
Enclosure.

Shawnee Indian Agency
Shawnee, Okla.,
Jan. 21, 1922.

Miss Hattie Mason,
c/o George Butler,
Avery, Okla.

Dear Miss Mason:

This is in reply to your letter of Jan. 13th, in which you state that you and James intend to get license to marry just as soon as you can.

Having attended schools like you have, you should realize that it is not right for you to live with James unless he is eligible to be married and that to be legal, you should by all means secure the usual license.

Sac & Fox – Shawnee
1846-1924   Volume XI

Your case will be watched to see that you do what you say you will do and I trust that you will do right in the matter

Very truly yours,

J. L. Suffecool
SUPERINTENDENT

JJ:EV

Sac and Fox-Shawnee – <u>DIVORCES</u>

January 21, 1901 – May 1, 1924

Sac & Fox – Shawnee
1846-1924   Volume XI

[The letter below typed as given]

Tecumseh Okla

Jan 21th 1901

Agent Patrick

Dear sur   I write you for information regarding Indian land when Divorced from Joe Melot he gave me a hundred and twenty acres of his land but I havent any papers to show that this land is mine   will you please inform me what I am to do to get a patient of this land in my name   will oblige me very much by answering soon

Yours respt

Louise Melot

****

G. A. OUTCELT
ATTORNEY AT LAW

TECUMSEH, O. T.   2/9/   *1901*

Hon Lee Patrick

   Sac and Fox O.T.

Dear Sir: You will doubtless remember Joseph Melot and the divorce suit he had with his wife some three years ago – also that the Court by its order set off to her 80 acres of his land. He executed a deed before you in accordance with the Courts order but the deed has been misplaced. Would you recognize a deed acknowledged before a Notary Public. Joe Melot has recently received injury in the shape of a broken leg and will not be able to be out for some time. It will be a great convenience to all the parties if this acknowledgement would be good. Please advise me.   Yours truly   G.A. Outcelt

Sac & Fox – Shawnee
1846-1924   Volume XI

Divorce of
Maggie Mathews.

Shawnee Oklahoma,
Marth 6th, 1916.

Horace J. Johnson, Supt.
    Sac and Fox Indian School,
        Stroud, Oklahoma.
Sir:-

Attached herewith you will find a certificate signed by the Clerk of the Court of Pottawatomie County in regard to the Mathew-Pickett divorce. There was no record of any proceedings for a divorce shown on the records at that place.

I also asked Jesse Pickett if there was any divorce made or given between he and this woman, and he said that there was not, That they lived together a while and then just quit like all the Indians done at that time.

Very respectfully
[Name Illegible]
U.S. Farmer.

Sac and Fox Indian School,
Stroud, Oklahoma, July 21, 1919.

Albert Moore,
    C/o Mr. Collins,
        Cushing, Oklahoma.

Dear Albert:

This is to advise you that I am this day taking with me to Shawnee with other papers your decree of Divorce and at any time when you want this paper you may get it from Mr. Deaver who is new Superintendent for the Sac and Foxes.

I am sending this letter to Mr. Collins as I do not know where to address you.

Very Truly Your Friend,
Horace J Johnson
Special Supervisor.

Sac & Fox – Shawnee
1846-1924   Volume XI

Shawnee Indian Agency
Shawnee, Oklahoma
April 10, 1922

Mr. W. W. Janes
Purcell, Oklahoma

Dear Sir:

    Replying to your letter of April 4, in which you advise this office that a Court Decree entered in a divorce suit gave you the custody of your five children and that your former wife, Lillie L. Janes, nee Bohner, has married again, and requesting us to not recognize any demands that she may make upon this office in behalf of the children, you are advised that, in order for us to have something tangible to work on, it will be advisable for you to furnish us the Copies of Court decrees you mention. These can be kept in our permanent files in this office.

    Very truly yours

    J. L. Suffecool
    Superintendent

JJ

Shawnee Indian Agency,
Shawnee, Oklahoma,
February 23, 1923.

Mrs. Pansy V. Jones,
  Poplar Bluff, Mo.

Dear Madam:

    This is to acknowledge receipt of your letter of February 20, in which you inclose certified copy of the decree of the divorce granted you by the courts, in which the custody of your children has been placed with you.

    In this connection, you are advised, that with the annuity payments are made to the Sac & Fox Indians, the share belonging to the children will be paid to you instead of to the father as heretofore.

    In connection with the withdrawing of the children's share of the Tribal trust funds, you are advised that we could not make any recommendation to the Indian Office without first making proper investigation of the circumstances in the case and securing such information as will give us knowledge of the conditions, which can be used to justify us in making any recommendations.

It is necessary that the parent applying for the childrens[sic] share of the Tribal trust fund, to secure legal guardianship of the children by the proper courts, as stated in our former letter, you are advised, that it is not deemed advisable to establish any precedent in allowing parents to withdraw children's share of the Tribal trust fund for the reason that it is unfair to the other minor members of the tribe; and that it is the intention of the Government to with-hold the minor's share until they reach their majority.

It is to be regretted that you are placed under the circumstances that you are, caused by the divorce from your husband and it should not become necessary for you, or the father to resort to the use of the children's funds for their support, as all children should under most any conditions be provided for by the parents, and it is believed that the support of the children could be obtained from the father of the children and through the proper courts upon the proper presentation to that court.

Very truly yours,

J. L. Suffecool
Superintendent

JJ:EV

Shawnee Indian Agency
Shawnee, Oklahoma,
December 18, 1923.

Mr. John T. Levergood, Attorney
Shawnee, Oklahoma.

Dear Sir:

I am inclosing herewith my official check #17987 payable to your order for $25.00 representing your fee for professional services rendered in the Martha Logan Vs. Charlie Logan divorce.

Very truly yours,

Incl.

_____

J. L. Suffecool
R-Mc
Superintendent.

Sac & Fox – Shawnee
1846-1924   Volume XI

Shawnee Indian Agency.
Shawnee, Oklahoma.
May 1, 1924.

Mr. Walter Mathews, Lawyer,
Cushing, Oklahoma.

Dear Sir:

This is to acknowledge receipt of your letter and another signed by Jess Rice concerning the matter of securing a divorce for him. It would appear that Edward Rice has little justification for a divorce and that I can not see my way clear to assist him in the matter. If he cares to take the matter into court he may do so on this own resources without any recommendations from this office.

As a matter of his inherited interest in Ottawa County, which is unrestricted land. I am not in a position to make any recommendation in this matter, inasmuch as the land is not within this jurisdiction and is unrestricted.

Very truly yours,

A. W. Leech,
Superintendent.

R/Mc

Sac and Fox-Shawnee –
ESTATES LOG BOOK VOLUME 1 INDEX
1891-1902

Sac & Fox – Shawnee
1846-1924   Volume XI

Note: This listing of names was originally an index for Estates Log Book Volume 1. Their page numbers would not coincide with the typed work now. Check the Index at the back of the book for each name. You'll have to scan the list, the names were not alphabetized.

Name	Pg	Name	Pg	Name	Pg
Ah-Quaw-Saw	44	Duncan, Robt	50	Ingalls, Bessie	37
		Davis, Bessie	50	" W<u>m</u>	38
Butler, Lizzie	10	" Marie	51	" Lucy	38
Black, Nancy	11	" Jefferson	51	" John J.	38
Black, Lucy	12	" Rachel	51	" Horace	39
Black, James	12				
Brown, Josephine	13	Eaton, Cassie	14	Jones, Emily	55
Buffalohorn, Clara	13	Ellis, Katie	14		
Buffalohorn, Mamie	13	Ellis, Mabel	17	Ke-Waw-Haw	1
Butler, Benj	14	Ely, Samuel	205	Keokuk, Phoebe	57
Brown, Eva	15				
Butler, Mollie	16	Falls, Emily	22	Long, Thomas	40
Baker, Timothy	17	Fox, Joseph	23	Long, Agnes	43
Bigwalker, Florence	18	Franklin, Susan	32	Lee, Bessie	43
Bigwalker, John W	18			Lunt, Lina B	206
Bear, James	44	Grass, Geo	3		
Bass, Samuel	46	Groinhorn, Charlie	24	Madison, Richard	2
Bass, Carrie	46	Grass, John	35	Madison, Susan	3
Bear, Mollie	48	Givens, Joshua	42	Mitchell, Egbert	3
		Grant, John	204	Mason, Nellie	15
Carter, Louise	10	Grant, Thomas	205	Martin, Betsy	19
Carter, Martha	10	Gra-law-tha-wa-me	206	McKosito, Alma	21
Conger, Silas	11			Maw-Mel-Lo-Han	25
Conger, Jasper	11	Hull, William	2	McKosito, Barbara	26
Conger, William	11	Hull, Lucy	2	McKosito, Moses	26
Conger, Julia Black	12	Hunter, John	2	Messawot, Julia	26
Conger, Julia	16	Harrison, Martha	4	Messawot, Alma	27
Conger, Martha	23	Hawk, Richard	4	Morris, Harriet	27
Conger, Hattie	23	Hawk, Maggie	4	Mokohoko	28
Cheekos-kuk	34	Hawk, James	4	McKuk, John	29
Conger, Hattie	47	Hawk, John	5	McClellan, Oscar	30
Conger, May	47	Hunter, Geo.	14	" Geo B	30
Coon, Dennis	47	Hawk, Samuel	16	" Thom	31
Cuppahe, Chief	54	Hall, Eudora	17	" Rebecca	31
Cuppahe, Mary	54	Hall, Rufus	32	Marshal, Gabriel	32
		Hoag, Lucy	34	Mock-E-Naw	33
Dunn, Lewis	21	Herdford, Martha	35	Mitchell, James	33
Dunn, Ralph	22	Hoag, Enoch	36	Morris, Martha	39
Dunn, Albert	41	Hallowell, Nannie	206	Morton, Oliver P	42
Duncan, Ada	41	Harrison, Rufus	55	My-Ah-Pe-Me-Gre-Me	
Duncan, May	48	Harris, Francis	55		203
" Lottie	49	Hallowell, Harry Falk	209	Murray, Kirwin	207
" David	49	Hamilton, William	211	" May	207
" Alice	50				

Sac & Fox – Shawnee
1846-1924   Volume XI

Note: This listing of names was originally an index for Estates Log Book Volume 1. Their page numbers would not coincide with the typed work now. Check the Index at the back of the book for each name. You'll have to scan the list, the names were not alphabetized.

Name	Page	Name	Page
Mohee, John	211	Senache, Fred	22
" Christian	211	Scott, Joseph	34
		Stanley, Popo	36
Neal, Moses	28	Senache, Fred	45
Neal, Mary	28	Senache, Anna	45
Neal, Kishko	29	Sha-Que-Quot, Jerome	46
Neal, Mary (Tohee)	200	Squirrel, Carrie	202
No-Ah-Tom	210		
No heart, Joseph	210	Taylor, Susan	7
Naw-A-No-Way	212	Turner, Clarence	8
" , Susan		Turner, Fannie	8
	212	Turner, Thomas	8
		Tohee, William	202
Ocean, Bettie	37	Tohee, Mary	202
		Townsend, Ed	212
Powers, Fannie V	5	Thrift, W$^{\underline{m}}$	213
Plumb, Mary	6		
Pattaqua, Mamie	9	Vetters, Lucy	204
Pennock, W$^{\underline{m}}$	9		
Pennock, Hester	9	Washington, Albert	
Perkins, Bishop W	9	(Ne-Po-Pe)	1
Pickett, Mary	10	Washington, Mary	1
Pattaqua, Charlotte	24	Washington, Geo.	1
Pickett, Clarence	33	Wah-Taw-Sah	11
Patrick, Lee (Tohee)	200	Wheeler, Eva	21
Pah-Ne-Me	201	Was-Ko-Pah-She-Toe	25
		Walker, Elmer	29
Randall, Fannie	5	McClellan, Oscar	30
Red Rock	6	McClellan, Geo. B	30
Ridge, Jesse	6	McClellan, Thomas	31
Rice, Jack O	20	McClellan, Rebecca	31
Rubideau, Fannie	210	Marshall, Gabriel	32
		Meek-E-Naw	33
Sherman, Lucy Anderson		Wa-Pe-Ko-Hol	44
	6	Wolf, John	52
Smith, Oda	7	" Jane	54
Strubble, Geo.	7	Wyman, Bertha	52
Sullivan, John L	7	" Esau	52
Shaw, Edward	13	" Peter	53
Smith, Martha	15	Wilson, James	53
Smith, Alex	18	Wah-to-Gramme	203
Sherman, Anne Anderson		Whitewater, James	208
	19	Whitecloud, Jefferson	208
Stanley, Mattie	20		

Sac and Fox-Shawnee –
ESTATES LOG BOOK VOLUME 1
1891-1902

Sac & Fox – Shawnee
1846-1924 Volume XI

1

Washington, Albert – Ne-po-pe
    Allottee No. 459
S.E.1/4 9-17-6
    Died May 10th 1895
Heirs – Junetta Davis, daughter – 8 years of age, whose mother is Deborah Rhodes
At his death he was the husband of Ida Smith. She died, left her father Webster Smith, sole heir to her share in this estate.

1

Washington, Mary – Naw-ko-se-quah
    Allottee No. 460
SW/4 – 3-17-6
    Died Sept 10th 1892
Heirs – George Washington, only son

1

Washington, George – Paw-She-Saw-Ha
    Allottee No. 458
NE/4 – 9-17-6
    Died April 30, 1898
Heirs – Junetta Davis, grand daughter, daughter of Albert Washington and Deborah Rhodes.

1

Ke-Was-Haw
    Allottee No. 539
SE/4 – 19-18-6
    Died January 1891
Heirs – Julia Hodge, Mother
    May Grass Sister, adult
    Inez Bass

2

Hull, William – Saw-Swah-Wah
    Allottee No. 39
SW/4 – 31-19-6
    Died Mar. 18, 1899
Heirs – Lucy Hull – wife
    Henry Hull – Son – minor
    Ben Hull   "   "

Sac & Fox – Shawnee
1846-1924   Volume XI

2

Hull, Lucy – Aw-Paw-She
    Allottee No. 40
SE/4 – 2-17-6
    Died April 5th 1899
Heirs – Henry Hull – Son – minor
    Ben   "   "   "

2

Hunter, John – Nah-Saw-Waw-che-lah
    Allottee No. 515
E/2 and Lots 3, 4, SW/4–19-18-6
    Died Aug 25, 1891
Heirs – Robt. Hunter Father, Sole Heir.

2

Madison, Richard – Me-Ah-She-Nah-Ne
    Allottee No. 535
S/2 and Lots 1, 2 NE/4-3-17-6
    Died July 20, 1893
Heirs – Susan Madison – Mother
    Bettie Wilson – (Fox) 1/2 Sister
    Henry Madison – a minor
Son of another 1/2 Sister, Wy-You-Wa-Jua

3

Madison, Susan – Ah-She-Tah
    Allottee No. 534
SE/4 3-17-6
    Died Jan 30, 1894
Heirs –

3

Mitchell, Egbert – Chah-yah-kaw-se
    Allottee No. 504
SE/4 – 11-17-6
    Died Jan. 30, 1894
Heirs – Kah-No-Se – Father, died before allotment
    Mary Plumb, Mother, Dead
    Minnie Plumb, Daughter of Mary Plumb, 1/2 Sister of Egbert Mitchell and Sole heir

Sac & Fox – Shawnee
1846-1924   Volume XI

3

Grass, George – Paw-Pas-Ko-Kuck
    Allottee No. 28
S/2 and Lots 1, 2, NE/4 2-18-5
    Died April 13, 1899
Heirs – Mary Grass Wife
    Silas Grass, A son by TiCora Grass, former wife.

4

Harrison, Martha – Kish-Sah-Saw
    Allottee No. 425
SE/4-29-17-6
    Died September 1893
Heirs – Benj Harrison, Husband and Sole Heir

4

Hawk, Richard – Chaw-Kaw-Pe
    Allottee No. 471
NE/4 32-18-6
    Died Mar. 24, 1899
Heirs – Samuel Hawk, Father (Dead)
    See Heirs of Samuel Hawk

4

Hawk, Maggie – Naw-No-We
    Allottee No. 524
SW/4 34-18-6
    Died Mar. 24, 1899
Heirs – James Hawk- Husband, (Dead)
    Silas Hawk Son

4

Hawk, James – Pen-E-Tal-Lo-Kut
    Allottee No. 523
SE/4 33-18-6
    Died Mar. 26, 1899
Heirs – Silas Hawk – Son Minor
    Ida Mansur – Daughter
    Mary Mansur –   "   Minor

5

Hawk, John – No-Tah-Naw
    Allottee No. 526
NW/4 34-18-6
    Died Oct. 4, 1893
Heirs – James Hawk – Father (Dead)   See his heirs

Sac & Fox – Shawnee
1846-1924   Volume XI

Powers, Fannie V.
    Allottee No. 548
SE/4 SE/4 10-12-4
NE/4 NE/4 15-12-4
SW/4 SW4 11-12-4
NW/4 NW/4 14-12-5
    Died Nov 28, 1894
Heirs – None known.

Randall, Fannie – Kit Toe
    Allottee No. 422
NE/4 26-16-6
    Died May 17, 1897
Heirs – Penashe – Husband
    Stephen Harrison, Son
    Leona Franklin, Daughter
    Amar Black, Son
    Paul Randall, Son Minor

Red Rock, Abby – Aw-Saw-Waw-Se
    Allottee 447
SE/4 14-17-6
    Died Dec. 10, 1898
Heirs – thought to be Andrew Barker and his half brother who live at Iowa City Iowa.

Plumb, Mary – Pe-Wah-Tah
    Allottee No. 545
Lot 3 and SE/4 SE/4 22-18-6
S/2 SW/4 22-18-6
    Died June 8, 1894
Heirs – Minnie Plumb – Daughter, Minor

Ridge, Jesse – O-Sha-Ke
    Allottee No. 375
NW/4 33-17-6
    Died June 13, 1899
Heirs – Edward Mathews, Brother Sole Heir

Sac & Fox – Shawnee
1846-1924   Volume XI

6
Sherman, Lucy Anderson
    Allottee No. 146
S/2 NW/4 3-11-4
N/2 SW/4 3-11-4
    Died June 20, 1894
Heirs – Ozhe-Ock-Pense Husband
    Frank Davis Half brother

7
Smith, Oda – Ok-O-Maw-Quah
    Allottee No. 34
SE/4 2-16-6
    Died Mar. 24, 1899
Heirs – Webster Smith Father

7
Strubble, George – Se-Po-Ah-S[??]
    Allottee No. 507
E/2 and Lots 4 & 5 SW/4 18-18-6
    Died Mar. 13, 1899
Heirs – Isaac Strubble

7
Sullivan, John L. – Mal-Lo-Chah
    Allottee No. 439
NW/4 11-12-4
    Died April 4, 1891
Heirs – Maggie Sullivan Wife
    Naomi Sullivan Daughter
    Lewis Sullivan Son

7
Taylor, Susan – No-Tah-Sagne
    Allottee No. 449
E/2 NE/4 30-14-6
W/2 NW/4 29-14-6
    Died Oct. 1, 1896
Heirs – Benj Harrison Nephew
    Fannie Randall Niece (dead)   (See her heirs)

8
Turner, Clarence – We-We-Nes
    Allottee No. 527
SW/4 29-18-6
    Died Jan. 1895
Heirs – Thomas Turner Son (Dead)   (See his heirs)

Sac & Fox – Shawnee
1846-1924   Volume XI

8
Turner, Fannie – Maw-She-Kah
    Allottee No. 528
NW/4 29-18-6
    Died Mar. 13, 1891
Heirs – Clarence Turner – Husband (dead)
    Thomas Turner – Son   (dead)

8
Turner, Thomas – Muck Kose
    Allottee No. 529
SW/4 19-18-6
    Died March 15th 1899
Heirs – Not fully determined, thought to be Ke-nah-num-mo-quah, a sister of Fannie Turner who lived at Nadeau Kan but who has since died and left a husband, who has also died and left a brother, now at Nadeau.

9

Pattaqua, Mamie
    Allottee No. 133
NW/4 33-11-4
    Died Feb. 5, 1895
Heirs – Bertha Pattaqua Daughter Minor
    Addie Pattaqua   "   "
*Separated from husband, William Pattaqua, before death

9

Pennock, W^{m} – Was-Waw-Ko
    Allottee No. 482
NW/4 11-11-6
    Died June 24, 1902
Heir – David Pennock Son minor

9

Pennock, Hester – Sheck-Ko-Kah
    Allottee No. 483
SW/4 11-11-6
    Died Aug. 1894
Heirs – William Pennock Husband (dead)
    David Pennock, Son

9

Perkins, Bishop W. – Me-ah-me-sah
    Allottee No. 486
NW/4 18-18-6
    Died Feb. 27, 1893   Heirs – Isaac Strubble

Sac & Fox – Shawnee
1846-1924   Volume XI

10
Pickett, Mary – Paw-Haw-Che-Quah
    Allottee No. 446
NW/4 21-11-4
    Died Dec. 13, 1893
Heirs – Jack Bear, Father
*Separated from husband Jesse Pickett before death and left no children.

10
Butler, Lizzie
    Allottee No. 298
SW/4 2-10-4
    Died Oct 25, 1898
Heirs – Benj Butler Father (dead)   (See his heirs)

Carter, Louise – Pe-Than
    Allottee No. 323
E/2 & Lots 1, 2 NW/4 19-17-6
    Died April 1, 1899
Heirs Frank Carter Husband
    Bertha Carter Daughter (Minor

10
Carter, Martha
    Allottee No. 324
E/2 and Lots 3, 4 SW/4 19-17-6
    Died July 4, 1891
Heirs – Frank Carter Father

11
Conger, Silas – Pe-Ah-Chew-Wah
    Allottee No. 381
SE/4 26-16-6
    Died Mar. 27, 1901
Heirs – Jay Conger Father (Sole Heir)

11
Conger, Jasper – Nah-Naw-Au-Pe
    Allottee No. 383
SW/4 27-16-6
    Died Nov. 26, 1894
Heirs – Jay Conger Father & Sole heir

Sac & Fox – Shawnee
1846-1924   Volume XI

Conger, William – No-Tem-O-Shuk
    Allottee 384
SE/4 27-16-6
    Died Sept. 20, 1891
Heirs – Jay Conger, Father (Sole heir)

Wah-Taw-Sah
    Allottee No. 175
S/2 NE/4 12-11-4
N/2 SE/4 12-11-4
    Died Mar. 28, 1891
Heirs – Sarah Ellis, Wife (Sole heir)

Black, Nancy – Waw-Waw-Ko
    Allottee No. 521
NE/4 28-18-6
    Died Sept. 15, 1892
Heirs – Julia Black Conger – Sister (dead) (See her heirs)

Conger, Julia Black – Mah-Ne-Ash-Ko-Tah
    Allottee No. 381
SW/4 26-16-6
    Died Aug. 11, 1900
Heirs – Andrew Conger Husband
        Pearl Conger Daughter (Minor)

        Waw-pe-se-taw
Black, Lucy – Naw-Pe-Se-Saw
    Allottee No. 214
SE/4 7-16-6
    Died July 2, 1892
Heirs – James Black, Husband (Dead)
       Mary Cup paw he Sister (Dead)
Not blood Ke-Ke-Tah-Kah – was Bro. (Dead)
Heirs – Mary (Cuppawhe) left a daughter, Caroline Dunn.
(Ke-Ke-Tah-was) left one son, Paul Gokey.
Caroline Dunn and Paul Gokey would heir 1/2 of Lucy Black allotment.
Bal. to heirs of James Black.

Sac & Fox – Shawnee
1846-1924   Volume XI

12
Black, James – Ah-Squah-Sup-Pit
    Allottee No. 213
E/2 and Lots 3 & 4 SW/4 7-16-6
    Died Aug. 25, 1892
Heirs – * No wife. No children
His mother's name was Waw-Paw-No-Quah
His father's name was Sha-Was-Ka-Kuk
Sha-Was-Ka-Kuk had one brother, Ma-She-Na, who has one son, W$^{\underline{m}}$ Parkinson, now living who would be James Black's own cousin.

13
Brown, Josephine – Waw-Waw-Sam-O-Quah
    Allottee No. 52
NE/4 20-11-4
    Died Aug. 15, 1900
Heirs – John Brown, Husband
    Thomas Brown, Son
    Harry Brown, Son
    Beulah Brown, Dau.
    Mary E Brown, Dau.

13
Buffalohorn, Clara – Quah-Quah-Che
    Allottee No. 86
NE/4 17-16-6
    Died Nov. 15, 1895
Heirs – Thomas J Buffalohorn – father and sole heir

13
Buffalohorn, Mama
    Allottee No. 87
SE/4 20-11-4
    Died Dec. 30, 1893
Heirs – Thomas J Buffalohorn – father and sole heir

13
Shaw, Edward – Mah-Tah-Wah-Quah
    Allottee No. 89
NW/4 28-11-4
    Died April 13, 1900
Heirs – W$^{\underline{m}}$ Shaw – Father, Sole Heir.

Sac & Fox – Shawnee
1846-1924   Volume XI

14
Butler, Benj. – Pen-Nah-He-Sr
    Allottee No. 293
NW/4 29-17-6
    Died June 30, 1902
Heirs – Edward Butler Son
        George Butler Son
        Jane Butler Dau

14
Eaton, Cassie
    Allottee No. 264
NE/4 17-11-4
    Died Aug. 14, 1890
Heirs – Cassie Rogers, Mother

14
Hunter, George – Wah-Maw-Nah-To-Mah
    Allottee No. 511
E/2 and Lots 3, 4 SW/4 31-18-6
    Died May 15, 1899
Heirs – Lillie G. Hunter, wife
        Robt Hunter – Father

14
Ellis, Katie – Ken-Ne-Sue
    Allottee No. 359
NW/4 12-18-5
    Died Jan. 20, 1900
Heirs – Jesse Kakaque Husband
        Maud Kakaque Dau (Minor)

15
Smith, Martha – Ke-Wah-Aw-Koque
    Allottee No. 32
SE/4 30-17-6
    Died Mar. 28, 1899
Heirs – Webster Smith Husband
        Frank Smith Son
        Benj Smith Son
        Charley Smith Son
        Rachel Smith Dau

Sac & Fox – Shawnee
1846-1924   Volume XI

15

Mason, Nellie – Nah-Kah-Pique
    Allottee No. 289
SW/4 5-17-6
    Died Mar. 1897
Heirs – Eudora Hall – Mother (dead)
    Edith Mason – Sister
    Grace Mason – Sister
    Rachel Hall   1/2 Sister
    Sam Brown   1/2 Brother
    Amos Black   1/2 Brother

15

Brown, Eva – Mock-Kut-Taho-Soque
    Allottee No. 24
S/2 NW/4 10-11-4
N/2 SW/4 10-11-4
    Died Nov. 29, 1892
Heirs – Sam Brown   1/2 Brother
    Amos Black   1/2   "
    Grace Mason   1/2 Sister
    Edith Mason   1/2   "

16

Hawk, Samuel – Nah-Waw-To-Nah
    Allottee No. 469
SW/4 33-18-6
    Died Nov. 17, 1899
Heirs – Eunice Hawk   wife
    Stella Hawk   Dau
    James Hawk   Son (dead)   (See Heirs of James Hawk)

16

Butler, Mollie – Waw-Se-Tal-O-Quah
    Allottee No. 296
N/2, SE/4, Lot 1 SW/4 11-10-4
    Died April 10, 1899
Heirs – George Butler – Son   Minor
    Edward Butler – Son   "
    Jane Butler   – Dau   "

16

Conger, Julia – Nah-Ne-Ash-Ko-Lah
    Allottee No. 387
SW/4 26-16-6
    Died May 3, 1893
Heirs – Henry Appletree – Husband

George Oliver Morten, Son
Clifford H Morten   Son

17

Baker, Timothy – Pe-Ap-Paw-Haw
    Allottee No. 411
SE/4 9-16-6
    Died March 21, 1899
Heirs – Eva Baker – wife
    Martha Baker   Dau. minor
    Sole heirs

17

Ellis, Mabel – Waw-Sah-Que
    Allottee No. 357
SE/4 12-18-5
    Died Aug. 10, 1900
Heirs – Sarah Ellis   Mother
    Jackson Ellis   Bro
    Stella Ellis   Sister
    Clara Ellis   Sister (minor
    Laura Ellis   Sister   "
    Maud Kakaque   Niece
    Anna McKardo

17

Hall, Eudora – Kish-Cut-Che
    Allottee No. 288
SE/4 5-17-6
    Died Mar. 13, 1899
Heirs – Harry Hall, Husband
    Edith Mason   Dau
    Grace Mason   Dau
    Rachel Hall   Dau

18

Bigwalker, John W. – Mon-Mol-Wah
    Allottee No. 198
Lots 1 & 4, NE/4 10-18-5
Lots 2 & 3 & S/2 SE/4 10-18-5
    Died April 20, 1899
Heirs – Sarah Bigwalker   Wife
    Dolly McClellan   Dau
    Jennie Bigwalker   Dau
    Lillie Bigwalker   Dau
    Maud Bigwalker   Dau (Minor
    Esther Bigwalker   Dau – Minor

Sac & Fox – Shawnee
1846-1924   Volume XI

Margaret Bigwalker Dau

18
Bigwalker, Florence – Paw-Ke
    Allottee No 212
S/2 SW/4 10-11-5
N/2 NW/4 15-11-5
    Died Feb. 26, 1894
Heirs – William Pennock 1/2 Bro (dead)
(Had same father – Nah-Ko-Twy-TuckS)   See heirs William Pennock

18
Smith, Alex
    Allottee No. 38
Lots 2 & 3 NW/4 30-18-5
Lots 4 & 5 E/2 SW/4 30-18-5
    Died Dec. 20, 1890
Heirs – Webster Smith, father, sole heir

19
Martin, Betsy – Waw-Saw-Hol-Lo-Quah
    Allottee No. 99
NE/4 33-11-4
    Died Dec. 31, 1894
Heirs – Left no husband
    At-Ton-No-To Son died before allotment and left three children viz:
        Frances Martin
        Julia Sullivan
        Alice Grant
        Waw-Naw-Som-O-Quza
    daughter, who died before allotment and left two
    children, as follows:-
        William Bear Son
        Barbara McKosito Dau dead
See heirs of Barbara McKosito

19
Sherman, Annie Anderson
    Allottee No. 147
S/2 Lots 1&2 NE/4 4-11-4
    Died Jan. 20, 1894
Heir – Tecumseh Sherman, father and sole heir

Sac & Fox – Shawnee
1846-1924   Volume XI

20

Stanley, Mattie – Mah-Teck-Co
    Allottee No. 256
NE/4   21-11-5
    Died Feb. 16, 1902
Heirs – She left no husband or children. She had one brother James Littlebear a Shawnee, who is dead but who left the following names children as his heirs:

Shoney Littlebear	Son	
George Littlebear	Son	
Eliza Littlebear	Dau	
Stella Little Ax	Dau	
Mattie Logan	Dau	
James Littlebear	Son	Minor
Lillie Littlebear	Dau	Minor
Lucy Littlebear	Dau	Dead

    (Lucy Littlebear left two minor children
See what rights Maggie Tyner has.

20

Rice, Jack O. – Muc-Cut-Tah-O-Soqu[sic]
    Allottee No. 231
NW/4   9-11-6
    Died Nov 22 1900
Heirs – Left no wife or children
    Lizzie Rice, Mother
    Edward Rice   Brother } Only Heirs
    Cora Bear   Sister

21

McKosito, Alma – Tan-No-Saque
    Allottee No. 104
SW/4   17-11-5
    Died Feb. 20, 1894
Heirs – No father or mother
    Jessie Pickett 1/2 Bro & sole heir

21

Wheeler, Eva – Mal-Lah-Ko-Wah
    Allottee No. 448
S/2 NW/4   1-11-4
N/2 SW/4   1-11-4
    Died Jan. 30, 1894
Heirs – No father or mother
    Enoch Hoag, Bro (dead)   See Heirs of Enoch Hoag

Sac & Fox – Shawnee
1846-1924   Volume XI

21

Dunn, Lewis – Tah-Kaw-Ko
  Allottee No. 117
NE/4 – 14-11-5
  Died April 12, 1899
Heirs – Jesse Carter – father & sole heir.

22

Dunn, Ralph – Nah-Aw-Taw-Waw-Pah-Mah
  Allottee No. 114
SW/4 12-11-5
  Died Oct. 7, 1898
Heirs – Caroline Dunn wife
    Ada Duncan   Dau (dead   (See heirs Ada Duncan)

22

Falls, Emily – Waw-Kaw-Pe
  Allottee No. 270
SW/4 15-16-6
  Died Feb. 19, 1900
Heirs – Left no husband
    Grover Falls,   Son
    Sam Falls   Son
    Annie Falls   Dau.

22

Senache, Fred – Much-E-Se-A-To
  Allottee No. 5
NW/4 12-10-4
  Died June 5, 1896
Heirs – Sarah Bear   Mother
    Mammie Pattequa Sister Dead
    Anna Senache   Sister Dead
    Oliver P Morton   Bro   Dead
See heirs, Mammie Pattequa, Anna Senache and Oliver P Morton

23

Conger, Martha – Maw-La-Lo-Wah-Quah
  Allottee No. 385
NE/4 23-16-6
  Died Nov. 5, 1893
Heirs – Jay Conger Son, sole heir

23

Conger, Hattie – Aw-Yaw-Che
  Allottee No. 386
SE/4 15-16-6

Sac & Fox – Shawnee
1846-1924 Volume XI

Died May, 1893
Heirs – Jay Conger Father and Sole heir.

23

Fox, Joseph – Maw-Ko-Shah-Pol-Lah-Shaw
    Allottee No. 233
Lots 1 & 2 and E/2 NE/4 11-18-5
    Died Nov. 5, 1899
Heirs – Bettie Fox Wife
    Dick Ellis Bro Shawnee
    Kate Ellis Sis Shawnee
    Mary Pa-paw Sis Kaw Agency

24

Pattaqua, Charlotte – Pe-She-Ke-She-Quah
    Allottee No. 434
NW/4 14-16-6
    Died May 31, 1902
Heirs – Gertrude Brown Mother
    Oscar Givens Brother
    Eveline Givens Brother
    Lydia Grant Sister
    Lucy Thurman Sister

24

Groinhorn, Charley – Kish-Ko
    Allottee No. 112
SE4 32-11-4
    Died June 1, 1897
Heirs – Left no father
    Jane Shaw Mother
    Milford Groinhorn Brother
    Fannie Lasley Sister

25

Maw-Mel-Lo-Han
    Allottee No. 356
Lots 1 & 2 and S/2 NE/4 1-18-5
    Died Dec. 1, 1890
Heirs – Sarah Ellis Wife
    Annie McKosito Dau
    Katie Ellis Dau Dead
    Jackson Ellis Son
    Stella Ellis Dau
    Clara Ellis Dau Minor
    Laura Ellis Dau Minor
    Mattie Ingalls Dau

Sac & Fox – Shawnee
1846-1924   Volume XI

See heirs Katie Ellis

25

Waw-Ko-Dah-She-Toe
    Allottee No. 547
Lot 1 SE/4 7-18-6
Lot 1 SW/4 17-18-6
Lots 3 & 2 NE/4 18-18-6
    Died June 20, 1890
Heirs – Mary Plumb   Mother   Dead
        Minnie Plumb   Sister (Sole heir)

26

McKosito, Barbara – Mesh-Ke-Ah-Ko-Quah
    Allottee No. 102
NE/4 Lots 3&4 20-11-5
    Died Jan. 1894
Heirs – Undecided, under investigation.

26

McKosito, Moses – Kah-Com-Mo-Saque
    Allottee No. 103
SE/4   6-11-5
    Died Jan. 7, 1898
Heirs – Che-Quam-Me-go-co, father   died before allotment.
        Lydia Walker   Mother   Dead
        Ben Walker   1/2 Bro
        Leo Walker   1/2 Bro
        Guy Walker   1/2 Bro   Minor
        Elmer Walker   1/2 Bro   Minor
        Ira Walker   1/2 Bro   Minor

26

Messawot, Julia – Nah-Cut-To-Shah
    Allottee No. 372
NE/4 33-17-6
    Died Feb. 24, 1894
Heirs – Linda Messawot   Dau   Sole Heir

27

Messawot, Alma – Ko-Pe-Wah
    Allottee No. 373
SE/4 23-17-6
    Died April 7, 1897
Heirs – Julia Messawot   Dead
        Linda Messawot   Sis & Sole heir

Sac & Fox – Shawnee
1846-1924   Volume XI

27

Morris, Harriet – My-Yah-Wah-Quah
    Allottee No. 64
SW/4 6-18-6
    Died Dec. 24, 1895
Heirs – Alice Morris   Dau
    Thomas Morris   Son   Minor
    Grover Morris   Son   Minor
    Susan Morris   Dau   Minor
    Edward Morris   Son   Minor
Harriet Morris had two husbands, one died before allotment and from the other she was separated before death.

28

Neal, Moses – We-She-Kaw-Mah-E-Que
    Allottee No. 465
SE/4 20-18-6
    Died May 1, 1895
Heirs – Henry Clay, Father, Sole heir

28

Mokohoko, Flora – Waw-Waw-Taw-Quah-She
    Allottee No. 158
SE/4 Lot 2 NW/4 7-11-5
NE/4 Lot 3 SW4 7-11-5
    Died April 30, 1897
Heirs – No husband
    Louisa Mack   Daughter by Wm Pattequa
    Dickson Duncan   Son by David Duncan
        (Only heirs)

28

Neal, Mary – We-Ke-Aw
    Allottee No. 462
NE/4 29-18-6
    Died Mar. 3, 1899
Heirs – Jesse Carter, husband
    Victor Neal   Son
    Osidore Neal   Son
        (Only heirs)

29

Neal, Kishko
    Allottee No. 464
SE/4 10-17-6
    Died Mar. 29, 1891
Heirs – Henry Clay   Father   (Sole heir.)

Sac & Fox – Shawnee
1846-1924   Volume XI

Walker, Elma – Waw-Push-Shaw-Kol
    Allottee No. 193
N/2 NW/4 12-11-4
S/2 SW4 1-11-4
    Died Feb. 20, 1894
Heirs – Kup-Pash-Ka   Mother died before allotment
    Clarence Pickett   Father (dead
    Jesse Pickett   1/2 Bro   (Sole heir)

McKuk, John – Mah-Kuk
    Allottee No. 259
SW4 32-12-6
    Died Mar. 28, 1894
Wah-Waw-To-Sah, uncle, being brother of John McKuk's father
Heirs thought to be – Wm Davenport   Nephew
        Nancy Davenport   Niece
            (Over)
        Seba Davenport   Grand-niece
        ------ Davenport   Grand-nephew
    All of Toledo, Iowa

McClellan, Oscar – Que-Quah-Lah-Ke-Kuk
    Allottee No. 477
NE/4 23-18-6
    Died Mar. 12, 1899
Heirs – Thomas McClellan   Fath.   dead
    Mus-Quaw-Ke-A-Quah   Moth dead
    John McClellan   Uncle
    Flora Davis   Aunt
    Edward McClellan   Uncle
        (Only heirs)

McClellan, Geo B – Chaw-Kah-Ne-Mah
    Allottee No. 474
SE/4 23-18-6
    Died Jan. 2, 1894
Heirs – John McClellan   Son
    Flora Davis   Dau
    Edward McClellan   Son
        (Only heirs)

Sac & Fox – Shawnee
1846-1924   Volume XI

31

McClellan, Thomas – Puch-E-Shin
    Allottee No. 484
Lots 1&2 and SE/4   NE/4 22-18-6
    E/2   SE/4 22-18-6
Lots 1&2   SE/4 15-18-6
    Died April 7, 1899
Heirs – No wife nor children
    John McClellan   Bro
    Flora Davis   Sis
    Edward McClellan Bro

31

McClellan, Rebecca – Nah-Aw-Ke-Ke
    Allottee No. 485
NE/4 27-18-6
    Died April 5, 1899
Heirs – Thomas McClellan   Husb. dead
    David Johnson, Son, died in 1894, leaving a wife, Ella Dupres and a son named Arthur Johnson at Nadeau, Kansas.
    Thomas McClellan's heirs get 1 half.
    Ella Dupres & David Johnson get the other half.

32

Franklin, Susan – Ne-Paw-Saque
    Allottee No. 410
SE/4 6-16-6
    Died Feb. 15, 1899
Heirs – No husband
    Fryor Franklin   Son   Minor
      (Sole heir)

32

Marshall, Gabriel – Waw-Waw-She
    Allottee No. 400
NE/4 27-16-6
    Died Oct. 9, 1891
Heirs – No ~~husband~~ wife nor children
    Ket-to-ne-quah, mother, full sister to Rachel Davis, she being dead the estate goes to her nearest relative, who is Jay Conger.
    (See heirs of Rachel Davis).
  Me Kah taw in Iowa.

Sac & Fox – Shawnee
1846-1924   Volume XI

32
Hall, Rufus – Wah-Shaw-Nah
    Allottee No. 292
SW/4 32-18-6
    Died May 30, 1902
Heirs – Harry Hall,   father   (Sole heir)

33
Pickett, Clarence – Ne-Kot-Lo-Ko-Hach
    Allottee No. 444
NW/4 22-16-6
    Died Nov. 2, 1892
Heirs – Jesse Pickett   Son   (Sole heir)

33
Mitchell, James – Mah-Ke-Koh-Nah-Wah
    Allottee No. 503
NE/4 11-17-6
    Died Aug. 20, 1891
Heirs – (Father and mother dead.)
    Supposed to be a 1/2 brother of Clarence Pickett, if so Jesse Pickett would be the heir. Investigate further

33
Mock-E-Naw
    Allottee No. 47
NW/4 15-17-6
    Died Sept. 28, 1890
Heirs – Cora Ward   Mother   (Sole heir)

34
Cheekos-Kuk-Kah-Tah-Ko-Wah
    Allottee No. 1
Lot 3 & E/2 & NE/4 SE/4 35-19-5
Lot 1   SW/4 35-19-5
Heirs – Ah-nah-me   Son (dead)
Ah-nah-me was an Iowa Sac & Fox and was not allotted here, he left a wife Lindy Rogers, who is sole heir of Mary Cheekos-kuk

34
Scott, Joseph – Puh-Pah-Sko-Se-Taw
    Allottee No. 398
Lots 3 and 4 & E/2 SW/4 18-17-6
    Died Oct. 7, 1901
Heirs – Jim Scott   Father   (Sole heir)

Sac & Fox – Shawnee
1846-1924   Volume XI

34
Hoag, Lucy – Pe-Ke-Haw
    Allottee No. 365
Lot 3 & W/2   NE/4 7-18-6
Lot 2 & NW/4 SE/4 7-18-6
    Died April 10, 1897
Heirs – Enoch Hoag, Husband (dead only relative – See his heirs

35

Grass, John – Mo-Law-Kaw
    Allottee No. 223
Lots 3 & 4 and E/2 SW/4 30-17-6
    Died Mar. 3, 1901
Heirs – Left no wife nor children
    Ke-nah-po   Fath dead
    Ah-Paw-hah-mo-que   dead
Ah-Paw-hah-mo-que had one sister named Pen-way-tah, dead, survived by one son, Jesse James.
Ke-nah-po had one brother, Chuck-E-maw-E-say, dead, who was the father of Sarah Bigwalker.
Heirs would be:
        Jesse James   1st cousin
        Sarah Bigwalker   1st cousin

35

Herdford, Martha – Wa-Pal-Ah-Wah-Nah
    Allottee No. 157
NW/4 23-17-6
    Died Jan, 1895
Heirs – Wah-Naw-Ke Sis dead
Wah-waw-ke, had one child, Gertrude Brown, who is now living and who is the sole heir

36
Hoag, Enoch – My-Aw-Che
    Allottee No. 364
SW/4 7-18-6
    Died April 11, 1897
Heirs – Kish-Kut-Tup-Pe-Wa   Fath (dead
    Nah-Kah-pe-ah   Moth (dead
    Moe-Lah-ko-wah   Sis died without leaving husband or issue
    Kish-Kut-tup-pe-wa had brothers and sisters as follows:-
            Chief M\$c\$Kosito   Bro
            David Wakolle   Bro
            Edgar Mack   Bro
            Judith Houston   Sister
The above are uncles and aunt to Enoch Hoag and his only heirs

36
Stanley, Popo – Po-Po
    Allottee No. 225
Lots 4, 5 & 6   SE/4 21-11-5
Lots 2 & 3   SW/4 21-11-5
Lots 1 & 2   SE/4 22-11-5
    Died Dec. 30th 1896
Heirs – Mattie Stanley   Wife dead
        Carrie Littlebear   Sister
        Thomas J Buffalohorn Bro.
          (Only heirs)
See heirs of Mattie Stanley

37

Ocean, Bettie – Se-Taw-Me
    Allottee No. 401
SE/4 23-16-6
    Died Aug. 20, 1892
Heirs – Opy-O-Sah   Fath. dead
    Opy-o-sah has one sister named, (Pe-to-Pe) Martha Morris, dead, survived by two sons – Benj. Franklin, living and Muck-ko-tah-new-me-ke-wah, dead, survived by two children, Alex Jefferson and Maggie Tyner both living.

37

Ingalls, Bessie – Naw-Saw-Paw-Meque
    Allottee No. 337
Lots 1 & 2 and E/2 NW/4 7-16-6
    Died Feb. 16, 1896
Heirs – William Ingalls   Nephew (dead
        Sadie Ingalls   Niece
See heirs of William Ingalls

38
Ingalls, William – Mo-Ke-Tah-Hot
    Allottee No. 340
SW/4 10-16-6
    Died Aug. 18, 1902
Heirs – Mattie Ingalls   Moth
        Sadie Ingalls   Sis. Minor
        Henry Ingalls   1/2 bro. Minor

Sac & Fox – Shawnee
1846-1924 Volume XI

38

Ingalls, Lucile – Naw-Aw-Ten-O-Kaque
    Allottee No. 336
NW/4   8-16-6
    Died Dec. 20, 1891
Heirs – John J. Ingalls   Husb.   dead
           Bessie Ingalls   Dau   dead
           Horace Ingalls   Son   dead
See heirs of the above

38

Ingalls, John J. – Waw-Ko-Mo
    Allottee No. 335
NE/4   14-17-6
    Died Feb. 20, 1892
Heirs – Bessie Ingalls   Dau   dead
           Horace Ingalls   Son   dead
See heirs of the above

39

Ingalls, Horace – Pe-Shaw-Kaw
    Allottee No. 338
Lot 7 NW/4   27-11-4
Lots 8&9 SE/4   27-11-4
Lots 5&6 SW4   27-11-4
    Died Jan. 1, 1895
Heirs – Mattie Ingalls   Wife
           Sadie Ingalls   Dau   minor
           William Ingalls   Son   dead
Mattie Ingalls, wife and Sadie, daughter, are only heirs

39

Morris, Martha – Pe-To-Pe
    Allottee No. 402
SE/4   5-16-6
    Died Dec. 14, 1892
Heirs – Benj. Franklin   Son
           Muck-ko-tah-nah-nem-me-ke-wah, son who died leaving two children
                   Alex Jefferson   Son
                   Mattie Tyner   Dau

Sac & Fox – Shawnee
1846-1924   Volume XI

40
Long, Thomas – Waw-Paw-Ko-Huck
    Allottee No. 209
SW/4   NE/4   22-11-5
SE/4   NW/4   22-11-5
Lots 3,4&5   SE/4   22-11-5
    Died July, 1898
Heirs – Left no wife nor children   Meu-wa-quot was a brother who died before allotment. He left one son, Nat-ko-twy-tuk who also died before allotment and who left surviving one son, William, who has since died, leaving David Pennock, a minor as the one heir of Thomas Long's. Men-na-quot also left one daughter named, Check-e-qua, dead but has a daughter, M-jish-ke, now living at Nadeau Kansas, and who would share equally with David Pennock in the Estate of Thomas Long.

    By
  M jish ke   { Instead of "Check e qua" – "Waw wa sum mo qua" was daughter of Men a quot and mother of M jish ke. Check e qua was younger
  Dec.31-04   dau. and sister of "Waw wa sum mo qua" left

41
Dunn, Albert – Maw-Maw-Kaw-She
    Allottee No. 116
NW/4   12-11-5
    Died Feb. 5, 1900
Heirs – Left no father nor mother   No wife nor children
    Ada Duncan Sis.   Dead   (Only her)
See heirs of Ada Duncan

41
Duncan, Ada – Ah-Pah-Che-Kah-Taw-Quaw
    Allottee No. 119
Lots 3&4   NW/4   6-11-5
Lot 4   SW/4   31-12-5
SE/4   31-12-5
    Died April 2, 1901
Heirs – Richard Duncan Husb.
    McKinley Duncan Son (since died, thus leaving Richard Duncan sole heir

---

applies to 1/2 of Agnes Long.

Waw Paw [illegible… – paper torn]
no wife, no Child

One brother Men o quot [illegible… - paper torn] allotment. He left a <u>Son</u> Naw ko twy [illegible… - paper town] who also died before allotment, and who left a son William Pennock (Waw saw ko) who died - - - and left a son David Pennock who shares 1/3 of said land.

Sac & Fox – Shawnee
1846-1924 Volume XI

Men o quot also left two daughters Chuck e qua, dau died and left Josephine Brown (Waw-waw son o quah) (named after Aunt) who died Aug 15 1900 and left John Brown (husband) and Thomas, Harry & Beulah my children who share 1/3 together.

Waw waw sum o quah   dau of Men o quot and sister to Chuck e qua died about 1872 and left Mjishke at Nadeau, Kas, now living who shares a 1/3 interest

Brothers:
- Thomas Long
- Men o quot died before any of his children about 1864 not sure
  - Na Ko twy tock (died about 1885)
  - Chuck e qua (died about 1875)
  - Waw waw som o quah (Died about 1872)
    - William Pennock { David Pennock
    - [illegible]
    - Josephine Brown (Waw waw som o qua)
    - M jish ke

By M jish ke – Laura [Illegible] and Mary Hurr

Dec 31-1904

42

Morton, Oliver P – Kaw-Ke-Ka-Toe
　　Allottee No. 203
SE/4 28-11-4
　　Died Aug. 5, 1895
Heirs – Carrie J Morton　wife
　　Clifford H Morton　Son
　　Geo. Oliver Morton　Son Minor
　　Mamie Morton　　　Dau, Minor

42

Givens, Joshua – Waw-Se-Nah-a-Tah
　　Allottee No. 431
SE/4 34-17-6
　　Died Sept. 1898
Heirs – Gertrude Brown　Wife
　　Lydia Grant　　Dau
　　Isaac Givens　　Son
　　Eveline Givens　Son
　　Lucy Thurman　Dau
　　(only heirs)

43

Long, Agnes – Maw-Taw-Che
　　Allottee No. 210
SW/4　SE/4　15-11-5
SE/4　SW/4　15-11-5

Sac & Fox – Shawnee
1846-1924   Volume XI

NW/4 NE/4   22-11-5
NE/4 NW/4   22-11-5
    Died Aug. 1, 1896
Heirs – Thomas Long   Husb. dead
    George, Man-a-Taw-a,   bro dead
See heirs of the above.

43

Lee, Bessie – Ke-Waw-Ho-Que
    Allottee No. 71
SE/4 4-11-4
    Died June 18, 1894
Heirs – Left no husband nor children. Father nor mother.
        Jesse Lee – Sister
        Tecumseh Sherman   Bro
        Ida Rubedeaux   Sister
    Philip Lee   (only Heirs)

44

Ah-Quaw-Saw
    Allottee No. 436
SW/4 14-16-6
    Died Feb. 10, 1891
Heirs – Joshua Givens   Fath. dead
See heirs of Joshua Givens.

44

Bear, James – Wah-Neck-Ko-Wah
    Allottee No. 238
NE/4 10-10-4
    Died Aug. 11, 1896
Heirs – Neither father, mother, brother nor sister.
      Mollie Bear, wife   (Dead)
        (Sole heir)
See heirs of Mollie Bear.

44

Wa-Pe-Ko-Hol
    Allottee No. 420
NE/4 34-17-6
    Died Aug. 25, 1890
Heirs – No Wife
    Mary Sha-que-quot

45

Senache, Fred – Much-E-Se-a-Po
    Allottee No. 5
NW/4 12-10-4
    Died June 15, 1896
Heirs – No wife or children
    Sarah Bear   Moth.
    Alma Senache   Sis. (dead)
    Mamie Pattaqua   Sis. (dead)
    Oliver P Morton   Bro. (dead)
See heirs of Anna Senache
   "   "   " Mamie Pattequa
   "   "   " Oliver P Morton

45

Senache, Anna – Waw-Such-Che
    Allottee No. 4
S/2   NE/4   22-14-6
N/2   SE/4   22-14-6
    Died July 2, 1897
Heirs – Wiley Uribes   Husb.
    Sarah Bear   Moth
See   { Oliver P Morton   Bro. dead
heirs { Mamie Pattequa   Sis. dead
The children of Oliver P. Morton
are: Clifford H. Morton   Son
    Geo. Oliver Morton   Son Minor
    Mamie Morton   Dau Minor
The children of Mamie Pattequa
are: Bertha Pattequa   Dau
    Addie Pattequa   Dau.

46

Bass, Samuel – Ah-She-Kaw
    Allottee No. 516
SE/4   16-17-6
    Died April 3, 1899
Heirs – Inez Bass   Wife
    Cora Bass   Dau. Minor
    Lee Bass   Dau. Minor
    Ione C. Bass Dau. Minor

46

Bass, Carrie – Che-Kaw-Mah-Quah
    Allottee No. 518
SE/4   31-18-6
    Died April 5, 1899

Sac & Fox – Shawnee
1846-1924   Volume XI

Heirs – Inez Bass   Mother
       Cora Bass   Sister
       Lee Bass   Brother
       Ione C. Bass   Sister
    (Only heirs)

46

Sha-Que-Quot, Jerome – Waw-Pas-She-Te-Pah
    Allottee No. 218
SW/4 21-16-6
    Died May 1893
Heirs – Tecumseh Sherman, father and sole heir

47

Conger, Hattie – Aw-Yaw-Che
    Allottee No. 386
SE/4 15-16-6
    Died Nov. 1893
Heirs – Jay Conger, Fath, Sole heir

47

Conger, May – Mesh-Shaw-Che
    Allottee No. 389
NE/4 22-16-6
    Died Nov. 12, 1893
Heirs – Charles Crane,   Fath, Sole heir

47

Coon, Dennis – Ah-Ske-Puck-Ka
    Allottee No. 184
NW/4 25-12-4
    Died June 5, 1902
Heirs – No wife or children
    Ella Carter, Sister
      (Sole heir)

48

Bear, Mollie – Waw-Se-Tal-O-Quah
    Allottee No. 296
N/2 SW/4   11-10-4
Lot 1 and SE/4 SW/4 11-10-4
    Died April 10, 1899
Heirs – Edward Butler, Son
    George Butler, Son (Minor
    Jane Butler   Dau (Minor

Sac & Fox – Shawnee
1846-1924   Volume XI

48

Duncan, May – No-Taw-Ko-Se-Quah
    Allottee No. 137
NE/4   22-17-6
    Died April 18, 1902
Heirs – Dickson Duncan   1/2 Bro   Minor
        Allen G. Thurman   1/2 Bro   Minor

48

Dunn, Ralph – Nah-Aw-Taw-Waw-Pah-Nah
    Allottee No. 114
SW/4   12-11-5
    Died Oct. 7, 1898
Heirs – Caroline Dunn   Wife
By a former wife, Annie Nullake, he had two children:
                Ada Nullake   Dau   Dead
                Albert Dunn   Son   Dead
See heirs of Ada Nullake and Albert Dunn

49

Duncan, Lottie – Ah-Nah-Me-Ne-Quah
    Allottee No. 136
SE/4   15-17-6
    Died April 5, 1899
Heirs – David Duncan   Husb.   dead
        May Duncan   Dau   dead
See Heirs of David Duncan and May Duncan.

49

Duncan, David – Ken-No-Tup-Pe
    Allottee No. 135
NW/4   22-17-6
    Died April 10th 1899
Heirs – No wife living at his death.
  By 1st wife, Flora Mokohoko, he had one son, Dickson Duncan (minor
  By 2nd wife, Lucy Thurman, he had one son, Allen G. Thurman, (minor
  By 3rd wife, Lottie Duncan, he had one daughter, May Duncan, now dead.

50

Duncan, Alice – Kap-Pol-Law
    Allottee No. 138
SE/4   7-11-5
    Died Mar. 18, 1901
Heirs – William Bear   Husband
        Richard Duncan   Brother
            (Sole heirs)

Sac & Fox – Shawnee
1846-1924   Volume XI

50

Duncan, Robt – Pah-Kob-No-Pe
    Allottee No. 139
NE/4 7-11-5
    Died Jan. 6, 1898
Heirs – Alice Duncan   Sister (dead
    Richard Duncan   Bro
See Alice Duncan heirs

50

Davis, Bessie – Waw-So-Sah
    Allottee No. 352
NW/4 32-17-6
    Died June 15, 1897
Heirs – Jesse James – Husband
    Jefferson Davis – Father (dead
(See heirs of Jefferson Davis.

51

Davis, Marie – Ke-Waco-To-Quah
    Allottee No. 353
SE/4 21-17-6
    Died Sept. 25, 1899
Heirs – Jefferson Davis   Fath. (dead
See heirs of Jefferson Davis

51

Davis, Jefferson – Mah-Kah-Kat
    Allottee No. 341
NE/4 21-17-6
    Died Nov. 1900
Heirs – Mary Hurr – wife
    Robt Davis, Son   (minor)
    Osville Davis   Son
    Jane Johnson, Dau (dead
Jane Johnson was survived by a son, Orlando Johnson, minor
    Osville Davis died

51

Davis, Rachel – Ke-Kaw-Saque
    Allottee No. 348
NE/4 28-17-6
    Died Jan. 1, 1902
Heirs – No husband or children
    Ne-Ma-Ko-Whah, brother dead, survived by son, Jay Conger – Sole and only heir of Rachel Davis

52

Wolf, John – Ke-Om-Mo-What
    Allottee No. 206
Lots 4,5,6   13-11-5
S/2 NE/4   13-11-5
    Died April 1894
Heirs – James Wolf   Son minor

52

Wyman, Bertha – Chuch-E-Quah
    Allottee No. 415
NW/4   11-16-6
    Died Nov. 25, 1899
Heirs – Henry Hunter   Husband
       Mary W Hunter   Dau. dead
Mary W. Hunter died Jan. 30, 1902, leaving Henry Hunter, Sole heir

---

52

Wyman, Esau – Mah-Taw-Waw-Kaw-Pe
    Allottee No. 416
SE/4   11-16-6
    Died Sept. 15, 1898
Heirs – Timothy Baker – Fath – Dead
  See heirs of Timothy Baker

53

Wyman, Peter – Nah-Ko-Te-It
    Allottee No. 418
NW/4   7-17-6
    Died Mar. 26, 1899
Heirs – Eva Baker   Mother
       Bertha Wyman Sister Dead
       Reuben Wyman Bro
       Jacob Wyman   Bro
       Martha Mathews 1/2 Sister
See heirs of Bertha Wyman

53

Wilson, James – Waw-Paw-Ko-Las-[??]
    Allottee [No.] 532
SW/4   27-18-6
    Died Dec. 14, 1892
Heirs – Bettie Fox, wife
       Harry Madison   son
The mother of Harry Madison was, My-you-waw-que, who died before allotment.

Sac & Fox – Shawnee
1846-1924   Volume XI

54

Wolf, Jane – Sau-E-Quah
  Allottee No. 208
S/2 SE/4 12-11-5
N/2 NE/4 13-11-5
  Died May 15, 1892
Heirs – John Wolf Husband dead
  James Wolf Son Minor

54

Cuppahe, Chief – Cup-Paw-He
  Allotee[sic][sic] No. 195
W/2 SE/4 14-11-5
E/2 SW/4 14-11-5
  Died Jan. 4, 1892
Heirs – Caroline Dunn Pickett (Dau
    (Sole heir)

54

Cuppahe, Mary – Maw-Taw-Ko-La-Que
  Allottee No. 196
SE/4 2-11-5
  Died May 1, 1895
Heirs – Caroline Dunn Picket (Dau
    (Sole heir)

55

Jones, Emily
  Allottee No. 12
NE/4 Sec 10-11-6
  Died June 1896
Heirs – Henry C. Jones

55

Harrison, Rufus
  Allottee No. 427
NW/4 10-16-6
  Died June 24th 1899
Heirs – Benjamin Harrison

55

Harris, Francis – Ah-Ne-Pe-Ah-No
  Allottee No. 473
NW/4 33-18-6
  Died 1899
Heirs – Tap-pe-no-wa, Moth died before allotments
  Joseph Harris   Fath. Dead before [illegible]

Mary Harris 1/2 sister
Moses Harris 1/2 brother
   (Only heirs

56

James Black – Ah-Squah-tup-pit
   Allottee No. 213
E/2 & Lots 3&4 SW/4 7-16-6
   Died August 25, 1892
Heirs – No wife no children
   James Parkinson 1st Cousin
   Ben Harrison 1st Cousin
   Kit toe (dead) 1st Cousin
   leaving as heirs the following
   Tom Penashe husb – 1/9
   Leona Franklin dau 1/18
   Steven Harrison son 1/18
   Amos Black son 1/18
   Paul Randall son 1/18

56

Townsend
   Allottee No. 64
E^2 of NE^4 14-17-3
Heirs – Shar-tar-cher mother 1/2
   Maggie White sister 1/2
Townsend died. 1/2 of his allotment went to his mother and the other 1/2 to his half sister, Maggie White. She died, her share in this allotment went to her mother, Emma Perry. her sister Jennie Lincoln, her brothers Farrah Roubideaux, Sam Perry they share equally.

57

Phoebe Keokuk   Allottee No. 261
Lots 3 and 4 and E/2 SW/4 – 31-17-6
   Died May 18th 1893
Heirs –
   Moses Keokuk – Husband sharing 1/3 Int.
   Marie A Fear (nee Keokuk) – dau " " "
   Alice Lee (nee Keokuk) – dau " " "

Sac & Fox – Shawnee
1846-1924   Volume XI

200
Tohee, William
    Allottee No. 1
Lots 6 and 7   –   8-17-3
    Died Feb. 2, 1892
Heirs – Maggie White Horse   Wife
        Charley Tohee   Son
        Dave Tohee, Jr.   Son

200
Patrick, Lee (Tohee)
    Allottee No. 5
N/2   NW/4   17-17-3
    Died June 20, 1891
Heirs – David Tohee, Father
    (Sole heir)

200
Neal, Mary (Tohee)
    Allottee No. 9
E/2   SW/4   9-17-3
    Died Dec. 1, 1895
Heirs – David Tohee, Father
    Sole heir.

201

Pah-Ne-Me
    Allottee No. 6
S/2   SW/4   28-16-1
    Died Jan 5, 1894
Heirs – Squirrel, first husband died before allotment, Mary Squirrel, now wife of Robt. Small, was ~~only~~ child of this marriage. Gerry Squirrel was also child of this marriage. Gerry Squirrel died and left as his heirs, Julia Tohee, wife, and Wah-to-gram-me, daughter, as he died before his mother, Pah-ne-me, his child inherited his share in his mother's estate. The child, Wah-to-gram-me, died, leaving her mother, Julia Tohee her heir.
Coonskin was the second husband of Pah-ne-me. He is an Otoe and is now living. The heirs would be:-
    Coonskin   Husb.   1/3
    Mary Small   1/3
    Julia Tohee   1/3

Sac & Fox – Shawnee
1846-1924 Volume XI

202

Tohee, Mary
  Allottee No. 10
W/2 SE/4 9-17-3
  Died Mar. 20, 1899
Heirs – David Tohee   Husb.
  Gertie Kent   Dau. by (Sho-jo mon, who died before allotment)
  Edward Tohee had same father and mother as Gertie Kent is a minor and now living.

202

Squirrel, Carrie
  Allottee No. 12
W/2 SE/4 24-17-2
  Died Dec. 26, 1892
Heirs – Left Julia Tohee wife living by whom he had one daughter, Wah-to-gram-me, who died after the father and thus left Julia Tohee only heir

203

Wah-To-Gramme
  Allottee No. 14
E/2 SE/4 10-17-3
  Died Dec. 31, 1895
Heirs – Julia Tohee   Moth   (Only heir)

203

My-Ah-Pe-Me-Gre-Me
  Allottee No. 17
S/2 NW/4 15-17-2
  Died Jan. 20, 1896
Heirs – Joe Vetter   Husb.
  Shu-tah-char – Dau.
  Sam Vetter   Son
(The above are the only heirs)

204

Vetters, Lucy (Mon You A Me)
  Allottee No. 19
W/2 SW/4 15-17-2
  Died June 26, 1892
Heirs – a daughter, Emma Kirk, father unknown, Lucy Vetters married Clem Whitehorse when the above child was a few days old. The heirs are – Clem Whitehorse, Husb.
        Nahko   Fath;
        (Only heirs

Sac & Fox – Shawnee
1846-1924   Volume XI

204
Grant, John – Na-Ther-Me-Na
    Allottee No. 22
S/2   SW/4   20-16-1
    Died July 3, 1900
Heirs – Mary Grant   Wife
      Jane Ely   Dau
      Annie Nellie Grant   Dau
      Thomas Stanley Elwood Grant, Son died Dec. 11, 1900 and left a wife Mary McGlaslin Grant and one child, Vestina Grant. John Grant, also left a son, William Green or Grant who died at Red Rock Dec. 11, 1901 and who left a wife, Mary Green Grant and 3 children at Red Rock and also left three children by a former wife at Nadeau Kansas.

Children at Redrock	Anna Grant	At Nadeau
	Frank "	Eva Morris
	Thelma "	Ralph Green
		Jefferson "

205
Grant, Thomas Stanley
    Allottee No. 25
N/2   SW/4   29-16-1
    Died Dec. 11, 1900
Heirs – Mary McGlaslin Grant   Wife
      Vestina Grant   Dau
      (Only Heirs)

205
Ely, Samuel
    Allottee No. 27
S/2   NE/4   30-16-1
    Died July 2, 1892
Heirs – Albert Ely, Father,   (Only heir

206
Gra-Taw-Tha-Wa-Me
    Allottee No. 29
N/2   SW/4   15-17-3
    Died Jan. 10, 1894
Heirs – Hog-Gra-ah-Chey   Husb
      (Only heir known)

Sac & Fox – Shawnee
1846-1924 Volume XI

206
Lunt, Lina B
    Allottee No. 31
N/2 NE/4 21-17-3
    Died July 3, 1892
Heirs – Augre   Mother   Sole Heir
Susan Whitewater & Nettie Whitewater,
                J Jenson L G Red Rock

206
Hallowell, Nannie
    Allottee No 39
N/2 SE/4 21-17-3
    Died July 12, 1897
Heirs – Ben Hallowell   Husb.
    (heir to one-~~third~~) half
    Mary Rubedeaux   Moth
    Lizzie Hallowell   Half Sister
    Alice Deran   "   "
 (heirs to other half)

207

Murray, Kerwin
    Allottee No. 66
W/2 SE/4 11-17-3
    Died June July 6, 1894
[Heirs –] May Murray, wife – Died Jan. 15, 1900
    Charles C Murray   Son
See heirs May Murray

207

Murray, May
    Allottee No.
Died Jan. 15, 1900
SW/4 NE/4 ⎫
SE/4 NW/4 ⎬ 19-15-2
Heirs – Left no father, mother, brother or sister and no children
~~John Ford~~, John Grant and Thomas Dorian, 1ˢᵗ cousins   John Grant and Thomas Dorian are dead. See their heirs

Refer to Business Committee May Murray was sister of Kah in go hah Deroin, wife of Frank Deroin, Whitecloud, Kus[sic]
John Grant and May Murry[sic] had same mother dif. father

Sac & Fox – Shawnee
1846-1924 Volume XI

208
Whitewater, James
 Allottee No. 45
S/2 SW/4 Lot 3 – 7-16-3
 Died Feb. 19, 1893
Heirs – Birdie Deroin, wife (Otoe)
 Bessie Whitewater Dau.

208
Whitecloud, Jefferson
 Allottee No. 56
SW/4 NW/4 15-14-3
SE/4 SE/4 21-15-1
 Died Feb. 10, 1893
Heirs – Susan Whitecloud Wife
 Julia Kihiga Dau
 Mary Rubedeaux "
 Emma Whitecloud "
 Phoebe Whitecloud "
 Eliza Morris " (Whitecloud)
 Dora James Red Rock

208
Grant, Thomas Stanley
 Allottee No. 25
N/2 SW/4 29-16-1
 Died Dec. 11, 1900
Heirs – Mary McGlaslin Grant Wife
 Vestina Grant Dau

209
Grant, John
 Allottee No. 22
S/2 SW/4 20-16-1
 Died July 3, 1900
Heirs – Mary Grant wife
 Jane Ely dau
 Anne Nellie Grant dau
 Thomas Stanley Grant son died Dec. 11, 1900 (see his heirs)
 William Green Grant son died March 1901, was enrolled with Iowas at Nadeau, Kan, left a wife, Mary Green Grant, three children at Nadeau, Kan and two children at Red Rock, Okla.

Sac & Fox – Shawnee
1846-1924   Volume XI

Hallowell, Harry Falk
    Allottee No. 40
S/2   SE/4 21-17-3
    Died June 17, 1892
Heirs – Ben Hallowell, Father

210
Rubideau, Fannie
    Allottee No. 49
NW/4   SE/4
NE/4   SW/4 } 28-11-3
    Died Aug. 3, 1901
Heirs – Annie Perry   Mother
      Thomas White   Father   died before allotment
      Jennie Lincoln   1/2 sister
      Farrah Rubideau 1/2 brother
      George Rubideau 1/2 brother

210
No-Ah-Tom
    Allottee No. 51
S/2   NE/4 9-17-3
    Died Sept. 4, 1901
Heirs – No father, mother, wife nor children
      Robert Small, Grandson

210
Noheart, Joseph
    Allottee No. 53
N/2   NW/4 18-15-2
    Died Nov. 30, 1892
Heirs – No-Ah-Che-Me   mother   dead
No brothers or sisters
      Eliza White and Sha-tah-cher   sisters of No-Ah-Che-Me and Aunts of Joseph
Noheart (Only heirs)

211
Mohee, John
    Allottee No. 92
SE/4 NW/4
NW/4 SE/4 } 30-15-2
    Died May 13, 1892
Heirs – Father died before allotment
      Maggie Mohee Mother
        (Sole heir)

Sac & Fox – Shawnee
1846-1924   Volume XI

211

Mohee, Christian
    Allottee No. 93
SE/4   SW/4   10-17-2
SE/4   NW/4   24-17-2
    Died Jan 1893
Heirs – Charlie Mohee   Son
        Osmond Franklin   Son
      (Only heirs)

211

Hamilton, William
    Allottee No. 105
E/2   SE/4   9-17-3
    Died Jan. 1894
Heirs – Left no wife, children, father or mother. His father was
Muck-ga-he who had one brother, who was father of Vina Kashway, who is sole heir.

212

Townsend, Ed
    Allottee No. 64
E/2   NE/4   14-17-3
    Died Jan. 1894
Heirs – Tom White, father died before allotment
        Sha-tah-cher   Mother   1/2
        ~~(Only heir)~~
        Emma Perry   1/4
        Jennie Lincoln   1/8
        Farra[sic] Roubideaux   1/8

212

Naw-A-No-Way
    Allottee No. 77
E/2   SE/4   14-17-3
    Died Aug. 25, 1891
Heirs – Susan Naw-a-no-way   wife, dead – see her heirs
        Maggie Lincoln   dau
        Frank Kent   son
        Nellie Tohee   dau

212

Naw-A-No-Way, Susan
    Allottee No. 78
W/2   SE/4   14-17-3
    Died Aug. 7, 1896
Heirs – Moses husband
        Thomas Lightfoot   son

by a former husband
    Maggie Lincoln   Dau
    Frank Kent   Son
    Nellie Tohee   Dau

213

Thrift, William
    Allottee No. 286
E/2 NE/4 Sec 32 }
W/2 NW/4 Sec 33 } T18 R4
    Died April 2nd 1901
Heirs – Edna Falls   Dau

Sac and Fox-Shawnee –
ESTATES LOG BOOK VOLUME 2 INDEX
1911-1919

Sac & Fox – Shawnee
1846-1924 Volume XI

Note: This listing of names was originally an index for Estates Log Book Volume 2. Their page numbers would not coincide with the typed work now. Check the Index at the back of the book for each name. You'll have to scan the list, the names were not alphabetized.

Name	Page	Name	Page	Name	Page
Anigre		Duncan, May	134	Hull, Lucy	124
~~Augre~~	46	Davis, Frank	155	Harris, Irene	149
Appletree, Henry	185	Davis, Bessie	163	Harris, Joseph	151
		Davis, Rachel	164	Houston, Judith	161
Benson, Laura Ellis	14				
Black, Mary	17	Embler, Joseph	47	Ingalls, William	79
Brown, Julia	18	Ely, Jane	65		
Barker, Levi	58	Ellis, Katie	89	Johnson, Samuel	16
Bigwalker, Jennie	78			Johnson, Harry	32
Benson, Harry	81	Franklin, Benjamin	51	Johnson, Jane	33
Bear, Jack	88	Falls, Annie	74	Johnson, Mercie	34
Butler, Benjamin	93	Fox, Joseph	90	Jefferson, Carrie	152
Bear, James	94	Foster, Flora	173	Jones, Henry C, Jr.	156
Bass, Cora	97	Falls, Samuel	191		
Black, Amos	144			Kakaque, Deborah	30
Burgess, Maggie	106	Gibbs, Hiram	31	Kakaque, Dosh	52
Buffalohorn, Thomas		Grant, John	63	Kakaque, Walter	53
Jefferson	118	Grant, Annie Nellie	64	Keokuk, Phoebe	69
Bigwalker, Florence	137	Grant, Susie	76	Keokuk, Laura	70
Brown, Josephine	147	Gokey, Lizzie		Keokuk, Charles	71
Buffalohorn, Clara	154	nee Graeyes[sic]	116	Kebolte, Eliza White	87
Barker, Andrew	159	Givens, Gertrude	125	Kakaque, Logan	183
Big Ear, Theresa	170	Grayson, Watt	143		
Bigwalker, Sarah	187	Guthrie, Mollie	157	Long, Thomas	10
		Grass, George	160	Long, Agnes	11
Conger, Silas	5	Grant, Ulysses S	181	Logan, Hattie	37
Coon, Nancy	15	Grant, Stella	182	Lunt, Lina B	48
Carter, Lewis	42	Givens, Isaac	189	Logan, John A	128
Carter, Sadie	43			Logan, Mary E	120
Carter, Louise	49	Hollowell, Benjamin	19	Logan, Clarence	186
Conley, Luke	2	Hawk, Silas	23	Lee, Grace	190
Conger, Jasper	119	Hog-gra-ah-chey	45	Logan, Leona	195
Conger, Jay	120	Hunter, Robert	50		
Conger, William	121	Hodge, Mary	75	Mah-tha-pwa	4
Conger, Hattie ~~120A~~	140	Hodge, Julia	83	Madison, Harvey	35
Crane, Charles	130	Hull, William	85	Miller, Ruth	9
Crane, Lizzie	131	Harris, Frances	86	Morris, Caroline	27
Curtis, Nancy	174	Hawk, Richard	99	Mathews, Della	54
Connolly, Liza	178	Hawk, Samuel	108	Mathews, Walter	55
		Hawk, James	110	Murray, Charles C	60
Dupee, Mary	1	Hollowell, Nannie	111	Murray, Kirwin	61
Davis, Marie	73	Hollowell, Irene	112	Murray, May	62
Duncan, Lottie	182	Hall, Harry	115	Mitchell, Egbert	72
Duncan, David	133	Hull, John	123	Messawat, Julia	80

Sac & Fox – Shawnee
1846-1924   Volume XI

Note: This listing of names was originally an index for Estates Log Book Volume 2. Their page numbers would not coincide with the typed work now. Check the Index at the back of the book for each name. You'll have to scan the list, the names were not alphabetized.

Name	Page	Name	Page	Name	Page
Mack, Edgar	82	Rogers, Linda	166	Wakole, Ella	192
Moore, Samuel S	84				
Mason, Grace	98	Smith, Webster	6		
Morton, Clifford	100	Shaquequot, Cora	8		
Morton, Oliver P	101	Sullivan, Neoma	25		
Morton, Melissa	102	Shaquequot, Henry	36		
Mansur, Mary	109	Seaborn, Lena	44		
Maw-mel-lo-haw	113	Sha-th-cher	105		
Manatowa, George	122	Starr, Hellen	117		
Mansur, Rhoda	141	Smith, Cora			
Mansur, Hannah	142	nee Bear	138		
McKuk, John	158	Sampson, Jennie	148		
Mokohoko, Flora	162	Sullivan, Bion	165		
Mohee, Charley	167	Squirrel, Mary	168		
Moses, John	180	Small, Charley Howard or			
McKosato, Chief	184	Charley Howard Lightfoot			
McKosato, Amanda	193		171		
		Starr, Hiram	177		
Neal, Victor	28				
Nahashe, John	95	Thorp, Charlotte	56		
Nahashe, Susan	96	Thorp, Hiram	57		
Nahmoswe, William	146	Tohee, Lee Patrick	92		
Neal, Pearl	172	Townsend	104		
Nullake, Walter	194	Thurman, Lucy	127		
		Thurman, Mary	175		
Pattequa, Bertha	24				
Pattequa, Mamie	26	Vetters, Joe	91		
Plumb, Mary	39				
Pattock, Eunice	107	Ward, Artemus	3		
Pattequa, Charlotte	126	Washington, George	12		
Pennock, William	135	Washington, Mary	13		
Pennock, Hester	136	Wolf, James	22		
Peel, Samuel W	144	Wolf, John	20		
Pickering, Julia		Wolf, Jane	21		
nee Falk	169	Washington, Juanitta	29		
Pickett, Caroline	179	Waw-ho-pah-she-toe	38		
Pate, Rachel	188	Walker, Andrew	40		
		Wolf, Jerome	41		
Randall, Paul	7	Whitecloud, Jefferson	67		
Redrock, Abby	59	Whitecloud, Lizzie	68		
Roubidoux, Mary	66	Whitecloud, Albert	77		
Rice, Lizzie	139	Walker, Lidia	113		
Rice, Edith		Wah-taw-sah	145		
nee Appletree	153	Wakole, Rufus	150		

Sac and Fox-Shawnee –
ESTATES LOG BOOK VOLUME 2
1911-1919

Sac & Fox – Shawnee
1846-1924 Volume XI

Mary Dupee

Land Sold   No Hearing Necessary

Luke Conley

Report Mailed July 3, 1915

June 2, 1911 –
Jack Bear testimony. Leo Walker interpreter
Supported by those signing affidavits.

Artemus Ward (Nah Kus Ke)

1911
Mar 29   Issued notices of Hearing to determine Heirs
May 1   Witnesses and principal appeared for hearing M̱cKosito & John Brown
                                                            Present a disinterested
" "   Statement of Case by Supt.
" "   Nora Barker (Kan pawk) sworn
" "   Leo Walker sworn as interpreter
" "   Chief M̱cKosito & John Brown disinterested persons by request.
" "   Cora Ward sworn
" "   Matilda Givens (Much a ho) sworn
" "   Andrew Barker Sworn
" "   John Brown Sworn

Report Approved Land Sales 109166-1911. J.W.H.
Mailed – to Washington Dec 18-1911
Jan 2-1912
Approved Jan 6, 1912

Nora Barker, - All

Claims:-
May 1   Chief M̱cKosito 1/2 day as disinterested person   Due 2^{00}
      John Brown   1/2 "   "   "   "   " 2^{00}
      Leo Walker   1/2 "   " Interpreter   " 2^{00}

No costs paid

Sac & Fox – Shawnee
1846-1924   Volume XI

4

Maw-tah-pwa

1911
Mar 29   Issued Notice of Hearing to determine Heirs.
May 1   Hugh Wakolle sole heir fails to appear a/c of sickness
"   "   John Brown sworn and testified
"   "   Chief McKosito "   "   "
"   "   Logan Kakaque "   "   "
"   "   Hugh Wakolle appears, was sworn and testified
"   "   Mrs. "   "   "   "   "   "
"   "   David Wakolle   "   "   "   "

Land Sale
109168-1911
J.W.H.
Jan 1-1912
Approved Jan. 6, 1912

Claims:
May 1	Chief McKosito 1/2 day disinterested			Due	2.00
" 1	John Brown 1/2 " "			"	2.00
" 1	Leo Walker 1/2 " "			"	2.00
" 1	Logan Kakaque 1/2 " "			"	2.00

Report Approved
Land Sales 109168-1911   J.W.H.
dated Jan. 6, 1912.

Hugh Wakole,   All

No costs paid

5

Silas Conger (Pe-ah-chea-wah)

1911
Mar 29   Issued Notice of Hearing to determine heirs
May 2   Statement of Case by Supt.
"   "   Andrew Conger sworn and testified
"   "   Leo Walker sworn as interpreter
"   "   Wm G. Foster   "   " witness
"   "   John Brown   "   "   "
"   "   Mamie Jennings "   "   "
"   "   George O Morton one of the interested parties fails to appear

Mailed 8/16/11

Andrew Conger – 1/2
George O. Morton – 1/2

Sac & Fox – Shawnee
1846-1924   Volume XI

Report of Land-Sale Approved:-
Land Heirship 73333-1911
　　　　　　130118-1912
　　　　　　106929-1912
　　　　　　34272-1913
W.D.G. dated July 19, 1913.
Andrew Conger Paid $6.00
Geo O. Morton　　"　$6.00

May 7	Leo Walker interpreter 1/2 day	Pd	2.00
	John Brown witness disinterested – 1/2 day	"	2.00
	Wm G. Foster　"　　"　1/2 "	"	2.00
Present:	Chief McKosito	"	2.00
	David Wakolle	"	2.00
	Logan Kakaque et al.	"	2.00

Costs Paid

6

Webster Smith (Waw-pe-ko-hal)

　　1911
Mar 29　Issued notice of Hearing to determine heirs.
May 2　Statement of Case by Supt.
"　2　All interested persons appeared in person.
"　2　Chief McKosito, David Wakolle, Logan Kakaque & John Brown
　　　appear as disinterested persons
　　　Wm G Foster
　　　~~Frank Smith~~　Sworn as interpreter
　　　Ben Smith　　Sworn and testified
　　　Frank Smith　Sworn and testified
　　　Charley Smith　"　　"　　"
　　　Rachel Franklin　"　　"　　"
　　　Harry Benson　　"　　"　　"
　　　Logan Kakaque　"　　"　　"
　　　John Brown　　"　　"　　"

　　　　　Charley Smith　　Due 2.00
　　　　　Rachel Franklin　　"　2.00
　　　　　Benjamin Smith　　"　2.00

　　　Frank Smith Paid $2.00
　　　Harry Benson　"　$2.00

Report approved Jan. 22, 1913
Land 76153-1911
108749-1912
W.D.G. dated 1/16/13

　　　Claims
May 2　Wm G. Foster interpreter　1/2 day　　Paid 2.00
"　"　Logan Kakaque　　　　1/2　"　　　　　　　　Due 2.00

Sac & Fox – Shawnee
1846-1924   Volume XI

"	"	John Brown	1/2 "		"	2.00
"	"	Chief McKosito			"	2.00
"	"	David Wakolle		Paid 2.00		

    Frank Smith, son, inherits 1/5 of Estate
    Benjamin Smith   "   "   1/5 "   "
    Charley Smith   "   "   1/5 "   "
    Harry Benson   "   "   1/5 "   "
    Rachel Franklin, dau "   1/5 "   "

7

Paul Randall (Mah ko che)

  1911
Mar 29 Issued notice of Hearing to determine heirs
May 3 Statement of Case by Supt.
" " Tom Penashe only interested party appears, was sworn & testified
" " John Brown sworn & testified
" " Isaac Strubble   "   "   "
" " Leo Walker, sworn as interpreter.

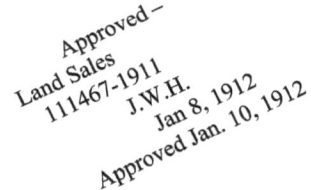

Approved –
Land Sales
111467-1911
J.W.H.
Jan 8, 1912
Approved Jan. 10, 1912

  Tom Panashe[sic], All

  Claims:
May 3 Leo Walker, Interpreter   Due 2.00
" " Isaac Strubble   disinterested witness " 2.00
" " John Brown " " " 2.00
" " Chief McKosito   " 2.00
" " David Wakolle   " 2.00
" " Logan Kakaque   " 2.00

No Costs Paid

8

Cora Sha que quot   (Naw-haw-she-taw)

  1911
Mar 29 Issued notice of hearing to determine heirs
May 3 All interested persons fail to appear. They being res. of Iowa.
" " Wm. G. Foster sworn as Interpreter.

Sac & Fox – Shawnee
1846-1924   Volume XI

"	"	Statement of case by Supt.
"	"	Affidavit of Ella Wakolle read & made part of record.
"	"	Isaac Strubble sworn and testified.
"	"	Affidavits of Chief McKosito, David Wakolle & Logan Kakaque taken.

      Pa-Phia-na   3/10 of estate
      Ne-pau-sa-qua 3/10   "   "
      Ma-ke-so-pe-at 3/10   "   "
      Pone-wya-tah   1/10   "   "

Mailed 3/27/1912

      Report approved Jan. 24, 1913
      Law 30955-12, W.D.G.
         dated 1/20/13

Claims

May 3	Wm. G. Foster, Interpreter	Due	2.00
" "	Ella Wakolle, witness	"	2.00
" "	Isaac Strubble "	"	2.00
" "	Chief McKosito "	"	2.00
" "	David Wakolle "	"	2.00
" "	Logan Kakaque "	"	2.00
" "	U.S. Grant Looking up witnesses for Interested parties.	"	2.00

No Costs Paid.

9

Ruth Miller (Ke wah ka me)

1911
Mar 29	Issued notice of hearing to determine heirs.
May 3	Interested Party Appearing; Ida Spooner.
" "	Paul Gokey fails to appear.
" "	Wm. G. Foster sworn as Interpreter.
" "	Ida Spooner Sworn and Testified.
" "	Maggie Parkinson Harris sworn & testified
" "	Wm Pattequa " "
" "	U. S. Grant " "
" "	Paul Gokey Sworn & testified.

Mailed 8/16/11

      Ida Miller (Spooner) 5/6
      Paul Gokey   1/6
        Report Approved Nov. 14, 1912
        Law 73061-11, 107352-12, F.E. dated 11/12/12

        Paul Gokey   Paid $\$2^{\underline{65}}$
        Ida Spooner Due $11^{\underline{35}}$

Sac & Fox – Shawnee
1846-1924   Volume XI

Claims:
May 3   Wm G. Foster – Interpreter   1/2 day Paid 2⁰⁰
 " "   U. S. Grant   witness   "   Due   2.00
 " "   Wm Pattequa   "   "   " .65   " $.35
 " "   Maggie Parkinson Harris witness   "   "
Present:
         Chief Mᶜ Kosito   Due   2⁰⁰
         David Wakolle   "   2⁰⁰
         John Brown   "   2⁰⁰
         Logan Kakaque, etal.   "   2⁰⁰

---

10   "Costs Paid" Thomas Long (Wan-saw-ko-huk)

All Witness fees & Mileage Paid by sole heir to Estate except Alex Connolly Interp. who is paid by Govt on July 21, 1913,

           1913
May 20   Issued Notices
June 23   Hearing Held.
                     Persons Present:-   { no witness fees a/c }
                     Bertha Hodsdon, nee Long, Int. Person { being sole heir.   }
Paid Apr 11 1914 }   Laura Carter   "   " } Paid
by Bertha Hodsdon   Elmer Manatowa   "   " }
   1 1/2 das/22 miles Paid Alex Connolly Interp & Disint Wit
See Authority   Paid Logan Kakaque, Disint. Wit.
                     W. M. Hodsdon, Stenog
                     Thomas P. Myers, Guardian Ad-Litem for minors
                     Horace J Johnson, Supt & S.D.A.
June 23   Hearing Continues to June 23, 13 a/c insufficient time to complete case
June 24   Persons Present:-
(1/2 day)   Paid Bertha Hodsdon, nee Long, Int. Wit
                     Paid Laura Carter   "   "
          See above Elmer Manatowa   "   "
                     Paid Alex Connolly, Disint. Wit & Interp.
                     Paid Logan Kakaque Disint. Wit.
                     W. M. Hodsdon, Stenog.
                     Paid William & Foster, Disint. Wit.
                     Thomas P. Myers, Guardian Ad-Litem for minors
                     Horace J Johnson, Supt & S.D.A.
June 24, 1913 Hearing Continued to July 21st, 1913 to secure additional evidence
July 21st.   Hearing Held:- Persons Present:-   { no witness fees a/c }
                     Bertha Hodsdon, nee Long-Int. Person { being sole heir.   }
Paid Apr 11 1914   Laura Carter 1 da & 21 miles   do Paid
by Bertha Hodsdon   { Paid Auth. 11 85-14
See Authority   1 day 2.⁰⁰ Alex Connolly, Interpreter –Govt { dated Feb. 21, '14
                     Paid Chief Mᶜ Kosato, Disint. Wit.
                     Paid William Harris,   do   do
                     Paid Logan Kakaque   do   do   Revision of Approved Report

Sac & Fox – Shawnee
1846-1924   Volume XI

Paid Thomas P. Myers, Guard.-Ad-Litem
W.M. Hodsdon, Stenog.   as to name of heir from
E. Robitaille, Atty. for Bertha Hodsdon, nee Long
Horace J. Johnson, Supt. & S.D.A.   Hodson to <u>Hodsdon</u>

Report Mailed Sept. 19, 1913

Land-Sales 10595-12
1120 -14
Bertha Hodsdon, nee Long Sole heir.   F.I.P.
Report Approved   dated Jan 24, 19[??]
L-Sales 10595-12
113294-13
F.I.P. dated Dec 10, 1913

<u>Agnes Long (Maw-taw-che)</u>

'Costs Paid' 1913

May 20   Issued Notices.
June 23 Hearing Continued to June 24, 1913 account
         lack of time to take case up
June 24 Hearing Continued to July 21st, account lack of
         time to take case up
July 21 Hearing Held.

All Witness fees & Mileage Paid by sole heir to Estate except Alex Connolly Interp. on July 21, 1913, who is paid by Govt

         Testimony and record introduced at hearing to determine
heirs of Thomas Long to be used in connection with determination
of heirship of Agnes Long.

Report Mailed Sept. 19, 1913

Bertha Hodsdon, nee Long – Sole heir

                Report Approved
Costs:-   L-Sales 10595-12
See Thomas Long   113294-13
  No. 10   F.I.P. dated Dec. 10, 1913.

Revision of Approved Report as to name of heir from
Hodson to <u>Hodsdon</u> : Land-Sales 10595-12
                                       1120-14,'
                      dated Jan. 24, 1914.

[Name Blocked With Paper]

Mar 29   Issued notice of Hearing to determine heirs
         Leo Whistler appointed guardian ad litem for David Pennock, Thomas,
         Harry & Mary Brown.
May 4   All interested parties, adult, John Brown and Mjishke appeared in person.
 " "   and the minors, David Pennock, Thomas, Harry & Mary Brown by their

Sac & Fox – Shawnee
1846-1924   Volume XI

"	"	guardian ad litem Leo Whistler present.
"	"	Mjishke sworn and testified.
"	"	Leo Walker " as interpreter
"	"	Wm Pattequa " " " Pottawatomie & Sac.
"	"	John Brown " and testified.
"	"	Isaac Strubble sworn and "
"	"	Logan Kakaque " and "
"	"	Chief McKosito " " "
"	"	Recalled Logan Kakaque " "
"	"	" M jish ke " "
"	"	" Isaac Strubble " "
"	"	Edgar Mack sworn and testified
"	"	Frank Keesis " " "

Claims:
May 4	Leo Walker Interpreter 1 day
" "	Wm Pattequa "
" "	Leo Whistler Guardian ad litem.
" "	Isaac Strubble witness
" "	Logan Kakaque "
" "	Chief McKosito "
" "	Edgar Mack "

Present: U.S. Grant, Edward McClellan, Wm G. Foster et al.

No Costs Paid.

[Name Blocked With Paper]

Mar 29	Issued notice of Hearing to determine heirs
May 4	Continued to May 5 – 8 a.m.
May 5	Case stated by Supt.
" "	Leo Walker & William Pattequa sworn as interpreters
" "	Affidavits of Laura Carter read and made part of record.
" "	Leo Whistler appeared as guardian ad litem for minors.
" "	M-jish-ke and John Brown only interested parties that appeared.
" "	Motion granted on application of Leo Whistler, John Brown and Mjishke to permit evidence introduced in hearing of heirship of Thomas Long, May 4, 1911, to enter into record in this case so far as it affects the interests of Thomas Long's heirs.
" "	Mjishke sworn & testified
" "	John Brown " " "
" "	Logan Kakaque " " "
" "	William Pattequa " " "
" "	U.S. Grant " " "

Sac & Fox – Shawnee
1846-1924   Volume XI

Claims:

No Costs Paid

12

George Washington (Paw-she-paw-ho)

1911
Apr. 1 Issued notices of hearing to determine heirs
May 5 Continued to June 12, 1911. Attorney for Mrs. Pickett at [illegible]
        Also no gdn ad litem for Juanita Washington
"   6 Issued new notices
June 12
    "   Case stated by Supt.
    "   Leo Walker sworn as interpreter
    "   All interested parties present except Caroline Pickett
    "   Caroline Pickett appears
    "   Deborah Kakaque Sworn & testified
    "   Lee Patrick   "   "   Wm G. Foster Int.
    "   Isaac Strubble   "   "
    "   Caroline Pickett sworn & testified
    "   Case continued to June 13, 1911.
June 13   "   resumed
"   "   Caroline Pickett testified
"   "   Jacob Wyman sworn & testified
"   "   Henry Hunter   "   "
"   "   Lizzie Crane   "   "
"   "   ~~Caroline Pickett recalled~~ → Lee Bass
"   "   U.S. Grant sworn & testified
"   "   Mary Hurr   "   "
"   "   Edward McClellan "
"   14 Leona Franklin   "   "
"   "   William Pattequa   "   "
"   "   Matilda Givens   "   "
"   "   Eunice [Illegible] "   "
"   "   Alex Connolly   "   "
"   "   Anna Matthews   "   "
"   "   Deborah Kakaque recalled

GrDau
Juanita Washington, inherits entire Estate.
Report Approved April 3, 1912.
Land-Sales 12903-1912
J.W.H. dated Mar 29, 1912

Present: Chief McKosito, David Wakolle, Jack Bear, Logan Kakaque

No Costs Paid

13

Mary Washington (Waw-ko-se-quah)

1911
Apr 1 Issued notice of hearing to determine heirs.
May 5 Continued to June 12-1911. Attorney for Mrs. Pickett
        and Junita[sic] Washington Gdn ad litem absent.
"   6 Issued new notices

Sac & Fox – Shawnee
1846-1924   Volume XI

June 12

    Juanita Washington, gr.dau
    inherits entire estate

    Report Approves April 3, 1911
      Land-Sales 12903-1911
    J.W.H. dated Mar. 29, 1912.

14

<u>Laura Ellis Benson</u>

1911
Apr. 27 Issued notice of Hearing to determine Heirs
May 31 Continued to June 1, 1911 a/c of absence of principals.
June 1 Harry Benson present, sworn and testified
  " " John Brown sworn   "   "
  " " Jack Bear   "   "   "
  " " Leo Walker Interpreter
      Sarah Ellis not present a/c of being sick:

Present as disinterested persons:

Mailed Dec. 21-11

    Chief McKosito
    David Wakolle
    John Brown
    U.S. Grant   <u>All Costs paid</u>
    Logan Kakaque
    Edward Mathews
    Wm Pattequa
    Jack Bear

Land Sales 110629 J.W.H. Approved Jan. 6, 1912

                        Report Approved
                        Land Sales 110629-1911
                        J.W.H. dated Jan. 6, 1912

Harry Benson 1/2 – Int.
Sarah Ellis   1/2   "

15

<u>Nancy Coon</u>

1911
Apr 27 Issued notice of Hearing to determine Heirs
June 1 Case called and stated by Supt.
  " " Paul Gokey sworn and testified
  " " John Brown   "   "   "
  " " William Pattequa " "   "
  " " Leo Walker Interpreter

Sac & Fox – Shawnee
1846-1924   Volume XI

Present as disinterested persons:
See Sheet 14.

Land Sales
110539 – 1911
J.W.H.
Dec. 30 – 1911
Approved Jan. 6, 1912

Ford Dec 21 - 11

<u>All Costs paid</u>
Report Approved.
Land Sales 110539-1911   J.W.H.
dated Jan. 6, 1912

Paul Gokey, All.

16

<u>Samuel Johnson</u>

1911
Apr 27   Issued notice of Hearing to determine Heirs.
June 2   Case stated by Supt.
    Interested party – Emily Johnson Present
        Sworn and testified.
    U.S. Grant Sworn and testified.
    Logan Kakaque "   "   "
    Leo Walker Interpreter.

Mailed Feb. 19 - 1912

Present: Edward Mathews
    John Brown
    Logan Kakaque
    U.S. Grant,
        Emily Johnson, widow
        inherits entire Estate.
Report Approved April 2, 1912
Land-Sales 18116-1912 J.W.H.

No Costs Paid

17

<u>Mary Black</u>

1911
Apr 27   Issued notice of Hearing to determine Heirs.
June 3   Interested parties absent –
  "   Leo Walker appointed Gdn ad litem of Carl, Amos Jr. & Bertha Black
  "   Case stated by Supt. and testimony introduced.
  "   Leo Walker Sworn as Interpreter.
  "   U.S. Grant Sworn & testified   (No others present)

Sac & Fox – Shawnee
1846-1924   Volume XI

		"	Logan Kakaque sworn & testified
June	3		Continued to June 12 – 1911
"	12		Case called and stated –

        Present: Amos Black and Leo Walker Gdn ad litem
                Chief McKosito, David Wakolle, Wm Pattequa
                U.S. Grant, Edward Mathews.

Costs Paid Mailed Feb. 19 - 1912

      "   Amos Black sworn and testified
      "   Leo Walker, " as Interpreter

        All Costs Paid

        Report approved May 10, 1913
        Land Heirship 18311-1912 S.Y.T.

        Amos Black husband 1/4 of Estate
        Amos Black, Jr. Son   3/8 " "
        Bertha Black, Dau   3/8 " "

18

Julia Brown

    1911

Apr	27	Issued Notice of Hearing to determine heirs
June	6	
May	29	Continued to June 16, 1911.
June	2	" " June 23, 1911
June	23	Called and stated by Supt as 1st Nat'l Bank Cushing
"	"	William L. Harris previously applied Gdn ad litem present.
"	"	Geo. T. Brown Interested Party Present.
"	"	Geo. T Brown Sworn & Testified
"	"	Edward Butler " "
"	"	Milton Carter " "
"	"	Wm L. Harris " "
"	"	Affidavit of William G. Foster & Frank Carter

Mailed

Land Sales 109167 Approved Jan 6, 1912

Costs Paid

                              Report Approved Jan. 6, 1912
                              Land Sales 109167.

George T. Brown,	5/15 Int.
Noble H. Brown,	2/15 "
Pearl Brown.	2/15 "
William T. Brown,	2/15 "
Elsie F. Brown,	2/15 "
Lorena J. Brown,	2/15 "

Sac & Fox – Shawnee
1846-1924   Volume XI

19

"Costs Paid"

Benjamin Hallowell

1911
Apr 27   Issued Notice of Hearing to determine Heirs
June 7
May 29   Continued to June 17, 1911
June 2   Continued to June 24, 1911
"   24   Case called and stated by Supt @ [Illegible] Hotel Perkins.
"   "   Only Interested party present – Emma Kent.
"   "   Emma Kent Sworn & Testified.
"   "   David Tohee   "   as Interpreter
"   "   David Tohee   "   testified   Costs Paid
"   "   John Roubidoux sworn & testified.

New Hearing required.
1913.
Sept. 18   Notices Issued for continuation
Oct 20   Hearing Continued to Oct. 30, '13 a/c Supt. not being able to be present
Oct 30   Hearing Held:-
Report Mailed Nov. 3, 1913
          Persons Present:-   Paid $2.00 [Illegible]
          Lizzie DeRoin, Int. Witness   #9061-14, 30597-14 Approved.
          Emma Kent, Int. Witness   dated 4/[?]/14 Report – Heirship
          David Tohee, Disint. Wit. – Govt.   Paid $5.00 [illegible] with as above
          Frank Kent, Disint. Wit. – Govt.   La Paid 4-13, E.
          Robert Small, Interpreter, – Govt. dated 2/21/14 uth 1185

Costs:- See Hearing for Nannie Hollowell - #111.

                now DeRoin
         Lizzie Hollowell – 1/3 int.
         Emma Kent   – 2/3 int.

20

John Wolf

1911
May 6   Issued Notices
June 14

         See Case #22

         Agreement by Interested parties to Conduct
         hearing in Case of James Wolf and allow
         same evidence in this case

Papers Mailed July 14, 1915 No Report

Sac & Fox – Shawnee
1846-1924   Volume XI

Jane Wolf

Papers ~~Report~~ Mailed July 14, 1915 No ~~Report~~

1911
May 6   Issued Notices
June 14

See Case No 22

Agreement by interested parties to Conduct hearing in Case of James Wolf and allow same evidence in this case.

22

James Wolf

1911
May 6   Issued Notices
June 14   Case called and Stated.
Oliver Jackson contestant present
Geo W. Pattock Intersted party present.
Wm. G. Foster, interpreter sworn
Oliver Jackson sworn & testified.
Interested parties agreed to let testimony in Case of James Wolf determine heirship also in Cases of John and Jane Wolf
Case continued to 8 a.m. June 15, 1911

June 15   Oliver Jackson resumed testimony
"   "   Isaac Strubble sworn & testified on behalf of Plaintiff
"   "   Benj Harrison   "   "   "   "
"   "   Hattie Logan   "   " on her own behalf.
"   "   Mary McCoy   "   "   "   "   "
"   "   Edward Mathews   "   " behalf of Geo W. Pattock.
"   "   William Pattequa   "   "   "   "
"   16   Leo Walker sworn as interpreter
"   16   Chief McKosito   "   " as Disinterested Witness
"   "   Continued to June 27 – 1911
"   27   No Costs Paid

Silas Hawk (Ut tah quos)

1911
May 26   Issued Notices.
June 27   Case called and stated by Supt. Continued to June 28
  "   account of absence of interested party.
  " 28   Ida Mansur Interested party present.
  " "   Ida Mansur or Butler sworn & testified
  " "   Alex Connolly sworn as Interpreter

Sac & Fox – Shawnee
1846-1924   Volume XI

"   "   Isaac Strubble sworn and testified.
"   "   Edgar Mack   "   "   "

		mi	ex
Present	Wm Pattequa - uninterested	3^{00}	2^{00}
	Edgar Mack "	3^{00}	"
	Alex Connolly Interpreter	1^{00}	
	Isaac Strubble Disinterested	3^{00}	2^{00}
	Ida & Edward Butler		

July 22 Forwarded to Indian Office
   Report Approved
   Determined by Department.

   Land Contracts, Cl. 209483 N.R. Sept. 22, 1911
    Approved Sept. 29, 1911

   Ida Butler, nee Mansur ----- All.

      No Costs paid.

24

Bertha Pattequa

1911
Aug 17   Issued Notices of Hearing
Sept 18 Not Present,
Oct 19   Issued Notice of Hearing –
Nov. 28 Wm Pattequa sworn & testified,
   Wm G. Foster   "   as Interpreter
   Sarah Bear   "   & testified
   Alex Connolly   "   "   "
   Leo Whistler   "   "   "
   Wm Pattequa recalled.

Present =
 Chief McKosito
 John Brown
 David Wakolle
 Logan Kakaque
 Jack Bear
    etal.
  Wm Pattequa Paid $2^{00} to each
    Wm G. Foster
    Alex Connolly
    Leo Whistler.

Report Approved Land Sales 106208-1911 J.W.H. Jan. 2 – 1912 Approved Jan. 6, 1912 William Pattequa ----- All.

Costs Paid

Costs paid

Sac & Fox – Shawnee
1846-1924   Volume XI

25

Neoma Sullivan

1911
Sept 8   Issued Notices of Hearing.
Oct 19   Peahmaske and Albert Ketche Shawno
         Continued to November 27, 1911
         Alex Connolly sworn as Interpreter - Govt
Nov 27   Pe ah maw ske   sworn & testified – Pd 3/15/15   (1 day & 48 miles 6.80)
         Albert Ketche Shawno   "   and testified   Pd 3/15/15   (1 day & 48 miles 6.80)
         Louis Sullivan   "   "   "   Pd 3/15/15   (1 day & 20 miles 4.00)
         Maggie Harris   "   "   "   Pd 3/15/15   (1 day & 20 miles 4.00)
         Paul Gokey   "   "   "   Pd 3/15/15   (1 day & 23 miles 4.36)
         David Wakolle   "   "   "   Gov't.
         Logan Kakaque ⎫
         John Brown   ⎬ sworn statement   Gov't.
                        ⎭   Gov't.

Report Approved:- Land-Heirship 65845-13
F.E; dated Mar. 26, '14.

Pe-ah-ma-she – 1/3 Int.
Albert Ketch-show-no – 2/3 Int.

Claims:-   4.50
                                                  3
  David Wakolle 1 days attendance 25 miles 13.50 Gov't.
  Logan Kakaque 1   "   "   "   "   Gov't.
  John Brown   1   "   "   "   "   Gov't.
                                 8 registers   80¢
Settled 3/11/15 No Costs paid   1 Cert Copy Marriage Record 75¢
Auth dated 3/5/15 Due W.C. Kohlenberg for registering 8 notices of Hearing .80
                   "   "   "   "   fees on Cert of Marriage -   .75
                                            Total Due W.C.K.   1.55

26

Mamie Pattequa

1911
Nov 28   See No. 24 (P24)
         Same testimony; same heirs;

Land Sales
106209-1911
J.W.H.
Jan 2 – 1912
Approved Jan. 6, 1912

Costs Paid

Sac & Fox – Shawnee
1846-1924   Volume XI

Report Approved.
Land Sales 106209-1911
J.W.H., dated Jan. 6, 1912

    William Pattequa,   All.

27

Caroline Morris

1911
Dec 19   Issued Notices –
1912
Jan 26   Case Called –
Thomas Morris interested party present – sworn & testified

William G. Foster Interpreter	Pd " $1^{\underline{75}}$	"	"	15 mi
U.S. Grant Witness	Pd " $1^{\underline{75}}$	"	"	15 mi
William Pattequa -	Pd " 2^{30}	"	"	26 mi
David Wakolle	Pd " $2^{\underline{40}}$	"	"	28 mi

    Costs divided with Victor Neal heirs paid Each 1/2
    Based on mileage and $^\$2^{00}$ per day

Mailed 2/19/1[?]

Thomas Shaw Morris, husband
inherits entire Estate

Report Approve Dec. 3, 1912
  Law 180140-1912 W.D.G.
  dated Nov. 29, 1912

28

Victor Neal

1911
Dec 19   Issued Notices.
1912
Jan 16   Case Called

U.S. Grant Called sworn & testified	15 mi	1/2 day	$1^{\underline{75}}$
David Wakolle " " "	28 "	1/2 "	$2^{\underline{40}}$
William G. Pattequa " " "	26 "	1/2 "	2.30

Thomas P. Myers appeared as Guardian ad litem for Pearl Neal.
Lilly Neal failed to appear
William G. Foster sworn as Interpreter   15 mi 1/2 da $1^{\underline{75}}$

Mailed- 2/19-12

Sac & Fox – Shawnee
1846-1924   Volume XI

Report Approved Apr 19, 1913
Land Heirship 18364-1912, 43475-1913, *"Costs Paid"*
W.D.G. dated Apr.

Report Approved Apr. 19, 1913 Law 18364-1912 W.D.G.

Lilly Neal, Widow – 1/2
Pearl Neal, Dau.   – 1/2

29

"Costs Paid"   Juanitta Washington

1912
June 13   Issued notices
July 22   Hearing Continued until July 23rd
July 23   Hearing Held
  Persons Present:-
  Thomas P. Meyers Guardian ad litem Sadie Rhodes
1 day- 15 miles $3^{50} Mary Hurr   Grand mother
1 day- 23 miles 4^{30} Bettie Groinhorn Disinterested Person
1 day-   2^{00} Alex Connolly – Interpreter & "   "
no costs charged against
estate of Deborah Kakaque   Walter M. Hodsdon – Stenographer
  Horace J Johnson Supt.

Report Mailed Aug. 8, 1912.   Witness Fees paid 9/16/12
  Sadie Rhodes sole heir.
  Report Approved Jan. 11, 1913.
  Law 80312-1912 S.Y.T. dated Jan'y. 9, 1913

---

30   *"Costs Paid"*   Deborah Kakaque

1912
June 13   Issued Notices
July 22   Hearing Held
  Persons Present:-
Costs charged against Estate of Juanitta Washington Fees Paid 9/16/12
  Thomas P. Meyers Guardian Ad litem for Sadie Rhodes
  Mary Hurr – Mother
  Bettie Groinhorn – Disinterested Person
  Alex Connolly – Interpreter & Disinterested Person
  Walter M Hodsdon – Stenographer
  Horace J Johnson Supt.

Report Mailed Aug. 8, 1912

Sac & Fox – Shawnee
1846-1924   Volume XI

Sadie Rhodes sole heir

Report approved January 23, 1913.
Law 80310-1912 W.D.G. dated
January 20, 1913

31

"Costs Paid"

Hiram Gibbs

1912
June 17   Issued Notices
July 24   Hearing held.
          Persons Present:-   Amos Black Jr
          Thomas P. Meyers Guardian Ad-litem for Bertha Black

27½ miles 1 day	4$\frac{75}{}$	Logan Kakaque
18 miles 1 day	3$\frac{80}{}$	Lindy Rogers
12 " 1 day	3$\frac{20}{}$	Amanda Starr
17½ " 1 day	3$\frac{75}{}$	Amos Black
22 " 1 day	4$\frac{20}{}$	Alice Hunter
		~~Henry Hunter~~
	2$\frac{00}{}$	Alex Connolly – <u>Gov't</u>.

Report Approved 4200-14. 80309-12 F.E. dated Aug. 19, 1914

Report Mailed Aug. 8, 1912.

Logan Kakaque	1/18
Gilbert Gibbs	17/90
Manda Starr	17/90
Linda Brown	17/90
Alice Hunter	17/90
Amos Black	7/135
Amos Black Jr	37/540
Bertha Black	37/540

Government Witness paid Sept 30, 1913, Auth. 87065, dated Aug. 22, 13.

32

"Costs Paid"

Harry Johnson

1912
June 19   Issued Notices
July 22   Hearing Continued until July 23, 1912.
 "   23   Hearing Continued until Aug 3, 1912.
                    Orlando Johnson sick.
Aug 3rd   Hearing continued to Jan. 23, 1913.
                    Orlando Johnson sick.
  1913
Jan. 23   Hearing Held:
          Persons Present:- } no fees actually paid as he inherits
½ day & no mileage 1.$\frac{00}{}$ Orlando Johnson } entire estate
½ day & no mileage 1.$\frac{00}{}$ Mary Hurr, disinterested witness.
½ day   1.$\frac{00}{}$ Leo Whistler,   "   "   Gov't.
½ day   1.$\frac{00}{}$ Alex Connolly, Interpreter & Dis Wit. Gov't.

Sac & Fox – Shawnee
1846-1924   Volume XI

Mileage charged to
Marie Davis Estate #73

Horace J Johnson, Supt & S.D.A.
Walter M. Hodsdon, Stenog

Costs Divided among Estates of:
Harry Johnson #32
Jane Johnson #33
Mercie Johnson #34

Orlando Johnson sole heir.
Report mailed March 15, 1913.

Report approved May 31, 1913.
Land Heirship 36395-1913. J.D.C.
Government Witnesses paid Sept 30, 1913. Auth. 81065, dated Aug. 22, '13.

"Costs Paid"   Jane Johnson   **33**

June 19	Issued Notices
July 22	Hearing Continued until July 23, 1912.
" 23	Hearing Continued until Aug 3, 1912.
	Orlando Johnson sick.
Aug 3	Hearing continued to Jan. 23, 1913.
	Orlando Johnson sick.
1913	
Jan. 23	Hearing Held:-

Persons Present:- Orlando Johnson } no fees actually paid as he inherits entire estate
Mary Hurr, disinterested witness.
Leo Whistler,   "   "   Gov't.
Alex Connolly, Interpreter   Gov't.
Horace J Johnson, Supt
Walter M. Hodsdon, Stenog

Costs Divided among Estates of:
Harry Johnson #32
Jane Johnson #33
Mercie Johnson #34

Orlando Johnson sole heir.
Report mailed March 15, 1913.

Report approved June 6, '13.
Land Heirship 36466-1913
J.D.C.

Report approved May 31, 1913.
Land Heirship 36395-1913. J.D.C.
Government Witnesses paid Sept 30, '13. Auth. 81065, dated Aug. 22, '13.

Sac & Fox – Shawnee
1846-1924   Volume XI

34   *"Costs Paid"*   <u>Mercie Johnson</u>

1912
June 19 Issued Notices
July 22 Hearing Continued until July 23, 1912.
" 23   Hearing Continued until Aug 3rd, 1912.
                     Orlando Johnson sick.
Aug 3rd Hearing continued to Jan. 23, 1913.
                     Orlando Johnson sick.

1913
Jan. 23 Hearing Held:-
         Persons Present:- } no fees actually paid as he inherits
         Orlando Johnson } entire estate
         Mary Hurr, disint. witness.
         Leo Whistler, "   "   - Gov't.
         Alex Connolly, Interpreter   - Gov't.
         Horace J Johnson, Supt
         Walter M. Hodsdon, Stenog

     Costs Divided among Estates of:
         Harry Johnson #32
         Jane Johnson #33
         Mercie Johnson #34
         Orlando Johnson sole heir.
         Report mailed March 15, 1913.

     Report approved May 31, 1913.
     Land Heirship 36395-1913. J.D.C.
Government Witnesses paid Sept 30, 1913. Auth. 81065, dated Aug. 22, '13.

---

35 *"Costs Paid"*   <u>Harvey Madison</u>

1912
June 21 Issued Notice.
July 22 Hearing Continued until July 23, 1912.
" 24   Hearing held
         Persons Present:-
½ day 1⁰⁰   Mary Hurr – Aunt – Paid
½ day 1⁰⁰   Bettie Groinhorn – Aunt Paid   Gov't.
{ ½ day 1⁰⁰ Paid in Case of Juanitta Washington. } Alex Connolly – Interpreter & Disinterested Person – Paid
         Walter M Hodsdon – Stenographer
         Horace J Johnson Supt.
Mileage paid in case of
Juanitta Washington

Report Mailed 8/16/12

Sac & Fox – Shawnee
1846-1924 Volume XI

Bettie Groinhorn, Aunt		1/3 of Estate
Mary Hurr	"	1/3 " "
Me-Ough-kaw	"	1/3 " "

Report Approved Jan. 9, 1913.
Law 82681-1912 S.Y.T. dated Jan'y. 4, '13.

Witness fees of:
Mary Hurr and Bettie Groinhorn paid under Auth. Ed. Indus 19061-14, 30597-14, C.H.S., dated Apr 6, '14.

---

36   "Costs Paid"   Henry Shaquequot

1912
June 22   Issued Notices
July 26   Hearing Held

Persons Present:-

1 Da 27 ½ Miles	4^{75}	Grace Lee	Widow — See Notation Below
1 Da 27 ½ Miles	4^{75}	Katie Shaquequot	Dau
1 Da 16 "	3^{60}	Mary Wyman	StepDau – Gov't.
		Philip Lee	Husband of Widow
1 Da	2^{00}	Alex Connolly	Interpreter – Gov't.

Report Mailed Aug. 5, 1912.

Grace Lee   1/2 of Estate
Kate Shaquequot 1/2 of Estate

Report approved June 25, 1913
Land-Heirship
73182-1913,
21697-1913-
5272-1913,
79432-1912 M.H.W.

Government Witnesses paid Sept. 30, '13, Auth. 81065, dated Aug. 22, '13
No Witness fees to Kate Shaquequot or Grace Lee necessary for the reason that both heirs have a 1/2 int. in the estate of Henry Shaquequot

Sac & Fox – Shawnee
1846-1924   Volume XI

Hattie Logan

"Costs Paid"

1912
July 5th Issued Notices
Aug 6   Hearing Held
          Persons Present:-
1 Da 14 Mile $3^{\underline{40}}$ Clarence Logan   son
½ Da 25½ Miles 3^{55} Shoque
1 Day $2^{\underline{00}}$ Alex Connolly   Interpreter
                              Horace J Johnson   Supt.

9/1/12 Witness Fees Paid Auth. 84478-12

Report Mailed Aug. 1912.

Clarence Logan,   son,   1/2 of Estate
Theresa Logan,   Gr-Dau   1/6 "   "
John Crane,   Gr. Son, 1/6 "   "
Harry Crane,   Gr. Son, 1/6 "   "

Report Approved Nov. 23, 1912.
Law 84292-1912, L.L. dated
Nov. 21, 1912.

Waw-ko-pah-she-toe

Costs Paid

1912
July 8   Issued notices
Aug 12   Hearing Continued until Jan. 15, 1913 on a/c
          insufficient time.
1913
Jan. 15   Hearing Held
          $15^{\underline{20}}$ Persons Present:- To be paid from   } Paid Auth Edwd Indus
2 day & 1½ Miles   Minnie Barada — Waw-ko-pah-she-toe } 19061-14. 30547-14
To be paid from   Bettie Groinhorn estate only   C.H.S. dated 4/6/14
Egbert Mitchell est only ^{75}
2 days & 27½ miles   Grace Lee To be paid from Waw-ko-pah-she-toe } Paid Auth Edwd Indus
                                            estate only   } 19061-14. 30547-14
                                 Isaac Strubble   Gov't.   C.H.S. dated 4/6/14
Report Mailed Mar. 12, 1914.   Pe-pique   -Gov't.
                                 U.S. Grant   -Gov't.
                                 Alex Connolly   -Gov't.
                                 Horace J Johnson
                                 Walter M Hodsdon

Sac & Fox – Shawnee
1846-1924 Volume XI

Costs divided among estates of
Egbert Mitchell #72
Waw-ko-pah-she-toe #38

Government Witnesses paid Sept. 30, '13 Auth. 81065, Aug. 22, '13.
  Grace Lee nee Shaquequot – 1/2
  Katie Shaquequot -   1/2

Mary Plumb   39

Costs Paid

1912
July 8   Issued notices
Aug 12   Case continued until Aug 13th
 "   13   Case continued until Aug 15th
 "   15   Case continued

              Aug 12   Persons Present:-
½ da 1^{00} Alex Connolly, Gov't.
½ day & 112 Miles 12^{20} Minnie Barada } No Witness fees or mileage necessary a/c of being sole heir

              Aug 13   Persons Present:-
½ da 1^{00} Alex Connolly Gov't
½ da $1^{\underline{00}}$ Frank Carter } Paid Auth dated Sept 12, 1914.
½ da $1^{\underline{00}}$ Pe pe qua (Edward Matthews)-Gov't
½ da $1^{\underline{00}}$ Minnie Barada } No Witness fees or mileage necessary a/c of being sole heir

1 da+21 miles 4.10 Aug 15   Isaac Struble[sic]- Gov't.
1 da+16 miles $3^{\underline{60}}$ Jane Harrison- Gov't.
1 da $2^{\underline{00}}$ Alex Connolly- Gov't.

Report Mailed October 26, 1912.

          Minnie Plumb, nee Barada
          inherits entire estate.

          Report approved Dec. 14, 1912.
          Law 108756-1912, M.H.W. dated 12/12/'12
Government Witnesses paid Sept 30, '13, Auth. 81065, Aug. 22, '13.

---

40   Andrew Walker

No Costs

1912
July 13   Issued Notices
Aug 15   Hearing Held
              Persons Present:-

Sac & Fox – Shawnee
1846-1924   Volume XI

No Fees nor Milage[sic] allowed

Elmer Walker — Father
Edith Walker — Mother
Alex Connolly — Interpreter

Elmer Walker- 1/2 Int.
Edith Walker- 1/2 Int.

Report Mailed August 15, 1912

Estate distributed under authority from Indian Office 82811-13, dated May 17, 1913, and 47766-1913.

{ No Declaration by Secretary of the Interior necessary as Andrew Walker was not allotted

---

Jerome Wolf   41

Costs Paid   *Report Mailed June 24, 1915.*

1912
July 16   Issued notices
Sept 25   Hearing Held
           Persons Present:-
2 da+7½ Mi   4$\underline{75}$ Eunice Pattock } Dep to Credit under Auth of May 11, '14
2 da+14½ Mi   5$\underline{45}$ Edward Matthews – Gov't.
2 da   4$\underline{00}$ Alex Connolly – Gov't.
2 da+7½ Mi   4$\underline{75}$ Oliver Jackson } Paid under Auth of May 11, '14
2 da+21 Mi   6$\underline{10}$ Isaac Struble – Gov't.
                                   Continued to Sept. 26th
"   26   Hearing concluded to Feb. 10, 1913

   1913
Feb 10   Persons Present:-
No Witness fees or Mileage   Jim Peters
         do   Sa-ke-na-we-que
         do   Eunice Hawk
1 day   2$\underline{00}$ Alex Connolly   Interpreter – Gov't.
No Witness fees nor Mileage   Minnie Barker
                              Walter M Hodsdon, Stenogr.
                              Horace J Johnson Supt.

Government Witnesses paid Sept 30, '13, Auth. 81065, Aug. 22, '13.

           Report Approved in
           Law-Heirship 71403-15, E.G.T.,
           dated Oct. 1, 1915.

           Lydia Grant, --------- 1/2 Interest.
           Sa-ke-na-wa-que, --- 1/2   "

Sac & Fox – Shawnee
1846-1924   Volume XI

42

"Costs Paid"   Lewis Carter

1912
July 31   Issued Notices
Sept 27   Hearing Held
                    Persons Present:-   Sole heir-No Witness fee or
1 da+22 Miles $4²⁰   Milton Carter ⎫ mileage necessary
1 da+22 Miles   4²⁰   Ella Carter   ⎬ Brought by Milton Carter-No
1 da+21 Miles   4¹⁰   Frank Carter ⎭ Witness fees or mileage
1 da   2⁰⁰   Alex Connolly-Gov't.   Mileage See Note below
                    Walter M. Hodsdon – Stenog.
                    Horace J Johnson Supt. & S.D A.

Costs divided among the estates of
            Lewis Carter
            Louise Carter
            Sadie Carter
    Milton Carter, father, inherits entire estate.

Report Mailed December 7th, 1912

            Report approved Jan. 2, 1913.
            Law 126314-1912. W.D.G. dated 12/23/'12.

            Frank Carter appeared to testify in his dec. Wife's case,
            Louise Carter & also testified in Lewis Carter estate.
            Milton Carter appeared to testify in Lewis & Sadie Carter
            Cases, and also testified in Louise Carter estate.
            As Frank Carter testified in Milton Carter's Cases and Milton
            Carter testified in Frank Carter's Case, no fees should be allowed
            either of them. There are no funds to the credit of any of these
            estates.

Government Witness paid Sept. 30, '13. Auth. 81065, Aug. 22, '13.

43

"Costs Paid"   Sadie Carter

1912
July 31   Issued Notices
Sept 27   Hearing Held
                Persons Present:-
                    Milton Carter
                    Ella Carter
                    Frank Carter
                    Alex Connolly
        See Hearing for Lewis Carter #262
                    Walter M. Hodsdon, Stenog.

Sac & Fox – Shawnee
1846-1924   Volume XI

Horace J Johnson, Supt. & S.D.A.

Report Mailed December 7th, 1912

Milton Carter inherits entire estate

Report Approved Jan. 2, 1913.
Law 124568-1912, W.D.G. dated 12/23/'12.

Government Witnesses paid
Sept 30, '13, Auth. 81065, Aug 22, '13.

---

44   "Costs Paid"   Lena Seaborn

1912
Aug. 6   Issued notices
Sept 9   Case called.   Paid. Auth
          Persons Present:-   Ed. Indus.
1 Day 38^M $5^{80} Wm Seaborn   1906: 14, 30597 '14
1 Day 62^M 8^{20} Albert D Kenyon   C.H.S. dated
1 Day 36^M 5^{60} Jennie Cofer   4/6/'14.

         Testimony taken and case continued to Sept. 10, 1912
½ Day 1^{00} Mary McCoy   Paid Above Auth.   *Report Mailed July 18, 1913.*
½ Day 1^{00} Alex Connolly – Gov't.
½ Day 1^{00} Jennie Cofer   } Paid
½ Day 1^{00} Albert D. Kenyon } Above Auth.
         Certified copy of Patent covering allotment
Paid { of Lena Seaborn, $1.^{00} Paid by check #498,
         on 1st. Natl Bnk Stroud, Okla, dated July 12, '13.
                William Seaborn – Husband – 1/2
                Isabel Kenyon – Daughter – 1/2

                         July 18, 1912 } Called by Supt to give evidence
36 Miles 3^{60} Jennie Cofer   } regarding Homestead } Paid Auth Above

Government Witnesses paid Sept. 30, '13, { Report approved Land-Heirship
Auth. 81065, Aug. 22, 1913.   17698-10, 89123-13, 97113-13 F.E.
                                            dated Oct. 3, 1913.
                                            Report modified in Law-Heirship
                                            17698-10, F.E-dated Dec. 15, 1914,
                                            to exclude William M. Seaborn
                                            from a homestead right in
                                            this allotment

Sac & Fox – Shawnee
1846-1924   Volume XI

45

"Costs Paid"   Hog-gra-ah-chey

1912
Aug. 7   Issued Notices
Oct. 7   Hearing held

1 day & 2½ Miles 2^{25}	
1 day & 50 Miles 7^{00}	
1 day & 6 Miles 2^{60}	
1 day & 3½ Miles 2^{35}	
1 day & 5½ Miles 2^{55}	
1 day & 5½ Miles 2^{55}	
{ See #48 for Costs of $^{\$}70^{00}$ }	

Persons Present:-
David Tohee-Gov't.
Charles Kihega-Gov't.
Frank Kent – Govt.
Robert Small, Interpreter & Guardian-Ad-Litem for Mary Small, minor
Joseph Springer-Govt. & Disin Person
Sophie Embler } ½ from 45 } Paid $1.27 Auth. Edwd
            } ½   "   47 } Indus 19061-14, 305097-14 C.H.S.
                              dated 4/6/14

Walter M. Hodsdon, Stenographer
Horace J Johnson, Supt. & S.D.A.

Report Mailed Dec. 23, 1913.
Additional Evidence submitted Jan 25, 1915.

Costs Divided among the Estates of
Hog-gra-ah-chey
Augre
Joseph Embler
Lina B. Lunt

Report Approved in Law-Heirship 64964-15 F.W.S., dated June 30, 1915.

Sophie Embler – 1/2
Mary Ford Small – 1/4
Tom Hartico   – 1/4

Paid Jan. 24-1914
Check No 606 on 1st Natl. Bnk. of Stroud, Okla.

Certified copy of Marriage License & Return of Marriage of Thomas Young and Josephine DeRoin – 55 Cents.

Government Witness fees paid Sept 30, '13, Auth. 81065, Aug. 22, 1913.

46

"Costs Paid"   ~~Augre~~ Anigre

1912
Aug. 7   Issued Notices
Oct. 7   Hearing held
            Persons Present:-
            David Tohee – Govt
            Charles Kihega – Govt
            Frank Kent – Govt.
            Joseph Springer – Gov't.

Sac & Fox – Shawnee
1846-1924   Volume XI

Robert Small Interpreter of Guardian-Ad-Litem
for Mary Small, Minor
Gov't.

Costs   See Hearing for Hog-gra-ah-chey #45

Government Witness fees
paid Sept. 30, '13. Auth. 81065
Aug. 22, 1913

Report Mailed Jan. 22, 1914
Additional Evidence submitted Jan. 25, 1915.

Tom Hartico – 1/2
Mary Ford Small – 1/2

Paid Feb. 2, 1914
Check No 622 on 1st Natl. Bnk. of Stroud, Okla.

{ Certified copy of Application for Marriage License
Marriage License and Certificate of Marriage
of Tom Hartico and Anigre or Augie Ford. $1.$\underline{25}$

Report Approved in
Law-Heirship 64963-15, F.W.S.
dated June 30, 1915.

"Costs Paid"   Joseph Embler   47

1912
Aug. 7   Issued Notices
Oct. 7   Hearing held
         Persons Present:-
         David Tohee – Govt
         Charles Kihega – Govt
         Frank Kent – Govt.
         Robert Small, Interpreter of Guardian-Ad-Litem for Mary
                                                              Small, minor
         Joseph Springer – Govt
         Sophie Embler   } Paid 1\underline{28}$ under Auth
                           dated 2/6/'14

Report Mailed Dec. 24, 1913

         Walter M Hodsdon, Stenographer
         Horace J Johnson, Supt. & S.D.A.

Costs – See Hearing for Hog-gra-ah-chey #45

         Sophie Embler (Kish-tah-che-um) sole heir.

Government Witness fees paid
Sept. 30, '13. Auth. 81065, Aug. 22, '13
            Report Approved: Law-Heirship 153587-13
            E.G.T. dated Feb. 21, 1914.

Sac & Fox – Shawnee
1846-1924   Volume XI

48

"Costs Paid"   Lina B. Lunt

1912
Aug. 8   Issued Notices
Oct. 7   ~~Case Continued~~   Hearing Held:-

    Oct. 7th   Persons Present:-
        David Tohee – Gov't.
        Charles Kihega – Gov't
        Frank Kent – Gov't.
        Joseph Springer – Gov't.
        Robert Small Interpreter ~~of Guardian-Ad-Litem for~~ – Gov't
1 day & 50 Miles 7^{00} Susan Whitewater – Gov't   ~~Mary Small~~

    Walter M Hodsdon, Stenog
    Horace J Johnson, Supt. & S.D.A.
Costs – See Hearing for ~~[Name Illegible]~~ #45
    Hog-gra-ah-chey

Report Mailed Jan. 23, 1914

Government Witness fees paid
Sept. 30, '13   Auth. 81065   Aug 22, 13

    Susan Whitewater, Wife of Dec. father – 1/2
    Nettie Whitewater, Gr. Dau of Dec. father – 1/2

Report approved Law-Heirship 9097-14,
S.H.E. dated Feb. 21, 1914.

49

"Costs Paid"   Louise Carter

1912
Aug 27   Issued notices
Sept. 27   Hearing Held
    Persons Present
    Frank Carter
    Milton Carter - See #42
    Alex Connolly – Gov't.
Costs:- See Hearing for Lewis Carter #42

Report Mailed Dec. 2nd 1912

    Thos. P. Myers, Guard-ad-litem for
        Bertha Carter, Minor
    Walter M Hodsdon, Stenog
    Horace J Johnson, Supt & S.D.A.

    Frank Carter   1/3 int.
    Bertha Carter   2/3 int.

Sac & Fox – Shawnee
1846-1924   Volume XI

Report Approved Jan. 2, 1913.
Law 123565-1912; 123879-1912,
W.D.G. dated 12/23/'12.
Government Witness fees paid Sept. 30, '13.
Auth. 81065, Aug. 22, '13.

50

"Costs Paid" Robert Hunter

1912
Sept. 6   Issued notice
Oct. 14   Case Continued until Oct. 15, 1912
 "   15   Hearing Held
           Persons present:-
22 M + 1 Day 4.$\underline{20}$ Henry Hunter
21 M + 1 Day 4.$\underline{10}$ Isaac Struble – Gov't.
     1 Day 2.$\underline{00}$ Alex Connolly – Gov't.
21 M + 1 Day 4.$\underline{10}$ Nora Barker – Gov't.

Government Witness fees paid
Sept 30, 13, Auth. 81065, Aug. 22, '13.

Report Mailed Feb. 13, 1914

            Henry or Harry Hunter- 1/5
            Emma Hunter   - 1/5
            Harrison Hunter   - 1/5
            Gertrude Hunter   - 1/5
            Daniel S. Hunter   - 1/5

    Report Approved Law-Heirship 17690-14, S.H.E.
        dated Apr. 1, 1914.

51

"Costs Paid" Benjamin Franklin

1912
Sept. 7   Issued notices.
Oct. 14   Hearing Held.
15 M+1 Da   3$\underline{50}$ Leona Wyman   ⎫
16 M+1 Da   3$\underline{60}$ Osmond Franklin   ⎬
17 ½ M+1 Da 3$\underline{75}$ Randall Franklin ⎭
            Thomas P Meyers Guardian ad litem
                         for Harding, George and
                         Alex Franklin Minors, &
                         Fryor Franklin Brown, minor.
   1 Da   2$\underline{00}$ Alex Connolly ⎫ Interpreter and Disinterested-Gov't.
   1 Da   2$\underline{00}$ Leo Whistler ⎭   Witnesses – Gov't.

Paid. Auth Ed. Indus 19061-14, 30597-14, C.H.S; dated 4/6/'14.

            Leona Wyman   1/8
            Osmond Franklin 2/21

149

Sac & Fox – Shawnee
1846-1924   Volume XI

Report as modified approved Jan'y. 6, 1913, Law 126329-12 W.D.G.

Randall Franklin 2/21
Christine Boyd, nee Franklin 2/21
Harding Franklin 2/21
Geo. R. Franklin 2/21
Alex Franklin 2/21
Fryor Franklin Brown 2/21

} *Modified as below*

Report mailed Dec. 7, 1912

Government Witness fees paid Sept. 30, '13, Auth. 81065, Aug. 22, 1913.

Leona Wyman Franklin 1/8
Osmond Franklin 1/8
Randall Franklin 1/8
Christine Boyd, nee Franklin 1/8
Harding Franklin 1/8
George R. Franklin 1/8
Alex Franklin 1/8
Fryor Franklin Brown 1/8

---

52   "Costs Paid"   Dosh Kakaque

1912
Sept 12   Issued Notices
Oct. 21   Hearing Held
          Persons present:-   19061-14
                                                           C.H.S.
1 day 27½ miles 4^{75} Logan Kakaque } Paid Auth. Ed Indus 30597-14 dated Apr 6 '14
1 day 18 miles   3^{80} Lindy Brown   } Paid   do   do   do
1 day 12 miles   3^{20} Amanda Starr } Paid   do   do   do
1 day 22 miles   4^{20} Alice Hunter } Paid   do   do   do
1 day ~~18 miles~~ 2^{00} Sam Brown- Gov't.
1 day 17½ miles 3^{75} Amos Black   } Deposited do   do   do
                                            to Credit.
                            Thomas P. Myers:- Guardian-ad-Litem
                                               for Amos Black Jr. and
                                               Bertha Black
       1 da   2^{00} Alex Connolly   Interpreter- Gov't.
                            Horace J Johnson: Supt & S.D.A.
                            Walter M Hodsdon: Stenographer

Paid Jan. 24-1914

Check No 604   Logan Kakaque   1/6 of Estate
on 1st Natl.   Lindy Brown   1/6 "   "
Bank of Stroud,   Amanda Starr   1/6 "   "
     Okla.   Alice Hunter   1/6 "   "
                    Gilbert Gibbs   1/6 "   "
                    Amos Black   1/18 "   "   Government Witness fees
                                                      paid Sept. 30, '13, Auth.
                    Amos Black Jr   1/18 "   "   81065, Aug. 22, 1913.

Sac & Fox – Shawnee
1846-1924   Volume XI

Report Mailed Feb. 13, 1913

Bertha Black   1/18 "   "

Report approved May 10, 1913,
Land-Heirship 21769-1913
S.Y.T.

53

"Costs Paid"   Dosh Kakaque

1912
Sept 12   Issued Notices
Oct. 21   Case Continued until Oct. 22nd, 1912.
            Persons Present:-
{ No fees nor   Logan Kakaque
  Mileage   Sam Brown
  No fees nor   Alex Connolly   Interpreter- Gov't.
  Mileage   Thomas P. Myers   Guardian-ad-litem for Sadie Rhodes
                 Horace J Johnson   Supt & S.D.A.
↑ See Dosh Kakaque hearing   Walter M Hodsdon   Stenographer

Paid Jan. 24-1914

Check No2. 603   Application for Marriage License
on 1st National   Certified copy of Marriage license
Bank of Stroud,   and Certificate $1.00
Oklahoma

                       Logan Kakaque, father- 1/2
                       Sadie Rhodes, Dau of dec. Wife- 1/2

Report Mailed June 5, 1913

Government Witness fees   Report approved
paid Sept. 30, '13, Auth.   Law-Heirship 71910-13. E.A.U.
81065, Aug. 22, 1913.   dated Feb. 21, 1914.

54
                    No fees from   Della Mathews
1912   Estate to be paid
Sept. 14   Issued Notices
Oct. 28   Continued until Nov. 25, 1912.
           Interested parties not present.
Nov. 25   Interested parties not present. Hearing Continued to
           April 3, 1914.
1914
Apr. 3   Hearing Held:-
             Persons Present :-
               Isaac Struble, Disint. Person Gov't.
               Alexander Connolly Inter. of Disint. Person Gov't.
               Logan Kakaque Disint Person – Gov't.
               Walter M. Hodsdon Stenog.

Sac & Fox – Shawnee
1846-1924   Volume XI

Horace J Johnson Supt

Costs: "Gov't Witnesses" See Flora Mokohoko- $162.

55

"Costs Paid" Walter Matthews

1912
Sept 14   Issued Notices
Oct 28   Hearing Held.
1 day 31 Miles 5^{10} Nannie Matthews } Paid Auth. Edw. Indus 19061-14
                                            30597-14 C.H.S. dated 4/6/14
1 day 2^{00} Alex Connolly- Gov't Guardian-Ad-Litem for
                    Thomas P. Myers }   Annie Matthews
                    Horace J Johnson   Supt & S.D.A
                    Walter M Hodsdon   Stenog

1914
Apr 3   Isaac Struble, Disint. Person (Gov't) Paid from No. 54
                                                  162, 163 of 164
          Alexander Connolly, Interp. (Gov't)   do   do   do

Paid Jan. 24, 1914
Check No 607   ⎧ Certified copies of records as to:
on 1st National   ⎨ Application for License for Marriage
Bank of   ⎩ of License. $1.^{00}
Stroud, Okla.

Report Mailed Apr. 28, 1914

Government Witness fees paid Sept.
30, 1913, Auth. 81065, Aug. 22, 1913.

Nannie Matthews- 1/3
Annie Matthews - 2/3

56

Charlotte Thorp

1912
Sept 23   Issued Notices
Nov. 4   Case Continued until Nov. 25, 1912
          Supt absent from Agency
Nov. 25   Interested parties not present Continued to May 5, '13
1913
May 5   ⎧ Hearing Held. See Case #57, Hiram P Thorp
        ⎨ Testimony taken in Hiram Thorp Case #57.
        ⎩ to apply in this case also. Certified copies to be made for this case.
1914
Dec. 10   Further evidences secured from
          Mary McCoy and Alexander Connolly (See #57)   *Report Mailed December 18, 1914*
          The following persons inherit the balance of the allotment of

152

Sac & Fox – Shawnee
1846-1924   Volume XI

Charlotte Thorp now under control of Government:-
  James Thorp   – 1/4 Int
  Mary Wilson, nee Thorp   – 1/4 "
  Adaline Rhodd, nee Thorp – 1/4 "
  Edward Thorp   – 1/4 "

The following persons were the heirs of Charlotte Thorp
at time of death:-   The interest partitioned
  Hiram P. Thorp   – 1/3   ⎫ by Court to these parties
  George Thorp   – 2/15 ⎬ was void under deed appr.
  James Thorp   – 2/15 ⎭ by Dept. by themselves
  Mary Wilson, nee Thorp   – 2/15 ⎫
  Adaline Rhodd, nee Thorp – 2/15 ⎬ Still under control of Gov't.
  Edward Thorp   – 2/15 ⎭ Receive 1/4 interest each.

Report approved Law-Heirship 136686-14, F.W.S. dated Jan. 25, 1915.

Requested Auth. to settle 12/21/14.
Paid by Check #991 on 1st Natl. Bk. Stroud, Okla: $3.50

Certified copy of Partitionment proceedings and Certificates from Clerk of Cty Ct Pottawatomie Cty Tecumseh Okla $3.50 *Paid*

Paid by check #994 on 1st Natl Bk Stroud, Okla: $5 [illegible]

Certified copy of record concerning Divorce proceedings from Clerk of District Ct of Pott. Cty Tecumseh Okla   .35 *Paid*
                                        Total - - - - - - - $3.85

57

"Costs Paid"   Hiram Thorp

1912
Sept 23 Issued Notices
Nov. 4   Case Continued until Nov. 25, 1912
         Supt absent from Agency
Nov. 25 Interested parties not present
         Continued to May 5, 1913.
1913
May 5   ~~Min~~ Hearing Held:-
         Persons Present-

1 day & 33½ miles 5.^{35} Minnie Rider, nee Thorp, Int. Wit
1 day & 21 miles   4.^{10} Frank Thorp, Int. Wit
1 day & 27½ miles 4.^{25} Geo. Thorp. Int. Wit.
1 day & 21 miles   4.^{10} Mary Wilson, Int. Wit.
1 day   2.^{00} Alex Connolly Interpreter – Gov't *Disinterested person*
                  Horace J Johnson, Supt
                  Walter M Hodsdon, Stenog
                  Thomas P Myers G.A.L. for minors

Paid Auth. Ed. Indus 19061-14, 30597-14, C.H.S. dated 4/6/'14

153

Sac & Fox – Shawnee
1846-1924   Volume XI

Government Witness fees
paid Sept. 30, 1913, Auth. 81065,
Aug. 22, 1913

Report Mailed
Dec. 21, 1914

1914
Dec. 10 1 day 2^{13} Mary McCoy disinterested witness Paid 3/15/15
"   "   1 day 2^{00} Alexander Connolly disinterested Witness Paid 3/15/15
             Thomas P Myers G.A.L. for minors

Requested auth to settle 12/21/14
Paid by check# 4057 on 1st Natl Bk Chandler, Okla ~~dated~~ pay to order of Clerk of Cty Ct Pottawatomie Cty

Certified copy of Marriage Record of Hiram P Thorp & Julia Mixon from Clerk of Cty Ct Pott. Cty Tecumseh Okla $1^{25}
affidavit showing no marriage license issued to Hiram P. Thorp up to 1900 from same Court as above - - - - - - - $.25$
                                            Total - - - - - - - - $\overline{\$1.^{50}}$

Julia Mixon, nee Thorp – 1/3   Minnie Rider nee Thorp – 1/15
~~Minnie Rider, nee Thorp- 1/15~~   Frank Thorp-   1/15
Fannie Grayson -   1/15   George Thorp-   1/15
James Thorp-   1/15   Mary Wilson nee Thorp   1/15
William Lasley Thorp-   1/15   Adaline Rhodd, nee Thorp- 1/15
Edward Thorp-   1/15   Roscoe Thorp-   1/15

Report Approved in Law-Heirship 48940-12, 33771-15. F.W.S. dated May 22, 1915

[Note: Charlotte and Hiram Thorps' information was given again.]

58
                                            Levi Barker
   1912   Costs Paid
Oct 5   Notices Issued
Nov 11   Case Continued until Nov. 25, 1912.
            Supt absent from Agency
Nov. 25   Interested Parties not Present.
            Case Continued to Dec. 28, 1912.
Dec. 28   Hearing Held
                 Persons Present:-   Sole heir. No Witness fees
1 day & 21 miles 4^{10} Andrew Barker } or mileage necessary.
1 day & 21 miles 4^{10} Nora Barker   } Paid under auth dated Sept 12
1 day & 21 miles 4^{10} Cora Ward   } 1914, from Andrew Barker
                            Walter M Hodsdon, Stenog. account
                            Horace J Johnson, Supt & S.D.A
1 day 2^{00} Alex Connolly, Interpreter Gov't

                            Andrew Barker, sole heir

Sac & Fox – Shawnee
1846-1924   Volume XI

Report mailed Jan. 14, 1913.

Report approved Feb. 12, 1913
Law 6151-1913, 67285-1913
W.D.G. dated Feb. 11, 1913

Government Witness fees paid Sept. 30, 1913, Auth. 81065, Aug. 22, 1913 fees paid Sept. 30, 1913, Auth. 81065, Aug. 22, 1913

Abby Redrock

Costs Paid

1912
Oct. 5   Notices issued.
Nov. 11 Case Continued until Nov. 25, 1912.
         Supt absent from Agency
Nov. 25 Case Continued until Jan. 13, 1913
1 day & 27 miles 4.^{70} Richard Duncan } Paid Auth Ed. Indus 19061-14, 30597-14, C.H.S. dated 4/6/14

1913
Jan. 13 Case Continued until Jan 15, 1913
Jan. 15 Hearing held.

Report Mailed July 8, 1915.

Persons Present:-
2 das   4.^{00} Andrew Barker } Deposited to Credit Same Auth as above
No fees or mileage   Chief McKosato
No fees   Alex Connolly, Interpreter.

Report Approved in
Law-Heirship 77369-15, E.G.T.
dated August 14, 1915.

Na-wa-ke-ke, Sole heir.

Charles C. Murray (no funds)

1912
Oct. 14 Issued notices
Nov. 18 Hearing held
         Persons Present
           Emily Roubidoux
           David Tohee
           Frank Kent
           Robert Small – Interpreter
           Walter M Hodsdon Stenog. & Guardian-ad-litem
             for Kirwin Murray, Franklin Murray, Pearl Murray,
             Kate Murray, Vestina Murray, & Velinda Murray, minors

Report Mailed May 21, 1913

Sac & Fox – Shawnee
1846-1924   Volume XI

Horace J Johnson, Supt & S.D.A.
Joseph Springer

Costs – See Hearing for Kirwin Murray #61.

Emily Roubidoux, nee Murray-	1/3
Kerwin[sic] Murray	1/9
Franklin Murray	1/9
Pearl Murray	1/9
Vestina Murray	1/9
Kate Murray	1/9
Velinda Murray	1/9

Report approved Aug. 16, 1913,
Land Heirship 6554-'13, J.B.K.

Government Witness fees paid
Sept. 30, 1913, Auth. 81065, Aug. 22, '13

Kirwin Murray

Report Mailed July 7, 1915.

1914.
Dec. 5   Notices issued
1915.
Jan. 5   On a/c insufficient time to take case up same is continued to Jan. 6, 1915.
Jan. 6   Hearing Held:- Persons Present:-

½ day & 3½ miles	1.$\underline{35}$	Emily Roubidoux, Inter' person
½ day	1.$\underline{00}$	Charlie Watson, Witness (possibly Int.)
See Case #169		Joseph Springer, Interp – Govt.
See Case #169		David Tohee, Disint. Witness – Govt.
½ day & 40 miles	5$\underline{00}$	Mary Green Grant (possibly Inter. person)
½ day & 40 miles	5$\underline{00}$	Frank English-(Inter person possibly)
½ day & 40 miles	5$\underline{00}$	Mary Grant (do do do)
½ day & 40 miles	5$\underline{00}$	Zolo Grant do do do
½ day & 40 miles	5$\underline{00}$	Anna Grant do do do
½ day & 40 miles	5$\underline{00}$	Mary Hana qua do do do
See Case #169		Frank Kent, Disint. person – Govt
½ day & 40 miles	5$\underline{00}$	Robert Small, Disint. person – Govt

Walter M. Hodsdon, Guardian-ad-litem for minor heirs
Horace J. Johnson, Supt & S.D.A. S.D.A.

Report Approved
Law-Heirship
12056-30-12
76610-16
Dated 10-7-16

Frank O. English	9/36	Interest
Charles Watson	9/36	"
Emily Roubidoux	6/36	"
Kirwin Murray	2/36	"
Franklin Murray	2/36	"

Sac & Fox – Shawnee
1846-1924   Volume XI

Pearl Murry[sic]	2/36	"
Vestina Murray	2/36	"
Kate Murray	2/36	"
Velinda Murray	2/36	"

[Charles C. Murray, page 156, given again.]

[61]

Kirwin Murray

1912
Oct. 14 ~~Costs Paid~~ Issued notices
Nov. 18   Case Continued until Nov. 19, 1912
   Nov. 18 Persons Present:-
        David Tohee
        Joseph Springer
Report Mailed June 16, 1913. Frank Kent
        Robert Small, Interpreter
        Walter M. Hodsdon, Guardian ad litem for William Jr
        Franklin, Pearl, Vestina, Kate & Velinda Murray
        Horace J Johnson, Supt & S.D.A.
        Emily Roubidoux
   Nov. 19- Persons Present:-

1 day & 2½ miles	2^{25}	Maggie Lincoln – Gov't
2 days & 4 miles	8^{00}	Mary Grant } Pay 1/3 from 61, " " " 62, " " " 63 } Paid 2^{66} Auth Ed Indus 19061-14, 30597-14, C.H.S. dated 4/6/14
3 days & 3½ miles	6^{35}	Robert Small, Interpreter-Gov't.
		Walter M. Hodsdon, Stenog & Guardian-Ad-Litem for above minors
		Horace J Johnson, Supt. & S.D.A.
2 days & 4 miles	8^{00}	Zolo Grant } Pay 1/3 from 61, " " " 62, " " " 63 } Paid 2^{66} Auth Ed Indus 19061-14, 30597-14, C.H.S. dated 4/6/14
3 days & 3½ miles	6^{35}	David Tohee – Gov't.
3 days & 2½ miles	6^{25}	Frank Kent – Gov't.
3 days	6^{00}	Joseph Springer – Gov't.
2 days & 3½ miles	4^{35}	Emily Roubidoux } ~~Pay 1/3 from 60~~, " " " 61, " " " 62 } Paid 2^{18} Auth Ed Indus 19061-14, 30597-14, C.H.S. dated 4/6/14

Government Witness fees
paid Sept. 30, 1913, Auth
81065, Aug. 22, 1913.

Costs Divided among the
Estates of:-
Kirwin Murray   #61
May Murray   #62
Charles C. Murray   #60
John Grant   #63

Sac & Fox – Shawnee
1846-1924 Volume XI

62

1912 — *Costs Paid* — May Murray — *Report Mailed July 7, 1915.*
Oct. 14   Issued notices
Nov. 18   Case Continued until Nov. 19, 1912

Nov. 19 -   Persons Present:-
    David Tohee – Gov't.
    Frank Kent – Gov't } Paid 2^{67} Auth-Ed. Indus, 19061-14,
    Mary Grant   } 30597-14, C.H.S. dated 4/6/14
    Emily Roubidoux } Paid 2^{17} Same Auth as above
    Robert Small, Interpreter – Govt.
    Zolo Grant } Paid 2^{17} Same Auth. as above
    Walter M Hodsdon, Stenog & Guardian-ad-litem for Wm Jr &
    Harvey Atkins, Frank & Thelma Grant, Kirwin, Franklin, Pearl,
    Vestina, Kate & Velinda Murray, minors.
    Horace J Johnson, Supt. & S.D.A.
    Joseph Springer – Gov't.

Costs:- See Hearing for Kirwin Murray #61.
      Frank English
Government Witness fees
paid Sept. 30, 1913, Auth.
81065, Aug. 22, 1913.

    Frank O. English 1/2 Interest
    Charles Watson   1/2   "

Heirs declared in Law-Heirship
76611-15, 39030-16, 89336-16, S.E.B.
Dated 10-7-16.   Probate fees pd 10/14/16.

63

1912 — *Costs Paid* — John Grant — *Report Mailed July 14, 1915.*
Oct. 10   Issued notices
Nov. 19   Case Continued to Nov. 20, 1912.

    Nov. 19 – Persons Present:-
      Mary Grant   David Tohee-Gov't
                          Joseph Springer-Gov't.
      Zolo Grant   Frank Kent-Gov't.
      Walter M Hodsdon-Stenog & Guardian-ad-litem for
      Vestina Grant, Wm Atkins Jr, Harvey Atkins, Frank
      Grant, Thelma Grant
      Robert Small, Interpreter – Gov't.

Sac & Fox – Shawnee
1846-1924   Volume XI

Horace J Johnson, Supt & S.D.A.
Mary Grant ⎱ Paid Each $2.⁶⁹ under Auth.
Zolo Grant ⎰ Edw. Indus 19061-14, 30597-14,
Joseph Springer – Gov't.   C.H.S. dated 4/6/14.
Robert Small, Interpreter-Gov't.
Walter M. Hodsdon, Stenog & Guardian-ad-litem for
                                    above minors.
Horace J Johnson, Supt. & S.D.A
David Tohee-Gov't
Frank Kent-Gov't.

Costs:- See Hearing for Kirwin Murray #61

Government Witness fees paid	Law-Heirship
Sept. 30, 1913, Auth. 81065, Aug. 22,'13	78911-1915 F.E.

Notice of declaration to heirs 1-15-17

Name	Share
Mary Grant	9720/25920
Mary Harragara (Mary McGlaslin Grant)	2160/25920
Vestina Grant	3240/25920
Ralph Green	1079/25920
Eva Hoogradora	do
Anna Grant	1074/25920
Frank Grant	do
Thelma Grant	do
William Atkins Jr	1650/25920
Harvey Reed Atkins	do
Susie Deroin	1200/25920
Baxter Atkins	750/25920
Louise Brien	5/ 25920
Mary Brien	do
Josie Brien	do
Thaddeus Brien	do
Josephine Deroin Young	450/25920

Probate fees pd 12/5/16

64

<u>Annie Nellie Grant</u>

Report Mailed July 14, 1915.

1912
Oct. 15 Issued Notices
Nov. 19 Case Continued

Law-Heirship 79154-1915 F.E.
Nov. 25, 1916.

William Atkins Jr	11/36 Int.
Harvey Reed Atkins	11/36 "
Susie Deroin (or Zolo Grant)	8/36 "
Josephine (Deroin) Young	3/36 "

Sac & Fox – Shawnee
1846-1924   Volume XI

Baxter Atkins   3/36   "

Probate Fees pd 12/5/16
Notice of declaration mailed to heirs 12/21/16
Personal Estate distributed 12/21/16

65

Jane Ely   *Report Mailed July 14, 1915.*

1912
Oct. 15   Issued Notices
Nov. 19   Case Continued

Law-Heirship
79224-1915, 62334-1916
F.E. dated 11/25/16

Notice of Declaration to heirs 1-15-17

Mary Grant,	1/4 or 216/864 Int.
Vestina Grant	1/4 or 216/864 "
Eva Hoogradora	43/864 "
Ralph Green	43/864 "
Anna Grant	42/864 "
Frank Grant	do
Thelma Grant	do
Louise Brien	1/864
Mary Brien	do
Josie Brien	do
Thaddeus Brien	do
Susie Grant Deroin	48/864
William Atkins Jr	66/864
Harvey Reed Atkins	66/864
Josephine Deroin Young	18/864
Baxter Atkins	do

Probate fees pd 12/5/16

66

"Costs Paid"   Mary Roubidoux

1912
Nov. 25   Issued notices
          1913
Jan. 6   Case Continued to Jan. 7, 1913, a/c Supt. not being present
          1913
Jan. 7   Hearing Held:-
          Persons Present:-
          Robert Roubidoux
          Julia Kihega
          Robert Small
          Joseph Springer
          David Tohee

Sac & Fox – Shawnee
1846-1924   Volume XI

Walter M. Hodsdon, Guard.-Ad-Litem for Sevinah
                    & Sophie Roubidoux
Horace J Johnson, Supt. & S.D.A.

Report Mailed July 21, 1915

Costs divided among Estates of
  Jefferson Whitecloud #67
  Mary Roubidoux   #66
  Lizzie Whitecloud   #68

Report approved Aug. 21, 1913.
Land Heirship 84626-13, 90583-13, J.B.K.

Robert Roubidoux, husband 7/18 int.
Sevinah Roubidoux, Dau.   11/36 int.
Sophie Roubidoux, Dau   11/36 int.

Government Witness fees
paid Sept. 30, 1913, Auth.
81065, Aug. 22, 1913

67

"Costs Paid"   **Jefferson Whitecloud**

1912
Nov. 25   Issued Notices
1913
Jan 6   Case Continued to Jan. 7, 1913, a/c Supt. not being present
1913
Jan 7   Hearing Held.
       Persons Present:-

2 days & 3 Miles 4^{30}	Robert Roubidoux	Pay ½ from No. 67	Paid $\$2^{15}$ Auth Ed. Indus 19061-14,
2 days & 8 Miles 4^{80}	Susan Whitecloud	Pay ½ from No. 67	30597-14, C.H.S. dated 4/6/14 Paid $\$2^{40}$ Auth as above
2 days & 43 Miles 8^{30}	Julia Kihega	" " " " 68	Paid $\$4^{15}$ Same Auth as above
2 days & 3½ Miles 4^{25}	Robert Small – Gov't.		
2 das	4^{00}	Joseph Springer – Gov't.	
2 days & 3½ Miles 4^{25}	David Tohee – Gov't		

       Walter M Hodsdon, Guardian-ad-Litem for
              Sevinah & Sophie Roubidoux.
       Horace J Johnson, Supt & S.D.A.

Report Mailed June 15, 1914

Report approved Law-Heirship 68036-14, F.E. dated July 7, 1914

       Costs divided among the Estates of
         Jefferson Whitecloud #67
         Mary Roubidoux   #66
         Lizzie Whitecloud   #68
               Susan Whitecloud- 1/3

Government Witness fees   Dora E. Hudson- 1/9
paid Sept. 30, 1913, Auth.   Julia Kihega-   1/9

Sac & Fox – Shawnee
1846-1924   Volume XI

81065, Aug. 22, 1913
Emma Fawfaw-   1/9
Phoebe Black-   1/9
James H. Morris-   1/27
Charles H. Morris-   1/81
Eliza F DeRoin-   1/81
James A Morris-   1/81
George L. Morris-   1/81
Herman Morris-   1/81
Samuel R. Morris-   1/81
Robert Roubidoux-   7/162
Sevinah Roubidoux-   11/324
Sophie Roubidoux-   11/324

---

68   "Costs Paid"   Lizzie Whitecloud

1912
Nov. 25   Issued Notices
1913
Jan. 6   Hearing Continued to Jan. 7, 1913, a/c Supt not being present.
1913
Jan. 7   Hearing Held:-
           Persons Present:-
           Robert Roubidoux } Paid $2¹⁵ Auth Ed. Indus 19061-14, 30597-14, C.H.S. dated 4/6/14
           Susan Whitecloud } Paid $2⁴⁰ Auth as above
           Julia Kihega   } Paid $4¹⁵ Same Auth as above
           David Tohee- Gov't.
           Joseph Springer- Gov't.
           Robert Small- Gov't.
           Walter M. Hodsdon, Stenog & Guard-Ad-Litem for
                          Sevinah & Sophie Roubidoux
           Horace J Johnson, Supt.
      Costs divided among Estates of:-
           Jefferson Whitecloud   #67
           Mary Roubidoux   #66
           Lizzie Whitecloud   #68

Government Witness fees paid
Sept. 30, 1913, Auth. 81065, Aug. 22, 1913
           Susan Whitecloud-   1/3
           Dora E Hudson-   1/9
           Julia Kihega-   1/9
           Emma Fawfaw-   1/9
           Phoebe Black-   1/9
           James H. Morris-   1/27
           Charles H. Morris-   1/81
           Eliza F DeRoin-   1/81

Report Mailed May 14, 1914

Report approved Law-Heirship 57991-14 F.W.S. dated June 5, 1914

Sac & Fox – Shawnee
1846-1924   Volume XI

James A Morris-   1/81
George L. Morris-   1/81
Herman Morris-   1/81
Samuel R. Morris-   1/81
Robert Roubidoux-   7/162
Sevinah Roubidoux-   11/324
Sophie Roubidoux-   11/324

"Costs Paid"   Phoebe Keokuk   69

1912
Nov. 26   Issued Notices
1913
Jan. 13   Hearing Held-
          Persons Present:-

1 da & 6 miles	$2^{\underline{60}}$	John E. Keokuk Paid Witness & mileage fees $1^{\underline{30}}$ July 21, '13
No fees for mileage		Marie A Fear
1 da & 6 miles	$2^{\underline{60}}$	Robert (Peyton) Keokuk Paid Witness & mileage fees 87¢ July 21, '13
1 da & 6 miles	$2^{\underline{60}}$	Fannie K. Foote Paid Witness & mileage fees 87¢ July 21, '13
1 da & 14 miles	$3^{\underline{40}}$	Fannie Nadeau- Gov't.
1 day	$2^{\underline{00}}$	Leo Whistler- Gov't.
		Horace J Johnson, Supt
		Walter M Hodsdon, Stenog

Costs divided among estates of:-
Phoebe Keokuk #69
Laura Keokuk   #70
Charles Keokuk #71

Marie A Fear-   1/3
Alice Lee-   1/3
Mary A Keokuk-   1/6
Frank Keokuk   1/24
John Earle Keokuk   1/24
Robert Peyton Keokuk   1/24
Fannie Foote, nee Keokuk   1/24

Report Approved June 23, 1913, Land-Heirship 55152-1913, 62288-1913 J.B.K.

Report Mailed Apr 29, 1913

Witness and Mileage fees paid July 21, '13 from Estate
Government Witness fees paid Sept. 30, 1913, Auth. 81065, Aug. 22, '13

---

70   "Costs Paid"   Laura Keokuk

1912
Nov. 26   Issued Notices
1913
Jan. 13   Hearing Held

Sac & Fox – Shawnee
1846-1924 Volume XI

Persons Present:-
Fannie K. Foote   Paid 86¢ Witness & Mileage fees July 21, '13
Robert Peyton Keokuk   Paid 86¢ Witness & Mileage fees July 21, '13
Fannie Nadeau – Govt
Leo Whistler – Govt
Horace J Johnson, Supt
Walter M. Hodsdon, Stenog
Costs divided among Estates of:-
  Phoebe Keokuk #69
  Laura Keokuk   #70
  Charles Keokuk #71

Robert Peyton Keokuk-   1/2
Fannie Foote, nee Keokuk 1/2

Report Mailed Apr 29, 1913
Report Approved June 23, 1913, Land-Heirship 55152-1913, 62288-1913 J.B.K.

{ Certified Copy of Divorce Decree of Laura and
  Charles Keokuk - - - - - - - - - - - - - 65 cents.
  Paid under Auth. 54447 dated May 2, 1913-Paid 5/15/13.

Witness and Mileage fees paid July 21, '13 from Estate
Government Witness fees paid Sept. 30, '13, Auth. 81065, Aug. 22,'13

71

"Costs Paid"   Charles Keokuk

1912
Nov. 27   Issued Notices
1913
Jan. 13   Hearing Held
          Persons Present:-
          Fannie K. Foote   Paid 87¢ Witness & Mileage fees July 21, '13
          Robert Peyton Keokuk   Paid 87¢ Witness & Mileage fees July 21, '13
          Fannie Nadeau – Govt
          John E Keokuk   Paid $1.30 Witness & Mil. fees July 21, '13
          Leo Whistler – Govt
          Horace J Johnson, Supt
          Walter M. Hodsdon, Stenog

Report Approved June 23, 1913, Land-Heirship 55150-1913, 55614-1913 J.B.K.

          Costs divided among Estates of:-
            Phoebe Keokuk #69
            Laura Keokuk   #70
            Charles Keokuk #71

Report Mailed Apr 29, 1913

          Fannie Foote, nee Keokuk 1/2 of 1/2 or 1/4 of whole estate
          Robert Peyton Keokuk-   1/2 of 1/2 or 1/4 of whole estate

Witness and Mileage fees paid July 21, '13 from Estate
Government Witness fees paid Sept. 30, '13, Auth. 81065, Aug. 22,'13

72

Egbert Mitchell

1912
Dec 6   Issued Notices
1913
Jan. 14   Case Continued until Jan. 15, 1913.

Jan. 14   Persons Present:-
2 days & 112 Miles $15^{20}	Minnie Barada	Pay from Waw-ko-pah-she-toe
2 das & 27½ Miles 6^{75}	Grace Lee	Estate only
2 das & 21 Miles 6^{10}	Isaac Strubble- Govt	
2 das & 14½ Miles 5^{45}	Edward Mathews (Pe-pique)- Govt	
2 das & 13½ Miles 5^{35}	U.S. Grant Requested by Supt to be present at hearing - Govt	
2 das & 23 Miles 6^{30}	Bettie Groinhorn To be paid from Egbert Mitchell Estate only.	
2 das & 25½ Miles 6^{55}	Jesse Pickett- Govt	
½ day $1^{00}	Leo Walker- Govt	
No fees of Mil	Chief McKosato	
2 das 4^{00}	Alex Connolly-Interpreter-Govt.	

Jan 14   Persons Present:-   Minnie Barada nee Plum- 1/2
    Alex Connolly Int-Govt
    Minnie Barada   Sadie Rhodes-   1/4
    Grace Lee   Frank Smith-   1/20
    Isaac Strubble- Govt   Benjamin Smith-   1/20
    Edward Mathews (Pe-pique)Govt   Charles Smith-   1/20
    U. S. Grant- Govt   Rachel Franklin nee Smith 1/20
    Bettie Groinhorn   Edith Brain, nee Benson 1/40
    Jesse Pickett-Govt   Clara Benson, nee Ellis- 1/40
2 das & 4 miles $4^{40} Chief McKosato
Jan. 7   John Roubidoux   Testimony taken at Perkins, Okla by Supt- Govt

(Report Mailed March 12, 1914)

    Costs divided among Estates of Egbert Mitchell #72
    & Wah-ko-pah-she-toe[sic] #38
Government Witness fees paid Sept. 30, '13, Auth. 81065, Aug. 22, '13

73

Marie Davis   (No funds)

1912
Dec. 10   Issued notices
1913
Jan, 22   Hearing Held:-
    Persons Present:-
1 da & 19 miles 3^{90} Mary Hurr
1 da & 19 miles 3^{90} Orlando Johnson
    Thos. P. Myers, Guard-Ad-Litem for Sadie Rhodes
1 da   2^{00} Leo Whistler-Govt
1 da   2^{00} Alex Connolly-Govt

Sac & Fox – Shawnee
1846-1924   Volume XI

Horace J Johnson, Supt
Walter M. Hodsdon, Stenogist[sic]

as modified Report Approved May 31, 1913, Land-Heirship 36465-1913, J.D.C.

Mary Hurr, nee Davis, mother	7/18 of Estate	} Modified as below
Robert Davis, Brother	5/18 " "	
Orlando Johnson,	5/18 " "	
Sadie Rhodes	1/18 " "	

Report mailed March 15, 1913.

Mary Hurr, nee Davis - 11/27 of Estate
Robert Davis   - 8/27   "   "
Orlando Johnson   - 8/27   "   "

Government Witness fees paid
Sept. 30,'13, Auth. 81065, Aug. 22,'13

---

74   *Costs Paid*   Annie Falls

    1912
Dec 10   Issued notices
    1913
Jan. 23   Hearing Held:-
                 Persons Present:-
½ da & 20 miles 3⁰⁰   Frank Smith } No witness fees or mileage necessary a/c being sole heir
½ da   1⁰⁰   Leo Whistler, disint witness - Govt
½ da   1⁰⁰   Alex Connolly, Interpreter & Witness - Govt
½ da & 24 miles 3⁴⁰   Amanda McKosato
                      Horace J Johnson, Supt.
                      Walter M Hodsdon, Stenogr.

Report mailed January 29, 1913

Frank Smith sole heir

Report approved Feb. 12, 1913.
Law 16109-1913, W.D.G. dated
Feb. 11, 1913.

Government Witness fees paid
Sept. 30,'13, Auth. 81065, Aug. 22,'13

                  "Costs Paid"   Mary Hodge   75

    1912
Dec. 10   Issued notices
    1913
Jan. 24   Hearing Held:-

Sac & Fox – Shawnee
1846-1924 Volume XI

                Persons Present:

1 da & 11½ miles 3^{15}	Andrew Conger	⎫ Paid Auth. Ed. Indus 19061-'14,
1 da & 11½ miles 3^{15}	Inez Bass	⎭ 30597-14. C.H.S. dated 4/6/'14.
1 da 2^{00}	Alex Connolly, Int. & Dis. Wit-Govt.	
	Thos. P. Myers, Guard-Ad-Litem for	
	Florence Grass, minor	
	Horace J Johnson, Supt	
	Walter M Hodsdon, Stenogr.	
Sept. 11 1 day 2^{00}	Sarah Ellis, Disint. Witness. ~~Gov't~~	no mileage allowed [illegible] request by Sept. to get testimony
	Florance Grass, Inherits all	

Report Mailed Aug. 13, 1913

Government Witness fees paid Sept. 30,'13,
Auth. 81065, Aug. 22,'13

                Report Approved
                    Law-Heirship 113285-13, S.A.U.
                    dated Sept. 23, 1914
                ~~Report~~ Declaration of Department modified in
                  Law-Heirship 113285-13, 26061-14, F.W.S.
                  dated 11/13/14.

---

76   "Costs Paid"   <u>Susie Grant</u>

1912
Dec. 21 Issued Notices
1913
Jan. 23 Hearing Held.

                Persons Present:-

1 da & 7½ miles 2^{75}	Saginaw Grant	⎫ Paid Auth. Ed. Indus 19061-'14, ⎭ 30597-14. C.H.S. dated 4/6/'14.
1 day 2^{00}	Leo Whistler, Disin Wit- Govt	
1 day 2^{00}	Alex Connolly, Disin. Wit- Govt.	
	Horace J Johnson, Supt.	
	Walter M. Hodsdon, Stenog.	

                Saginaw Grant, husband, 1/2 of Estate
                John Scott, father,   1/2 "   "

                Report mailed March 11, 1913.
                Report approved June 3, 1913.
                Land-Heirship 34323-1913, J.B.K.

Government Witness fees paid
Sept. 30,'13, Auth. 81065, Aug. 22,'13

Sac & Fox – Shawnee
1846-1924   Volume XI

Paid Jan. 24, '14
Check No. 605
on 1st Natl.
Bank. of Stroud,
Okla.

{ Certified Copy of Marriage License
and Certificate of Marriage . . . . 75 cts.
(Paid by Saginaw Grant, Auth. request
should be made to reimburse Grant) }

Albert Washington   (No funds)   77

1913
Jan. 2   Issued Notices
Feb. 3   Hearing Held:-
Persons Present:-

1 da & 19½ miles	3^{25}	Charles Smith
1 da & 20 miles	4^{00}	Frank Smith
1 da & 19½ miles	3^{25}	Benjamin Smith
1 da & 16 miles	3^{60}	Rachel Franklin
1 da & 14½ miles	3^{45}	William G. Foster, dis. Witness
1 day	2^{00}	Alex Connolly, Interpreter of Disin Wit-Govt

⎫ Requested by Interested
⎭ parties to be present (for Rachel Franklin & William G. Foster)

Walter M Hodsdon, Stenog.
Horace J Johnson, Supt
Thomas P. Myers, Guardian-Ad-Litem for
   Sadie Rhodes, minor.

Government Witness paid Sept. 30, 1913,
Auth. 81065, Aug. 22, 1913

Report Mailed Sept. 13, 1913

Sadie Rhodes-   1/2
Frank Smith-   1/10
Benjamin Smith   1/10
Charles Smith-   1/10
Rachel Franklin- 1/10
Edith Brown, nee Benson- 1/20
Clara Benson, nee Ellis - 1/20

---

78   *"Costs Paid"*   Jennie Bigwalker

1913
Feb. 14   Issued Notices
Feb. 24   Hearing Held
Persons Present:-

1 da & 29½ miles	4^{25}	Sarah Bigwalker
1 da & 29½ miles	4^{25}	Dollie McClellan
1 day	2^{00}	Lelia Bigwalker
1 day & 32 miles	5^{20}	Mamie Jennings
1 day & 16 miles	3^{60}	Osmond Franklin

Sac & Fox – Shawnee
1846-1924   Volume XI

1 day	2^{00}	Alex Connolly, Int. of Disin Wit- Govt
1 day	2^{00}	Leo Whistler, Disin Wit.-Govt
		Walter M. Hodsdon, Stenog.
		Horace J Johnson, Supt

Sarah Bigwalker	1/7
Dollie McClellan	6/35
Lelia Bigwalker	6/35
Esther Bigwalker	6/35
Mamie F. Jennings	6/35
Osmond Franklin	6/35

Report Mailed Apr. 17, 1913

Report approved May 12, 1913,   Government Witness fees
Land-Heirship 49809-1913, J.B.K.   paid Sept. 30, 1913, Auth.
~~Report approved May 12, 1913.~~   81065, Aug. 22, 1913

79

"Costs Paid" William Ingalls

1913
Mar. 18   Issued Notices
April 19   Hearing Held-
　　　　　Persons Present-   Paid Auth Ed Indus 19061-14,
1 day & 25 ½ miles 4^{55}　Mattie Ingalls }　30597-14, C.H.S. dated 4/6/14
1 day　2^{00}　Alex Connolly, Int. of Dis Wit-Govt
1 day　2^{00}　Leo Whistler, Disin Wit- Govt
　　　　　Horace J Johnson, Supt.
　　　　　Walter M. Hodsdon, Stenogr.

Report approved June 19, 1913, Land-Heirship 63901-1913, J.B.K.

Report Mailed May 17, '13

Mattie Ingalls	1/3
Sadie Ingalls	1/3
Henry Ingalls	1/3

Government Witness fees paid
Sept. 30, 1913, Auth. 81065, Aug. 22,'13

80

Julia Messawat   (No funds)

1913
Mar. 18   Issued Notices
Apr. 21   Hearing Held.
　　　　　Persons Present: No Witness fees or mileage
1 day & 17½ miles 3^{75}　Linda LaBelle } necessary a/c being sole heir.
1 day & 20 miles 4^{00}　Sarah Ellis, Disin. Wit.
1 day　2^{00}　Alex Connolly, Int. of Dis. Wit-Govt
　　　　　Horace J Johnson, Supt & S.D.A
　　　　　Walter M. Hodsdon, Stenogr.

Sac & Fox – Shawnee
1846-1924   Volume XI

Linda LaBelle, nee Mesawat
inherits entire estate.

Report Mailed June 14, 1913

Report Approved July 19, 1913,
Land-Heirship 71461-1913. F.E.

Government Witness paid Sept. 30, 1913,
Auth. 81065, Aug. 22, 1913

81

"Costs Paid"   Harry Benson

1913
Mar. 19   Issued Notices
Apr. 22   Continued to May 26, 1913.
dMay 26   Hearing Held.
           Persons Present   Paid under Auth of 2/6/14.
1 day & 28½ miles 4^{85} Edith Brown   ~~Paid Auth Ed Indus 19061-14,~~
1 day   2^{00} Jane Harrison, Disin Wit. ~~30597-14. C.H.S. dated 4/6/14~~
1 day   2^{00} Alex Connolly, Int of Wit- Govt   No mileage present in Govt.
                             Horace J Johnson, Supt   office and requested
                             Walter M. Hodsdon, Stenog.   by Sept to get testimony.

May 26,'13 Hearing Cont. to June 7,'13 a/c all int. parties not present.
1 day & 30 miles 5^{00}
June 7, '13   Clara Benson}   Paid. See above Auth.
Persons Present-

Paid { Certified Copy of Marriage License and
      Certificate of Marriage . . . . $1.[??]

       Clara Benson- Wife – 1/2
       Edith Brown-mother – 1/2

Government Witness paid Sept. 30,1913,
Auth. 81065, Aug. 22,1913

Report Mailed June 14, 1913

Report Approved
Law-Heirship
41505-13
144521-13.
E.A.U.
dated Mar. 9, 1914.

82

"Costs Paid"   Edgar Mack

1913
Mar. 19   Issued notices
Apr. 28   Hearing Held.
           Persons Present:
1 day & 24½ miles 4^{45} Sarah Mack   ⎫   Paid Auth. Ed. Indus.
1 day & 25 miles   4^{50} Elbert Mack   ⎬   19061-14, 30597-14,
1 day & 24½ miles 4^{45} Charley Mack ⎭   C.H.S. dated 4/6/14.
1 day   2^{00} Alex Connolly, Int. of Disin Wit. Govt
1 day & 26 miles   4^{60} Hugh Wakolle, Dis. Wit.} Brought by Int Parties } Paid
                                                        Auth same as above-Mack's
                              Walter M Hodsdon, Stenog.

170

Sac & Fox – Shawnee
1846-1924   Volume XI

Horace J Johnson, Supt.

Sarah Mack-Wife- One-third (1/3)
Elbert Mack-Son- One-third (1/3)
Charley Mack-Son- One-third (1/3)

Report Mailed June 28, 1913

Government fees paid Sept 30, 1913
Auth. 81065, Aug. 22, 1913

Report Approved Law-Heirship 82651-13, E.A.U.
dated Feb. 26, 1914.

83

"Costs Paid"   Julia Hodge

1913
Mar. 19   Issued notices
Apr. 30   Hearing Continued to May 1st. Supt. absent from Agency
May 1   Hearing Held
         Persons Present
1 day & 11½ miles 3$\underline{15}$ Inez Bass
1 day & 7½ miles 2$\underline{75}$ Olive Jackson, Disin Wit Brought by Int Parties
1 day   2$\underline{00}$ Alex Connolly   Int of Disin Wit-Govt
                                      Walter M. Hodsdon, Stenogr
                                      Horace J Johnson, Supt.

Paid Auth.
Ed. Indus
19061-'14,
30597-14,
C.H.S. dated
4/6/14.

Report Mailed Sept. 15, '13

Inez Bass, Dau 1/2 Int.
Florence Grass, Gr. Dau 1/2 Int.

Report approved Law-Heirship 112485-1913, F.E.
dated Nov. 3, 1913.

Government Witness fees paid
Sept. 30,'13, Auth. 81065, Aug. 22,'13

84

"No Costs"   Samuel L. Moore

1913
Mar. 19   Issued notices   to ~~Mar. 26, '14~~ Sept. 10, 1913
May 5   Hearing Continued Interested Parties not Present
Sept. 10 ~~1913~~
~~Mar. 26~~   Hearing Held
         (Persons Present: Testimony introduced at hearing to
         determine heirs of ~~Watt Grayson~~ Grace Mason. Case
         No. ~~143~~ 98, to apply in this Case also.)
         Isaac Strubble, Disint. person
         William G. Foster, Disint. person
         Thomas P. Myers, Guardian-ad-Litem for Hattie and

171

Sac & Fox – Shawnee
1846-1924 Volume XI

Ellen Mason, minors.
Walter M. Hodsdon, Stenog
Horace J. Johnson, Supt. & S.D.A.

Ellen Mason – 1/2 of Estate
Hattie Mason – 1/2 of Estate

Report Mailed Oct. 7, 1914

Report Approved Law-Heirship
10055-1914, F.W.S. dated Nov. 5, 1914.

85

Hull, William

1913
Mar. 27 Issued notices   to Mar. 21, 1914
April 28 Hearing Continued- ⋀ No Witnesses Present
1914
Mar. 21 Hearing Held:-
    Persons Present:
    Isaac Struble, Disint. Person, Govt
    Jane Harrison, Disint. Person Govt
    Alexander Connolly, Interpreter of Disint. Person Govt
    Walter M. Hodsdon, Stenog.
    Thomas P. Myers, Guardian-Ad-Litem for
      Ben Hull, minor
    Horace J. Johnson, Supt.

Costs: See George Manatowa #122

Report Mailed May 4, 1914

Ben Hull Mansur, sole heir.

Report Approved.
  Law-Heirship 50944-13, F.W.S.
  dated May 29, 1914.

86

Francis Harris

1913
Apr. 18 Issued Notices
May 19 Interested Parties not present Hearing Continued to July 23, 1913
July 23 Hearing Held:-
    Persons Present:-

1 day and 30½ miles 5⁰⁵	Moses Harris, Int. Wit	Paid Auth. Ed. Indus. 19061-14, 30597-'14 C.H.S. dated 4/6/14
1 day and 30½ miles 5⁰⁵	Liza Martin, Disint. Wit.	
1 day and 13½ miles 3³⁵	Ulysses S. Grant, Disint. Wit.	
	William Pattequa, Disint. Wit.	No Witness or mileage allowed Member of Bus Comm
1 day 2⁰⁰	Alex Connolly, Interpreter- Govt	

Sac & Fox – Shawnee
1846-1924   Volume XI

Horace J Johnson, Supt.
W. M. Hodsdon, Stenog.

Mary Harris – 1/2 interest
Moses Harris – 1/2   "

Report Mailed May 4, 1914

Report Approved
Law-Heirship 105882-13, F.E. dated Nov. 29,'13

87

Eliza White Kebolte (No funds)

1913
Apr 30   Issued Notice
June 2   Hearing Held:-
         Persons Present:-

1 day & 40 miles 6^{00}	Sam Ellis — Not entitled to Witness & mileage fees for the reason
~~1 day & 40 miles 6^{00}~~	Fred Vetter } that he was not summoned to appear at hearing a/c
1 day & 40 miles 6^{00}	Mary McGlaslin being a minor, & a Guardian-ad-litem unappointed.
1 day & 3½ miles 2^{35}	David Tohee, Disint Witness-Govt
1 day 2^{00}	Joseph Springer Int. of Disint. Witness- Govt
	Arza B. Collins, U.S. Farmer
	Horace J Johnson Supt

Report Mailed Dec. 2, 1913

Charles Kebolte- 1/2
Sam Ellis-   1/2

Government Witness fees paid
Sept. 30, 1913, Auth. 81065, Aug. 22,'13

Report Approved, Law-Heirship 144638-13,
E.A.U. dated Mar. 4, 1914.

88

Jack Bear $22^{50} Request auth. to settle Wit. fees.

1913
May 5   Issued Notices
June 9 Hearing Held:-
        Persons Present:-

1 day & 32 miles 5^{20}	Mamie Jennings
1 day & 31½ miles 5^{15}	George O Morton
1 day & 30 miles 5^{10}	William Bear
1 day 2^{00}	Edward Matthews { no mileage- Present in Office & requested by Supt to give testimony
1 day & 31½ miles 5^{15}	Sarah Bear
1 day 2^{00}	Alex Connolly, Int. of Disin Person- Govt
	Walter M. Hodsdon, Stenog
	Horace J Johnson, Supt

173

Sac & Fox – Shawnee
1846-1924   Volume XI

June 10, 1913
1 day   2⁰⁰   John Brown { no mileage- Present in Office & requested by Supt to give testimony

Report Mailed Dec. 10, 1913

Sarah Bear -   1/4
William Bear -   1/4
Mabel Wakole -   1/4
George Oliver Morton - 1/8
Mamie F. Jennings,
   nee Morton -   1/8

Report Approved:- Law-Heirship 147044-13 E.G.T. dated Jan. 3, '14

Government Witness fees paid
Sept. 30,'13, Auth. 81065, Aug. 22,'13

Katie Ellis (No funds)   89

1913
May 31   Issued notices
July 1   Hearing Held:-
             Persons Present:-
             James H Wright
             Alex Connolly, Disint. Witness & Interp
             Bettie Groinhorn, Disint Witness
             Chief McKosato, Disint Witness
             Thomas P. Myers, Guard-Ad-Litem for
                Maude Kakaque, minor
             Horace J Johnson, Supt
             W. M. Hodsdon, Stenog

Report Mailed Aug. 25, 1913

Jesse Kakaque - -   1/2 interest
Maude Kakaque - -   1/2   "

Report Returned- No Authority for
Department to Determine Heirs, as land
has been sold. (Law-Heirship 131617-13
   F.E. dated Jan. 8, 1914)

90

Joseph Fox (No funds)

1913
May 31   Notices Issued
July 1   Hearing Held
             Persons Present:-
             James H. Wright
             E. L. Conklin
             Alex Connolly, Disint. Witness & Interp
             Bettie Groinhorn, Disint. Witness
             Chief McKosato, Disint. Witness

174

Sac & Fox – Shawnee
1846-1924   Volume XI

Horace J Johnson, Supt
W. M. Hodsdon, Stenog.

1913
July 1   Hearing Continued on account of all interested parties not being present:- To July 10, 1913.

1913
July 10   Persons Present:- At Shawnee.
Thomas W. Alford, Disint. Wit.
Jennie Cegar   "   "
John Snake   Interpreter

Bettie Fox - -	1/2 Interest	
Sallie Ellis - -	1/36	"
Sargeant Ellis	1/36	"
Frank Ellis	1/36	"
Mary James	1/12	"
Katie Ellis	1/12	"
Peter Brady	1/12	"
Little Jim	1/24	"
Cora Starr	1/12	"
Charley Bob	19/864	"
Pem-mah-com-se	17/864	

Report Mailed Aug. 25, 1913

Report Returned- No Authority for Department to Determine Heirs, as land has been sold. (Law-Heirship 110771-13 F.E. dated Jan. 8, 1914)

91

Costs Paid   Joe Vetters

1913
June 12   Issued Notices
July 14   Hearing Held:-
          Persons Present:-

½ day & 3½ miles 1^{35}	Annie Perry Tohee, Int. Witness	
½ day & 40 miles 5^{00}	Mary Murdock McGlaslin, Int. Witness	
½ day 1^{00}	Joseph Springer, Disint. Witness-Govt	
½ day & 40 miles 5^{00}	John Moses, Disint. Witness-Govt	
½ day & ~~miles~~ 1^{00}	David Tohee, Disint. Witness	No mileage fees as he-Govt testified in case of Lee Patrick Tohee-Govt.
½ day & 2 miles 1^{20}	Jacob Dole, Interpreter-Govt	
	Horace J Johnson, Supt.	
	W. M. Hodsdon, Stenog	

*Paid. Auth.
Ed. Indus
19061-14,
30597-14
C.H.S. dated 4/6/14*

Costs Divided among Estates of:-
Joe Vetters -   No. 91
Lee Patrick Tohee- No. 92

~~Government Witness fees paid
Sept. 30,'13, Auth. 81065, Aug. 22,'13~~
Government Witnesses paid under
Auth. 1185, dated Feb. 21, 1914.

Report Mailed May 18, 1914.

Sac & Fox – Shawnee
1846-1924   Volume XI

Paid by Ck #753 dated 6/1/14 on 1st Natl Bk. Stroud, Okla.
auth dated 5/25/14

Certified Copy of Marriage License & Certificate of Marriage of Joe Vetters or Joseph Vetter & Miss Nesojame- 55 Cents

Nesojame Vetters- 1/3 Int.
Annie Perry Tohee- 1/3 Int.
Mary Murdock McGlaslin- 1/9 Int.
Fred Vetters - 1/9 Int.
Lucy Ruth Vetters-1/9 Int.

Report Approved:- Law-Heirship 60508-14, F.E., dated June 17, '14.

92

"Costs Paid"   Lee Patrick Tohee

1913
June 12   Issued Noticed
July 14   Hearing Held:-
          Persons Present:-

EA ~~1 day & miles~~ David Tohee
½ day & 40 miles 5.00
~~1 day & miles~~ 1.00 "Little" Dave Tohee Jr-Govt
½ day
~~1 day & miles~~ 1.00 Annie Perry Tohee-Govt
½ day
~~1 day & miles~~ Jacob Dole, Interpreter-Govt
          Horace J Johnson, Supt
          W. M. Hodsdon, Stenog

Report Mailed July 23, '13

Costs Divided among Estates of:-
Joe Vetters - No. 91
Lee Patrick Tohee -No. 92

David Tohee, father Inherits entire Estate.

Report approved Aug. 13, 1913,
Land-Heirship 91387-1913, 92350-1913
F.E.

~~Government Witness fees paid Sept. 30,'13, Auth. 81065, Aug. 22,'13~~
Government Witnesses paid under
Auth. 1185, dated Feb. 21, 1914.

93

Costs Paid   Benjamin Butler

1913
June 23   Issued notices
July 23   Hearing Continued on account of interested parties not being present.
          Continued to Sept. 8, 1913.
Sept. 8   Hearing Held:-

Sac & Fox – Shawnee
1846-1924   Volume XI

Persons Present:-
Edward Butler, Int. Witness
George Butler, Int. Witness
Jane Foster, nee Butler, Int. Witness
Alex Connolly, Interpreter of disint Wit-Govt
Sarah Bear, Disint. Witness – Govt.
Horace J Johnson, Supt
Walter M. Hodsdon, Stenog.

Mileage   ½ day 1⁰⁰
allowed   ½ day 1⁰⁰
in James   ½ day 1⁰⁰
Bear Case ½ day 1⁰⁰
          ½ day 1⁰⁰

Paid under auth dated Sept. 12, 1914

~~Government Witness fees paid Sept. 30,'13, Auth. 81065, Aug. 22,'13~~

Report Mailed Feb. 5, 1914.

Edward Butler - - 1/3
George Butler - - 1/3
Jane Foster, nee Butler—1/3

Report Approved:-
Law-Heirship 14017-14,
F.W.S., dated Mar. 27, '14

Government Witnesses paid under Auth. 1185, dated 2/21/14.

94

Costs Paid   James Bear

1913
June 23   Issued notices
July 23   Hear Continued on account of interested parties not being present. Continued to Sept. 8, 1913.
Sept. 8   Hearing Held:-
          Persons Present:-

½ day & 25½ miles 3⁵⁵   Edward Butler, Int. Witness
½ day & 12½ miles 2⁷⁵   George Butler, Int. Witness
½ day & 19 miles 2⁹⁰   Jane Foster, nee Butler, Int. Witness
½ day   1⁰⁰   Alex Connolly, Interpreter & disin. Witness-Govt
½ day   1⁰⁰   Sarah Bear, Disint. Witness
                        Horace J Johnson, Supt
                        Walter M. Hodsdon, Stenog.

Paid-Auth Edw. Indus 19061-14, 30597-14, C.H.S. dated 4/6/14

No mileage allowed Present in Office & requested by Supt to give testimony

~~Government Witness fees paid Sept. 30,'13, Auth 81065, Aug. 22,'13~~
Government Witnesses paid under Auth 1185, dated Feb. 21, 1914.

Report Mailed January 16, 1915.

         Edward Butler -   1/3 Int.
         George Butler-   1/3 Int.
         Jane Foster, nee Butler- 1/3 Int.
              Report Approved in
              Law-Heirship 7981-15, T.W.S.
              dated March 1, 1915

95

John Nahashe — "Costs Paid"

1913
- July 15 — Issued Notices
- Sept 8 — Hearing continued to Oct. 1, 1913 account of interested Parties not being present.
- Oct. 1 — Hearing Held:-

Persons Present:-

1 day	2^{00}	Alex Connolly, Interpreter- Govt
1 day 31½ miles	5^{15}	Sarah Bear- Disint. Witness- Govt
1 day & 33 miles	5^{30}	Jane Shaw- Disint. Witness- Govt.

} Paid under Auth. 1185 dated 2/21/14

Report Mailed Oct. 28, 1913.

Costs Divided Among Estates of:-
  John Nahashe - #95
  Susan Nahashe- #96

  William Nahashe- 1/2 int
  Emma Nahashe - 1/2 int.

Report Approved:-
  Law-Heirship 137565-13
  F.E. dated Dec. 12, 1913

96

Susan Nahashe — "Costs Paid"

1913
- July 15 — Issued notices
- Sept 8 — Hearing continued to Oct. 1, 1913 account of interested parties not being present
- Oct. 1 — Hearing Held:-

Persons Present:-
  Alex Connolly- Interpreter- Govt.
  Sarah Bear- Disint. Wit. - Govt.
  Jane Shaw- Disint Wit. - Govt.

} Paid under Auth. 1185 dated 2/21/14

Costs:- See John Nahashe - #95

Report Mailed Oct. 28, 1913.

William Nahashe- ½ int
Emma Nahashe- ½ int.

Report Approved:-
  Law-Heirship 137826-13, F.E. dated Dec. 12, '13

Sac & Fox – Shawnee
1846-1924   Volume XI

Cora Bass

1913
Aug 5   Issued Notices
Sept 8   Hearing continued to Sept 9,'13 account of interested parties not being present
Sept 9   Hearing Held:-
Persons present:-

1 day & 19½ miles	$3^{\underline{25}}$	Charley Smith, Inter. Witness Pd 3/15/15
1 day & 11½ miles	$3^{\underline{15}}$	Inez Bass, Inter Witness Pd 3/15/15
1 day	$2^{\underline{00}}$	Alex Connolly, Interpreter of Disint. Witness Govt
1 day	$2^{\underline{00}}$	Bettie Groinhorn, Disint. Witness } Present in Office & Requested to give testimony Govt
		Horace J Johnson, Supt
		Walter M. Hodsdon, Stenog
1 day	$2^{\underline{00}}$	Isaac Strubble Mileage No fee- Govt Present in Office and requested to give testimony on account of insufficient testimony at Hearing

Report Mailed Oct. 5, 1913

Charley Smith Husband 1/2
Inez Bass, Mother   1/6
Ione C Bass Sister   1/6
Lee Bass   1/6

Report Approved:-
Law-Heirship 119800-13, F.E. dated Feb. 5,'14.

Government Witness fees under Auth. 1185, dated 2/21/14.

"Costs Paid"

Grace Mason

1913
Aug 5   Issued Notices
Sept. 10   Hearing Held:-
Persons Present:-

½ day	$1^{\underline{00}}$	William G. Foster, Interpreter of Disint. Wit.- Govt
½ day	$1^{\underline{00}}$	Isaac Strubble, Disint. Witness- Govt

Horace J Johnson, Supt.
Walter M Hodsdon, Stenog
Thomas P. Myers, Guardian-Ad-Litem
for Ellen Mason and Hattie Mason,
minor heirs:-

Report Mailed Oct. 6, 1913

Ellen Mason- 1/2 of Estate
Hattie Mason 1/2 of Estate
Report approved: Law-Heirship
119811-13, F.E. dated Feb. 5,'14.

Government Witness fees paid under Auth. 1185, dated 2/21/14

Sac & Fox – Shawnee
1846-1924   Volume XI

99

No Costs 1913 — Richard Hawk

Aug. 5   Issued Notices
Sept. 10   Hearing Continued until Oct. 13, 1913, on account of all interested parties not being present
Oct. 13   Hearing Continued to Dec. 2, 1913, a/c Interested Parties not being present
Dec. 2   Hearing Held
    Testimony taken in Unice Paddock Case, No. 107, applicable to this Case

    George W. Paddock-   1/9
    Stella Grant, nee Hawk- 4/9
    Ida Butler   - - - - - 4/9

Report Mailed Aug. 27, 1914

Report Approved Law-Heirship
94053-1914, F.W.S. dated Oct. 10, 1914.

100

Costs Paid 1913 — Clifford H. Morton

Aug 5   Issued Notices
Sept. 10   Hearing Held:-
    Persons Present:-

1 day & 31½ miles 5^{15}	George O. Morton, Inter. Witness	Pay ½ from #100, " " " #101
1 day & 32 miles 5^{20}	Mamie Jennings, Inter Witness	Pay 1/3 from 100, " " " 101
½ day 1^{00}	William G. Foster, Interpreter Govt	" " 102
½ day 1^{00}	Isaac Strubble, disint Witness Govt	No Mileage allowed these three persons as they were present in Office & requested by Supt to give testimony
½ day 1^{00}	Sarah Bear, Disint. Witness Govt	
	Horace J Johnson, Supt	
	Walter M. Hodsdon, Stenog.	

Report Mailed Dec. 13, 1913

Costs Divided Among Estates of:
    Clifford H. Morton   #100
    Oliver P. Morton   #101
    Mellisa Morton   #102

George Oliver Morton-   1/2
Mamie F. Jennings, nee Morton- 1/2

Report Approved June 8, 1914, Law-Heirship 149437-13, F.E. dated 6-8-14

Government Witness fees paid under Auth. 1185, dated 2/21/14

Sac & Fox – Shawnee
1846-1924   Volume XI

{ George Oliver Morton and Mamie Jennings not entitled to any mileage and witness fees in this case as they both inherit an equal interest therein.

101

Oliver P. Morton

1913
Aug. 5   Issued Notices
Sept. 10 Hearing Held:-
　　　　Persons Present:-
　　　　George O. Morton, Inter. Witness $2⁵⁸   Fees not paid as claimant is an heir to 1/3 of Estate
　　　　Mamie Jennings, Inter Witness $2⁶⁰   "   "
　　　　William G. Foster, Interpreter - Govt
　　　　Isaac Strubble, disint Witness - Govt
　　　　Sarah Bear, Disint. Witness - Govt
　　　　Horace J Johnson, Supt
　　　　Walter M. Hodsdon, Stenog.

Costs- See Hearing for Clifford H. Morton- #100

Report Mailed Dec. 12, 1913

　　　　George Oliver Morton- 1/3
　　　　Mamie F Jennings nee Morton- 1/3
　　　　George Littlebear- 1/6
　　　　Florien Littlebear- 1/6

Government Witness fees paid under Auth. 1185, dated 2/21/14

　　　　Report Approved:- Law-Heirship
　　　　62215-14, F.E. dated July 3, 1914.

---

102 *"Costs Paid"*

Mellisa Morton

1913
Aug. 5   Issued Notices
Sept. 10 Hearing Held:-
　　　　Persons Present:-   Sole heir
　　　　Mamie Jennings, Int. Witness } Witness fees unnecessary
　　　　William G. Foster, Interpreter Govt
　　　　Isaac Strubble, Disint. Witness. Govt
　　　　Sarah Bear, Disint. Witness. Govt   *Report Approved*
　　　　Horace J Johnson, Supt   *Law-Heirship*
　　　　Walter M. Hodsdon, Stenog.   *149438-13, 56812-14*
　　　　 E.G.T. dated June 11, '14

Costs: See Hearing for Clifford H. Morton- #100

Sac & Fox – Shawnee
1846-1924   Volume XI

Report Mailed Dec. 13, 1913

Mamie F. Jennings, nee Morton- All

Government Witness fees paid under
Auth. 1185, dated 2/21/14

103

"Costs Paid"   Maw-mel-lo-haw

1913
Aug. 11   Issued Notices
Sept. 11 Hearing Held:-
          Persons Present

1 day & 30 miles	5.00	Sarah Ellis, Int. Wit
1 day & 25½ miles	4.50	Mattie Ingalls, Int. Wit
1 day & 30 miles	5.00	Jackson Ellis, Int. Wit.
1 day & 24½ miles	4.45	Anna McKosato, Int. Wit
1 day & 30 miles	5.00	Clara Benson, Ind. Wit
1 day & 21½ miles	4.85	Edith Brown, Int. Wit.
1 day	2.00	John Brown, Disint. Wit.
1 day	2.00	Alex Connolly, Int. of Disint. Wit-Govt

Paid. Auth. Ed.
Indus 19061-14,
30597-14, C.H.S.
dated 4/6/14.

Present in Office & requested by Supt to give testimony, no mileage allowed   -Govt

Thomas P. Myers, Guardian-Ad-Litem for
Maude Kakaque, minor
Horace J Johnson, Supt
W. M. Hodsdon, Stenog.

John Brown & Alex Connolly- Govt Wit paid under Auth. 1185, dated 2/21/14.

Report Mailed Jan. 17, 1914

Sarah Ellis- 25/64
Mattie Ingalls- 3/32
Anna McKosato, nee Ellis- 3/32
Jackson Ellis-   3/32
Stella Ellis-   3/32
Clara Benson, nee Ellis 15/128
Edith Brown, nee Benson 3/128
Maud Kakaque   5/96
Jesse Kakaque   1/24

Report Approved Law-Heirship 8218-14, 13257-14, F.W.S. dated May 11, 1914

104

"Costs Paid"   Townsend

1913
Aug. 6   Issued Notices
Sept. 15 Hearing Held:
          Persons Present:-

½ day & 40 miles	5.00	Jennie Fawfaw, Inter. Wit.
½ day	1.00	Joseph Springer, Interpreter of Disint. Wit.-Govt
½ day	1.00	Frank Kent, Disint. Wit.-Govt
½ day	1.00	Wm Fawfaw, Disint. Wit.-Govt

Paid. Auth. Ed. Indus 19061-14, 30597-14, C.H.S. dated 4/6/14.

no mileage Present & requested by Supt to testify

W.M. Hodsdon, Guardian-Ad-Litem for Fred

Sac & Fox – Shawnee
1846-1924   Volume XI

½ day & 40 miles 5⁰⁰

and Lucy Vetter minors
Horace J Johnson, Supt
Sam Ellis, Int. Wit. } ½ from #104
                      ½   "   #105

Report Mailed Dec. 3, 1913

Paid $2⁶⁰
auth. Ed. Indus
19061-14, 30507-14
C.H.S. dated 4/6/'14

Costs Divided among Estates of:
    Townsend #104
    Sha-th-cher #105

    Sam Ellis- 1/2
    Annie Perry, nee Rubideau- 1/2

    Report Approved:-
        Law-Heirship 144062-13, F.E.
                dated Feb. 11, '14.

Government Witnesses paid under Auth. 1185
dated 2/21/14.

105

"Costs Paid"   Sha-th-cher

1913
Aug. 6   Issued Notices.
Sept 15   Hearing Continued to Sept. 16,'13 a/c Supt not being able to be present
Sept. 16 Hearing Held.
          Persons Present:-
          Joseph Springer, Interpreter-Govt.
          Sam Ellis, Int. Witness   no costs held out for reason that Sam Ellis is sole heir.
          Frank Kent, Disint. Wit-Govt.
          Wm Fawfaw, Disint. Wit.-Govt
          W.M. Hodsdon, Stenog & Guardian-Ad-Litem for Fred
          & Lucy Vetter, minors
          Horace J. Johnson, Supt.

Report Mailed Dec. 2, 1913

Costs: See Townsend #104.

        Sam Ellis – Sole heir
            Report Approved
        Law-Heirship 143573-13, F.E. dated Feb. 11, '14

Government Witness fees paid under Auth.
1185, dated 2/21/14

---

106   *"Costs Paid"* Maggie Burgess, nee Mohee

1913
Aug. 13   Issued Notices.
Sept. 15 Hearing Continued to Sept. 16,'13 a/c Supt not being able to be present.

183

Sac & Fox – Shawnee
1846-1924   Volume XI

Sept. 16   Hearing Held
        Persons Present:-

½ day & 40 miles 5⁰⁰ William Burgess, Int. Wit. } Paid. Auth. Ed. Indus 19061-14, 30597-14, C.H.S. dated Apr 6, 1914.
½ day & 2½ miles 1²⁵ Frank Kent, Disint. Wit.- Govt } Paid Auth 1185 dated 2/21/14
~~Wm Fawfaw~~
W.M. Hodsdon, Stenog. & Guardian-Ad-Litem for Frank, Roy, and Mark Burgess, minors.

½ day & ~~miles~~ 1⁰⁰ Charley Tohee-Disint. Wit-Govt } Present & requested by Supt to testify no mileage
Horace J Johnson, Supt. Paid Auth. 1185 dated 2/21/14.

Report Mailed Sept. 22, 1913.

Report Approved:-
Law-Heirship 117752-13, F.E.
dated <u>Jan. 12, 1914.</u>

William Burgess- 1/3
Frank Burgess- 2/9
Roy Burgess- - 2/9
Mark Burgess- - 2/9

"Costs Paid"   <u>Unice Paddock, nee Hawk</u>   107

1913
Sept. 11   Issued Notices
Oct. 13   Hearing Continued to Dec. 2, 1913 a/c interested parties not being present
Dec. 2   Hearing Held:-
        Persons Present:-

1 day & 11 miles 2⁷⁵ George W. Paddock, Int. Wit. } Paid under Auth of 2/6/14.
1 day   2⁰⁰ Sarah Ellis, Disint. Wit.(Govt) } no mileage allowed Present in Office and requested by Supt to testify.
1 day   2⁰⁰ Alex Connolly, Disint. Wit & Inter (Govt) } no mileage allowed Present in Office and requested by Supt to testify
1 day   2⁰⁰ Edward McClellan, Dist. Wit (Govt)
Horace J Johnson, Supt
Dec. 10th   W. M. Hodsdon, Stenog
1 day & 7½ miles 2⁷⁵ Stella Grant, nee Hawk, Int. Witness } Paid under Auth of 2/6/14.

Government Witnesses paid under Auth. 1185
  dated 2/21/14.

Report Mailed Aug. 25, 1914.

        George W. Paddock- 1/3
        Stella Grant, nee Hawk- 1/3
        Ida Butler - - - - - - - - - - 1/3

Report Approved. Law-Heirship
  94292-1914, F.W.S. dated Oct. 10, 1914.

Sac & Fox – Shawnee
1846-1924   Volume XI

108

Samuel Hawk

1913
Sept. 11 Issued Notices
Oct. 13   Hearing Continued to

Land Sold- No Hearing necessary

109

Mary Mansur

1913
Sept. 12 Issued Notices
Oct. 13   Hearing Continued to

No Estate- No Hearing necessary

110

James Hawk

1913
Sept. 12 Issued Notices
Oct. 13   Hearing Continued to

Land Sold- No Hearing necessary

111

"Costs Paid" ### Nannie Hollowell

1913
Sept. 18 Notices Issued
Oct. 20   Hearing Continued to Oct. 30,'13 a/c Supt. not being able to be present.
Oct. 30   Hearing Held:- Persons Present:-

1 day & 2½ miles 2²⁵	Emma Kent, Int. Witness	Pay 1/3 from #111
1 day & 40 miles 6⁰⁰	Lizzie DeRoin, Int. Witness	" " " #112
1 day & 40 miles 6⁰⁰	Richard Roubidoux, Int. Witness	" " " #19
1 day & 3½ miles 2³⁵	David Tohee, Disint. Witness-Govt.	
1 day & 2½ miles 2²⁵	Frank Kent, Disint. Witness-Govt.	
1 day & 3½ miles 2³⁵	Robert Small, Interpreter- Govt.	

Paid 75 Cts Auth Ed. Indus 19061-14, 30597-14, C.H.S. dated 4/6/14
Paid $2⁰⁰ Same auth as above
Paid Same Auth as above
Paid. Auth 1185, dated 2/21/14

Costs Divided among estates of:-

Report Mailed Nov. 3, 1913

Nannie Hollowell- #111
Irene Hollowell- #112
Benjamin Hollowell- #19
Except that "Richard Roubidoux" should be paid
from estate of "Nannie Hollowell" only

Lizzie Hollowell, now DeRoin	5/12
Emma Kent	1/3
Richard Roubidoux	1/12
Mitchell DeRoin	1/18
Joseph DeRoin	1/18
William DeRoin	1/18

Report Approved:-
Law-Heirship
139847-13,
F.E. dated
May 6, 1914.

Sac & Fox – Shawnee
1846-1924 Volume XI

112

Irene Hollowell

"Costs Paid"

1913
Sept. 18   Notices Issued.
Oct. 20   Hearing Continued to Oct. 30, '13 a/c Supt not being able to be present.
Oct. 30   Hearing Held:-
   Persons Present:-
   Lizzie DeRoin, Int. Witness } Paid $2.00 Auth Ed. Indus 19061-14, 30597-14, C.H.S. dated 4/6/14
   Emma Kent, Int. Witness } Paid 75 cts, Same Auth as above
   David Tohee, Disint. Witness-Gov't.
   Frank Kent, Disint. Witness-Gov't. } Paid. under Auth 1185, dated 2/21/14
   Robert Small, Interpreter-Gov't.

Report Mailed Nov. 3, 1913

Costs:-   See Hearing for Nannie Hollowell #111

   Lizzie Hollowell, now DeRoin   1/3
   Emma Kent   2/3
Report Approved Law-Heirship 140426-'13, F.E.
dated Feb. 25, '14.

113

Lidia Walker

1913
Sept. 19   Issued Notices   Leo Walker-   1/5 Int.
Oct. 27   Hearing Held:-   Benjamin Walker-   1/5 Int.
          Persons Present:-   Guy Walker-   1/5 Int.
1 day & 22½ miles 4$\underline{25}$ Leo Walker, Int. Wit.   Elmer Walker-   1/5 Int.
1 day & 22½ miles 4$\underline{25}$ Benjamin Walker, Int. Wit   Ira Walker-   1/5 Int.
1 day & 30½ miles 5$\underline{05}$ Guy Walker, Int. Wit   } Paid. under Auth 1185, dated 2/21/14   **Report Mailed Mar 18, 1914**
1 day & 44 miles 6$\underline{40}$ Ira Walker, Int. Wit.
1 day & 23½ miles 4$\underline{55}$ Rosa Appletree, Disint Witness- Gov't   Paid under Auth. 1185 dated 2/21/14
1 day & 30½ miles 5$\underline{05}$ Liza Martin, Disint. Witness-Govt.   Paid under same auth. as above
½ day & 22 miles 3$\underline{20}$ Ella Carter, Int. Witness.   Paid under auth. dated Sept 11, 1914
½ day & 21 miles 3$\underline{10}$ Laura Carter, Disint. Wit. } not to be paid from estate or by Govt.
1 day & 23½ miles 4$\underline{35}$ George Appletree, Interpreter- Govt   Brought by a claimant Ella Carter   Paid under Auth. 1185 dated 2/21/14
½ day   1$\underline{00}$ Mary McCoy, Interpreter- Govt.
Oct. 27   ½ day   1$\underline{00}$ Hearing Continued to secure additional evidence
Oct. 28   Alex Connolly, Disin Witness-Govt   Pay 1 day f[??] all
Nov. 10   ½ day & 30½ miles 4$\underline{42}$ Liza Martin, Disint. Wit.   } Paid under auth dated Sept 11, 1914
½ day & 22½ miles 3$\underline{35}$ Rosa Appletree, Disint. Wit.
½ day   1$\underline{00}$ Logan Kakaque, Disint. Wit.   } Present in Office & requested by Supt to give testimony.   Paid under auth dated Sept 11, 1914
½ day & 25½ miles 3$\underline{55}$ Caroline Pickett, Disint Wit   } Paid under auth dated Sept 11, 1914
½ day & 38 miles 4$\underline{80}$ Elmer Walker Interested Witness
½ day & 23½ miles 4$\underline{55}$ George Appletree, Interpreter- Govt
Nov. 11   ½ day & 16 miles 2$\underline{60}$ Jane Bentley Disint Wit. } not to be paid from estate or by Govt.   Brought by a claimant Ella Carter
½ day   1$\underline{00}$ Mary McCoy, Interpreter- Govt.

Sac & Fox – Shawnee
1846-1924 Volume XI

Nov. 19 ½ day	1.00	Milton Carter, Disint Wit	no mileage allowed Did not make special trip to testify in case / Brought by a claimant Ella Carter
½ day & 29½ miles	3.25	Dollie McClellan Disint Wit	no mileage allowed / not entitled to be paid from estate or Gov't.
Nov. 20 ½ day	1.00	Joe Carter, Disint. Wit.	Did not make special trip to testify in case
" " ½ day	1.00	Samuel Houston	not to be paid by estate or by Gov't. / Brought by a claimant Ella Carter
½ day	1.00	Alex Connolly Interp-Govt.	
Dec. 18		Chief McKosato, Disint. Wit.	No Witness fees or mileage / a/c being Member of Business Committee
½ day	1.00	Alex Connolly Interp-Govt.	Leo Walker- 1/5 Benjamin Walker-1/5;
1914			no witness fees or mileage Present in Office and
Mar. 17		John Brown	Guy Walker-1/5 Elmer Walker- 1/5;
		George Appletree, Interpreter requested to give testimony took like four minutes.	Ira Walker-1/5 / Report Approved:- Law-Heirship / 31860-14, F.W.S. dated Apr 6, 1914

114

Amos Black

1913
Dec. 27   Notices Issued.
1914
Jan. 30   Hearing Continued to Jan. 31, 1914 a/c Supt. being necessarily absent from Agency
Jan. 31   Hearing Held:-
Persons Present:-

½ day & 17½ miles 2.75   Julia Black, nee Sullivan , Inter Witness Paid under auth. Sept. 12, 1914
½ day   1.00   Sarah Bigwalker, Disint. Witness Mileage allowed in Harry Hall Case
½ day   1.00   Alex Connolly, Interpreter and Disint Witness-Gov't.
                          Horace J Johnson, Supt & S.D.A.
                          Walter M. Hodsdon, Stenographer
                          Thomas P. Myers, Guardian-Ad-Litem
                          for Amos Black Jr and Bertha Black, minors

Julia Black, nee Sullivan-1/3
Amos Black Jr.   -1/3
Bertha Black   -1/3

Report Mailed Mar. 14, 1914
Report Approved:- Law-Heirship 29608-14, F.W.S. dated June 11, 1914

115

Harry Hall

1913
Dec. 24   Notices Issued.
1914
Jan. 30   Hearing Continued to Jan. 31, 1914 a/c Supt. being necessarily absent from Agency Office
Jan. 31   Hearing Held:-

Sac & Fox – Shawnee
1846-1924   Volume XI

Persons Present:-

½ day & 22 miles 3²⁰	Rachel Pate, nee Hall, Inter. Witness
½ day & 29½ miles 3²⁵	Sarah Bigwalker do do
½ day & 29½ miles 3²⁵	Dollie McClellan do do
½ day & 32 miles 4²⁰	Mamie F. Jennings do do
½ day & 16 miles 2⁶⁰	Osmond Franklin, do do
No fees or mileage	John Brown, Disint. Witness } No witness fees or mileage allowed. Requested to be excused from testifying at hearing account of not knowing sufficient about decedent & his relations.
	William Harris, Disint. Witness }
½ day 1⁰⁰	Alex Connolly, Interperter[sic] of Disint. Witness - Govt
½ day & 22 miles 3²⁰	Henry Hunter, Disint. Witness-Govt
	Horace J Johnson, Supt and S.D.A.
	Walter M. Hodsdon, Stenographer.

Report Mailed Apr. 9, 1914

Rachel Pate, nee Hall-	1/2	1/2
Sarah Bigwalker-	1/14	1/12
Dollie McClellan-	3/35	1/12
Lelia Bigwalker-	3/35	1/12
Esther Bigwalker-	3/35	1/12
Mamie F. Jennings-	3/35	1/12
Osmond Franklin-	3/35	1/12

Declaration made Law-Heirship 85279-14 44190-14 F.W.S. dated Aug 27, 1914

116

<u>Lizzie Gokey, nee Graeyes</u>

1914

Jan. 7   Notices Issued.
Feb. 7   Hearing Held:-
        Persons Present:-

1 day & 23 miles 4³⁰	Paul Gokey, Int. Wit. Paid under auth. Sept. 12, 1914
1 day & 21 miles 4¹⁰	Laura Carter, Disint Wit- Govt.
No fees or mileage	William Pattequa, Disint. Wit. Member of Business Committee
1 day 2⁰⁰	Alex Connolly, Disint. Wit & Inter-Gov't.
	Horace J Johnson, Supt & S.D.A.
Feb. 11	Walter M. Hodsdon, Stenog.
½ day 1⁰⁰	Joe Carter, Disint. Wit. Requested by Supt. to give testimony-Gov't.
Mar. 30 ½ day 1⁰⁰	Eveline Givens Requested by Supt to give testimony-Gov't.

Request for Auth to settle forwarded 2/23/15.
  Settled 3/11/15
  Auth 3/5/15

{ Clerk of Cty. Court Lincoln Cty, Chandler, Okla. Certified copy of Application and Affidavit for Marriage License, Marriage License and Certificate of Marriage of Paul Gokey to Lizzie Givens. . . . . 75 cts

Eveline Givens	1/3 Int.
Ethline Carter	2/9 Int.
Leona Gokey	2/9 Int.
Agnes Gokey	2/9 Int.

Report Mailed Nov. 10, 1914

Sac & Fox – Shawnee
1846-1924   Volume XI

Heirs declared in Law-Heirship 123590-1914
F.W.S. dated May 6, 1915.
   Paul Gokey---------------1/4 Interest.
   Leona Gokey-------------1/4   "
   Agnus Gokey-------------1/4   "
   Ethline Carter-------------1/4   "

         (Correct spelling   **117**
     Hellen Starr (Helen Starr) Land Records
1914   19814-1914, C.W.B.
Jan. 11 Notices Issued.   dated Mar. 2, 1914)
Feb. 11 Hearing Held:-
    Persons Present:-
1 day & 12 miles $3^{\underline{20}}$ Hiram P. Starr, Inter Wit. ⎤ Paid under auth.
1 day & 87 miles $10^{\underline{80}}$ Sarah Pettit, Disint. Wit. ⎦ dated Sept. 12, 1914.
1 day & 18 miles $3^{\underline{80}}$ Sam Brown, Disint. Wit.-Govt.
1 day $2^{\underline{00}}$ Alex Connolly, Disint. Wit. & Interpreter-Govt.
    Horace J. Johnson, Supt. & S.D.A.
    W.M. Hodsdon, Stenog.
    (Original Estate of Helen Starr:-)
    Hiram P. Starr- 1/2
    Frank Smith- 1/10
    Benjamin Smith- 1/10
    Charley Smith----1/10
    Rachel Franklin,   *Report Mailed*
     nee Smith--------1/10 *January 28, 1915.*
    Clara Benson, nee Ellis---1/20
    Edith Brown--------1/20
    (Estate of Helen Starr now under control of Gov't:-)
    Frank Smith-1/5; Benjamin Smith-1/5;
    Charley Smith-1/5; Rachel Franklin, nee Smith-1/5;
    Clara Benson, nee Ellis-1/10; & Edith Brown-1/10

---

118 $2^{\underline{00}}$ No funds Thomas Jefferson Buffalohorn
 1914
Feb. 7 Notices Issued.
March 9 Hearing Continued until Mar. 31, 1914, a/c interested parties
    not being present.
Mar. 31 Hearing Held:-
    Person Present:-
    Grace Lee, Inter Person ⎫ See Clara Buffalohorn #154
    Thomas P. Myers, Guardian-ad-Litem for minor heir
    Logan Kakaque, Disint. Person-Govt. ⎫ Requested by Supt to be present
    Alexander Connolly, Interp & Disint. Person
    Isaac Struble, Disint. Person- Gov't ⎫ Requested by Supt to be present
    Walter M. Hodsdon, Stenog.

Sac & Fox – Shawnee
1846-1924   Volume XI

Horace J. Johnson, Supt.

Costs:- See Edith Rice- #153 – "Govt. Witnesses"

Request for Auth to settle $2^{00} forwarded 2/23/15 from Clara Buffalohorn account settled 3/6/15 Auth dated 3/5/15

Register of Deeds, Pottawatomie Cty-Tecumseh, Okla. Certified Copy of Fee Simple Patent from U.S.A. to Thomas Jefferson Buffalohorn $1^{00} and Certified Copy of Warranty Deed from Thomas Jefferson Buffalohorn to Mamie Buffalohorn $1^{00} Total- $2^{00}

Grace Lee- 1/2 of Estate
Mamie Buffalohorn- 1/2 of Estate

Report Mailed October 9, 1914.

Report Approved, Law-Heirship
111102-14, E.G.T. dated
Nov. 11, 1914.

Jasper Conger

1914
Feb. 18   Notices Issued
March 20   Hearing Held:
   Persons Present;-

1 day & 11½ miles $3^{15} Andrew Conger, Inter. Person } Paid under Auth. dated 9/12/14
1 day & 21 miles $4^{10} Isaac Struble, Disint. Person- Govt.
1 day & 16 miles $3^{60} Jane Harrison, Disint. Person- Govt.
1 day $2^{00} Alexander Connolly, Interpreter-Govt.
                  Walter M. Hodsdon, Stenog.
                  Horace J Johnson, Supt.

Report Mailed May 22, 1914.

Costs Divided Among Estates of:-
   Jasper Conger - #119
   William Conger - #121
   Jay Conger - #120
   Hattie Conger - #140

Report Approved:- Law-Heirship 60650-14 F.E. dated Aug. 18, '14.

   Andrew Conger – 1/2
   George Oliver Morton – 1/2

Jay Conger

1914
Feb. 18   Notices Issued
Mar 20   Hearing Held:-

Sac & Fox – Shawnee
1846-1924   Volume XI

Persons Present:-
Andrew Conger, Inter Person } Paid from Jasper Conger #119
Isaac Struble, Disint. Person-Govt.
Jane Harrison, Disint Person- Govt.
Alexander Connolly, Interpreter- Govt
Walter M. Hodsdon, Stenog
Horace J Johnson, Supt.

Report Mailed May 21, 1914.

Costs:- See Jasper Conger #119

Andrew Conger- 1/2
George Oliver Morton- 1/2

Report Approved:-
Law-Heirship
60628-14
F.E.
dated Aug. 18, '14.

121

William Conger

1914
Feb. 18   Notices Issued
Mar. 20 Hearing Held:
Persons Present:-
Andrew Conger, Inter Person } Paid from Jasper Conger, #119
Isaac Struble, Disint. Person- Govt
Jane Harrison, Disint. Person- Govt
Alexander Connolly, Interpreter-Govt
Walter M. Hodsdon, Stenog.
Horace J Johnson, Supt.

Report Mailed May 23, 1914.

Costs:- See Jasper Conger #119

Andrew Conger- 1/2
George Oliver Morton- 1/2

Report Approved:-
Law-Heirship, 60661-14, F.E.
dated Aug. 18, '14

122

$10^{40}

George Manatowa

1914
Feb. 18   Notices Issued.
March 21 Hearing Held:-
Persons Present:-
1 day & 21 miles 4[10]   Laura Carter, Inter Person

Sac & Fox – Shawnee
1846-1924   Volume XI

1 day & 22 miles	4^{20}	Elmer Manatowa, Inter Person
1 day	2^{00}	Bertha Hodsdon, Inter Person
1 day	2^{00}	Isaac Struble, Disint Person- Govt (No Mileage)
1 day	2^{00}	Jane Harrison, Disint Person- Govt (No Mileage)
1 day	2^{00}	Alexander Connolly, Interpreter & Disint Person- Govt

      Walter M. Hodsdon, Stenog
      Horace J Johnson, Supt.

Costs "Gov't Witnesses" Divided among Estates of:-
  George Manatowa - #122
  John Hull - #123
  Lucy Hull - #124
  William Hull - # 85

 Laura Carter, nee Manatowa- 1/3
 Bertha Hodsdon, - 2/9
 Elmer Manatowa - 2/9
 Lorena Manatowa - 2/9

Report Mailed April 30, 1914.

Report Approved:- Law-Heirship 8241-14, E.G.T. dated May 19, '14.

123

John Hull

 1914
Feb. 18 Notices Issued.
March 21 Hearing Held:-
  Persons Present:-
  Isaac Struble, Disint Person- Govt
  Jane Harrison, Disint Person- Govt
  Alexander Connolly, Interpreter & Disint Person- Govt
  Thomas P. Myers, Guardian-Ad-Litem for
  Ben Hull, minor
  Walter M. Hodsdon, Stenog
  Horace J Johnson, Supt.

Costs:- See George Manatowa #122

 Ben Hull Mansur sole heir

Report Mailed May 5, 1914.

Report Approved:- Law-Heirship 8241-14, E.G.T. dated May 19, '14.

124

Lucy Hull

 1914
Feb. 18 Notices Issued
March 21 Hearing Held:-
  Persons Present:-
  Isaac Struble, Disint Person- Govt
  Jane Harrison, Disint Person- Govt
  Alexander Connolly, Interpreter & Disint Person- Govt
  Thomas P. Myers, Guardian-Ad-Litem for

Sac & Fox – Shawnee
1846-1924   Volume XI

Ben Hull, minor
Walter M. Hodsdon, Stenog
Horace J Johnson, Supt.

Report Mailed Apr. 30, 1914.

Costs:- See George Manatowa #122

Ben Hull Mansur – All.

*Report Approved:-
Law-Heirship 49504-14
F.W.S. dated May 22, '14.*

125

Gertrude Givens

1914
Feb 20   Notices Issued
Mar 23   Hearing Held:-
         Persons Present:-   To be paid from 125 ~~& 126~~

½ day & 13½ miles	2$\underline{35}$	Lydia Grant, Inter. Person	} Paid under auth-9/12/14
1 day & 14½ miles	3$\underline{25}$	Isaac Givens, Inter Person	Paid under auth-9/12/14
1 day & 14½ miles	3$\underline{25}$	Allen G. Thurman, Inter. Person	To be paid from 125 ~~& 126~~ Paid 1st under auth-9/12/14
1 day & 19½ miles	2$\underline{95}$	Theresa Smith. Inter Person	Paid 1st under auth-9/12/14 To be paid from 125 ~~126~~ & 127
		Thomas P. Myers, Guardia-Ad-Litem for Jennie Thurman, minor	To be paid from 125 ~~126~~ & 127
1 day	2$\underline{00}$	Isaac Struble, Disint Person- } No Mileage - Govt	
1 day	2$\underline{00}$	Alexander Connolly, Interpreter & Disint. Person- Govt	
		Walter M. Hodsdon, Stenog	
		Horace J Johnson, Supt.	
Mar. 28		John Brown, Inter. Person	} Witness & Mileage fees paid from Josephine Brown- No. 147

Costs- Divided Among Estates of:-   Gertrude Givens- #125
                                    Charlotte Pattequa- #126
                                    Lucy Thurman - #127

Paid by Check #779 on First Natl. Bank of Stroud, Okla. dated 7/18/14
Auth dated 6/24/14

{ Certified copy of Petition for Divorce & Dismissal of Case, of John Brown & Gertrude Brown or Gertrude Givens-----$1.$\underline{85}$

John Brown.............1/3 Int.
Lydia Grant.............1/6 "
Eveline Givens..........1/6 "
Isaac Givens............1/6 "
Jim Scott...............8/135 "

Report Mailed Apr. 30, 1914.

Sac & Fox – Shawnee
1846-1924 Volume XI

    Allen G Thurman......29/1080 "
    Roy V. Thurman.......29/1080 "
    Theresa Smith..........29/1080 "
    Jennie Thurman........29/1080 "

Report Approved:-
Law-Heirship
124456-14
E.G.T.
dated Dec. 15, 1914.

---

126   No Costs   <u>Charlotte Pattequa</u>

1914
Feb. 20   Notices Issued
Mar 23   Hearing Held:-
    Persons Present:-
        Lydia Grant, Inter. Person
        Allen G. Thurman, Inter Person
        Theresa Smith, Inter Person
        Isaac Givens, Inter. Person
        Isaac Struble, Disint Person- Govt
        Alexander Connolly, Interpreter & Disint Person- Govt
        Walter M. Hodsdon, Stenog
        Horace J Johnson, Supt
        Thomas P. Myers, Guardian-ad-Litem for
        Jennie Thurman, minor

1 day & 25½ miles 4⁵⁵   William Pattequaw, Disint. Person- Govt

Costs: See Gertrude Givens - #125.

Report Mailed November 17, 1914.

    Jim Scott......................112/1350 Int.
    Allen G. Thurman............203/5400 Int.
    Roy V. Thurman..............203/5400 Int.
    Theresa Smith nee Thurman. 203/5400 Int.
    Lydia Grant.....................7/30 Int.
    Eveline Givens.................7/30 Int.
    Isaac Givens....................7/30 Int.
    John Brown....................1/15 Int.

Report Approved:- in Law-Heirship 124973-14 E.G.T. dated Jan. 28, 1915.

Lucy Thurman

127

1914
Feb. 20 Notices Issued
SSSMar 23 Hearing Held:-
 Persons Present:-
  Allen G. Thurman, Inter Person } Paid $1.72 under Auth. dated 9/11/14
  Theresa Smith, Inter Person } Paid 1.97 under Auth. dated 9/11/14
  Thomas P. Myers, Guardian-ad-Litem for
  Jennie Thurman, minor
½ day   1.00   Lydia Grant, Disint. Person- Govt
  Isaac Struble, Disint Person- Govt (Mileage paid from 125 & 126)
  Alexander Connolly, Interpreter & Disint Person- Govt
  Walter M. Hodsdon, Stenog
  Horace J Johnson, Supt

Costs:- See Gertrude Givens- #125.

Report Mailed November 12, 1914.

  Jim Scott............................65/180 Int.
  Allen G. Thurman..................29/180 "
  Roy V. Thurman...................29/180 "
  Theresa Smith, nee Thurman.....29/180 "
  Jennie Thurman....................29/180 "

Report Approved:- Law-Heirship 123575-1914, F.W.S., dated 1/9/15.

128

John A. Logan

1914
Feb. 21 Notices Issued.
Mar. 24 Hearing Continued to Mar. 25, 1914 at 9A.M. a/c insufficient time to take case up today
Mar. 25 Hearing Held:
 Persons Present:-
1 day 13½ miles   3.35   Clarence Logan, Inter Person } To be paid from this Estate only. Paid under auth. dated Sept. 11, 1914
1 day & 27½ miles   4.75   Logan Kakaque, Disint. Person-Govt
1 day   2.00   Alexander Connolly, Interpreter of Disint Person-Govt
1 day   2.00   Isaac Struble, Disint. Person-Govt.
  Thomas P. Myers, Guardian-ad-Litem for minor heirs
  W. M. Hodsdon, Stenog.
  Horace J. Johnson, Supt.

Costs:- "Gov't Witnesses" Divided Among Estates of:-
  John A. Logan- #128
  Mary E. Logan- #129
  Charles Crane- #130

Report Mailed June 3, 1914.

Sac & Fox – Shawnee
1846-1924   Volume XI

Lizzie Crane-   #131
William Pennock #135
Hester Pennock #136
Florence Bigwalker #137

Clarence Logan-1/2
John Crane   -1/6
Harry Crane   -1/6
Theresa Logan -1/6

Report Approved:- Law-Heirship 63260-1914, F.E. dated June 22, 1914.

129

Mary E. Logan

1914
Feb. 21 Notices Issued.
Mar. 24 Hearing Continued to Mar. 25, 1914 at 9A.M. a/c insufficient time to take case up today
Mar. 25 (Hearing Held:) See Case No. 130.
Testimony taken in Charles Crane Case, No. 130, to apply in this case also)
Clarence Logan, Disint. Person (Paid from No. 128)
Isaac Struble, Disint. Person- Govt.
Alexander Connolly, Interp of Disint Person-Govt
Thomas P. Myers, Guardian-ad-Litem for minor heirs
Logan Kakaque, Disint. Person-Govt
W.M. Hodsdon, Stenog.
Horace J Johnson, Supt.

Costs:- "Govt Witnesses", See John A. Logan #128

Theresa Logan-1/3
John Crane   -1/3
Harry Crane   -1/3

Report Mailed June 4, 1914.
Report Approved:- Law-Heirship 63161-14, E.G.T. dated July 15, 1914,
Report Modified:- Law-Heirship 63161-14, 89088-14, E.G.T. dated Dec. 15, 1914.
Proportionate share of heirs not changed

Sac & Fox – Shawnee
1846-1924   Volume XI

130

Charles Crane

1914
Feb. 21 Notices Issued.
Mar. 24 Hearing Continued to Mar. 25,'14 at 9A.M. a/c insufficient time to take case up this day
Mar. 25 Hearing Held:
   Persons Present:-
   Clarence Logan, Disint Person (Paid from No. 128)
   Isaac Struble, Disint. Person- Govt
   Alexander Connolly, Interpreter of Disint. Person-Govt
   Thomas P. Myers, Guardian-ad-Litem for minor heirs
   W.M. Hodsdon, Stenog
   Horace J Johnson, Supt
   Logan Kakaque, Disint Person- Govt

Report Mailed June 5, 1914.

Costs:- "Gov't Witnesses"- See John A. Logan #128

   John Crane- 47/108
   Harry Crane- 47/108
   Theresa Logan- 7/54

Report Approved in Law-Heirship 64669-14, F.E. dated March 22, 1915

Requested auth. to settle 2/23/15
Settled 3/11/15
Auth. dated 3/5/15
   Certified copies of:-
   Marriage License and Certificate of Marriage of
   Charles Crane and Mary E. Logan- .45¢
   Clerk of Cty. Court, Lincoln Cty., Oklahoma

131

Lizzie Crane

1914
Feb. 21 Notices Issued
Mar. 24 Hearing Continued to Mar. 25,'14 a/c insufficient time to take case up today
Mar. 25 Hearing Held:
   Persons Present:-

1 day & 30 miles 5.00 Sarah Ellis, Inter Person
1 day & 29 miles 4.20 Susan Appletree, Inter. Person
1 day & 13½ miles 3.45 Alice Grant, Inter Person

   To be paid from this Estate only
   Paid under Auth dated Sept 12, 1914

   Isaac Struble, Disint Person- Govt
   Alexander Connolly, Interpreter of Disint Person-Govt
   Logan Kakaque, Disint Person- Govt
   Thomas P. Myers, Guardian-ad-Litem for minor heirs
   W.M. Hodsdon, Stenog
   Horace J Johnson, Supt.

Report Mailed June 10, 1914.

Costs:- "Govt Witnesses", See John A. Logan #128

Sac & Fox – Shawnee
1846-1924 Volume XI

Sarah Ellis- 1/3
John Crane- 1/6
Harry Crane- 1/6
Alice Grant, nee Morris-1/15
Thomas Morris-   1/15
Grover Morris-   1/15
Susan Appletree, nee Morris 1/15
Edward L. Morris-   1/15

Report Approved:- Law-Heirship 65912-1914, F.W.S dated June 29, 1914.

132

Lottie Duncan

1914
Feb. 21 Notices Issued
Mar. 24 Hearing Held:
Persons Present:

1 day	2⁰⁰	Allen G. Thurman, Inter Person	Paid under auth. dated Sept. 12, 1914
1 day	2⁰⁰	Alice Grant, Disint Person ~~(Govt)~~	No mileage ~~Paid~~ See #125 Paid under above auth.
1 day	2⁰⁰	Isaac Struble, Disint. Person Govt.	Mileage paid from No 131
1 day	2⁰⁰	Sarah Ellis, Disint. Person ~~Govt~~	Mileage paid from No 131 Paid under above auth.
		W.M. Hodsdon, Stenog.	
		Horace J Johnson, Supt	
1 day	2⁰⁰	Alexander Connolly, Interpreter- Gov't.	

Costs Divided Among Estates of:-
Lottie Duncan- #132
David Duncan- #133
May Duncan- #134

Report Mailed June 13, 1914.

Allen G. Thurman-   7/18
Dickson Mokohoko-   7/18
Sarah Ellis-   2/27
Alice Grant, nee Morris- 2/135
Thomas Morris-   2/135
Grover Morris-   2/135
Susan Appletree, nee Morris-2/135
Edward L Morris-   2/135
John Crane-   1/27
Harry Crane-   1/27

Report Approved:- Law-Heirship 68455-14, F.E. dated Aug. 18, 1914.

133

David Duncan

No Costs

1914
Feb. 21 Notices Issued
Mar. 24 Hearing Held:-
Persons Present:
Allen G. Thurman, Inter. Person
Sarah Ellis, Disint. Person-~~(Govt)~~

Sac & Fox – Shawnee
1846-1924   Volume XI

Isaac Struble, Disint. Person- Gov't.
Alexander Connolly, Interp. of Disint. Person- Gov't.
W. M. Hodson, Stenog.
Horace J. Johnson, Supt.

Report Mailed June 2, 1914.

Costs:- See Lottie Duncan #133

Report Approved:- Law-Heirship 63262-14, F.E. dated July 8, 1914.

    Dickson Mokohoko- 1/2
    Allen G. Thurman-   1/2

134

No Costs

May Duncan

1914
Feb. 21 Notices Issued
Mar. 24 Hearing Held:-
    Persons Present:
    Sarah Ellis, Disint. Person-(Gov't)
    Isaac Struble, Disint. Person-Gov't.
    Allen G. Thurman, ~~Disint~~ Inter. Person
    Alexander Connolly, Interp. of Disint. Person-Gov't.
    Walter M. Hodsdon, Stenog
    Horace J Johnson, Supt.

Costs:- See Lottie Duncan #132

Report Mailed May 29, 1914.

    Allen G. Thurman-   1/2
    Dickson Mokohoko- 1/2

    Report Approved
Heirship Determined Law-Heirship
60493-14   F.E. dated July 8, 1914.

135

William Pennock

1914
Feb. 23 Notices Issued
Mar. 25 Hearing Held:
    Persons Present:-
    Isaac Struble, Disint. Person- Gov't.
    Logan Kakaque, Disint. Person-Govt
    Alexander Connolly, Interpreter of Disint Person- Govt
    Thomas P. Myers, Guard.-Ad-Litem
    for David Pennock, minor
    W. M. Hodsdon, Stenog.
    Horace J. Johnson, Supt.

Sac & Fox – Shawnee
1846-1924   Volume XI

Mar. 30$^{½ day}$ 1^{00}Inez Bass } Present in Office & requested by Supt to give testimony
No Mileage. Paid fees under Auth dated Sept. 11, 1914.

Costs:- "Gov't. Witnesses":- See John A. Logan #128

    Inez Bass- 1/2 - now 1/3
    David Pennock- 1/2 - now 2/3

Report Mailed October 16, 1914
January 8, 1915.

    Report Approved in
    Law-Heirship 5699-1915,
    41409-1915, F.W.S., dated
    May 6, 1915.

136

No Costs   Hester Pennock

1914
Feb. 23 Notices Issued
Mar. 25 Hearing Held:-
    Persons Present:-
    Isaac Struble, Disint Person- Gov't.
    Logan Kakaque, Disint. Person- Gov't.
    Alexander Connolly, Interpreter of Disint Person- Gov't
    Thomas P Myers- Guardian-ad-Litem
    for David Pennock, minor
    Walter M. Hodsdon, Stenog.
    Horace J. Johnson, Supt.

Report Mailed January 8, 1915.

Costs:- "Gov't. Witnesses"- See John A. Logan #128

    David Pennock- 5/6 Int.
    Inez Bass-   1/6 Int.

    Report Approved in
    Law-Heirship 5700-1915,
    41408-1915, F.W.S., dated
    May 8, 1915.

137

No Costs   Florence Bigwalker

1914
Feb. 23 Notices Issued
Mar. 25 Hearing Held:-
    Persons Present:-
    Isaac Struble, Disint Person- Gov't.
    Logan Kakaque, Disint. Person- Gov't.
    Alexander Connolly, Interpreter of Disint Person- Gov't
    Thomas P Myers- Guardian-ad-
    Litem for David Pennock, minor

Sac & Fox – Shawnee
1846-1924   Volume XI

W.M. Hodsdon, Stenog.
Horace J. Johnson, Supt.

Costs:- "Gov't. Witnesses"- See John A. Logan #128

Report Mailed January 9, 1915.

David Pennock- 1/2 Int.
Inez Bass-   1/2 Int.

Report Approved in
Law-Heirship 5437-1915,
41410-1915, F.W.S., dated
May 8, 1915.

Inez Bass ——— 1/3 Interest.
David Pennock 2/3   "

---

138   18.90

Cora Smith, nee Bear

1914
Feb. 23 Notices Issued
Mar. 25 Hearing Continued to Mar. 26, 1914, a/c insufficient time
         to take case up today
Mar. 26 Hearing Held:-
         (Persons Present:-⅔ See Case No. 139 testimony taken in
         Lizzie Rice Case, No. 139, to apply in this Case also.)
Mar. 26 Frank Smith, Inter Person
Mar. 26 Edward Rice, Inter Person
         Isaac Struble, Disint. Person- Gov't.
         Logan Kakaque, Disint Person- Gov't.
         Alexander Connolly, Interp. of Disint Person- Gov't.
         Walter M. Hodsdon, Stenog
         Horace J. Johnson, Supt
         Frank Smith, Inter. Person

Report Mailed October 15, 1914.

Report Approved in Law-Heirship 45462-14, 135926-14, dated Mar. 1, 1915.

Costs:- See Lizzie Rice- #139

         Frank Smith--------1/2 Interest
         Edward Rice--------1/2 Interest.
Nov. 17 Notices Issued for Supplemental Hearing in accordance with instructions
         contained in Law-Heirship 115462-14 F.W.S.
Dec. 3 Supplemental Hearing Held:- Persons Present:-

Report re-submitted Dec. 4, 1914.

1 day & 20 miles 4⁰⁰   Frank Smith, Inter. Person   Paid 3/15/15
1 " & 27½ miles 4⁷⁵   Edward Rice,   do   do   Paid 3/15/15
1 day & 31½ miles 5¹⁵   John McClellan, Disint person Paid 3/15/15
1 day & 30 miles 5⁰⁰   William Bear,   "   "   Paid 3/15/15
1 day   2⁰⁰   Alexander Connolly, Interp- Gov't.

201

Sac & Fox – Shawnee
1846-1924 Volume XI

139

Lizzie Rice

1914
Feb. 23 Notices Issued
Mar. 25 Hearing Continued to Mar. 26, 1914, a/c insufficient time to take case up today
Mar. 26 Hearing Held:
Persons Present:

1 day & 27½ miles	4$\underline{^{75}}$	Edward Rice, Inter. Person	Paid under Auth. dated Sept. 12, 1914.
1 day & 20 miles	4$\underline{^{00}}$	Frank Smith, Inter. Person	
½ day	1$\underline{^{00}}$	Isaac Struble, Disint. Person- Gov't.	
½ day	1$\underline{^{00}}$	Logan Kakaque, Disint Person- Gov't.	
½ day	1$\underline{^{00}}$	Alexander Connolly, Interp. of Disint. Person- Gov't.	

Walter M. Hodsdon, Stenog
Horace J. Johnson, Supt.

Report Mailed November 6, 1914

Costs Divided Among Estates of:
  Cora Smith, nee Bear- #138
  Lizzie Rice   - #139

  Edward Rice---------3/4 Int.
  Frank Smith---------1/4 Int.

Nov. 17 Notices issued for a Supplemental Hearing in accordance with instructions contained in Law-Heirship 36508-1914, 121870-1914, F.W.S.
Dec. 3 Supplemental Hearing Held:-
Persons Present: { Same persons as appeared in Cora Smith, nee Bear Case, #138
Testimony introduced at Cora Smith, nee Bear supplemental Hearing, applicable to this case also.
Report approved Law-Heirship 36508-14, 131034-14, F.W.S. dated Feb. 5, 1915.

Report Re-submitted Dec. 4, 1914

140

Hattie Conger

1914
Feb. 18 Notices Issued
Mar. 20 Hearing Held
Persons Present:
Andrew Conger Inter Witness } Paid from Jasper Conger #119
Isaac Struble, Disint. Person- Gov't
Jane Harrison, Disint. Person- Gov't.
Alexander Connolly, Interpreter- Govt.
Walter M. Hodsdon, Stenog
Horace J Johnson, Supt

Report Mailed May 25, 1914

Report Approved Law-Heirship 60662-14, F.E. dated Aug. 18, 1914

Costs:- See Jasper Conger #119

Sac & Fox – Shawnee
1846-1924   Volume XI

Andrew Conger-   1/2
George Oliver Morton- 1/2

141

Rhoda Mansur

1914
Feb. 24 Notices Issued
Mar. 26 Hearing Held:
         Persons Present:

1 day & 25 miles	4^{50}	Ida Butler, Inter Person } To be paid from No. 141, 142 & 143 Paid under Auth dated Sept. 12,'14
		Thomas P. Myers, Guardian-ad-Litem for minor heir
½ day	1^{00}	Isaac Struble, Disint. Person -Gov't.
½ day & 16 miles	2^{60}	Jane Harrison, Disint. Person -Gov't.
½ day	1^{00}	Alexander Connolly, Interpreter- Gov't.
½ day	1^{00}	Logan Kakaque, Disint Person- Gov't. } Requested by Supt to be present
		W. M. Hodsdon, Stenog
		Horace J. Johnson, Supt

Report Mailed Dec. 29, 1914

Costs:- "Gov't Witnesses" Divided Among Estates of
    Rhoda Mansur- #141
    Hannah Mansur- #142
    Watt Grayson -#143

Requested auth. to settle 2/23/15
Settled 3/11/15
auth dated 3/5/15 { Certificate showing that County Records at Chandler, Okla. do not show adoption of Henry Hull & Ben Hull by Charles H. Mansur -Pay Clerk of Cty Court Chandler, Okla.

    Ida Butler------------------------ 44/90
    Sarah Thompson, nee Mansur- 23/90
    Ben Hull Mansur---------------23/90

142

Hannah Mansur

1914
Feb. 24 Notices Issued
Mar 26 Hearing Held:
        Persons Present:
        Ida Butler, Inter. Person } See No. 141 Paid $1.50 under auth. dated 9/11/14
        Jane Harrison, Disint. Person- Gov't.
        Isaac Struble, Disint. Person- Gov't.
        Alexander Connolly, Interpreter of Disint Person- Gov't.
        Logan Kakaque, Disint. Person- Gov't.} Requested by Supt to be present
        Walter M. Hodsdon, Stenog.
        Horace J. Johnson, Supt.

Costs-"Gov't Witnesses"- See Rhoda Mansur- #141

Sac & Fox – Shawnee
1846-1924   Volume XI

        Ida Butler- 7/9 Int.
        Stella Grant, nee Hawk- 1/9 Int.
        George W. Paddock- 1/9 Int.

Report Mailed Jan. 21, 1915

1915
Jan. 15   Isaac Struble, Disint. person
        Alexander Connolly, Interp. of Disint. person
Jan. 19   U. S. Grant, Disint. Person
        Lydia Grant, Disint. Person
        Alex Connolly, Interpreter.

143

Watt Grayson

1914
Feb. 24   Notices Issued
Mar. 26   Hearing Held:
        Persons Present:-

1 day & 32½ miles $5^{\underline{25}}$ Albert Moore, Inter. Person } Paid under auth. dated 9/12/14. To be paid
1 day & 25 miles $4^{\underline{50}}$ Ruth Moore, Inter Person } from this Estate Only.
        Ida Butler, Disinter. Person } Paid $1.^{\underline{50}}$ under auth dated 9/12/14 See No 141
        Thomas P. Myers, Guardian-ad-Litem for
        minor heirs
        Isaac Struble, Disint. Person- Gov't.
        Jane Harrison, Disint. Person- Gov't.
        Alexander Connolly, Interpreter- Gov't.
        Logan Kakaque, Disint Person- Gov't. (Requested by Supt to be present)
        Walter M. Hodsdon, Stenog
        Horace J Johnson, Supt.

Costs- "Gov't Witnesses"- See Rhoda Mansur- #141.
        Albert Moore- 1/4 Int.
        Ruth Moore-   1/4 "
        Sarah Thompson, nee Mansur- 1/4 "
        Ellen Manson-------------- 1/8 "
        Hattie Mason---------------1/8 "

Report Mailed Dec. 22, 1914.

        Declaration Made Law-Heirship
        138333-14 dated 2/16/15.

144

Samuel W. Peel

1914
Feb. 25   Notices Issued
Mar. 27   Hearing Continued to Mar. 27, 1914, a/c insufficient time to take case
Mar. 28   Hearing Held.   up to-day
        Persons Present:-

1 day & 23½ miles $4^{\underline{35}}$ Chief M$^{\underline{c}}$Kosato, Inter Person
1 day & 27 miles $4^{\underline{70}}$ Richard Duncan, Inter. Person

Sac & Fox – Shawnee
1846-1924   Volume XI

1 day & 24½ miles	4⁴⁵	Sarah Mack, Inter Person	
1 day & 25 miles	4⁵⁰	Elbert Mack, Inter Person	
1 day & 24½ miles	4⁴⁵	Charley Mack, Inter. Person	
1 day & 18 miles	3⁸⁰	Samuel L. Brown, Inter Person	
		Thomas P. Myers- Guardian-ad-Litem	
		for minor heirs	

Paid under Authority dated Sept 12, 1914.

1 day	2⁰⁰	Logan Kakaque, Disint. Person- Gov't.
1 day	2⁰⁰	Isaac Struble, Disint. Person- Gov't.
1 day	2⁰⁰	Alexander Connolly, Interpreter- Gov't.
		W. M. Hodsdon, Stenog.
		Horace J Johnson, Supt.

Mar. 28 Hearing Continued to Mar. 30, '14. a/c insufficient time to complete case on this date

Mar 30 Hearing Held:
  Persons Present;

½ day	1⁰⁰	Chief Mᶜ Kosato, Inter Person } *Paid under auth. dated Sept. 12, 1914*
½ day	1⁰⁰	Logan Kakaque, Disint. Person- Gov't.
½ day	1⁰⁰	Isaac Struble, Disint. Person- Gov't.
½ day	1⁰⁰	Alexander Connolly, Interpreter- Gov't.

See Case No. 150

Report Approved in Law-Heirship 79689-1915 T.E. dated Aug. 12, 1915

Chief Mᶜ Kosato------------1/3 Int.
David Wakole---------------1/3 "
Sarah Mack-----------------1/9 "
Elbert Mack----------------1/9 "
Charley Mack---------------1/9 "

Report Mailed July 16, 1915.

Costs:- "Gov't Witnesses" Divided Among Estates of:- Mar. 28,'14
  Samuel W. Peel- #144- March 28, 1914.
  Wah-taw-sah   - #145
  ~~William Nahmoswe- #146~~
  Josephine Brown- #147
  Jennie Sampson- #148
  Irene Harris   - #149

145

Wah-taw-sah

1914
Feb. 25 Notices Issued
Mar. 27 Hearing Continued to Mar. 27, 1914, a/c insufficient time to take case
Mar. 28 Hearing Held.   on this date
  Persons Present:-
1 day & 30 miles 5⁰⁰ Sarah Ellis, Inter Person } *No Witness or mileage to be paid a/c being sole heir.*
  Logan Kakaque, Disint Person- Gov't.
  John Brown, Disint. Person } *Mileage & Witness fees paid from 147*
  Alexander Connolly, Interp. of Disint. Person- Gov't.
  W. M. Hodsdon, Stenog.
  Horace J. Johnson, Supt.

205

Sac & Fox – Shawnee
1846-1924   Volume XI

Isaac Struble, Disint. Person- Gov't.

Costs: "Gov't. Witnesses" See Samuel W. Peel- #144
July 25   Alexander Connolly, Disint. Wit.-(~~Gov't.~~)
          Frank Carter, Disint. Wit- (~~Gov't.~~)

Report Mailed July 31, 1914.

Sarah Ellis- Sole heir.

Report Approved Law-Heirship
85280-14, F.W.S. dated Sept. 16,'14.

~~146~~

William Nahmoswe   *1.00 Gov't. next request after June 30, '14*

1914
Feb. 23   Notices Issued
Mar. 25   Hearing Continued to Mar. 27, 1914.
          a/c insufficient time to take case up to-day.

1914
Mar. 27   Persons Present:- Hearing Held:
1 day	2.00	Edward Rice, Inter Person — *Mileage paid from No. 138 & 139. Paid under auth. dated Sept. 12, 1914.*
1 day	2.00	Isaac Struble, Disint. Person- Gov't.
1 day	2.00	Logan Kakaque, Disint. Person- Gov't. — *Mileage paid from No. 138 & 139.*
1 day	2.00	Frank Smith, Inter Person- *Paid under auth. dated 9/12/14.*
1 day	2.00	Alexander Connolly, Interpreter- Gov't.
		W. M. Hodsdon, Stenog
½ day	2.00	Horace J Johnson, Supt.
Oct. 15		Alexander Connolly, Disint. Wit. — *Requested by Supt. to give additional testimony Gov't.*

                    Edward Rice......3/4 Interest
                    Frank Smith......1/4 Interest

Report Mailed October 16, 1914.

Nov. 17   Notices issued for a Supplemental Hearing in accordance
          with instructions contained in Law-Heirship 115288-1914, F.W.S.
Dec. 3   Supplemental Hearing Held:-
          No Costs for Supplemental hearing
          Persons present: { Same persons as
                             appeared in Cora Smith
                             nee Bear Case #138

          Testimony introduces in Cora Smith, nee Bear Case #138
          applicable to this Case also.

          Report Approved Law-Heirship
          115228-14, 131035-14, F.W.S. dated
          Feb. 5, 1915.

Report Resubmitted Dec. 4, 1914.

Josephine Brown

147

1914
Feb. 25 Notices Issued
Mar. 28 Hearing Held:-
    Persons Present:-

1 day & 28½ miles 4$\frac{85}{}$ John Brown, Inter Person } To be paid from 147 & 148 Equally Paid 2\frac{43}{}$ under auth. dated Sept. 12, 1914
1 day & 28½ miles 4$\frac{85}{}$ Thomas Brown, Inter Person Paid under auth. dated Sept. 12, 1914
    Thomas P Myers, Guardian-ad-Litem for minor heirs
    Isaac Struble, Disint. Person- Gov't.
    Logan Kakaque, Disint. Person- Gov't.
    Alexander Connolly, Interp of Disint Person- Gov't.
    Walter M. Hodsdon, Stenog
    Horace J Johnson, Supt.

Costs:- "Gov't. Witnesses". See Samuel W. Peel- #144

    John Brown............11/30 Int.
    Thomas Brown.........19/90 Int.
    Harry Brown...........19/90 Int.
    Mary E. Brown........19/90 Int.

Report Mailed Nov. 5, 1914.

Report Approved Law-Heirship 121226-14, F.W.S. dated Jan. 16, 1915.

148

Jennie Sampson

1914
Feb. 25 Notices Issued
Mar. 28 Hearing Held
    Persons Present

    John Brown, Inter Person } See No. 147. Paid 2\frac{42}{}$ under auth. dated ~~Dec.~~ Sept. 12, 1914
1 day & 16 miles 3$\frac{60}{}$ Emily Johnson, Inter Person Paid under auth. dated Sept. 12, 1914
    Logan Kakaque, Disint. Person- Gov't.

No mileage & Witness fees Member of Business Committee { Isaac Struble, Disint. Person- Gov't.
Chief McKosato, Disint Person- (~~Gov't~~.)
    Alexander Connolly, Interpreter- Gov't.
    W. M. Hodsdon, Stenog
    Horace J Johnson, Supt

Report Mailed July 8, 1915.

Costs:- "Gov't. Witnesses", See Samuel W. Peel- #144

    Report Approved
  in Law-Heirship 77370-15
  E.G.T., dated Aug. 11, 1915.

Emily Johnson, Sole heir.

149

Irene Harris

1914
Feb. 25   Notices Issued
Mar. 28   Hearing Held:-
    Persons Present:-
    Sarah Ellis, Disint. Person} Paid from Wah-tau-sak - #145
    Samuel L. Brown, Disint. Person} Paid from Samuel W. Peel- #144
    Alexander Connolly, Interp of Disint Person- Gov't
    W. M. Hodsdon, Stenog
    Horace J Johnson, Supt.
    Isaac Struble, Disint. Wit. - Gov't.
    Logan Kakaque, Disint. Wit. -Gov't.

Costs:- "Gov't Witnesses"- See Samuel W. Peel- #144

Requested auth. to settle 2/21/14
Paid Jan. 25, '15 by check #4056 on 1st Natl Bk Chandler, Okla.
[illegible]

{Certified copy of Petition for Divorce of Alex Jefferson from Irene Jefferson (Harris).
Certified copy of Decree of Divorce of Alex Jefferson from Irene Jefferson (Harris).
Clerk of District Court of Lincoln Cty, Chandler, Okla. 80¢
                                            Total-------$1.45

Report Mailed Oct. 5, 1914.

William H. Jefferson- All.

Report Approved Law-Heirship
109227-14, F.W.S., dated Nov. 24, 1914

150

Rufus Wakole

1914
Feb. 27   Notices Issued
Mar. 30   Hearing Held:-
    Persons Present:

1 day & 21½ miles 4⁸⁵   Anna Mᶜ Kosato, Inter Person Paid under auth. dated Sept. 12,'14
No mileage or witness fees Member of Bus. Comm. Chief Mᶜ Kosato, Disint Person- ~~Gov't~~} Requested by Supt to be present
½ day   1⁰⁰   Logan Kakaque, Disint Person. Govt.
½ day   1⁰⁰   Alexander Connolly, Interp. of Disint Person- Gov't.
½ day   1⁰⁰   Isaac Struble, Disint. Person- Gov't.
              W. M. Hodsdon, Stenog.
              Horace J Johnson, Supt
              Thomas P. Myers, Guardian-ad-Litem
              for minor heir

Costs:- "Gov't. Witnesses" Divided Among Estates of:
    Rufus Wakole- No. 150
    Joseph Harris- No. 151

Sac & Fox – Shawnee
1846-1924   Volume XI

Carrie Jefferson- No. 152
Paid ½ day from Samuel W. Peel- No. 144- Mar. 30, 1914.

Anna McKosato- 1/3
Grover Wakole- 2/3.

Report Mailed June 25, 1914.
Report Approved Law-Heirship 72150-1914, F.W.S. dated 7/15/14.

151

Joseph Harris

1914
Feb. 27   Notices Issued
Mar. 30   Hearing Held:
   Persons Present:-

1 day & 30½ miles 5⁰⁵	Liza Martin, Inter. Person	⎫ Paid under
1 day & 30½ miles 5⁰⁵	Moses Harris, Inter. Person	⎬ auth. dated
No mileage or witness fees Member of Bus. Comm.	Chief McKosato, Disint. Person- ~~Gov't~~. Requested by Supt. to be present	⎭ Sept. 12, 1914

   Logan Kakaque, Disint. Person, Gov't
   Isaac Struble, Disint. Person, Gov't
   Alexander Connolly, Interp of Disint. Person- Gov't
   W.M. Hodsdon, Stenog
   Horace J Johnson, Supt

Costs:- "Gov't. Witnesses"- See Rufus Wakole- No. 150

Report Mailed June 26, 1914.
Report Approved Law-Heirship 73125-14, F.W.S. dated July 24, 1914.

   Liza Martin, nee Harris-   1/3
   Mary Peacore, nee Harris- 1/3
   Moses Harris-   1/3

152

Carrie Jefferson

No funds 5⁰⁰

1914
Feb. 27   Notices Issued
Mar. 30   Hearing Held:-
   Persons Present:-

1 day & 30 miles 5⁰⁰ George Littlebear, Inter Person
   Thomas P. Myers, Guardian-ad-Litem
   for minor heir
   Logan Kakaque, Disint. Person- Gov't.
   Alexander Connolly, Interp of Disint Person, Gov't
   Isaac Struble, Disint Person- Gov't
   W.M. Hodsdon, Stenog
   Horace J Johnson, Supt

No fees or mileage Member of Bus. Comm. Chief McKosato, Disint Person, Gov't. Requested by Supt to be present

Costs:- "Gov't. Witnesses"- See Rufus Wakole- No. 150

Report Mailed June 26, 1914.

Sac & Fox – Shawnee
1846-1924 Volume XI

George Littlebear- 1/2
Florien Littlebear- 1/2

Report Approved Law-Heirship 73125-14, F.W.S. dated July 24, 1914.

153

Edith Rice, nee Appletree

1914
Feb. 28 Notices Issued
Mar. 31 Hearing Held:-
　　　　Persons Present:-

1 day & 27½ miles 4$^{\underline{75}}$		Edward Rice, Inter. Person Paid under auth. dated Sept. 12, 1914
		Thomas P. Myers, Guardian-ad-Litem for minor heirs
1 day	2$^{\underline{00}}$	Isaac Struble, Disint. Person- Gov't.
1 day	2$^{\underline{00}}$	Logan Kakaque, Disint. Person- Gov't.
1 day	2$^{\underline{00}}$	Alexander Connolly, Interp. of Disint Person- Gov't.
		Walter M. Hodsdon, Stenog
		Horace J Johnson, Supt.

Costs:- "Gov't. Witnesses" Divided Among Estates of:-
　　　　Edith Rice, nee Appletree-　　#153
　　　　Clara Buffalohorn　　-　　#154
　　　　Frank Davis　　-　　#155
　　　　Thomas Jefferson Buffalohorn- #118

　　　　Susie Rice--------1/3 Int.
　　　　Carrie Rice-------1/3 Int.
　　　　Lucien Rice------1/3 Int.

Report Mailed January 20, 1915.

1915
Jan. 13 ½ day Edward Rice - Inter person
　　　　½ day Liza Martin - Disint. person
　　　　½ day Edith Brown -   do   do
　　　　½ day Elmer Walker, Interpreter

Present in Office and requested by Supt to give testimony

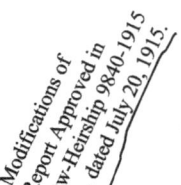
Modifications of Report Approved in Law-Heirship 9840-1915. L.L. dated July 20, 1915.

Edward Rice ---------- 1/3 Interest
Susie Rice　---------- 2/9　"
Carrie Rice　---------- 2/9　"
Lucien Rice　---------- 2/9　"

Sac & Fox – Shawnee
1846-1924 Volume XI

154

Clara Buffalohorn

1914
Feb. 28 Notices Issued
Mar. 31 Hearing Held:
   Persons Present:-
                                          To be paid from #118 & #154
1 day & 27½ miles 4$^{\underline{75}}$ Grace Lee, Inter Person Paid under Auth. dates Sept. 11, 1914
      Thomas P. Myers, Guardian-ad-Litem for minor heir
      Isaac Struble, Disint. Person- Gov't.
      Logan Kakaque, Disint. Person- Gov't.
      Alexander Connolly, Interp. of Disint Person- Gov't.
      Walter M. Hodsdon, Stenog
      Horace J Johnson, Supt.

Costs:- "Gov't. Witnesses"- See Edith Rice - #153.

Report Mailed October 9, 1914.

   Grace Lee, - 1/2 Interest
   Mamie Buffalohorn- 1/2 Interest.

   Report Approved- Law-Heirship
   111106-14, E.G.T., dated Nov. 11, 1914

155

Frank Davis

1914
Feb. 28 Notices Issued
Mar. 31 Hearing Held
   Persons Present:-
   Isaac Struble, Disint Person- Gov't
   Logan Kakaque, Disint. Person- Gov't.
   Alexander Connolly, Interp of Disint Person- Gov't
   Thomas P. Myers, Guardian-ad-Litem for minor heirs
   Walter M. Hodsdon, Stenog.
   Horace J. Johnson, Supt.

   "Gov't. Witnesses"
Costs:- See Edith Rice - #153

   Frank B. Davis - 1/2
   Harry Davis   - 1/2

Report Mailed June 25, 1914.
Report Approved Law-Heirship 72201-14, F.E. dated Sept. 15, 1914.

Sac & Fox – Shawnee
1846-1924   Volume XI

156

Harry C. Jones, Jr

1914
Mar. 2   Notices Issued
Apr. 1   Interested Parties not present
Hearing Continued to Dec. 30, 14
1914
Dec. 30   Hearing not held. Interested parties not present.
Dec. 30'14 Hearing continued to Jan. 18, 1915
Hearing Held:-
Persons Present:-

1 day	2^{00}	Alex Connolly, Disint person- Gov't.
1 day	2^{00}	Leo Whistler, Disint person- Gov't.

Thomas P. Myers, Guardian-ad-Litem
Horace J. Johnson, Supt.

Report Mailed January 19, 1915.

Emma Goodman - 1/2 Int.
Helen Jones - - - - -1/2 Int.

Heirs declared in Law-
Heirship 9005-15, F.W.S., dated
Feb. 25, 1915.

Helen Jones - Sole heir of
unsold portion (S/2 of NW/4 of 26-11-6)

157

Mollie Guthrie

1720

1914
Mar. 2   Notices Issued
Apr. 1   Hearing Held:-
Persons Present:-

1 day & 36 miles 5^{60} Leona Chandler, Inter Person Paid under auth. dated Sept 12, 1914
1 day 2^{00} Logan Kakaque, Disint. Person- Gov't.
1 day 2^{00} Alexander Connolly, Interp. of Disint Person- Gov't.
1 day 2^{00} Isaac Struble, Disint Person- Gov't.
W. M. Hodsdon, Stenog.
Horace J. Johnson, Supt.

Report Mailed October 22, 1914.

Leona Chandler, nee Graeyes - 1/2 Int.
Chela Fritz, nee Guthrie-------- 1/2 Int.

Requested auth. to settle 12/21/14.
{ Certified copy of record showing date of death of Guthrie or Henry Kah-us-sen-we, and who his heirs are.... $1.^{05}
Clerk of Cty Ct Lincoln Cty-Chandler, Okla.

Sac & Fox – Shawnee
1846-1924   Volume XI

1914
Nov. 17 Notice issued for a supplemental hearing in accordance with instructions contained in Law-Heirship 116014-14, F.E.
Dec. 3   Supplemental Hearing Held - Persons Present:-

½ day & 36 miles 5⁶⁰   Leona Chandler, Int. person Paid 3/15/15
½ day 36 miles 5⁶⁰   Laura Carter, disint. person Paid 3/15/15
½ day & 30 miles 5⁰⁰   William Bear, disint. person
½ day   1⁰⁰   Alexander Connolly, Interpreter- Gov't
Dec. 22 ½ day 1⁰⁰   Sarah Bear, disint. person } No mileage. Present in Office & requested by Supt to testify
"   21 ½ day 1⁰⁰   George O. Morton, Interpreter- Gov't.
Jan. 19 ½ day 1⁰⁰   1915 U. S. Grant, Disint. person } No mileage. Present in Office and requested by Supt. to testify. Sent by Int. persons.
Jan. 19 ½ day 1⁰⁰   Alex Connolly, Interp- Gov't.
Jan. 21 ½ day 1⁰⁰   Lilly Carter, Disint. person
Jan. 22 ½ day 1⁰⁰   Laura Carter, Disint. person
Jan. 22 ½ day 1⁰⁰   Alex Connolly Interp of Disint. person- Gov't

Report re-submitted January 25, 1915

Leona Chandler, nee Graeyes- 1/3 Int.
Shelah Fritz, nee Guthrie - - - - 1/3 Int.
Fryor Franklin Brown - - - - - - - 1/3 Int.

Report Approved in Law-Heirship 11060-15, 116014-14, F.E. dated June 14, 1915.

158
John McKuk

Report Mailed July 15, 1915.

1914
Mar. 2 Noticed Issued
Apr. 1 Hearing not held for reason that none of disinterested persons present knew decedent well enough to testify. Hearing referred to R.S. Russell, Supt. Sac & Fox Sanatorium, Toledo, Iowa, on whose reservation heirs of decedent reside.

Report Approved in
Law-Heirship 79320-15, 113241-15,
F.E., dated Nov. 11, 1915.

William Davenport, --------- 6/12 Int.
John Witonosee, ------------- 2/12 "
Ke-wa-sa-no-qua, ----------- 1/12 "
Ma-me-che, ------------------ 1/12 "
Ke-sha-sah, ------------------ 1/12 "
Mo-na-che-qua, ------------- 1/12 "

Sac & Fox – Shawnee
1846-1924   Volume XI

Andrew Barker

1914
Mar. 2   Notices Issued
Apr. 2   Hearing Held:
         Persons Present:

1 day & 19½ miles	3^{95}	Cora Smith, Inter Person Paid under auth. dated 9/11/14. Present in Office & requested by Supt to testify. Paid under above auth.
1 day	2^{00}	Minnie Barker, Inter. Witness
1 day	2^{00}	Isaac Struble, Disint. Person- Gov't.
1 day	2^{00}	Logan Kakaque, Disint. Person- Gov't.

         Ira Walker, Interpreter   No fee, Gov't. Employee
         W. M. Hodsdon, Stenog.
         Horace J Johnson, Supt.

Costs:- "Gov't. Witnesses"- Divided Among Estates of:
         Andrew Barker- #159
         George Grass - #160
         Judith Houston- #161

         Nora Barker   - 1/4 Int.
         Stella Barker - 1/4 "
         Cora Smith   - 1/4 "
         Phia-taw-na-ha- 1/4 "

Report Mailed October 19, 1914.
Report Mailed July 8, 1915.

George Grass

160 *No funds*

1914
Mar. 2   Notices Issued
Apr. 2   Hearing Held:
         Persons Present:

1 day & miles   Silas Grass, Inter. Person
                Thomas P. Myers, Guardian-ad-Litem for minor heir
                Isaac Struble, Disint. Person- Gov't.
                Logan Kakaque, Disint. Person- Gov't.
                W. M. Hodsdon, Stenog
                Horace J. Johnson, Supt.
                Ira Walker, Interpreter } See Case #159

Report Mailed Dec. 31, 1914.

Costs:- "Gov't. Witnesses"- See Andrew Barker- #159

         Silas Grass- 1/2 Int   1/2 Int.[sic]
         Florence Grass- ~~1/2 Int.~~

              Report Approved in
              Law-Heirship 2392-15, F.W.S.,
              dated March 12, 1915.

Sac & Fox – Shawnee
1846-1924   Volume XI

Silas Grass ------- 1/2 Interest
Andrew Conger -- 1/6   "
Florence Grass --- 1/3   "

161

No Costs from 1914 Estate

Judith Houston

Mar. 2 Notices Issued
Apr. 2 Hearing Held:
1 day & 25½ miles 4$\underline{^{55}}$ Samuel Houston, Inter Person
1 day & 25½ miles 4$\underline{^{55}}$ Madeline Carter, Inter. Person
                  Isaac Struble, Disint. Person- Gov't
                  Logan Kakaque, Disint. Person- Gov't.
                  Ira Walker, Interpreter } See Case #159
                  Walter M. Hodsdon, Stenog
                  Horace J. Johnson, Supt.

Costs:- "Gov't. Witnesses"- See Andrew Barker- #159

Samuel Houston- 1/2
Madeline Carter - 1/2

Report Mailed June 24, 1914.

Not necessary to pay Witness and mileage fees of Samuel Houston & Madeline Carter as both have equal interest in Estate (No funds to credit of Estate)

Report Approved July 15, 1914.
Law-Heirship 72149-1914, F.W.S.

---

162 *No Costs from 1914 Estate*

Flora Mokohoko

Mar. 2 Notices Issued
Apr. 3 Hearing Held:
        Persons Present:-
1 day & 29½ miles 4$\underline{^{25}}$ Dickson Mokohoko (Duncan), Inter Person
1 day & 25 miles 4$\underline{^{50}}$ Louisa Mack, Inter. Person
1 day   2$\underline{^{00}}$ Logan Kakaque, Disint. Person- Gov't
1 day   2$\underline{^{00}}$ Isaac Struble, Disint. Person- Gov't
1 day   2$\underline{^{00}}$ Alexander Connolly, Interp of Disint. Person- Gov't.
                  Walter M. Hodsdon, Stenog.
                  Horace J Johnson, Supt.

Costs:- "Gov't. Witnesses" Divided Among estates of:-
        Flora Mokohoko- #162
        Bessie Davis   - #163
        Rachel Davis   - #164
        Della Mathews   - #54

215

Sac & Fox – Shawnee
1846-1924 Volume XI

Louisa Mack- 1/2
Dickson Mokohoko- 1/2

Report Mailed June 24, 1914.

Not necessary to pay Witness & Mileage fees of
Dickson Mokohoko & Louisa Mack for reason
that both have equal interest in estate (no funds to credit of Estate)

163

Bessie Davis

Report Mailed July 8, 1915.

1914
Mar. 2 Notices Issued
Apr. 3 Hearing Held:-
    Persons Present:-

1 day & 17½ miles 3^{75}	Jesse James, Inter. Person	Paid under auth. dated Sept. 11, 1914.
1 day & 19 miles 3^{90}	Mary Hurr, Inter Person	
1 day & 19 miles 3^{90}	Robert Davis, Inter. Person	
1 day & 36½ miles 5^{65}	Robert Peyton Keokuk, Inter. Person	

Thomas P. Myers, Guardian-ad-Litem for minor heir
Isaac Struble, Disint. Person- Gov't.
Logan Kakaque, Disint. Person- Govt.
Alexander Connolly, Interp. of Disint. Person- Govt
Walter M. Hodsdon, Stenog.
Horace J. Johnson, Supt.

Costs:- See Flora Mokohoko- #162, "Gov't. Witnesses"
    Heirs declared in Law-Heirship
    76777-1915 S.E.B., dated Aug. 5, 1915.
    Heirs modified in Law-Heirship
    76777-15, 109156-15, S.E.B. dated Nov. 23, 1915.

Jesse James,	162/324	Int.
Sadie Rhodes,	36/324	"
Robert Davis,	44/324	"
Orlando Johnson,	8/324	"
Wa-so-sah,	27/324	"
Mary Hurr Davis,	47/324	"

164

Rachel Davis

1914
Mar. 2 Notices Issued
Apr. 3 Hearing Held:
    Persons Present:-

1 day & 11½ miles 3^{15}	Andrew Conger, Inter. Person	Paid under auth. dated Sept. 11, 1914
1 day & 31½ miles 5^{15}	George Oliver Morton, Inter. Person	

Logan Kakaque, Disint. Person- Govt
Isaac Struble, Disint Person- Govt
Alexander Connolly, Interp of Disint Person- Govt

Sac & Fox – Shawnee
1846-1924   Volume XI

Walter M. Hodsdon, Stenog
Horace J Johnson, Supt.

Costs:- "Gov't. Witnesses" See Flora Mokohoko #162

Andrew Conger - 1/2
George Oliver Morton- 1/2

Report Mailed January 11, 1915.

Report Approved March 8, 1915.
Law-Heirship 6814-15, F.W.S.

165

Bion Sullivan

1914
Nov. 30   Notices Issued
Dec. 30   Hearing Held:
          Persons Present:
Sole heir. No Witness fees or Mileage necessary { Albert Ketch-show-no, Interested person.
1 day 2^{00} Alexander Connolly, Interpreter of Disint. Person- Govt
          Walter M. Hodsdon, Stenographer.
          Horace J. Johnson, Supt & S.D.A.

Albert Ketch-show-no, inherits entire estate.

Report Approved Law-Heirship
2394-15, F.W.S., dated Jan. 28, 1915.

Report Mailed December 31, 1914.

166

Linda Rogers

1914
Nov. 30   Notices Issued
Dec. 30   Hearing Held:
          Persons Present:
1 day & 12 miles 3^{20} Amanda Starr, Interested person, pd 3/15/15
1 day & 2^{00} Alexander Connolly, Disinterested person- Govt
          Walter M. Hodsdon, Stenog.
          Horace J Johnson, Supt
          Thomas P. Myers, Guard-ad-Litem for minors
Dec. 30   Hearing Continued to Dec. 31, 1914 a/c ~~not~~ all interested parties
          not being present
Dec. 31   Continuation of Hearing Held:-
No Witness fees or Mileage { Persons Present:
          Amanda Starr, Interested person
1 day & 22 miles 4^{20} Alice Hunter, Interested person, Pd 3/15/15
1 day & 22 miles 4^{20} Henry Hunter, Disinterested person, Pd 3/15/15
1 day 2^{00} Alexander Connolly, Interpreter of Disint person- Govt
          Walter M. Hodsdon, Stenog

217

Sac & Fox – Shawnee
1846-1924   Volume XI

Report Approved in Law-Heirship 5436-1915, 41019-1915, F.W.S., dated May 14, 1915.

Horace J Johnson, Supt
Thomas P. Myers, Guardian-ad-Litem for minors

Samuel L. Brown- 1/2 Int.
Amanda Starr   - 1/8 Int.
Alice Hunter   - 1/8 Int.
Gilbert Gibbs - 1/8 Int.
Amos Black, Jr - 1/16 Int.
Bertha Black   - 1/16 Int.

Report Mailed January 9, 1915.

167

Charley Mohee

1914
Dec. 5   Notices Issued
1915
Jan. 4   Hearing Held:
           Persons Present:
1 day & 3½ miles 2$\underline{35}$ David Tohee, Disint Person- Gov't.
1 day & 2½ miles 2$\underline{25}$ Frank Kent, Disint Person- Gov't.   No mileage
½ day   1$\underline{00}$ Sallie Deroin, Disint Person- Gov't. } Present at hearing & reqst by Supt to testify
1 day   2$\underline{00}$ Joseph Springer, Disint Person & Interp- Gov't.   No mileage
½ day   1$\underline{00}$ Edmund Kent, Disint Person- Gov't. } Present at hearing & requested by Supt to testify
½ day   1$\underline{00}$ Mitchell Deroin, Disint Person- Gov't   do
           Walter M Hodsdon, Stenog & Guardian-ad-Litem for minors
           Horace J Johnson, Supt & SDA

           Osmond Franklin - 1/2 Int.
           Frank Burgess   - 1/6 Int.
           Roy Burgess   - 1/6 Int.
           Mack Burgess   - 1/6 Int.

Report Mailed January 13, 1915.

Frank Kent   ⎫ Gov't. Witnesses to be paid equally by Gov't. from estates
David Tohee   ⎬ of Charley Mohee and Mary Squirrell - Balance of Gov't.
Joseph Springer ⎭ witnesses certified but 1/2 day in Charley Mohee estate.

Report Approved Law-Heirship
6698-15 dated 3/9/15 F.W.S.

168

Mary Squirrell

1914
Dec. 5   Notices Issued
1915
Jan. 4   Hearing Held:
           Persons Present:-
½ day & 2½ miles 1$\underline{25}$ Robert Small, Disint person } Pay from estate of Mary Squirrell

Sac & Fox – Shawnee
1846-1924 Volume XI

See Charley	Frank Kent, Disint person- Gov't.	
Mohee Case	David Tohee, Disint person- Gov't.	
No. 167	Joseph Springer, Interp. of Disint person- Gov't.	No Mileage
Jan. 6 ½ day 1⁰⁰	Thomas Lincoln, Disint. person	Pay from estate of Mary Squirrell
Jan. 4	Walter M Hodsdon, Stenog and Guardian-ad-Litem for minor heirs	
	Horace J Johnson, Supt & S.D.A.	

Jack Small Lincoln - 1/2 Int
Elwood Small-   1/2 Int

Report Mailed January 12, 1915.

Requested auth. to settle 2/3/15 Settled 3/11/15 Auth. dated 3/5/15	Certified Copies of proceedings in connection with divorce of Robert Small from Mary Small or Mary Squirrell- $4⁰⁰ Send to Clerk District Court, Payne County, Stillwater, Okla.

Report Approved Law-Heirship
6427-15 6697-15 dated 3/8/15 F.W.S.

169

Julia Pickering, nee Falk

1914
Dec. 5   Notices Issued
         1915
Jan. 4   Hearing continued to Jan. 6, 1915 a/c insufficient time to take up case on this date
Jan. 6   Hearing Held:-
         Persons Present:-

½ day & 65 miles 7⁵⁰		Isaac Pickering, Int Person
½ day & 40 miles 5⁰⁰		John C. Falk, Inter. Person
½ day & 40 miles 5⁰⁰		Margaret Bassett, Inter Person
½ day	1⁰⁰	Mitchell Deroin, disint. person- Gov't.
½ day	1⁰⁰	Joseph Springer, Interp of Disint. person- Gov't.
½ day	1⁰⁰	David Tohee, Disint. person- Gov't.
½ day	1⁰⁰	Frank Kent, disint. person- Gov't.

Walter M. Hodsdon, Stenographer and Guardian-
ad-Litem for minor heir
Horace J Johnson, Supt. & S.D.A.

Report Mailed January 15, 1915.

Margaret Bassett- 1/4 Int.
John C. Falk -   1/4 Int.

Joseph Springer David Tohee Frank Kent Gov't. Witnesses	Nellie or Nora Pickering-3/8 Int. To be paid 1/2 day by Gov't. from estates of Julia Pickering nee Falk, and Kirwin Murray.

F.W.S.
Report Approved Law-Heirship 6962-15 dated March 11, 1915.

Sac & Fox – Shawnee
1846-1924 Volume XI

[170]

Theresa or Theresa Big Ear

Estate of Theresa Big Ear.
Report Approved in
Law-Heirship 78417-15, J. C., dated
Aug. 19, 1915.

Richard Roubidoux,	2520/17640	Int.
Sylvynia[sic] Van Valkenburg,	2520/17640	"
Louis Roubidoux,	2520/17640	"
Lizzie Barada, nee Roubidoux,	2520/17640	"
James Whitecloud,	2520/17640	"
I-cha-ne, or Mrs. John Walters,	360/17640	"
Charles Roubidoux,	360/17640	"
Felix Roubidoux,	360/17640	"
John Roubidoux,	360/17640	"
Sophie Roubidoux,	360/17640	"
Annie Suck-ko-pe-ah, nee Roubidoux,	168/17640	"
Charles Roubidoux,	64/17640	"
Kate Roubidoux,	64/17640	"
Joseph Roubidoux,	64/17640	"
Joseph Jeans,	120/17640	"
Edmore Jeans,	120/17640	"
Eliza Jeans,	120/17640	"
Mitchell DeRoin,	315/17640	"
John DeRoin,	315/17640	"
James DeRoin,	315/17640	"
George Carson,	105/17640	"
Frank Carson, Jr.,	105/17640	"
Joe Carson,	105/17640	"
Robert McGlaslin, (Over)	480/17640	"
Mary McGlaslin, (Harragara)	120/17640	Int.
Walter McGlaslin	120/17640	"
Charles McGlaslin	120/17640	"
John McGlaslin,	120/17640	"
Ida McGlaslin,	120/17640	"
Ella Smith, or Brown,	120/17640	"
Mary Gives Water Now, or Alice B. McGlaslin.	60/17640	"

1914
Dec. 5   Notices Issued
Jan. 5   Hearing Held:-
         Persons Present:-
1 day & __ miles   Jacob Blackhawk, Inter. person

Report Mailed January 14, 1915.

Sac & Fox – Shawnee
1846-1924   Volume XI

1 day & 40 miles 6^{00}		Mitchell Deroin, Inter. person
1 day	2^{00}	Joseph Springer, Disint person- Gov't.
1 day	2^{00}	David Tohee, Disint. person- Gov't.
1 day & 40 miles 6^{00}		Robert McGlaslin, Inter person
1 day & 40 miles 6^{00}		Charlie Watson, Disint person
1 day	2^{00}	Frank Kent, Disint. person- Gov't.
1 day & 40 miles 6^{00}		Sallie Deroin, Disint. person
		Walter M. Hodsdon, Guard-ad-Litem for minor and Stenographer
		Horace J. Johnson, Supt & S.D.A.
Jan. 6		Hearing Continued ~~to~~ Persons Present:-
½ day	1^{00}	Jacob Blackhawk, Int. person
½ day	1^{00}	Mitchell Deroin, Int. person
½ day	1^{00}	Joseph Springer, Inter & Disint. person- Gov't
½ day	1^{00}	David Tohee, Disint. person- Gov't.
½ day	1^{00}	Robert McGlaslin, ~~Disint~~. Inter person
½ day	1^{00}	Charles Watson, Disint. person
½ day	1^{00}	Frank Kent, Disint. person- Gov't.
½ day	1^{00}	Sallie Deroin, Disint. person
		Walter M. Hodsdon, Stenog & Guardian-ad-litem for minor
		Horace J. Johnson, Supt & S.D.A.
½ day	1^{00}	Robert Roubidoux, Disint. person- Gov't.

171

Charley Howard Small or Charley Howard Lightfoot

No Notice of Hearing Issued or testimony taken. Certified Copies of Testimony taken at hearing to determine heirs of Mary Squirrell, dec. Iowa, Okla. allottee #7, transmitted to Indian Office to be used in determining the heirs of the decedent with request that Notice of hearing and Hearing be waived in this case as decedent was not an allotted Indian he having a personal estate only. Mary Squirrell was the mother of decedent.

    Heirs declared in
    Land Sales 79600-11 J.W.H.
    dated Sep. 26. 1911.

Report Mailed January 14, 1915.

       Jack Lincoln -------- 1/2 Interest
       Edward Small ------ 1/2   "

172

Pearl Neal

    1914
Sept. 16   Informal hearing held
No Costs   Persons Present:-
       Claud Chandler, Disint. Person

Sac & Fox – Shawnee
1846-1924   Volume XI

Alex Connolly, Disint. Person
       or Lilly Neal
Lilly Gokey, ~~Disint~~. Person
              Interested
Horace J Johnson, Supt & S.D.A.
conducted informal hearing.

Report Mailed
October 8, 1914.

Lilly Neal- All.

Report Approved
Law-Heirship 110057-1914,
F.W.S. dated Dec. 19, 1914.
     (Pearl Neal was an unallotted Indian.)

173

Flora Foster, nee Grass

1915
June 1   Notices Issued
July 1   Hearing Held.

Report Mailed
July 2, 1915.

     Persons Present:
        William G. Foster, Interested Person.
        Alex Connolly, Disinterested   "
        Isaac Struble, Disinterested   "
        E. A. Upton, Examiner of Inheritance
        John Slaughter, Stenographer
        Aurelia Moran, Guardian-Ad-Litem for Minor Heirs.

        William G. Foster -------- 1/5 Interest
        Green Foster, -------------- 1/5   "
        Roy Foster, ---------------- 1/5   "
        Silas Grass, ---------------- 1/5   "
        Edna Foster, --------------- 1/5   "

     Report Approved in
     Law-Heirship 74639-15, E.G.T.,
     dated July 22, 1915.

174

Nancy Curtis

1912
June 1   Informal Hearing held.
     Persons present.
        Alex Connolly,   Disint. person.
        Alex Jefferson,   Interested person.
        Leo Whistler,   Disint. person.
        Frank Carter,   Disint. person.

Sac & Fox – Shawnee
1846-1924   Volume XI

Heirs declared in
Law, 61517-1912, 5225-1912,
W.D.G. dated Feb. 28, 1913.

Alex Jefferson,   Sole heir.

175

Mary Thurman

Hearing held at
Toledo, Iowa.

Report Approved in
Law-Heirship 92052-13,
J.D.C., dated Feb. 12, 1914.

Jim Scott,   Sole heir

176

Frank Carter

Report Mailed April 7, 1915.

1915
Mar. 9   Notice of Hearing Issued
Apr. 7   Hearing Held
  Persons present:
  Laura Manatowa, now Carter, Int. person
  Bertha Carter,   Interested person
  John Brown,   Disint. person
  Isaac McCoy,   Disint. person
  Mary McCoy,   Interpreter.
  Frank A. Winsor,   Stenographer
  Warner L. Wilmeth,   Examiner of Inheritance.

  Laura Carter,   1/2 Interest
  Bertha Carter,   1/2 Interest

  Report Approved in
  Law-Heirship 41681-1915,
  F.W.S., dated May 27, 1915.

177

Hiram Starr

1916
Feb. 26   Notice of Hearing Issued.
March 27   Hearing Held.
  Persons present:
  Manda Starr,   Interested person
  Daniel McCoy,   Disinterested person
  Alex Connolly,   Disinterested person

Sac & Fox – Shawnee
1846-1924   Volume XI

Aurelia Moran, Ass't Clerk and Guardian-Ad-litem for minor heirs
Horace J. Johnson, Supt. & S.D.A.

Manda Starr	3/9 Interest
Leona Starr	2/9 Interest
Mabel Starr	2/9 Interest
Ella Starr	2/9 Interest

Report mailed 7-14-16

Report approved:
Law-Heirship 78210-16 F.E.

178

Liza Connolly

1916
Feb. 26   Notice of Hearing Issued
May 6   Hearing Held.
    Persons present:
Alexander Connolly, Interested person
Isaac McCoy, Disint. person
Henry Jones, Disint. person
Louis Gokey, Interested person
Aurelia Moran, Ass't Clerk and guardian-ad-Litem for minor heirs
Horace J Johnson, Supt & S.D.A.

Alexander Connolly	7/21	Interest
Louis Gokey	2/21	"
Frank Gokey	2/21	"
Viola May Morris	2/21	"
Alvira Connolly	2/21	"
Charles Connolly	2/21	"
Grace Connolly	2/21	"
Edgar Connolly	2/21	"

Report mailed 5-27-16

Report approved:
Law-Heirship 60330-16 F.E.

179

Caroline Pickett

1916
July 24   Notice of hearing issued
Aug 28   Hearing held
    Persons present:
Jesse Pickett, Interested person
Alex Connolly, Disinterested person
Isaac Struble, Disinterested person

Sac & Fox – Shawnee
1846-1924   Volume XI

Aurelia Moran, Asst Clerk
Horace J Johnson, Supt & S.D.A.

Jesse Pickett   1/2 Interest
Lee Cup pahe   1/2 Interest

Report approved:
Law-Heirship 99083-16 R.T.B.

180

(John) Moses

Hearing held by Geo. A. Hoyo, Supt. at Otoe Agency on March 19, 1917

Heirs declared by Department May 16, 1917 in Probate 29631-17 J.R.V.
    Sophie Lincoln   1/2
    Martha Lightfoot   1/4
    Katie Roubidoux English   1/20
    Lizzie Roubidoux Homoratha 1/20
    Dan Whitecloud   1/20
    Sarah Whitecloud   1/20
    Louise Whitecloud   1/20
        Probate Fees Paid 5/24/17

181

Ulysses S. Grant

Hearing held by S.Y. Tutwiler, Examiner of Inheritance, July 3, 1917, Sac & Fox Agency, Oklahoma.

Heirs declared by Department in Probate 66839-17 F.E. Aug. 6, 1917
Lydia Grant   1/3
Austin Grant   1/6
Saginaw Grant 1/6
Fred Grant   1/6
Bessie Grant   1/6

Probate fees paid 8/13/17

182

Stella Grant

Hearing held by S.Y. Tutwiler, Examiner of Inheritance, July 3, 1917, Sac and Fox Agency, Okla.

   Heirs declared by Dept., in Probate 67215-17 F.E. 9-6-17.
Saginaw Grant,   14/36

Sac & Fox – Shawnee
1846-1924 Volume XI

Ah-ne-kowa Grant,   11/36
Charley Grant,   11/36

Probate fees pd 10-1-17

183

Logan Kakaque

Hearing held by S. Y. Tutwiler, Examiner of Inheritance, July 12, 1917
at Sac & Fox Agency, Okla.
   Heirs declared by Dept., in Probate 67789-17 F.E. 9-27-17
      Esther Wakole   1/2
      Jesse Kakaque   1/2

Probate fees pd. Nov. 1, 1917

184

Chief McKosato

Hearing held by S.Y. Tutwiler, Examiner of Inheritance,
July 10, 1916 at Sac and Fox Agency, Okla.
   Heirs declared by Department in Probate 67548-17 M.H.W.

Painter McKosato	5/20
Liza Harris Martin	5/20
Rosa Battice Appletree	5/20
Leo Walker	1/20
Benjamin Walker	1/20
Guy Walker	1/20
Elmer Walker	1/20
Ira Walker	1/20

Probate fees pd 11-19-17

185

Henry Appletree

Hearing held by S. Y. Tutwiler, Examiner of Inheritance, July 2, 1917
at Sac and Fox Agency, Okla.
   Heirs declared by Department in Probate 67302-17 J.R.V.
dated March 12, 1918.
Susan Appletree   All

Probate fees paid 3/18/18

Sac & Fox – Shawnee
1846-1924 Volume XI

186

Clarence Logan

Hearing held by Examiner of Inheritance June 26, 1917 at Sac and Fox Agency, Okla.
Heirs declared by Department in Probate 65887-17 J.R.V. dated March 14, 1918.

  Lucy Logan, dau.   all

Probate fees paid 4/1/18

187

Sarah Bigwalker

Hearing held by Examiner of Inheritance July 5, 1917 at Sac and Fox Agency, Okla.
Heirs declared by Department in Probate 66838-17 J.R.V. dated March 12, 1918.

Dollie Gokey	1/4
Lelia Bigwalker	1/4
Esther Bigwalker	1/4
Mamie F. Jennings	1/4

Probate fees paid 4/1/18
Funds disbursed 4/1/18

188

Rachel Pate

Hearing held by Examiner of Inheritance July 12, 1917 at Sac and Fox Agency, Okla.
Heirs declared by Department in Probate 67790-17, J.R.V. dated March 14, 1918.

Robert T. Pate	1/3
Robert Charles Pate	1/3
Harry Samuel Pate	1/3

189

Isaac Givens

Hearing held by Examiner of Inheritance July 9, 1917 at Sac and Fox Agency, Okla.
Heirs declared by Department in Probate 67718-17 dated March 14, 1918.

Eveline Givens	4/12
Lydia Grant	4/12
Allen G. Thurman	1/12

Sac & Fox – Shawnee
1846-1924   Volume XI

Roy V. Thurman	1/12
Theresa Thurman	1/12
Jennie Thurman	1/12

Probate Fees Paid 5/1/18

190

Grace Lee

Hearing held by Examiner of Inheritance Jan. 27, 1917 at Sac and Fox Agency, Okla.
Heirs declared by Department in Probate 65064-17 dated March 12, 1918.

Real estate:
Philip Lee	1/4
Mary Wyman	1/4
Kate Shaquequot	1/4
Mamie Buffalohorn	1/4

Personal Property:
Philip Lee	3/9
Mary Wyman	2/9
Kate Shaquequot	2/9
Mamie Buffalohorn	2/9

Probate Fees Paid 5/1/18

191

Samuel Falls

Hearing held by Examiner of Inheritance June 28, 1917 at Sac and Fox Agency Okla.
Heirs declared in Probate 65840-17 J.R.V. dated March 12, 1918.

Edna Falls	3/9
Clara Falls Morris	1/9
Robert Falls	1/9
Annie Falls	1/9
William Falls	1/9
Addie Falls	1/9
Kishko Falls	1/9

Probate Fee Paid Nov. 1, 1918

Sac & Fox – Shawnee
1846-1924   Volume XI

192

Ella Wakole

Hearing held by Examiner of Inheritance June 25, 1917
at Sac and Fox Agency, Okla.
Heirs declared by Department in Probate 65886-17
dated March 12, 1918.

David Wakole	2/6
Hugh Wakole	1/6
Jackson Wakole	1/6
Lucien Wakole	1/6
Grover Wakole	1/6

Probate Fees Paid 5/1/18

193

Amanda McKosato

Hearing held by Examiner of Inheritance July 10, 1917
at Sac and Fox Agency, Okla. Heirs declared by Department
in Probate 67439-17 dated March 12, 1918.

Painter McKosato	5/20
Liza Harris Martin	5/20
Rosa Battice Appletree	5/20
Leo Walker	1/20
Benjamin Walker	1/20
Guy Walker	1/20
Elmer Walker	1/20
Ira Walker	1/20

Probate Fees Paid 5/1/18

194

Walter Nullake

Hearing held by Examiner of Inheritance July 11, 1917
at Sac and Fox Agency, Okla.
Heirs declared by Department in Probate 72750-17
dated March 25, 1918.

Ida Nullake	3/9
Alice Nullake	2/9
Watt Nullake	2/9

Probate fees paid 4/8/18

Leona Logan

Hearing held by Examiner of Inheritance June 26, 1917
at Sac and Fox Agency, Okla.
Heirs declared by Department in Probate 65879-17 J.R.V.
dated March 6, 1918.
   Randall Franklin 1/6
   Christine Boyd   1/6
   Harding Franklin 1/6
   George R. Franklin 1/6
   Alex Franklin   1/6
   Lucy Logan   1/6
Probate fees paid 3/11/18

Cora Ward (Chah-kah-quah)

Hearing held by Examiner of Inheritance July 2, 1917
at Sac and Fox Agency, Oklahoma.
Heirs declared by Department in Probate 66962-17 JRV
dated 3/18/18.
  Nora Barker all
   Probate Fees Paid 11/1/18

Jessie Smith

Hearing held by Examiner of Inheritance and by Superintendent
Concluded 2/18/18
Heirs declared by Department in Probate 67988-17, 82628-18, 46049-18
95106-18 MHW dated 12/31/18
   Frank Smith Husband 3/6
   Ida Nullake Sister   1/6
   Philip Lee   Brother 1/6
   Stephen Harrison 1/2 Bro 1/6
    Probate Fee Paid 2/1/19

Sac & Fox – Shawnee
1846-1924   Volume XI

⑫ George Washington
⑬ Mary Washington
   3 days
{ Leo Walker 9^{00}
Chief McKosito 6^{00}
Logan Kakaque 6^{00}
David Wakolle 6^{00}
Jack Bear 6^{00}
Wm G. Foster 6^{00} }
Juanita Washington $^\$39^{00}$

⑭ Laura Ellis Benson
{ ~~Leo Walker~~ 2^{00}
~~Chief McKosito~~ 2^{00}
~~Logan Kakaque~~ 2^{00}
~~Jack Bear~~ 2^{00}
~~David Wakolle~~ 2^{00}
~~John Brown~~ 2^{00}
~~U.S. Grant~~ 2^{00}
~~Wm Pattequa~~ 2^{00} }
pd 8/4-11
Harry Benson $^\$6^{00}$
Sarah Ellis $^\$6^{00}$
Pd- 8/4/11

⑮ Mancy Coon
{ ~~Leo Walker~~ 2^{00}
~~Chief McKosito~~ 2^{00}
~~Logan Kakaque~~ 2^{00}
~~Jack Bear~~ 2^{00}
~~John Brown~~ 2^{00}
~~Wm Pattequa~~ 2^{00} }
Paul Gokey $^\$12^{00}$
Paid 8/5-11

③ Artemus Ward
  Nora Barker
{ Chief McKosito $^\$2^{00}$
John Brown $^\$2^{00}$
Leo Walker $^\$2^{00}$ }
Nora Barker $^\$6^{00}$

④ Maw-tah-pwa
  Hugh Wakolle
{ Chief McKosito $^\$2^{00}$
John Brown $^\$2^{00}$
Leo Walker $^\$2^{00}$
Logan Kakaque $^\$2^{00}$
David Wakolle $^\$2^{00}$ }
Hugh Wakolle $^\$10$

⑤ Silas Conger
  George O. Morton
  Andrew Conger
  ~~Mamie Jennings~~
{ ~~Chief McKosito~~ 2^{00}
~~John Brown~~ 2^{00}
~~Leo Walker~~ 2^{00}
~~Logan Kakaque~~ 2^{00}
~~David Wakolle~~ 2^{00}
~~Wm. G. Foster~~ 2^{00} }
Andrew Conger 6^{00}
Paid- 8/3/11
George O Morton 6^{00}
Paid- 8/21/11
~~Mamie Jennings 4~~
Paid 9/29-11

Sac & Fox – Shawnee
1846-1924   Volume XI

⑥ Webster Smith
{ Chief McKosito   2⁰⁰
  John Brown   2⁰⁰
  ~~Leo Walker~~
  Logan Kakaque   2⁰⁰
  David Wakolle   2⁰⁰
  Wm G. Foster   2⁰⁰ }

Pd 8/22/11
Frank Smith 2⁰⁰
Charley "   2⁰⁰
Rachel Franklin 2
Benj Smith   2
Pd 1/26/1 Harry Benson ~~Pd 8/21~~
Paid 9/29-11

⑯ Samuel Johnson
{ Leo Walker   3⁰⁰
  Logan Kakaque   3⁰⁰
  U.S. Grant   3⁰⁰
  John Brown   3⁰⁰
  Edward Mathews   3⁰⁰ }   Emily Johnson $15⁰⁰

⑰ Mary Black
{ ~~Leo Walker   3⁰⁰~~
  ~~Chief McKosito   2⁰⁰~~
  ~~Logan Kakaque   2⁰⁰~~
  ~~David Wakolle   2⁰⁰~~
  ~~U.S. Grant   2⁰⁰~~
  ~~Wm. Pattequa   2⁰⁰~~
  ~~Edward Mathews   2⁰⁰~~ }

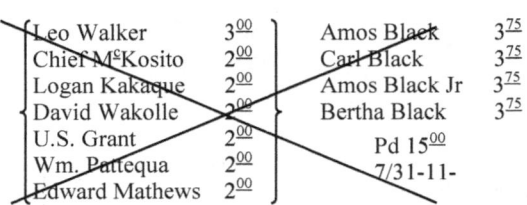

Amos Black   3⁷⁵
Carl Black   3⁷⁵
Amos Black Jr 3⁷⁵
Bertha Black   3⁷⁵

Pd 15⁰⁰
7/31-11-

⑳ John Wolf
㉑ Jane "
㉒ James "
{ [This is blank on original] }

㉓ Silas Hawk
{ Wm Pattequa   3⁰⁰
  Alex Connolly   1⁰⁰
  Isaac Strubble   3⁰⁰
  Edgar Mack   3⁰⁰ }   Ida Butler $10⁰⁰

Sac & Fox – Shawnee
1846-1924   Volume XI

May 1 - 2 - 3 - 4 - 5

	3	(1) 4	5	2 6	7	8	9
Chief McKosito	3^{00}	2^{00}	2^{00}	2^{00}	2^{00}	2^{00}	2^{00}
John Brown	2^{00}	2^{00}	2^{00}	2^{00}	2^{00}		2^{00}
Leo Walker	2^{00}	2^{00}	2^{00}		2^{00}	2^{00}	
Logan Kakaque	~~2^{00}~~	2^{00}	2^{00}	2^{00}	2^{00}	2^{00}	2^{00}
David Wakolle		2^{00}	2^{00}	2^{00}	2^{00}	2^{00}	2^{00}
Wm G. Foster			2^{00}	2^{00}		2^{00}	2^{00}
Isaac Strubble					2^{00}	2^{00}	
~~Ella Wakolle~~						2^{00}	
U.S. Grant						2^{00}	2^{00}
Wm Pattequa							2^{00}
~~Maggie Parkinson Harris~~							2^{00}
	8^{00}	10^{00}	12^{00}	10^{00}	12^{00}	16^{00}	14^{00}

⑦ Paul Randall
{ Chief McKosito 2^{00}
  John Brown 2^{00}
  Leo Walker 2^{00}
  Logan Kakaque 2^{00}
  David Wakolle 2^{00}
  Isaac Strubble 2^{00} }   Tom Penashe $$12^{00}$

⑧ Cora Shaquequet[sic]
{ Chief McKosito 2^{00}
  Leo Walker 2^{00}
  Logan Kakaque 2^{00}
  David Wakolle 2^{00}
  Wm. G. Foster 2^{00}
  Isaac Strubble 2^{00}
  U. S. Grant 2^{00} }
Pa Johia na 3^{50}
Ne pau sa qua 3^{50}
Pone wya tah 3^{50}
Make so peah 3^{50}

⑨ Ruth Miller
{ Chief McKosito 2^{00}
  John Brown 2^{00}
  Logan Kakaque 2^{00}
  David Wakolle 2^{00}
  Wm. G. Foster 2^{00}
  U.S. Grant 2^{00}
  Wm Pattequa 2^{00} }
11.35
Ida Spooner $$9^{25}$
Paul Gokey   ~~4^{75}~~
Paid 8/5/11   265

Sac & Fox – Shawnee
1846-1924   Volume XI

	12 & 13	⑭	⑮	⑯	⑰	⑱
Leo Walker	$9⁰⁰	2⁰⁰	2⁰⁰	3⁰⁰	3⁰⁰	$35⁰⁰
~~Leo Patrick~~	~~3⁰⁰~~					
Chief Mᶜ Kosito	6⁰⁰	2⁰⁰	2⁰⁰		2⁰⁰	29⁰⁰
Logan Kakaque	6⁰⁰	2⁰⁰	2⁰⁰	3⁰⁰	3⁰⁰	32⁹⁰
David Wakolle	6⁰⁰	2⁰⁰			2⁰⁰	16⁰⁰
Jack Bear	6⁰⁰	2⁰⁰	2⁰⁰			10⁰⁰
Wm G. Foster	6⁰⁰					17⁰⁰
U.S. Grant		2⁰⁰		3⁰⁰	3⁰⁰	18⁰⁰
John Brown (Washington)	$39⁰⁰		2⁰⁰	3⁰⁰		15⁰⁰
Wm Pattequa			2⁰⁰		2⁰⁰	3⁰⁰
Edward Mathews				3⁰⁰	2⁰⁰	5⁰⁰
Alex Connolly						1⁰⁰ 1⁰⁰
Isaac Strubble						3⁵⁰ 5⁰⁰ 6⁰⁰
Edgar Mack						3⁵⁰

	⑩ ④	⑪	
Chief Mᶜ Kosito	3⁰⁰		$17⁰⁰
John Brown	~~3⁰⁰~~	~~3⁰⁰~~	12⁰⁰
Leo Wakolle	3⁰⁰	3⁰⁰	16⁰⁰
Logan Kakaque	3⁰⁰	3⁰⁰	16⁰⁰
David Wakolle			12⁰⁰
Wm G Foster	3⁰⁰		11⁰⁰
Isaac Strubble	3⁰⁰		7⁰⁰
~~Ella Wakolle~~			~~2⁰⁰~~
U. S. Grant	3⁰⁰	3⁰⁰	10⁰⁰
Wm Pattequa	3⁰⁰	3⁰⁰	8⁰⁰
~~Maggie Parkinson~~			~~2⁰⁰~~
Edgar Mack	3⁰⁰		3⁰⁰
Edward Mᶜ Clellan	3⁰⁰		3⁰⁰
Leo Whistler Gau-ad-litem	3⁰⁰	3⁰⁰	6⁰⁰
	$30⁰⁰	15⁰⁰	$121⁰⁰

⑩ Thomas Long

Chief Mᶜ Kosito	3⁰⁰	David Pennock	7⁵⁰
Leo Walker	3⁰⁰	M Jish ke ⑧⁰⁰	7⁵⁰
Logan Kakaque	3⁰⁰	John Brown	2⁵⁰
Wm G. Foster	3⁰⁰	Thomas Brown	1⁶⁵
Isaac Strubble	3⁰⁰	Harry Brown	1⁶⁵
U.S. Grant	3⁰⁰	Mary Brown	1⁷⁰
Wm Pattequa	3⁰⁰		
Edgar Mack	3⁰⁰	Shih she wahno	3⁷⁵
Edward Mᶜ Clellan	3⁰⁰	Wish ta ah	3⁷⁵
Leo Whistler	3⁰⁰		

Sac & Fox – Shawnee
1846-1924   Volume XI

(11) Agnes Long

Leo Walker	3^{00}	
Logan Kakaque	3^{00}	
U. S. Grant	3^{00}	
Wm Pattequa	3^{00}	

Laura Carter	2^{50}
Bertha Manatowa	1^{65}
Elmer "	1^{65}
Lorene "	1^{70}
David Pennock	1^{75}
M jish ke	1^{75}
John Brown	1^{75}
Thomas Brown	.35
Harry "	.35
Mary "	.30
Shih she wahn o	1^{00}
Wich to ah	1^{00}

[Copy of Original]

CERTIFICATE.

I, W. C. Kohlenberg, Superintendent and Special Disbursing Agent, at Sac and Fox Agency, Oklahoma, do hereby certify that the above named _____

_____ the witnesses whose names are severally subscribed to the foregoing depositions, were by me first duly sworn to testify to the truth, the whole truth and nothing but the truth, in the hearing aforesaid, and that the depositions by them respectively subscribed were reduced to writing and subscribed by the respective witnesses in my presence, and the same were taken on the ___ day of _____, between the hours of ___ o'clock a. m. and ___ o'clock p.m., of said day and at the office of the Sac and Fox Agency, at Sac and Fox Agency, in the County of Lincoln and State of Oklahoma, as specified in the notice thereto attached, and that I am not attorney for any of the parties interested, and am disinterested in the said hearing.

I further certify that _____, interpreter, whose name appears subscribed to the above depositions was by me first duly sworn to correctly interpret the English language into the Indian and the Indian language into the English, in the hearing aforesaid and that the depositions by him subscribed were reduced to writing and subscribed by him in my presence.

_____
Supt. & Spl. Disb. Agent.

Sac and Fox Agency,
_____.

Sac & Fox – Shawnee
1846-1924   Volume XI

SCHEDULE OF FEES DUE INTERPRETER &
DISINTERESTED WITNESSES IN HEIRSHIP
CASES.
SAC AND FOX, OKLAHOMA, ALLOTTEES.

CASE NO.	DECEDENT.	HEARING HELD.	WITNESSES & INTERPRETER.	WITNESS & INTERPRETER FEES.	MILEAGE FEES.	TOTAL.
10	Thomas Long	July 21, 1913 at	Alex Connolly	2.00		2.00
11	Agnes Long	Sac & Fox Agcy.	(Interpreter)			
93	Benjamin Butler	Sept. 8, 1913 at	Alex Connolly, Int.	2.00		
94	James Bear	Sac & Fox Agcy.	and witness.			
			Sarah Bear	2.00		4.00
95	John Nahashe	Oct. 1, 1913 at	Alex Connolly, Int.	2.00		
96	Susan Nahashe	Sac & Fox Agcy.	Sarah Bear	2.00	3.15	
			Jane Shaw	2.00	3.30	12.45
97	Cora Bass	Sept. 9, 1913 at	Alex Connolly, Int.	2.00		
		Sac & Fox Agcy.	and witness.			
			Bettie Groinhorn	2.00		
			Isaac Strubble	2.00		6.00
98	Grace Mason	Sept. 10, 1913 at	William G. Foster,	1.00		
		Sac & Fox Agcy.	Int. and witness.			
			Isaac Strubble	1.00		2.00
			(Allowed 1/2 day in Morton cases.)			
100	Clifford H. Morton	Sept. 10, 1913 at	William G. Foster, Interpreter.	1.00		
101	Oliver P. Morton	Sac & Fox Agcy.	Isaac Strubble	1.00		
102	Mellisa Morton		Sarah Bear	1.00		3.00
103	Maw-mel-lo-haw	Sept. 11, 1913 at	Alex Connolly, Int.	2.00		
		Sac & Fox Agcy.	and witness.			
			John Brown	2.00		4.00
107	Unice Paddock, nee Hawk	Dec. 2, 1913 at	Alex Connolly, Int.	2.00		
		Sac & Fox Agcy.	and witness.			
			Sarah Ellis	2.00		
			Edward McClellan	2.00		6.00
113	Lidia Walker	Oct. 27, 1913 at	George Appletree,	2.00	2.35	
		Sac & Fox Agcy.	Interpreter.			
			Rosa Appletree	2.00	2.35	
			Liza Martin	2.00	3.05	13.75
				$39.00	$14.20	$53.20

I certify on honor that the above schedule shows the amount due witnesses and interpreters in various heirship hearings, as shown in schedule, held under this jurisdiction, in accordance with the Regulations made to carry our an Act of Congress approved June 25, 1910.

I further certify that where we were able to secure all the necessary data to satisfy the requirements from two disinterested witnesses, only these two are included in the schedule, but where complete and satisfactory evidence could not be obtained from two persons other witnesses as necessary were called and their names have been included. I further certify that the charges shown in this schedule represent only the charges incurred on account of disinterested witnesses for the Government and that in addition to this schedule there are fees of various persons for giving testimony including the heirs themselves, settlement of which will be made from the estate.

Supt. & S. D. A.
Sac & Fox Indian School, Oklahoma.
December 30, 1913.

VMH.

SCHEDULE OF FEES DUE INTERPRETER & DISINTERESTED WITNESSES IN HEIRSHIP CASES.
IOWA, OKLAHOMA, ALLOTTEES.

CASE NO.	DECEDENT.	HEARING HELD.	WITNESSES & INTERPRETER.	WITNESS & INTERPRETER FEES.	MILEAGE FEES.	TOTAL.
91	Joe Vetters	July 14, 1913 at Iowa Mission, Perkins, Okla.,	Jacob Dole, Int. David Tohee John Moses Joseph Springer	1.00 1.00 1.00 1.00	.20 4.00	8.20
92	Lee Patrick Tohee	July 14, 1913 at Iowa Mission, Perkins, Okla.,	Jacob Dole, Int. (Little) Dave Tohee, Jr. Annie Perry Tohee	1.00 1.00 1.00		4.00
104 105	Townsend Sha-th-cher	Sept. 16, 1913 at Iowa Mission, Perkins, Okla..	Joseph Springer, Int. and witness. Frank Kent William Fawfaw	1.00 1.00		3.00
106	Maggie Burgess, nee Mohee	Sept. 16, 1913 at Iowa Mission, Perkins, Okla.,	Frank Kent Charley Tohee	1.00 1.00	.25	2.25
19 111 112	Benjamin Hollowell. Nannie Hollowell Irene Hollowell	Oct. 30, 1913 at Iowa Mission, Perkins, Okla.,	Robert Small, Int. Frank Kent David Tohee	2.00 2.00 2.00	.35 .25 .35	6.95
				$18.00	$9.40	$27.40

I certify on honor that the above schedule shows the amount due witnesses and interpreters in various heirship hearings, as shown in schedule, held under this jurisdiction, in accordance with the Regulations made to carry our an Act of Congress approved June 25, 1910.

I further certify that where we were able to secure all the necessary data to satisfy the requirements from two disinterested witnesses, only these two are included in the schedule, but where complete and satisfactory evidence could not be obtained from two persons other witnesses as necessary were called and their names have been included. I further certify that the

Sac & Fox – Shawnee
1846-1924   Volume XI

charges shown in this schedule represent only the charges incurred on account of disinterested witnesses for the Government and that in addition to this schedule there are fees of various persons for giving testimony including the heirs themselves, settlement of which will be made from the estate.

Supt. & S. D. A.
Sac & Fox Indian School, Oklahoma.
December 30, 191 3 .

Sac and Fox-Shawnee –
LOG BOOK RECORDS
OF BIRTHS AND DEATHS - INDEX
1902-1919

Sac & Fox – Shawnee
1846-1924 Volume XI

Note: This listing of names was originally an index for Record of Births and Deaths. Their page numbers would not coincide with the typed work now. Check the Index at the back of the book for each name. You'll have to scan the list, the names were not alphabetized.

Appletree, Carrie	2
Alley, Enos	15
Black, James	101
Butler, Benjamin	101
Black, Amos Jr	2
Bigwalker Hull, Jennie	102
Buffalohorn, Jennie	103
Barker, Olive	4
Boyd, Lizzie	18, 107
Black, Emma	13, 107
Bigear, Theresa	107
Baker, Eva	107
Black, Fannie	16
Butler, Dewey	16
Brown, Elsie F	16
Barada, Newlyn	16
Bassett, Frank	15
Burgess, Earl N	15
Bass,	11
Black, Bertha	9
Brown, William Theodore	8
Bigear	102
Boyd, Rosie	21
Big ear	102
Boyd, Rosie	21
Brown, Julia	108
Benson, Laura (Ellis)	108
Butler, Carl	21
Brown, Lorena Julia	21
Black, Mary	108
Coon, Dennis	101
Carter, Lucy	2
Connolis, Katharine	2
Carter, Etheline	2
Carter, Jefferson	2
Crane, Carrie	102
Crane, Horace	103
Conger, Jay	104
Connolly, Edgar	3
Couteau, Carl	3
Crane, Harry & Horace	3
Cuppahe, Edwina	3
Connalis, Elizabeth	4
" "	4
Capper, Alfred Rodell	20
Cuppawhe, Henry	19
Carter, Andrew	19
Connalis, Joseph	19, 108
Crain, Mamie Lorena	12, 107
Curtis, Juanita Evalena	16
Connalis, Juanita	14, 108
Carter, Lola	14
" Dennis	12
Connalis, Leona	12
Cuppaha, Louis	12
Carter,	11
Clute,	9
Connalis, Remona	9
Couteau, Ernest Antoinne	9
Connalis, Pearl	9, 108
Che-naw-que-naw	6
Carlisle, John G	101
Crane, Charlie	101
Coon, Nancy	108
Casteel, Edith Clarence	22
Conallis, James	22
Duncan, ~~Richard~~ Lulu	1
Duncan, May	101
Davis, Mary	3, 101
Duncan, Robert	15, 107
" Lulu	1
Dupee, Louise	20
Dole, Joseph	107
Duncan, Morcealus	10
Dupee, Mabel	7
" Mary M.	6
" Maggie	5, 102
Davis, Flora	101
Dole, Willie	102
Dupee, Louisa	103
Dupee, Frederick	103
Dupee, Joe Lawrence	103
Duncan, Richard Jr	22
Ellis, Alex	101
Ellis, Edgar	4
Emmerson, Frederick William	18
Ellis, Katie	18
" Frank	14
Emerson, Edward Henry	13
Emerson,	9
Ely, George W.	6
Ely, Samuel L	102
Ellis, Minnie	22
Franklin, Ross	2, 101
Falls, Herbert	3, 101
Falls, William	18
Fox, Harry M	108
Franklin, Mary	13
Foster, Emma	12
Falls, Annie	12
" William	8
Franklin, Alex	8
Falk, Lawrence Dupee	7
Ford, Angeline	7
Folk, Frank	6
Franklin, Cora	20, 108
Franklin, Benjamin	108
Gokey, ~~Paul~~ Ross	1
" ~~Leo~~ Amelia	1
Grant, ~~Austin~~ Maxey	1
Givens, Charlotte	101
Goodell, Isaac	101
Grass, Sadie	13, 103
Grant, Amos	104
Gibbs, Augusta	3
Grass, Walter	3
Grass, Sadie	3
Goodell, Larona Modesta	19
Gokey, Rosetta	18
Grant, Myrtle	18

Sac & Fox – Shawnee
1846-1924 Volume XI

Note: This listing of names was originally an index for Record of Births and Deaths. Their page numbers would not coincide with the typed work now. Check the Index at the back of the book for each name. You'll have to scan the list, the names were not alphabetized.

Name	Page		Name	Page		Name	Page
Grant, Susie	107	"	William	101	Longshore, ~~Annie~~ Stella.E	1
Givens, Mary E	15, 107	"	Mary	8, 5, 102	Lasley, Florence	2
Gokey, Agnes	16	"	Della	14, 107	Lewis, Cecil Day	3
Grant, Ulyses S, Jr	20	"	Stella	18, 107	Logan, Sadie	3
Gokey, John	14	"	Leila	10	Longshore, Wilson	4
Grant, Shelah	14				Longshore, Ida	20, 107
Givens, Mary	11	Jefferson, Irene		101	Lewis, Paulena Montana	
Gokey, James	11	Jefferson, George		2, 101		19
Grayeyes, Leona	11	Jones, William Woodward			Labelle, Clifford E	19, 108
Gokey, Pauline	11			20	Longshore, Iola E	18
Grass, Mary	9	Jennings, Pearl Elizabeth			" Herbert	14
Gokey, Unice	9			19	Logan, Emma	11
Grant, Thomas Judge	5	Jones, Leona Mildred		18	Longshore, Harriet	12
Gokey, Lizzie	108	" William		107	Lewis, Glen Wyman	11
Gokey, Elmer	22	Jefferson, Omer		17	Logan, Ollie	9
		Jones, Frances Orales		17	Lincoln, Fullwood	7
Hunter, ~~Emma~~ George	1	" Leroy, Jr		14	Lincoln, Abraham	6
Harnes, ~~Sarah~~ Lulu	1	Jefferson, Emanuel		13	Lunt, Lina B	5, 102
Hall, Rufus	101	" Katherine		7, 8	Longshore, Theodore R	1
Hall, Carrie	2, 101	Jones, Henry Lee		21	Lucinda	102
Hamblen, Ada	2	Jones, Henry C, Jr		111	La-ton-shish-me	102
Hunter, George	2				Lincoln, Billie	103
Hunter, Robert	102	Keokuk, Charles H		102	Lincoln, Abraham, Jr	103
House, Guy Preston	107	Keokuk, J Earle		18	Miles, ~~Thomas J~~ Harold Isaac	1
Harrison, Josie	107	Kakaque, Dosh		107	McKosito, ~~Painter~~ Flossie	1
Hunter, George	15	Kihega, Francis		17, 107	" Horace	1, 101
Harris, Mamie Ruby	13	Kakaque, Walter		107	Mansur, Henny H	103
Hamblin, Grace	10	Kaw-Kaw-Keese		17	Mason, Olive	3
Hallowell, Jane	6, 102	Kent, Bessie Naw-a-no-way		17	Miles, Charles	3
Howard, Charley	5				McClellan, Benston	3
Ha~~ll~~, Harry	101	Kent, Theodore		20, 103	McCoy, Loreen	4
Hall, Jennie Bigwalker	101	Keokuk, D. Dennis		15	McKosito, Marion	17, 107
Harris, Battice	21	Kihega, Ozetta		14	McClellan, Pauline	20
Hallowell, Irene	102	" George		7	McClellan, Ernest	20
Hot-che-see	103	Kent, Edward L		7	Meek, Frances Cecelia	19
Hawk, Silas	108	" John		6	Moore, Mildred Elizabeth	
Harnes, Avis Eleanor	21	Kihega, Lina		6		19
Hensley, Guy Garfield	22, 108	Kirk, Emma		6, 102	Morton, Celester	19
Hamblen, Pauline	22	Keokuk, Moses		101	Mack, Lorena	18
Hallowell, Benjamin	108	Kent, Samuel		21	Miles, Howard Taft	18
Hunter, Mary	109	Keokuk, Dorothy Luella		22	Mansur, Gertie	17, 107
					Mathews, Cornelia	10, 107
Ingalls, ~~Mattie~~ Frank	1	Logan, ~~Clarence~~ Lucy		1	Mohee, Charlie	107

Sac & Fox – Shawnee
1846-1924 Volume XI

Note: This listing of names was originally an index for Record of Births and Deaths. Their page numbers would not coincide with the typed work now. Check the Index at the back of the book for each name. You'll have to scan the list, the names were not alphabetized.

McClellan, Ethel	107	
Masquot, Norwood	17	
McClellan, Ethel	16	
McCoy, Timothy	16	
Mathews, Annie	16	
Madison, Harvey	108	
McKinney, Daniel	15, 108	
Mack, Henrietta	15	
McKinney, Beatrice	14	
Mansur, Ella	14	
Meek, Ella Beatrice	14	
McKosito, Abi	13	
Murray, Velinda	12	
McClellan, Wallace	12	
McClellan, John B	11	
McCoy, Oran I	11	
McKinney, Lossen Fred	10	
Mo-so-qua	10	
McKosito, Charles Wakolle	10	
Mansur, Anna	9	
Murray, Kate	8	
McKinney, Ceceal	8	
Meek, Etta May	8	
Mason, William	8	
McKinney, Fred Lossen	8	
Murray, Louis	7, 103	
Murray, Kerwin	7	
Mohee, Richard	6, 103	
Mack, Clara	5	
McKinney, Myrtle May	21	
Mansur, May	101	
Mohee, John	103	
Murry, Kerwin	103	
Muc-cum-pem-e	103	
McKosito	21, 108	
McKosito, (Painter)	21, 108	
Masquat, Narcissus	21	
My-ah-che	22	
Mathews, Ray	22	
Neal, Iva	104	
Nullake, Sadie	4, 107	
Nullake, Alice	17	

Neal, Pearl	16
Nullake, John	12
Neal, Mary	12
Nawanoway, Theodore	10
Neal, Iva	5
Nawanoway	102
No ah tom	102
Nawanoway, Mary	103
Nawanoway, John	103
" Susan	103
" Dan	103
Nawanoway, Samuel	21
Nullake, Watt	22
O'Brien, Ruth	4
O'Brien, Lucille	20
O'Brien, Emily Lucinda	18, 107
" Edward	13
" Myrtle Myree	10
Parkinson, Roger	101
Patrick, Lee	5, 102
Peel, Samuel W	107
Pe-ah-me-squet	17
Pa-mo-thaw-haw	17
Pickering, George	15
Peah-twa-tah	10
Perry, Isaac	103
Rider, ~~Minnie~~ Ellen	1
" Jody Sylvester	4
Rhodes, Sadie	4
Rice, Bion	4
Roubideaux, Bessie	107
Rice, Samuel F	17, 107
Rider, Claud Eldridge	14
Roubidoux, Rufus	14
Rice, Lucian	10
Roubideaux, George	7
Smith, Thomas	101
Sherman, James	20
Scott, Winfield	19

Se-sa-ho	18
Sampson, Jessie	107
Strubble, Ione C	107
Smith, Cora (nee Bass)	107
Star, Leona	17
Starr, Charles	13
Springer, James	11
Starr, George	11
Studer, Ollie	10
Smith, Mattie	9
Small, Edward	7
Squirrel, Garrie	7
" Jane	6
" Charley Howard	5
Shar-tar-cher	108
Spooner, Beatrice	22
Sullivan, Bion	108
Tyner, ~~Claude~~ Stella	1
" Eugene E	101
Thurman, Harry	5, 102
Thurman, Sadie	5, 104
Thorp, Ernest	4, 101
Thorp, Rossetta	4, 101
Tyner, Johnson	5
Thorp, Bernice	20
Taylor, Willis Lee	19
Tyner, Ralph Benjamin	16
Tohee, William	13, 102
Thorp, Walter	13
Tyner, William B	12
Tohee	10
" Daniel	9, 102
Thorp, Myrtle Agnes	9
Tohee, Lee Patrick	5, 102
Thorp, Roscoe	5
Tohee, Daniel	5, 102
Thorp, Hiram	101
Tohee, Leah	102
" Jane	102
Task, Harry	102
Townsend, Ed	103
Tohee, Mary Neal	103
Tohee, Pauline	103

Sac & Fox – Shawnee
1846-1924 Volume XI

Note: This listing of names was originally an index for Record of Births and Deaths. Their page numbers would not coincide with the typed work now. Check the Index at the back of the book for each name. You'll have to scan the list, the names were not alphabetized.

Tohee, Margaret	103
Tyner, Alice	21
Taylor, Eugene Lewis	21
Tohee, Noah	22
Vetter, Lucy	8, 102
" Ida	7, 103
" Fred	6
" Sallie	6, 102
" Annie	103
Wakolle, ~~Hugh~~ William	1
" Jackson	2
White, Myrtle Amanda	2
White, Ida	102
Wyman, Lulu	103
Wolf, James	103
Walker, Evans	4
Wood, Theresa	107
" Ethelyn Gladys	20
White, Lahoma Edith	19
Wilson, Israel	19
Wakolle, Ben	17, 107
Whistler, Mary Frances	17
Walker, Willard	17
Williams, Elsie Marie	16
Wakolle, Glade	16
Waw-sha-law	20
Wyman, Belle	15
Wyman, Rosa	15
White, Leonard	15
Wood, Stella	14
Walker	13
Wyman, Charley	13
Williams, Hazel Faye	12
Walker, Mabel	11
Wakolle, Richard	11
Waw-paw-ko-huck	10
White, Talbert Glenore	9
Williams, Francis Martin	8
Wyman, Benjamin	8
Wakolle, Edgar	8
Whitecloud, Robert	6, 103
Wakolle, Allie	5
Whitecloud, Lizzie	102
Wah-to-gra-me	103
Wa-ho-nee-mie	103
Ward, Artemus	108
Wakolle, Cora	21
Walker, Frances	22
Ward, Carl	108

Sac and Fox-Shawnee –

LOG BOOK RECORDS OF BIRTHS

1902-1919

Sac & Fox – Shawnee
1846-1924   Volume XI

Record of Births among Indians of   Agency

Child's Number on this Record	Parents' Numbers on Family Register		Name	Date of Child's Birth	Sex of Child	Ages of Parents	Blood or Nationality of Parents	Tribe, or Allegiance by Citizenship, of Parents
	127	Father,	Richard Duncan			28	Sac and Fox	Sac and Fox
	128	Mother,	Allie F Duncan			25	"	"
1	129	Child,	Lulu Duncan	July 26, 1902	F		"	
	167	Father,	Pauley Gokey			31	Sac and Fox	Sac and Fox
	168	Mother,	Mary M Gokey			49	"	"
2		Child,	Ross Gokey	Aug 1, 1902	M			
	163	Father,	Lee Gokey			26[sic] 26	Sac and Fox	Sac and Fox
		Mother,	Lizzie Gokey				Western Miami	
3	166	Child,	Amelia Gokey	July 13, 1902	F			
	175	Father,	Austin Grant			22	Sac and Fox	Sac and Fox
	176	Mother,	Alice Grant			22	"	"
4	177	Child,	Maxey Grant	July 31, 1902	M			
	342	Father,	Edward McClellan not			24	Sac and Fox	Sac and Fox
	232	Mother,	Mattie Ingalls legally			31	"	"
5	236	Child,	Frank Ingalls married	Aug 26, 1902				
	158	Father,	Gilbert Gibbs not			21	Sac and Fox	Sac and Fox
	222	Mother,	Emma Hunter legally			22	Sac and Fox	Sac and Fox
6		Child,	George Hunter married	Oct 22, 1902				
		Father,	William Harnes				White	
	213	Mother,	Sarah Harnes			25	Sac and Fox	Sac and Fox
7		Child,	Lulu Harnes	Oct 18, 1902				
	279	Father,	Clarence Logan			24	Sac and Fox	Sac and Fox
		Mother,	Mattie Logan				Shawnee	
8	280	Child,	Lucy Logan	April 26, 1902				
		Father,	Charley Longshore				White	
	283	Mother,	Annie Longshore			22	Sac and Fox	Sac and Fox
9	287	Child,	Theodore Rosswell " ⎫					
10	288		Stella Elizabeth " ⎭	Sept 14, 1902				
	326	Father,	Thomas J Miles			42	Sac and Fox	Sac and Fox
	322	Mother,	Rhoda Miles			26	"	"
11	325	Child,	Harold Isaac "	July 20 - 2				
	357	Father,	Painter McKosato			40	Sac and Fox	Sac and Fox
	358	Mother,	Annie "			20	"	"
12	361	Child,	Horace "					
13	362		Flossie "	July 7 - 2				
		Father,					White	
	396	Mother,	Minnie Rider			26	Sac and Fox	Sac and Fox
14	397	Child,	Ellen "	May 20-2				
		Father,	Claude Tyner				Shawnee	
	445	Mother,	Maggie Tyner			26	Sac and Fox	Sac and Fox
15	447	Child,	Stella Tyner	Sept 14-2				
	451	Father,	Hugh Wakolle			34	Sac and Fox	Sac and Fox
	452	Mother,	Mabel "			27	"	"
16	456	Child,	William "	Jan 8 - 2				

Sac & Fox – Shawnee
1846-1924   Volume XI

2

Record of Births among Indians of   Agency

Child's Number on this Record	Parents' Numbers on Family Register	Name	Date of Child's Birth	Sex of Child	Ages of Parents	Blood or Nationality of Parents	Tribe, or Allegiance by Citizenship, of Parents
	457	Father, Jackson Wakolle			30	Sac and Fox	Sac and Fox
	458	Mother, Esther "			29	"	"
17	461	Child, Ruth "	Aug 6-2				
		Father,					
	1	Mother, Edith Appletree			24	Sac and Fox	Sac and Fox
18		Child, Carrie "	Jan 4, 1903	F		"	"
	201	Father, Harry Hall			37	Sac and Fox	Sac and Fox
		Mother, Jennie Hall			24	"	"
19		Child, Carrie Hall	Feb 15, 1903	F		"	"
	74	Father, Milton Carter			43	Sac and Fox	Sac and Fox
	75	Mother, Ellen Carter			41	"	"
20		Child, Lucy Carter	Feb 23, 1903	F		"	"
		Father, Joe Connalis				Shawnee	Shawnee
	94	Mother, Martha M Connalis			18	Sac and Fox	Sac and Fox
21		Child, Katharine "	Jan 9, 1903	F		"	"
	148	Father, Benjamin Franklin			44	Sac and Fox	Sac and Fox
	149	Mother, Leona "			33	"	"
22		Child, Ross "	Feb 22, 1903	M		"	"
		Father,					
	162	Mother, Lizzie Givens			24	Sac and Fox	Sac and Fox
23		Child, Ethline[sic] Carter	Feb 27, 1903	F		"	"
		Father,					
	196	Mother, Lydia Hamblin				Sac and Fox	Sac and Fox
24		Child, Ada "	Feb 25, 1903	F	25	"	"
	240	Father, Alex Jefferson			26	Sac and Fox	Sac and Fox
	209	Mother, Sarah Jefferson			26	"	"
25		Child, George "	Feb 26, 1903	M		"	"
		Father,				Sac and Fox	Sac and Fox
	222	Mother, Emma Hunter			22	"	"
26		Child, George "	Oct 27, 1903	M		"	"
		Father,					
	272	Mother, Fannie Lasley			27	Sac and Fox	Sac and Fox
27		Child, Florence "	Jan 7, 1903	F		"	"
	483	Father, Talbert White				Sac and Fox	Sac and Fox
		Mother,					
28		Child, Myrtle Amanda White	Nov 28, 1902	F		Sac and Fox	Sac and Fox
	36	Father, Amos Black				Sac and Fox	Sac and Fox
	37	Mother, Mary "				"	"
29		Child, Amos Jr "	Dec 20-1903	M		"	"
	74	Father, Joe Carter				Sac and Fox	Sac and Fox
	71	Mother, Madeline Carter			26	"	"
30		Child, Jefferson Carter	Sept 11-1903	M		"	"

Sac & Fox – Shawnee
1846-1924   Volume XI

Record of Births among Indians of   Agency

Child's Number on This Record	Parents' Numbers on Family Register		Name	Date of Child's Birth	Sex of Child	Ages of Parents	Blood or Nationality of Parents	Tribe, or Allegiance by Citizenship, of Parents
	95	Father,	Alex Connelly			48	Sac and Fox	Sac and Fox
	96	Mother,	Liza "			39	" " "	" " "
31		Child,	Edgar "	Mar 17-1903	M		" " "	" " "
	104	Father,	John Couteau			34	Sac and Fox	Sac and Fox
	105	Mother,	Lettie "			25	" " "	" " "
32		Child,	Carl "	Dec 18-1903	M		" " "	" " "
	108	Father,	Charley Crane			38	Sac and Fox	Sac and Fox
	109	Mother,	Mary L "			33	" " "	" " "
33		Twins Child,	Harry & Horace [Crane]	Aug 3-1903	M's		" " "	" " "
	116	Father,	Lee Cuppawhe			26	Sac and Fox	Sac and Fox
		Mother,					" " "	" " "
34		Child,	Edwina "	Oct 2-1903	F		" " "	" " "
	119	Father,	Frank Davis			31	Sac and Fox	Sac and Fox
	120	Mother,	Flora "			31	" " "	" " "
35		Child,	Mary "	Dec 1-1903	F		" " "	" " "
	141	Father,	Samuel Falls			22	Sac and Fox	Sac and Fox
	142	Mother,	Edna "			23	" " "	" " "
36		Child,	Herbert "	Aug 4-1903	M		" " "	" " "
		Father,						
	155	Mother,	Alice Gibbs			25	Sac and Fox	Sac and Fox
37		Child,	Augusta "	July 27-1903	F		" " "	" " "
		Father,						
	186	Mother,	Flora Grass			38	Sac and Fox	Sac and Fox
38		Child,	Walter Grass	Dec 21-1903	M		" " "	" " "
		Father,						
	190	Mother,	May Grass			29	Sac and Fox	Sac and Fox
39		Child,	Sadie Grass	Dec 28-1903	F		" " "	" " "
		Father,					Pottawatomie	Pottawatomie
	347	Mother,	Pauline Lewis			23	Sac and Fox	Sac and Fox
40		Child,	Cecil Day "	Oct 21-1903	M		" " "	" " "
	279	Father,	Clarence Logan			25	Sac and Fox	Sac and Fox
		Mother,						
41		Child,	Sadie "	Sept 15-1903			" " "	" " "
		Father,					Sac and Fox	Sac and Fox
	309	Mother,	Grace Mason			18	" " "	" " "
42		Child,	Olive "	Apr 10-1903			" " "	" " "
		Father,						
	322	Mother,	Rhoda Miles			27	Sac and Fox	Sac and Fox
43		Child,	Charlie "	Jan 4-1903			" " "	" " "
		Father,						
	339	Mother,	Dolly McClellan			29	Sac and Fox	Sac and Fox
44		Child,	Benston "	Aug 8-1904			" " "	" " "

Sac & Fox – Shawnee
1846-1924   Volume XI

4

Record of Births among Indians of   Agency

Child's Number on this Record	Parents' Numbers on Family Register	Name	Date of Child's Birth	Sex of Child	Ages of Parents	Blood or Nationality of Parents	Tribe, or Allegiance by Citizenship, of Parents
	371	Father, Walter Nullake			23	Sac and Fox	Sac and Fox
		Mother,					
45		Child, Sadie "	Aug 5-1903	F		" " "	" " "
		Father,					
	373	Mother, Lucy O'Brien			32	Sac and Fox	Sac and Fox
46		Child, Ruth "	Aug 10-1903	F		" " "	" " "
		Father,					
	396	Mother, Minnie Rider			27	Sac and Fox	Sac and Fox
47		Child, Jody Sylvester "	June 5-1903	M		" " "	" " "
		Father,					
	398	Mother, Deborah Rhodes			25	Sac and Fox	Sac and Fox
48		Child, Sadie "	Jan 1-1904	F		" " "	" " "
	432	Father, Hiram Thorp			52	Sac and Fox	Sac and Fox
		Mother,					
49		Child, Ernest "	Apr 10-1903	M		" " "	" " "
	437	Father, Frank Thorp			23	Sac and Fox	Sac and Fox
		Mother,					
50		Child, Rosetta "	July 20-1903	F		" " "	" " "
	465	Father, Ben Walker			22	Sac and Fox	Sac and Fox
	466	Mother, Dora "			21	" " "	" " "
51		Child, Evans "	Aug 21-1903	M		" " "	" " "
		Father, Joe Connolis				Sac and Fox	Sac and Fox
		Mother, Martha Connalis				" " "	" " "
52		Child, Elisabeth "	April 7-1904	F		" " "	" " "
		Father,				Sac and Fox	Sac and Fox
	10	Mother, Matilda Barker			32	" " "	" " "
53		Child, Olive Barker	Feb 1-1904	F		" " "	" " "
		Father,					
	133	Mother, Ruth Ellis			20	Sac and Fox	Sac and Fox
54		Child, Edgar Ellis	Mar 5-1904	M		" " "	" " "
	345	Father, Dan McCoy			28	Sac and Fox	Sac and Fox
		Mother,					
55		Child, Loreen McCoy	Feb 13-1904	F		" " "	" " "
		Father, Albert Rice				Pottawatomie	Pottawatomie
		Mother, Naoma Sullivan Rice				Sac and Fox	Sac and Fox
56		Child, Bion Rice	May 20-1904	M			
		Father,					
	94	Mother, Connalis, Martha M				Sac and Fox	Sac and Fox
57		Child, " Elizabeth	Apr-7-04	F		" " "	" " "
		Father, Charley Longshore				White	White
	283	Mother, Annie Longshore				Sac and Fox	Sac and Fox
58		Child, Wilson Longshore	Mar 19-04	M		" " "	

Sac & Fox – Shawnee
1846-1924 Volume XI

Record of Births among Indians of Agency

Child's Number on This Record	Parents' Numbers on Family Register		Name	Date of Child's Birth	Sex of Child	Ages of Parents	Blood or Nationality of Parents	Tribe, or Allegiance by Citizenship, of Parents
59		Father,	Claude Tyner				Shawnee	
	445	Mother,	Maggie Tyner				Sac & Fox	Sac & Fox
		Child,	Johnson Tyner	June 18-04	M			
	368	Father,	Victor Neal			75	Sac and Fox	Sac & Fox
		Mother,	Lilly Neal				Shawnee	" " "
60		Child,	Iva Neal	July 6	F			
	292	Father,	Elbert Mack				Sac and Fox	Sac and Fox
	293	Mother,	Laura Mack				Sac and Fox	Sac and Fox
61		Child,	Clara Mack	June 11-04	F			
		Father,						
	439	Mother,	Lucy Thurman				Sac and Fox	Sac and Fox
62		Child,	Harry [Thurman]	June 17-04	M			
		Father,						
	439	Mother,	Lucy Thurman				Sac and Fox	Sac and Fox
63		Child,	Sadie [Thurman]	June 18-04	F			
	451	Father,	Hugh Wakolle				Sac and Fox	Sac and Fox
	452	Mother,	Mable Wakolle				Sac and Fox	Sac and Fox
64		Child,	Allie Wakolle	June 20-04				
	342	Father,	Edward McClellan				Sac and Fox	Sac and Fox
	232	Mother,	Mattie Ingalls				Sac and Fox	Sac and Fox
65		Child,	Mary Ingalls	May 26-04	F			
		Father,	Dave Tohee Jr				Iowa	Iowa
		Mother,	Leah Tohee				Iowa	Iowa
66		Child,	Daniel Tohee	May 28-04	M			
	175	Father,	Austin Grant			23	Sac and Fox	Sac and Fox
	176	Mother,	Alice Grant			23	" " "	" " "
67		Child,	Thomas Judge Grant	Aug 4-04	M			
	432	Father,	Hiram Thorp	Aug 12-04			Sac and Fox	Sac and Fox
		Mother,	Julia Thorp				White	
68		Child,	Roscoe Thorp		M			
		Father,						
		Mother,	Mary Squirrel				Iowa	Iowa
69		Child,	Charley Howard	Nov 18-1890	M		Iowa	Iowa
		Father,	David Tohee				Iowa	Iowa
		Mother,	Mary Tohee				Iowa	Iowa
70		Child,	Lee Patrick	Apr 25-1891	M		Iowa	
		Father,						
		Mother,	Au-gre				Iowa	Iowa
71		Child,	Lina B Lunt	Mar 12-1891	F			
		Father,	Victor Dupee				Iowa	Iowa
		Mother,	Mary Dupee				Iowa	Iowa
72		Child,	Maggie Dupee	July 10-1891	F			

Sac & Fox – Shawnee
1846-1924 Volume XI

6

Record of Births among Indians of   Agency

Child's Number on this Record.	Parents' Numbers on Family Register	Name.	Date of Child's Birth.	Sex of Child	Ages of Parents	Blood or Nationality of Parents	Tribe, or Allegiance by Citizenship, of Parents
73		Father, Mother, Mary Squirrel Child, Jane [Squirrel]	Nov. 18-1890	F	17	Iowa	Iowa
74		Father, Sam Vetter Mother, Mary Vetter Child, Sallie Vetter	Apr 12-1892	F	22 23	Iowa Iowa	Iowa Iowa
75		Father, Joe Vetter Mother, Myap-pe-me-gra-me Child, Emma Kirk	Feb 18-1892	F	56 61	Iowa Iowa	Iowa Iowa
76		Father, John Ely Mother, Mary Ely Child, George W Ely	May 4-1892	M	61 58	Iowa Iowa	Iowa Iowa
77		Father, Benj Hallowell Mother, Nannie Hallowell Child, Jane Hallowell	Mar 30-1892	M	39 23	Iowa Iowa	Iowa Iowa
78		Father, Jefferson Whitecloud Mother, Susan Whitecloud Child, Robert Whitecloud	May 7-1892	M	47 36	Iowa Iowa	Iowa Iowa
79		Father, Jefferson Whitecloud grd father Mother, Child, Lina Kihega	July 17-1892		47	Iowa	Iowa
80		Father, Victor Dupee Mother, Mary Dupee Child, Mary M Dupee	July 26-1892		37 34	Iowa Iowa	Iowa Iowa
81		Father, Frank Kent Mother, Emma Kent Child, John Kent	Jan 12-1892			Iowa Iowa	Iowa Iowa
82		Father, Abraham Lincoln Mother, Maggie Lincoln Child, Abraham Lincoln	Oct 10-1892	M	44 43	Iowa Iowa	Iowa Iowa
83		Father, Mother, Maggie Mohee Child, Richard Mohee	Sept 15-1892	M	19	Iowa	Iowa
84		Father, Daniel Falk Mother, Julia Falk Child, Frank Folk[sic]	Apr 5-1893	M	34 34 23 23	Iowa Iowa	Iowa Iowa
85		Father, Sam Vetter Mother, Mary Vetter Child, Fred Vetter	June 13-1893	M	23 24	Iowa Iowa	Iowa Iowa
86		Father, Mother, Theresa Bigear Child, Che-naw-que-naw	June 14-1893	M	71	Iowa	Iowa

Sac & Fox – Shawnee
1846-1924 Volume XI

Record of Births among Indians of Agency

Child's Number on This Record	Parents' Numbers on Family Register		Name	Date of Child's Birth	Sex of Child	Ages of Parents	Blood or Nationality of Parents	Tribe, or Allegiance by Citizenship, of Parents
		Father,	Frank Kent			32 32	Iowa	Iowa
		Mother,	Emma Kent			18 18	Iowa	Iowa
87		Child,	Edward L Kent	Apr 25-1893	M			
		Father,						
		Mother,	Julia Squirrel			25 25	Iowa	Iowa
88		Child,	Garrie Squirrel	Dec 26-1892	M			
		Father,	Isaac Perry			40 40	Iowa	Iowa
		Mother,	Annie "			38 38	Iowa	Iowa
89		Child,	Che-naw-que-naw	June 14, 1893	F			
		Father,						
		Mother,	Nellie Naw-a-no-way			22 22	Iowa	Iowa
90		Child,	Mabel Dupee	Feb 2-1893	F			
		Father,						
		Mother,	Augre			24	Iowa	Iowa
91		Child,	Angeline Ford	Oct 12-1894	F			
		Father,						
		Mother,	Julia Falk			25	Iowa	Iowa
92		Child,	Lawrence Dupee Falk	Apr 2-1894	F			
		Father,						
		Mother,	Jennie Rubideaux			17	Iowa	Iowa
93		Child,	George Rubideaux	Sept 10-1894	M			
		Father,	Charley Kihega			32	Iowa	Iowa
		Mother,	Julia Kihega			17	Iowa	Iowa
94		Child,	George Kihega	Sept 11-1894	M			
		Father,	Abraham Lincoln			46	Iowa	Iowa
		Mother,	Maggie Lincoln			45	Iowa	Iowa
95		Child,	Fullwood Lincoln	Aug 21-1894	M			
		Father,	Charley Murry			18	Iowa	Iowa
		Mother,	Emily Murry			17	Iowa	Iowa
96		Child,	Kerwin Murry	Feb 25-1895				
	240	Father,	Alex Jefferson				Sac and Fox	Sac and Fox
	209	Mother,	Sarah Jefferson				Sac and Fox	Sac and Fox
97		Child,	Katharine Jefferson	Aug 24-04	F			
		Father,	Saml Vetter			27	Iowa	Iowa
		Mother,	Mary Vetter			28	Iowa	Iowa
98		Child,	Ida Vetter	Dec 21-1896	F			
		Father,	Victor Dupee			42	Iowa	Iowa
		Mother,	Mary Dupee			39	Iowa	Iowa
99		Child,	Louis Murray	Jan 2-1897	M			
		Father,	Robert Small			22	Iowa	Iowa
		Mother,	Mary Squirrel			26	Iowa	Iowa
100		Child,	Edward Small	Mar 9-1898	M			

Sac & Fox – Shawnee
1846-1924 Volume XI

8
Record of Births among Indians of   Agency

Child's Number on This Record	Parents' Numbers on Family Register		Name	Date of Child's Birth	Sex of Child	Ages of Parents	Blood or Nationality of Parents	Tribe, or Allegiance by Citizenship, of Parents
		Father,	Sam Vetter			29	Iowa	Iowa
		Mother,	Mary Vetter			30	Iowa	Iowa
101		Child,	Lucy Vetter	Feb 10-1898	F			
	148	Father,	Benjamin Franklin				Sac & Fox	Sac & Fox
	149	Mother,	Leona Franklin				Sac & Fox	Sac & Fox
102		Child,	Alex Franklin	Sept 4-1904	M			
		Father,						
	232	Mother,	Mattie Ingalls			32	Sac & Fox	Sac & Fox
103		Child,	Mary Ingalls	May 20-04	F			
	240	Father,	Alex Jefferson			27	Sac & Fox	Sac & Fox
	209	Mother,	Sarah Jefferson			25	Sac & Fox	Sac & Fox
104		Child,	Katharine Jefferson	Aug 24-04	F			
	457	Father,	Jackson Wakolle			31	Sac & Fox	Sac & Fox
	458	Mother,	Ester Wakolle			30	Sac & Fox	Sac & Fox
105		Child,	Edgar Wakolle	Mar 1-1904	M			
	487	Father,	Jacob Wyman			27	Sac & Fox	Sac & Fox
	488	Mother,	Mary Wyman			24	Sac & Fox	Sac & Fox
106		Child,	Benjamin Wyman	Apr 25-04	M			
	352	Father,	Arron McKinney				Sac & Fox	Sac & Fox
		Mother,					White	White
107		Child,	Fred Lossen McKinney		M		Sac & Fox	Sac & Fox
		Father,	George Brown				White	
	46	Mother,	Julia Brown			26	Sac & Fox	Sac & Fox
108		Child,	William Theodore	Sept 17-04	M		Sac & Fox	Sac & Fox
		Father,						
	306	Mother,	Edith Mason			20	Sac & Fox	Sac & Fox
109		Child,	William Mason	Sept 13-04	M		" " "	" " "
		Father,					White	White
	315	Mother,	Jennie Meek			34	Sac & Fox	Sac & Fox
110		Child,	Etta May "	Sept 23-04	F		" " "	" " "
	352	Father,	Arron McKinney			24	Sac & Fox	Sac & Fox
		Mother,					White	White
111		Child,	Ceceal McKinney	Sept 28-04	M			
		Father,	Charles Murray			27	Iowa	Iowa
		Mother,	Emily Murray			26	Iowa	Iowa
112		Child,	Kate Murray	July 11-04	F			
	141	Father,	Sam Falls				Sac & Fox	Sac & Fox
	142	Mother,	Edna Falls				Sac & Fox	Sac & Fox
113		Child,	William Falls	Oct 22-04	M			
		Father,	Frank Williams				White	White
	402	Mother,	Cassie Williams				Sac & Fox	Sac & Fox
114		Child,	Francis Martin Williams	Oct 20-04	M			

Sac & Fox – Shawnee
1846-1924 Volume XI

Record of Births among Indians of Agency

Child's Number on This Record	Parents' Numbers on Family Register		Name	Date of Child's Birth	Sex of Child	Ages of Parents	Blood or Nationality of Parents	Tribe, or Allegiance by Citizenship, of Parents
115	163	Father,	Leo Gokey			27 27	Sac & Fox	Sac and Fox
		Mother,	Lizzie Gokey				Miami	" " "
		Child,	Unice [Gokey]	Apr 5-04	F		Sac & Fox	" " "
		Father,	Talbert White				Sac & Fox	Sac and Fox
		Mother,					White	
116		Child,	Talbert Glenore White	Dec 6-04	M		Sac & Fox	Sac & Fox
		Father,	Andrew Conger				Sac and Fox	Sac and Fox
		Mother,	May Grass			29	" " "	" " "
117		Child,	Mary "	Dec 29	F		" " "	" " "
		Father,	Frank Thorp				Sac & Fox	Sac & Fox
		Mother,	Angeline Thorp				Pottawatomie	" " "
118		Child,	Myrtle Agnes Thorp	Dec 4-1904	F		Sac & Fox	" " "
		Father,	Dave Tohee, Jr				Iowa	Iowa
		Mother,	Leah Tohee				Iowa	Iowa
119		Child,	Daniel Tohee	May 28-04	M		Iowa	Iowa
		Father,	Clarence Logan				Sac and Fox	Sac and Fox
		Mother,	Mattie Logan				Shawnee	Sac & Fox
120		Child,	Ollie Logan	Feb 6-05	F		Sac & Fox	Sac & Fox
		Father,	Bud Connalis				Pottawatomie	
		Mother,	Mary Connalis				Sac & Fox	Sac & Fox
121		Child,	Pearl Connalis	Apr 22-04			" " "	" " "
		Father,	John Couteau				Sac & Fox	Sac & Fox
		Mother,	Lettie Couteau				" " "	" " "
122		Child,	Ernest Antoinne Couteau	Mar	M		" " "	" " "
		Father,	Joseph Connalis				Pottawatomie	
		Mother,	Martha M Connalis				S&F	Sac & Fox
123		Child,	Remona Connalis	Mar 22-05	F		S&F	" " "
		Father,	Amos Black				Sac & Fox	Sac & Fox
		Mother,					" " "	" " "
124		Child,	Bertha Black	Apr 6-05	F		" " "	" " "
		Father,	Benjamin Smith			24	Sac & Fox	Sac and Fox
		Mother,	Cora Smith				" " "	" " "
125		Child,	Mattie Smith	March 17-05	F		" " "	" " "
		Father,	Edward Butler				Sac & Fox	Sac & Fox
		Mother,	Ida Mansur				" " "	" " "
126		Child,	Anna Mansur	May 16-05	F		" " "	" " "
		Father,	Clute	July 31				
		Mother,						
127		Child,						
		Father,	Emerson	Sept 30				
		Mother,						
128		Child,						

255

Sac & Fox – Shawnee
1846-1924   Volume XI

10

Record of Births among Indians of .... Agency

Child's Number on this Record	Parents' Numbers on Family Register	Name	Date of Child's Birth	Sex of Child	Ages of Parents	Blood or Nationality of Parents	Tribe, or Allegiance by Citizenship, of Parents
		Father, Frank Nawanoway				Iowa	Iowa
		Mother, Emma L Nawanoway				Iowa	Iowa
129		Child, Theodore Nawanoway	Apr 3-1905	M			
		Father, Edward McClellan				Sac & Fox " " "	Sac and Fox " " "
		Mother, Mattie Ingalls					
130		Child, Leila [Ingalls]	June 15	F		" " "	" " "
		Father, Painter McKosito				Sac & Fox " " "	Sac and Fox " " "
		Mother, Annie "					
131		Child, Charles Wakolle "	June 15	M		" " "	" " "
		Father,				White	
		Mother, Lydia Hamblin				Sac & Fox " " "	Sac & Fox " " "
132		Child, Grace [Hamblin]	May 25-05	F			
		Father, John Scott				Iowa Sac & Fox	Iowa Sac & Fox
		Mother, Stella Barker				Sac & Fox	Sac & Fox
133		Child, Mo-so-qua	Mar 30-05	F			
		Father, Richard Duncan				Sac & Fox " " "	Sac and Fox " " "
		Mother, Allie Duncan					
134		Child, Morcealus Duncan	Aug 25-05	M			
		Father, Walter Mathews				Sac & Fox	Sac & Fox
		Mother, Nannie Mathews				Shawnee	Sac & Fox
135		Child, Cornelia Mathews	Sept 11-05	F			
		Father, Edward Studer				White	White
		Mother, Alice Studer				Sac & Fox	White
136		Child, Ollie [Studer]	June 23-05	M		" "	
		Father, Aaron McKinney				Sac & Fox	Sac & Fox
		Mother,				White	"
137		Child, Lossen Fred McKinney	Sept 25-05	M		Sac & Fox	Sac & Fox
		Father, Frank Smith				Sac & Fox " " "	Sac and Fox " " "
		Mother, Annie Smith					
138		Child, Peah-twa-tah	Oct 2-05	F		" " "	" " "
		Father, Frank Smith				Sac & Fox	Sac & Fox
		Mother, Annie Smith				Sac & Fox	Sac & Fox
139		Child, Naw-paw-ke-huck	Oct 2-05	M			
		Father, Daniel O'Brien				Pottawatomie	
		Mother, Lucy O'Brien				Sac & Fox " "	Sac & Fox " "
140		Child, Myrtle Myree O'Brien	Oct 9-05	F			
		Father, Edward Rice				Sac & Fox " " "	Sac and Fox " " "
		Mother, Edith Appletree (Rice)					
141		Child, Lucian Rice	Oct 3-05	M		" " "	" " "
		Father, Jake Dole				Iowa "	Iowa "
		Mother, Amelia Tohee					
142		Child, Tohee	Sept 28-05	M		"	"

256

Sac & Fox – Shawnee
1846-1924   Volume XI

Record of Births among Indians of _____ Agency

Child's Number on this Record	Parents' Numbers on Family Register	Name	Date of Child's Birth	Sex of Child	Ages of Parents	Blood or Nationality of Parents	Tribe, or Allegiance by Citizenship, of Parents
		Father, Omer D Lewis				Cherokee	Sac and Fox
		Mother, Pauline Lewis				Sac and Fox	" "
142[sic]		Child, Glen Wyman Lewis	Oct 12-05	M		" "	" "
		Father, Joe Carter				Sac and Fox	Sac and Fox
		Mother, Madaline Carter				" "	" "
143		Child,	Nov 3	M			
		Father, Hiram Starr				Sac and Fox	Sac and Fox
		Mother, Manda Scott				" "	" "
144		Child, George Starr	Nov 15-05	M		" "	" "
		Father, Paul Gokey				Sac and Fox	Sac and Fox
		Mother, Mary Gokey				" "	" "
145		Child, Pauline Gokey	Nov 19-05	F		" "	" "
		Father, Andrew Conger				Sac and Fox	Sac and Fox
		Mother, Inez Bass				" "	" "
146		Child, Bass	Oct 10-05	M		" "	" "
		Father, Paul Gokey					
		Mother, Lizzie Greyeyes				Sac and Fox	Sac and Fox
147		Child, Leona Greyeyes	Dec 28-05	F		" "	" "
		Father, Dan McCoy				Sac & Fox	Sac & Fox
		Mother, Mary McCoy				White	White
148		Child, Oran I McCoy	Dec 12-05	M			
		Father, Leo Gokey				Sac & Fox	Sac & Fox
		Mother, Lizzie Gokey	Nov 30-05			Miami	Miami
149		Child, James Gokey	~~Dec 9-0~~	M		Sac & Fox	Sac & Fox
		Father, Jackson Wakolle				Sac & Fox	Sac & Fox
		Mother, Esther Wakolle				" "	" "
150		Child, Richard Wakolle	Dec 30-1905	M		" "	" "
		Father, John McClellan				Sac & Fox	Sac & Fox
		Mother, Fanny McClellan				" "	" "
151		Child, John B McClellan	Jan 9-06	M		" "	" "
		Father, Eveline Givens				Sac & Fox	Sac & Fox
		Mother, Matillda Givens				" "	" "
152		Child, Mary Givens	Jan 5-06	F		" "	" "
		Father, Joseph Springer			42	Iowa	Iowa
		Mother, Josie Springer			37	Iowa	Iowa
153		Child, James "	Dec 12-05	M		"	"
		Father, Ben Walker				Sac & Fox	Sac & Fox
		Mother, Dora Walker				" "	" "
154		Child, Mabel Walker	Feb 3-06	F		" "	" "
		Father, Clarence Logan				Sac & Fox	Sac & Fox
		Mother, Mattie Logan				Shawnee	" "
155		Child, Emma Logan	Feb 27-06	F		Sac & Fox	" "

257

Sac & Fox – Shawnee
1846-1924   Volume XI

12

Record of Births among Indians of   Agency

Child's Number on This Record	Parents' Numbers on Family Register	Name	Date of Child's Birth	Sex of Child	Ages of Parents	Blood or Nationality of Parents	Tribe, or Allegiance by Citizenship, of Parents
156		Father, Charles Longshore				White	Sac & Fox
		Mother, Annie Longshore				Sac & Fox	Sac & Fox
156		Child, Harriet Longshore	Nov 30-1905	F		Sac & Fox	Sac & Fox
		Father, Lee Cuppaha				Sac & Fox	Sac & Fox
		Mother, Cuppaha				Kickapoo	" "
156[sic]		Child, Louis Cuppaha	Mar 6-06	M		Sac & Fox	" "
		Father, Bull Connalis				Mexican	Sac & Fox
		Mother, Mary Connalis				Sac & Fox	Sac & Fox
156		Child, Leona "	Apr 6-06	F		" "	"
		Father, Williams				White	
		Mother, Cassie Williams				1/2 blood	Sac & Fox
157		Child, Hazel Faye Williams	Apr 6-06	F		1/4 blood	Sac & Fox
		Father, Claude Tyner				Shawnee	Shawnee
		Mother, Maggie Tyner				Sac & Fox	Sac & Fox
158		Child, William B Tyner	June 13-06	M		Sac & Fox	
		Father, Samuel Falls				Sac & Fox	Sac & Fox
		Mother, Edna Falls				Sac & Fox	Sac & Fox
158[sic]		Child, Annie Falls	June 16-06	F		Sac & Fox	Sac & Fox
		Father, Jesse Kakaque				Sac & Fox	Sac & Fox
		Mother, Dolly M McClellan				Sac & Fox	Sac & Fox
159		Child, Wallace McClellan	June 11-06	M		Sac & Fox	Sac & Fox
		Father, Allen Crain				Seminole	Sac & Fox
		Mother, Alice M Crain				Sac & Fox	Sac & Fox
160		Child, Mayme Lorea Crain	June 28-06	F		Sac & Fox	Sac & Fox
		Father, Clarence Logan				Sac & Fox	Sac & Fox
		Mother, Mattie Logan				Shawnee	Shawnee
161		Child, Emma Logan	Mar 2-06	F		Sac & Fox	Sac & Fox
		Father, Victor Neal				Sac & Fox	Sac & Fox
		Mother, Lilly Neal				Shawnee	Sac & Fox
162		Child, Mary Neal	Aug 24/06	F		Sac & Fox	Sac & Fox
		Father, Walter Nullake				Sac & Fox	Sac & Fox
		Mother, Ida Rubideaux				Sac & Fox	Sac & Fox
163		Child, John Nullake	March 22-06	M		Sac & Fox	Sac & Fox
		Father, Wm G Foster				Sac & Fox	Sac & Fox
		Mother, Flora Foster				Sac & Fox	Sac & Fox
164		Child, Emma Foster	Aug 10-06	F		Sac & Fox	Sac & Fox
		Father, Charley Murray				Iowa	Iowa
		Mother, Emily Murray	1906			Iowa	Iowa
165		Child, Orlando Murray	Mar 18	F		Iowa	Iowa
		Father, Milton Carter				Sac & Fox	Sac & Fox
		Mother, Ella Carter				Sac & Fox	Sac & Fox
166		Child, Dennis Carter	Aug 26/06	M		Sac & Fox	Sac & Fox

Sac & Fox – Shawnee
1846-1924   Volume XI

Record of Births among Indians of _____ Agency

Child's Number on this Record	Parents' Numbers on Family Register	Name	Date of Child's Birth	Sex of Child	Ages of Parents	Blood or Nationality of Parents	Tribe, or Allegiance by Citizenship, of Parents
		Father, Austin Grant				Sac & Fox	Sac & Fox
		Mother, Alice Grant				Sac & Fox	Sac & Fox
167		Child, Sadie Grant	Aug 21-06	F		Sac & Fox	Sac & Fox
		Father, Jacob Wyman				Sac & Fox	Sac & Fox
		Mother, Mary Wyman				Sac & Fox	Sac & Fox
168		Child, Charley Wyman	Aug 4/06	M		Sac & Fox	Sac & Fox
		Father, Frank Thorp				Sac & Fox	Sac & Fox
		Mother, Angeline Thorp				Pottawatomie	Sac & Fox
169		Child, Walter Thorp	Nov 8/06	M		Sac & Fox	Sac & Fox
		Father, ____ Hames				White	Sac & Fox
		Mother, Sarah M Hames				Sac & Fox	Sac & Fox
170		Child, Mamie Ruby Hames	Nov 8/06	F		Sac & Fox	Sac & Fox
		Father, Ed Emerson	Dec 30			White	Sac & Fox
		Mother, Lena Emerson	1906			Sac & Fox	Sac & Fox
171		Child, Edward Henry Emerson		M		" "	Sac & Fox
		Father, Osmond Franklin				Sac & Fox	Sac & Fox
		Mother, Maude Franklin	Dec 24			Sac & Fox	Sac & Fox
172		Child, Mary Franklin	1906	F		Sac & Fox	Sac & Fox
		Father, Alex Jefferson				Sac & Fox	Sac & Fox
		Mother, Sarah Jefferson	1906			Sac & Fox	Sac & Fox
173		Child, Emanuel Jefferson	Jan 1	M		Sac & Fox	Sac & Fox
		Father, Painter McKosito				Sac & Fox	Sac & Fox
		Mother, Annie McKosito	1906			Sac & Fox	Sac & Fox
173[sic]		Child, Abe McKosito	Dec 25	F		Sac & Fox	Sac & Fox
		Father, Dan O'Brien				Pott	Sac & Fox
		Mother, Lucy O'Brien	1906			Sac & Fox	Sac & Fox
174		Child, Edward O'Brien	Dec 28	M		Sac & Fox	
		Father, Hiram Starr				Sac & Fox	Sac & Fox
		Mother, Mandy Starr	1907			Sac & Fox	Sac & Fox
176		Child, Charles Starr	Jan 20	M		Sac & Fox	Sac & Fox
		Father, Elmer Walker					
		Mother,	1907			Kickapoo	
177		Child,	Jan 14	F			
		Father, Saginaw Grant				Sac & Fox	Sac & Fox
		Mother, Susie Grant	1907			" "	" "
178		Child, Shelah Grant	Feb 7	F			
		Father, Dan Tohee Jr				Iowa	Iowa
		Mother,	1906			"	"
179		Child, William Tohee	Dec 31	M		"	"
		Father, Pheobe Whitecloud Black				Iowa	Iowa
		Mother, ____ Black	1907			"	"
180		Child, Emma Black	Feb 8	F		"	"

Sac & Fox – Shawnee
1846-1924   Volume XI

14

Record of Births among Indians of Sac & Fox Agency

Child's Number on this Record.	Parents' Numbers on Family Register	Name.	Date of Child's Birth.	Sex of Child	Ages of Parents	Blood or Nationality of Parents	Tribe, or Allegiance by Citizenship, of Parents
181		Father, Mother, Mary Roubidoux Child, Rufus Rubidoux[sic]	1906 Nov 20			Iowa "	Iowa "
182		Father, Mother, Julia Kihega Child, Ozetta Kihega	1906 Aug 31			Iowa "	Iowa "
183		Father, Leroy Jones Mother, Child, Leroy Jones, Jr	1907 Jan 5			Sac & Fox Sac & Fox	Sac & Fox Sac & Fox
184		Father, Paul Gokey Mother, Mary Gokey Child, John Gokey	1907 Feb 17.07[sic]	M		Sac & Fox " " " "	Sac & Fox " " " "
185		Father, Mother, Jennie Meek Child, Ella Beatrice Meek	1907 Feb 19	F		White Sac & Fox " "	White " " " "
186		Father, Joe Carter Mother, Madeline Carter Child, Lola Carter	1907 March 1	F		Sac & Fox do " "	Sac & Fox " " " "
187		Father, Ed Rider Mother, Minnie Rider Child, Claud Eldridge Rider	Jan 12/07	M		White Sac & Fox " "	White Sac & Fox " "
188		Father, Jim Wood Mother, Theresa Wood Child, Stella Wood	Mar 23/07	F		White Sac & Fox " "	White Sac & Fox " "
189		Father, Ed Butler Mother, Ida Mansur Child, Ella Mansur	Apr 5/07	F		Sac & Fox " " " "	Sac & Fox " " " "
190		Father, Jackson Ellis Mother, Ruth Ellis Child, Frank Ellis	Apr 20/07	M		Sac & Fox " "	Sac & Fox " "
191		Father, Mother, Lizzie McKinney Child, Beatrice McKinney	Feb 29/07	F		Sac & Fox	Sac & Fox
192		Father, Mother, Annie Longshore Child, Herbert Longshore	May 13/07	M		Sac & Fox " "	Sac & Fox " "
193		Father, Mother, Martha Connalis Child, Juanita "	May 13/07	F		Sac & Fox do	Sac & Fox do
194		Father, Edwd McClellan Mother, Mattie Ingalls Child, Della Ingalls Ind. Name Waw-p[?]-mo[?]	July 1/07	F		Sac and Fox	Sac & Fox

Sac & Fox – Shawnee
1846-1924   Volume XI

Record of Births among Indians of Sac & Fox Agency Oklahoma

Child's Number on this Record	Parents' Numbers on Family Register		Name	Date of Child's Birth	Sex of Child	Ages of Parents	Blood or Nationality of Parents	Tribe, or Allegiance by Citizenship, of Parents
		Father,	Jim Pickering				Otoe	On Census 1907
		Mother,	Julia Pickering	1907			Iowa	Iowa
195		Child,	George Pickering	June 4	M		"	"
		Father,	William Burgess					
		Mother,	Maggie Burgess	1907			Iowa	Iowa ----
196		Child,	Carl N Burgess	July 5	M		"	"
		Father,	Sam Bassett					
		Mother,	Margaret Bassett	1907			Iowa	Iowa On Census 1907
197		Child,	Frank Bassett	May 22	M		"	"
		Father,	William Alley				Iowa	Iowa
		Mother,	------- (Otoe)	1907			Otoe	----
198		Child,	Enos Alley	July 5	M		Iowa 1/2	
		Father,	James Tyner White				Sac & Fox	
		Mother,	Ada White	1907			--------	----
199		Child,	Leonard White	June 24	M		Sac & Fox	
		Father,	Elbert Mack					
		Mother,	Laura Mack	1907			Sac and Fox	Ind Name of child
200		Child,	Henrietta Mack	Sept 1	F			Mones-se-mo-ke-magree
		Father,	Jacob Wyman					Sac & Fox
		Mother,	Mary Wyman	Sept 12			Sac & Fox	Child's Indian Name
201		Child,	Rosa Wyman	1907	F			Ma-tah-she-qua
		Father,	John E Keokuk				Sac and Fox	
		Mother,	Mabel Keokuk	Sept 19			White	
202		Child,	D Dennis Keokuk	1907	M		Sac & Fox	
		Father,	Henry Hunter					
		Mother,	Alice Hunter				Sac & Fox	Sac and Fox
203		Child,	George Hunter	May 7/07	M		do	
		Father,	Osmond Franklin					
		Mother,	Maude Franklin	Erroneous See Item No 172				
-----		Child,	Mary "	Dec 24, 1906	F		Sac & Fox	Sac and Fox
		Father,	Isaac Givens				Sac & Fox	
		Mother,	Martha Givens				Sac and Fox	Sac & Fox
204		Child,	Mary E Givens	Dec 2/07	F		" " "	
		Father,	Richard Duncan				Sac and Fox	
		Mother,	Allie Fox Duncan				" " "	
205		Child,	Robert Duncan	Mar 15/07	F		" " "	Was-ko-se-mon
		Father,	Reuben Wyman					
		Mother,	Ada Strubble or	Dec 12			Sac and Fox	Ind Name of child
206		Child,	Belle Wyman [Strubble]	1907	F			Ke-wy-kah-me
		Father,	Aaron McKinney				Sac and Fox	
		Mother,	(White)	Dec 24			White	
207		Child,	Daniel McKinney	1907	M		Sac and Fox	

Sac & Fox – Shawnee
1846-1924   Volume XI

16
Record of Births among Indians of   Sac & Fox   Agency

Child's Number on This Record	Parents' Numbers on Family Register	Name	Date of Child's Birth	Sex of Child	Ages of Parents	Blood or Nationality of Parents	Tribe, or Allegiance by Citizenship, of Parents
208		Father, Jackson Wakolle Mother, Esther Wakolle Child, Glade Wakolle	1908 Jan 8	M	35 34	Sac & Fox "	Indian Name Jah-mo-was
209		Father, Fred Barada Mother, Minnie Barada Child, Newlyn Barada	1907 Oct 24	M		White Sac & Fox	Sac & Fox
210		Father, J M Curtis Mother, Fannie Curtis Child, Juanita Evalena Curtis	Jan 29 08	F		White Sac & Fox	
211		Father, Paul Gokey Mother, Lizzie Gokey Child, Agnes Gokey	1908 Feb 12	F		Sac and Fox	Sac and Fox
212		Father, Walter Mathews Mother, Nannie Mathews Child, Annie Mathews	1908 Feb 10	F		Sac & Fox Shawnee Sac & Fox	
213		Father, Dan McCoy Mother, Mary McCoy Child, Timothy McCoy	1908 March 11	M		Sac & Fox White	
214		Father, Fred Brown Mother, Brown, Julia Child, " Elsie F	Born Nov 11/1907	F		White Sac & Fox " " "	S & F
215		Father, George Butler Mother, Edith Butler Child, Dewey Butler	Mar 10 1908	M		Sac & Fox	Sac & Fox
216		Father, Mother, Tyner, Maggie Child, " Ralph Benjamin	Mar 11 1908	M		Sac & Fox Sac & Fox	
217		Father, Neal, Victor Mother, " Libby Child, " Pearl	Mar 30 1908	F		Sac & Fox Sac & Fox	Sac & Fox
218		Father, Williams Mother, " Cassie Child, Elsie Marie [Williams]	Mar 12, 1908	F	42	Sac & Fox Sac & Fox	Sac & Fox
		Father, John McClellan Mother, Fannie " Child, Ethel McClellan	May 1st, 1908	F		Sac & Fox " " " " " "	Sac & Fox
219		Father, Mother, Alice M Crain Child, Allen Lenard Crain	Apr 26/08	M		Sac and Fox " "	Sac & Fox
220		Father, Henry Black Mother, Phoebe Black Child, Fannie Black	May 1-08	F		Otoe Iowa	Otoe Iowa

Sac & Fox – Shawnee
1846-1924   Volume XI

Record of Births among Indians of Sac & Fox Agency

Child's Number on this Record	Parents' Numbers on Family Register	Name	Date of Child's Birth	Sex of Child	Ages of Parents	Blood or Nationality of Parents	Tribe, or Allegiance by Citizenship, of Parents
		Father, Charley Kihega			36	Iowa	Iowa
		Mother, Julia Kihega			31	"	"
221		Child, Francis Kihega	May 11/08	M		"	"
		Father, Edward Rice			37	Sac & Fox	
		Mother, Edith Appletree			29	"	
222		Child, Samuel F Rice	May 8, 08	M		"	
		Father, Hugh Wakolle			39	Sac & Fox	Sac & Fox
		Mother, Mabell "			30	"	
223		Child, Ben "	April 1, 08	M		"	
		Father, Ben Walker			26	Sac & Fox	Sac & Fox
		Mother, Dora "			25	"	
224		Child, Willard "	Apr 1, 08	M		"	
		Father, Leroy Jones 1909			23	Sac & Fox	Sac & Fox
		Mother,				White	"
224		Child, Frances Orales	Aug 5, 08	F		Sac & Fox	Sac & Fox
		Father, Frank Nawanoway Kent			47	Iowa	Iowa
		Mother, Emma " "			31	"	"
225		Child, Bessie " "	Aug 3, 08	F		"	"
		Father, Walter Nullake			27	Sac and Fox	Sac and Fox
		Mother, Jada Roubideaux				" "	" "
225		Child, Pe ah nu squet Alice Nullake	Aug 7-08	F		" "	" "
		Father, Hiram Star			25	" "	" "
		Mother, Manda Star Fa-mo-thaw-haw			35	" "	" "
226		Child, Leona Star	Sept 26/08	F		" "	" "
		Father, Alex Jefferson				Sac and Fox	Sac and Fox
		Mother, Sarah Jefferson				" "	" "
227		Child, Omer Jefferson	Oct 7/08	M		" "	" "
		Father, Edward George Butler				Sac and Fox	Sac and Fox
		Mother, Ida Mansur				" "	" "
228		Child, Gertie Mansur	Oct 3/08	F		" " "	" " "
		Father, Painter Mc Kosito			45	Sac and Fox	Sac and Fox
		Mother, Annie Mc Kosito			29	" "	" "
229		Child, Kaw-Kaw-Keese	Oct 15-08	M		" "	" "
		Father,				Sac and Fox	Sac and Fox
		Mother, Julia Masquot			25	" "	" "
230		Child, Norwood Masquot	Oct 17-08	M		" "	" "
		Father,					
		Mother, Lizzie Casteel				Sac and Fox	Sac and Fox
		Child, Elizabeth Casteel	Oct 26-08	F		" "	" "
		Father, Guy Whistler		M			Sac and Fox
		Mother, Margaret Whistler				White	
231		Child, Mary Frances Whistler	Nov 26-08	F			" "

Sac & Fox – Shawnee
1846-1924   Volume XI

18
Record of Births among Indians of Sac & Fox Agency

Child's Number on This Record	Parents' Numbers on Family Register	Name	Date of Child's Birth	Sex of Child	Ages of Parents	Blood or Nationality of Parents	Tribe, or Allegiance by Citizenship, of Parents
		Father, Dan O'Brien				Shawnee	Shawnee
		Mother, Lucy O'Brien			37	Sac and Fox	Sac and Fox
232		Child, Emily Lucinda O'Brien	11/28 '08	F		" " "	" " "
		Father, Randal Franklin				Sac and Fox	Sac and Fox
		Mother, Sora Ellis "				Shawnee	Shawnee
233		Child, Se-sa-ho	11/30 '08	M		Sac and Fox	Sac and Fox
		Father, Charley Longshore				White	White
		Mother, Annie "				Sac and Fox	Sac and Fox
234		Child, Iola E "	Dec 18-08	F		"	"
		Father, Austin Grant				Sac and Fox	Sac and Fox
		Mother, Alice "				"	"
234		Child, Myrtle Grant	Jan 7-09	F		"	"
		Father, J E Keokuk				Sac and Fox	Sac and Fox
		Mother, Mabel Keokuk				White	White citizen
235		Child, J Earle Keokuk	Jan 28-09	M		Sac and Fox	Sac and Fox
		Father, Leo Gokey			32	Sac and Fox	Sac and Fox
		Mother, Lizzie Gokey				Miama[sic]	
236		Child, Rosetta Gokey	Dec 8-08	F		Sac and Fox	Sac and Fox
		Father, Jackson Ellis			25	Sac and Fox	Sac and Fox
		Mother, Ruth Grayeyes Ellis			24	Sac and Fox	Sac and Fox
237		Child, Katie Ellis	Feb 19-09	F		Sac and Fox	Sac and Fox
		Father, ~~Arthur~~ Jones Artemus			19	Sac and Fox	Sac and Fox
		Mother, Pansy "				White	White
238		Child, Leona Mildred Jones	Feb 27-09	F		Sac and Fox	Sac and Fox
		Father, Thomas Miles			48	Sac and Fox	Sac and Fox
		Mother, Rhoda Miles			32	Sac and Fox	Sac and Fox
239		Child, Howard Taft Miles	March 8-09	M		Sac and Fox	Sac and Fox
		Father, Joe Boyd				Mexican	Mexican
		Mother, Christine F Boyd	Died March 23, 09		18	Sac and Fox	Sac and Fox
240		Child, Lizzie Boyd	March 5-09	F		Sac and Fox	Sac and Fox
		Father, Elbert Mack			32	Sac and Fox	Sac and Fox
		Mother, Laura Mack			27	Sac and Fox	Sac and Fox
241		Child, Lorena Mack	March 5-09	F		Sac and Fox	Sac and Fox
		Father, E H Emmerson				White	White
		Mother, ~~Alice Gertrude~~ Emmerson Lina			26	Sac and Fox	Sac and Fox
242		Child, Frederick William Emmerson	March 1-09	M		Sac and Fox	Sac and Fox
		Father, Falls, Samuel			27	Sac and Fox	Sac and Fox
		Mother, Edna Falls			28	Sac and Fox	Sac and Fox
243		Child, William Falls boy	Jan 3-09	M		Sac and Fox	Sac and Fox
		Father, Edward McClellan				Sac and Fox	
		Mother, Mattie Ingalls			37	Sac and Fox	Sac and Fox
244		Child, Stella Ingals[sic]	Feb 25-09	F		Sac and Fox	Sac and Fox

Sac & Fox – Shawnee
1846-1924   Volume XI

Record of Births among Indians of Sac & Fox Agency

Child's Number on this Record	Parents' Numbers on Family Register		Name	Date of Child's Birth	Sex of Chil. d	Ages of Parents	Blood or Nationality of Parents	Tribe, or Allegiance by Citizenship, of Parents
		Father,	John Isaac Goodell			19	Sac and Fox	Sac and Fox
		Mother,						
246		Child,	Larona Modesta "	3/22-09	F		Sac and Fox	Sac and Fox
		Father,	Bud Conalis[sic] Joe				American	------------
		Mother,	Martha Conalis			24	Sac and Fox	Sac and Fox
247		Child,	Joseph Conalis	4/5-09	M		Sac and Fox	Sac and Fox
		Father,	George Morton			23	Sac and Fox	Sac and Fox
		Mother,					Shawnee	Shawnee
247		Child,	Celester Morton	4/20-09	F		Sac and Fox	Sac and Fox
		Father,	Willis Taylor Ne-pa-so-qua				White	White
		Mother,	Gertie Taylor			20	Sac and Fox	Sac and Fox
248		Child,	Willis Lee Taylor	4-21-09	M		Sac and Fox	Sac and Fox
		Father,	H M LaBelle				Sioux	cen Filed under
24[sic]		Mother,	Linda LaBelle			24	Sac and Fox	Labelle Sac and Fox
248		Child,	Clifford E LaBelle	3-22-09	M		Sac and Fox	Sac and Fox
		Father,	Edgar Jennings				White	White
		Mother,	Mamie F Jennings			20	Sac and Fox	Sac and Fox
249		Child,	Pearl Elizabeth Jennings	6-8-09	F		Sac and Fox	Sac and Fox
		Father,	Albert Wilson				Mexican	
		Mother,	Mary Wilson			18	Sac & Fox	Sac and Fox
250		Child,	Israel Wilson	May 16, 1909	M		Sac and Fox	Sac and Fox
		Father,	Bill Scott				Sac & Fox	Sac & Fox
		Mother,	Helen Scott			16	Sac and Fox	Tama, City-Iowa Sac and Fox
251		Child,	Winfield Scott	Mar 24-09	M		Sac and Fox	Sac and Fox
		Father,	James Tyner White				Sac and Fox	Sac and Fox
		Mother,						
252		Child,	Lahoma Edith White	July 6, 1909	F		Sac and Fox	Sac and Fox
		Father,	Edwin L Moore			27	Sac and Fox	Sac and Fox
		Mother,	Claudia Moore				Cherokee	Cherokee
253		Child,	Mildred Elizabeth Moore	July 10, 1909	F		Sac and Fox	Sac and Fox
		Father,	Joseph Carter			37	Sac and Fox	Sac and Fox
		Mother,	Madaline Carter			31	Sac and Fox	Sac and Fox
254		Child,	Andrew Carter	Aug 28, 1909	M			
		Father,	D N Meek				White	White
		Mother,	Jennie Meek				Sac & Fox 1/2	Sac & Fox
255		Child,	Frances Cecelia Meek	Aug 21-09	F		Sac & Fox 1/4	Sac & Fox
		Father,	Omer D Lewis				Pottawatomie	Citizen Pottawatomie
		Mother,	Pauline Lewis				Sac & Fox	Sac & Fox
256		Child,	Paulena Montana Lewis	Oct 16-09	F		Sac & Fox	Sac & Fox
		Father,	Lee Cuppawhe		M	32	Sac & Fox	Sac & Fox
		Mother,	Ah-ke-na-nah-tho			37	Kickapoo	Kickapoo
257		Child,	Henry Cuppawhe	May 30-09				

Sac & Fox – Shawnee
1846-1924 Volume XI

20

Record of Births among Indians of   Sac & Fox   Agency

Child's Number on this Record.	Parents' Numbers on Family Register		Name.	Date of Child's Birth.	Sex of Child	Ages of Parents	Blood or Nationality of Parents	Tribe, or Allegiance by Citizenship, of Parents
		Father,	Levi W Jones			31		Sac & Fox, Okla
		Mother,	Mrs " " Jones					
258		Child,	William Woodward Jones	Nov 20, 1909	M			Sac & Fox, Okla
		Father,	Alex Jefferson			32	Sac & Fox	Sac & Fox, Okla
		Mother,	Savola Jefferson			32	Sac & Fox	Sac & Fox, Okla
259		Child,	James Thurman "	Nov 15, 1909	M			Sac & Fox, Okla
		Father,						
		~~Child~~ ~~Mother~~,	Pauline McClellan	Sept 28-09				Sac & Fox, Okla
260		~~Mother~~ ~~Child~~,	Dolly McClellan		F	35	Sac & Fox	Sac & Fox, Okla
		Father,	Frank Thorp			29	Sac & Fox (1/2)	
		Mother,	Angeline ~~Angie~~ Thorp				Pottawatomie	
261		Child,	Bernice Thorp	Dec 8-09	M			Sac & Fox, Okla
		Father,	John McClellan			41	Full Blood	Sac & Fox, Okla
		Mother,	Fannie McClellan			34	" "	" " "
262		Child,	Ernest McClellan	Sep 9, 1909	M			" " "
		Father,	Daniel O'Brien				Full Blood	Pottawatomie
		Mother,	Lucy O'Brien			38	Half-breed Indian blood	
263		Child,	Lucille O'Brien	Jan 16-10	F		Sac&Fox and Cherokee	Sac & Fox, Okla
		Father,	Charlie Longshore				White	White
		Mother,	Annie Longshore			28	Sac & Fox	Sac & Fox, Okla
264		Child,	Ida Longshore	Dec 18, 1908	F			Sac & Fox, Okla
		Father,	John T Capper			32	Sac & Fox	
		Mother,	Mabel Capper			25	White	
265		Child,	Alfred Rodell Capper	Feb 15, 1910	M			Sac & Fox, Okla
		Father,	Jim Wood				White	
		Mother,	Theresa Wood			23	Half-blood	
266		Child,	Ethelyn Gladys Wood	Feb 13, 1910	F			Sac & Fox, Okla
		Father,	Victor Dupee			54	Full Blood Iowa	
		Mother,						
267		Child,	Louis Dupee	Nov 26, 1909	M			Iowa
	Saginaw	Father,	~~Ulyses~~ S Grant, Char			54	Sac and Fox	
		Mother,	~~Lydia~~ Grant Stella			44	Sac and Fox	
268		Child,	Ulyses S Grant, Jr (Qua quaw tah)	Mar 28-10	M			
		Father,	Hugh Wakolle			40	Sac & Fox	Sac & Fox, Okla
		Mother,	Mabel Wakolle			31	Sac & Fox	Sac & Fox, Okla
269		Child,	Waw-sha-law	Apr 5, 1910	M			
		Father,	Blaine Kent					
		Mother,						
270		Child,	Theodore Kent	Feb 3, 1910	M			
		Father,	Osmond Franklin			27	Sac & Fox, Okla	
		Mother,	Rachel Franklin			22	" " "	
280 [sic]		Child,	Cora Franklin	Apr 29, 1910	F			

Sac & Fox – Shawnee
1846-1924   Volume XI

Record of Births among Indians of Sac & Fox, Okla. Agency

Child's Number on this Record	Parents' Numbers on Family Register	Name	Date of Child's Birth	Sex of Child	Ages of Parents	Blood or Nationality of Parents	Tribe, or Allegiance by Citizenship, of Parents
		Father, Aaron McKinney					
		Mother,			29	Sac & Fox (1/2)	
281		Child, Myrtle May McKinney	Apr 19, 1910	F			
		Father, David Harris			21	Sac & Fox	Sac & Fox, Okla
		Mother, Anna Harris			18	Sac & Fox	Sac & Fox, Okla
282		Child, Battice "	May 14, 1910				
		Father, Joe A Boyd				Mexican	
		Mother, Christine F Boyd			19	Sac & Fox	
283		Child, Rosie Boyd	May 11, 1910	F			
		Father, Painter McKosito			46	Sac & Fox (full)	
		Mother, Annie McKosito			30	" " " "	
284		Child, -------- McKosito	May 14, 1910	M			
		Father, Painter McKosito			46	Sac & Fox (full)	
		Mother, Annie McKosito			30	" " " "	
285		Child, -------- McKosito	May 14, 1910				
		Father, Jackson Wakolle			36	Sac & Fox (full)	
		Mother, Ester Wakolle			35	" " " "	
286		Child, Cora Wakolle (Pem-o-toe)	May 10, 1910	F			
		Father, George Butler			23	Sac & Fox (full)	
		Mother, Edith Butler			23	" " " "	
287		Child, Carl Butler	Jun 19, 1910	M			
		Father, Frank Nawanoway (Kent)				Iowa	Iowa
		Mother,					
288		Child, Samuel [Nawanoway]	May 28, 1910	M			
		Father, Harnes, William				White	
		Mother, " Sarah M			32	Sac & Fox	
289		Child, " Avis Eleanor	Aug 28-10	F			
		Father,					
		Mother, Maggie Tyner			33	Sac & Fox	
290		Child, Alice "	Dec 22-09				
		Father, Artemus Jones			20	Sac & Fox	
		Mother,					
291		Child, Henry Lee Jones	Sept 4, 1910	M			
		Father, Taylor, J W				White	
		Mother, Gertie Taylor			21	Sac & Fox	
292		Child, Eugene Lewis Taylor	1910	M			
		Father, George Masquat				Kickapoo	
		Mother, Juliet Masquat			27	Sac and Fox (full)	
293		Child, Narcissus Masquat	Oct 20, 1910	M			
		Father, George T Brown					
		Mother, Julia Brown			32	Sac & Fox (1/2)	
294		Child, Lorena Julia Brown (named after mother)	Oct 19, 1910	F			

Sac & Fox – Shawnee
1846-1924   Volume XI

22

Record of Births among Indians of _____ Agency

Child's Number on this Record	Parents' Numbers on Family Register	Name	Date of Child's Birth	Sex of Child	Ages of Parents	Blood or Nationality of Parents	Tribe, or Allegiance by Citizenship, of Parents
		Father, John Keokuk			31	Sac & Fox (half blood)	S & F
		Mother, Mabel "					
295		Child, Dorothy Luella "	Nov 5, 1910	F			
		Father, Ben Walker			27	Sac & Fox (f. b.)	S & F
		Mother, Dora "			26	" " " (f. b.)	S & F
296		Child, Frances "	June 27-10	F			
		Father, James Clarence Casteel				White	
		Mother, Elizabeth M°Kinney "				1/2 Sac & Fox	
297		Child, Edith Clarence "	Nov 7-10	F			
		Father, Jacob Wyman			33	Sac & Fox (f. b.)	S & F
		Mother, Mary Wyman			30	" " " (f. b.)	S & F
298		Child, (My-ah-che) Frank	Nov 22, 1910	M			
		Father, Walter Nullake			29	Sac & Fox	
		Mother, Ida (Nah-naw-ah-kah)					
299		Child, Watt "	Dec 5, 1910	M			
		Father, Harding Franklin				Sac & Fox	
		Mother, Nannie Mathews					
300		Child, Ray Mathews	Oct 18, 1910	M		Do not enroll here ←	
		Father, Fletcher Hensley					
		Mother, Minnie Rider Hensley					
301		Child, Guy Garfield Hensley	Dec 28, 1910	M			
		Father,					
		Mother, Martha Conallis				Sac & Fox	
302		Child, James Conallis	Jan 5, 1911	M			
		Father, Richard Duncan			35	Sac & Fox	
		Mother, Alice Fox Duncan			32	Sac & Fox	
303		Child, Richard Duncan Jr	Jan 18, 1911	M			
		Father, Jackson Ellis			28	Sac & Fox	
		Mother, Ruth Ellis			27	Sac & Fox	
304		Child, Minnie Ellis	Jan 27, 1911	F			
		Father, Hamblen, Frank W					
		Mother, " Lydia			33	Sac & Fox	
305		Child, " Pauline	Feb 1, 1911	F			
		Father, Tohee, Ed			28	Iowa	
		Mother,					
306		Child, " Noah	Nov 18, 1910	M			
		Father, Spooner, Irwin			20	Munsee	
		Mother, " Ida			19	Sac & Fox	
307		Child, " Beatrice	Feb 19, 1911	F			
		Father, Gokey, Leo			34	Sac and Fox	
		Mother,					
308		Child, " Elmer	Apr 13, 1911	M			

Sac & Fox – Shawnee
1846-1924 Volume XI

Record of Births among Indians of Agency

Child's Number on this Record	Parents' Numbers on Family Register		Name	Date of Child's Birth	Sex of Child	Ages of Parents	Blood or Nationality of Parents	Tribe, or Allegiance by Citizenship, of Parents
		Father,	Charley Kihega			39	Iowa (f. b.)	Iowa
		Mother,	Julia Kihega			34	" " "	"
309		Child,	Lillian L Kihega	June 4, 1911	F		" " "	
		Father,	Charley Smith			26	S & F (F. B.)	S & F, Okla
		Mother,	Theresa Smith			16	" " "	" " "
310		Child,	Grace Smith	June 3, 1911	F		" " "	
		Father,	Guy Whistler			23	S & F (f.b.)	Sac & Fox, Okla
		Mother,	Maggie Whistler				White	" " "
311		Child,	John Whistler (Che-ko-skuk)	June 20-11	M			"
		Father,	Randall Franklin			22		
		Mother,	Doris Franklin					
312		Child,	" Franklin (boy)	July 6/11	M			
		Father,	Robert Roubidoux					
		Mother,	Emily Roubidoux			33	Iowa	Iowa
313		Child,	Magdalene Roubidoux	Apr 26-11	F		"	"
		Father,	Frank Nawanoway			50	Iowa	Iowa
		Mother,	Emma Nawanoway			34	Iowa	"
314		Child,	Rachel Nawanoway	June 3-11	M		Iowa	
		Father,	Scott, William				Sac & Fox (Ia)	
		Mother,	Scott, Helen			18	" " Okla	
315		Child,	Scott,	October '11	M	18		
		Father,	Grass, Silas				Sac & Fox	Sac & Fox, Okla
		Mother,	Grass, Ada				" " "	" " "
316		Child,	" Silas, Jr	June 24, 1911	M	1 [sic]	" " "	
		Father,	Cuppawhe, Lee	Mar 1911	M	33	Sac & Fox	Sac & Fox, Okla
		Mother,						
317		Child,	Cuppawhe, Lee Jr	March 1911	M		" " "	
		Father,	Franklin, Randall			22	Sac & Fox	Sac & Fox, Okla
		Mother,	"					
318		Child,	" Randall, Jr	July 6-1911	M		"	
		Father,	Murdock, William				Kickapoo	
		Mother,	Murdock, Etta			20	S & F (f.b.)	Sac & Fox, Okla
319		Child,	" Edison	Aug 3, 1911	M			
		Father,	Appletree, Henry			38	S & F (f.b.)	Sac & Fox, Okla
		Mother,	Appletree, Susan			19	" " " "	" " "
320		Child,	Appletree, Eugenia	May 27-1911	F			
		Father,	Falls, Samuel			29	S & F (f.b.)	Sac & Fox, Okla
		Mother,	" Edna			30	" " " "	" " "
321		Child,	" Addie	Aug 17, 1911	F			
		Father,	Nawanoway, Blaine			18	Iowa	
		Mother,	" Rosa				Shawnee	
322		Child,	" Ben	Aug 9, 1911	M			

Sac & Fox – Shawnee
1846-1924 Volume XI

24

Record of Births among Indians of   Agency

Child's Number on this Record	Parents' Numbers on Family Register	Name	Date of Child's Birth	Sex of Child	Ages of Parents	Blood or Nationality of Parents	Tribe, or Allegiance by Citizenship, of Parents
		Father, Carter, Joe			39	Sac & Fox	Sac & Fox, Okla
		Mother, " Madaline			33	" " "	" " "
325		Child, " Della	Aug 23-11	F			
		Father, Morris, Thomas			25	Sac & Fox	Sac & Fox, Okla
		Mother, " Caroline			20	" " "	" " "
326		Child, " Evelyn	Aug 31-11	F			
		Father, Harry Hunter			34	Sac & Fox	Sac & Fox, Okla
		Mother, Alice Hunter			32	" "	" " "
327		Child, Mary Hunter	Aug 28-11	F			
		Father, Dan McCoy			36	Sac & Fox	Sac & Fox, Okla
		Mother, Mary "				White	
328		Child, Elburne "	Sept 20-11	M			
		Father, Ernest Wright				White	
		Mother, Irene Wright			18	Sac & Fox	Sac & Fox, Okla
329		Child, Cedro "	Oct 10-11	M			
		Father, Austin Grant			31	Sac & Fox	Sac & Fox, Okla
		Mother, Alice Grant			31	" " "	" " "
330		Child, Nona Grant	Sept 19-11	F			
		Father, Alex Jefferson			35	Sac & Fox	Sac & Fox, Okla
		Mother, Sarah "			35	" " "	
331		Child, Benjamin Franklin Jefferson	Nov 7-1911	M			
		Father, Edgar Jennings			24	White	
		Mother, Mamie Jennings			23	Sac & Fox	Sac & Fox, Okla
332		Child, Cecelia Maybell "	Nov 6, 1911	F			
		Father,				Shawnee	
		Mother, Maggie Tyner			35	Sac & Fox	Sac & Fox, Okla
333		Child, Raymond Tyner	Oct 19, 1911	M			
		Father, McClellan, John			43	Sac & Fox	Sac & Fox, Okla
		Mother, " Fannie			36	" " "	
334		Child, McClellan, Mamie	Dec 23, 1911	F			
		Father, Clarence Casteel				White	
		Mother, Lizzie "			29	Sac & Fox	Sac & Fox, Okla
335		Child, Reba "	Dec 25, 1911	F			
		Father, Painter McKosito			49	Sac & Fox	Sac & Fox, Okla
		Mother, Annie "			33	" " "	" " "
336		Child, Matilda "	Jan 17, 1912	F			
		Father, Frank Thorp			31	Sac & Fox	Sac & Fox, Okla
		Mother, " Thorp				Pottawatomie	
337		Child, Minnie Thorp	Jan 26, 1912	F			
		Father, Dickson Duncan			25	Sac & Fox	Sac & Fox, Okla
		Mother, Lilly Neal				Shawnee	
338		Child, Alice Duncan	Jan 2, 1912	F	(Not taken up on current roll Taken up later by order IO		

270

Sac & Fox – Shawnee
1846-1924   Volume XI

Record of Births among Indians of _____ Agency

Child's Number on this Record	Parents' Numbers on Family Register	Name	Date of Child's Birth	Sex of Child	Ages of Parents	Blood or Nationality of Parents	Tribe, or Allegiance by Citizenship, of Parents
		Father, Silas Grass			29	Sac & Fox	Sac & Fox, Okla
		Mother, Ada Grass			24	" " "	" " " "
339		Child, Emery "	Feb 6, 1912	M			
		Father, Elmer Walker			27	Sac & Fox	Sac & Fox, Okla
		Mother,					
340		Child, Andrew "	Jan 25, 1912	M			
		Father, Saginaw Grant			25	Sac & Fox	Sac & Fox, Okla
		Mother, Stella Grant			23	" " "	" " " "
341		Child, Ah ne ko wa Grant	Feb 24, 1912	M			
		Father, Levi M Jones			34	Sac & Fox	Sac & Fox, Okla
		Mother,				White	
342		Child, Robert Dwight Jones	Mar 6-12	M			
		Father, Harris, David			24	Sac & Fox	Sac & Fox, Okla
		Mother, " Annie G			21	" " "	" " " "
343		Child, " George William	Mar 28-12	M			
		Father, Sponer[sic], Irwin			22	Munsee	
		Mother, " Ida			20	Sac & Fox	Sac & Fox, Okla
344		Child, " Mary Elizabeth	Mar 13-12	F			
		Father, Starr, Hiram			29	Sac & Fox	Sac & Fox, Okla
		Mother, " Mandy			39	" " "	" " " "
345		Child, " Mabel	Feb 28-12	F			
		Father, Taylor				White	
		Mother, " Gertie			23	Sac & Fox	Sac & Fox, Okla
346		Child, " Sarah Harriet	Apr 5-12	F			
~~345~~		Father, Longshore, [Illegible]			31	Sac & Fox	Sac & Fox, Okla
		Mother, "				White	
347		Child, " Edward	May 3-12	M			
		Father, McCoy, David			20	Sac & Fox	Sac & Fox, Okla
		Mother, " Lizzie			21	do	do
348		Child, " David, Jr	May 16=12	M		"	"
		Father, Springer, Joseph			48	Iowa	Sac & Fox, Okla
		Mother, " Josie			43	do	do
349		Child, " Grace	June 19-12	F			"
		Father, Meek				White	
		Mother, " Jennie			42	Sac & Fox	Sac & Fox, Okla
350		Child, " Marie Fern	June 7, 1912	F		do	do
		Father, Joe Boyd					
		Mother, Christine F Boyd			21	Sac & Fox	
351		Child, Cora "	Aug 15, 1912	F			
		Father,					
		Mother, Connalis, Martha			27	Sac & Fox	
352		Child, Connalis, Viola Marie	Aug 6, 1912	F		" "	

271

Sac & Fox – Shawnee
1846-1924   Volume XI

26
Record of Births among Indians of   Agency

Child's Number on this Record	Parents' Numbers on Family Register	Name	Date of Child's Birth	Sex of Child	Ages of Parents	Blood or Nationality of Parents	Tribe, or Allegiance by Citizenship, of Parents
353		Father, Mah-ke-kiah Jim Scott Jr Mother, Martha Givens nee Baker Child, Waw-sah-ko;	Aug 26, 1912	F	20	Sac and Fox(Iowa) Sac and Fox(Okla)	Tama City Iowa Indian Reported by Collins
354		Father, Jackson Wakolle Mother, Esther Wakolle Child, Grace Wakolle	July 31, 1912	F	39 38	Sac and Fox Sac and Fox Sac and Fox	Reported by mother
355		Father, Claud Chandler Mother, Leona Chandler Child, Claudia Elizabeth Chandler	Sept 18, 1912	F	29	Cherokee Sac and Fox	Reported by father
356		Father, Jacob Dole Mother, Amelia Dole Child, Peter Dole	Sept 17, 1912	M	25 27	Iowa Iowa	Reported by Collins
357		Father, Albert D Kenyon Mother, Isabel Kenyon, nee barney[sic] Child, Jewel Virginia Kenyon	Nov 25, 1912	F	18	Sac & Fox Sac & Fox	Reported by mother
358		Father, Ira Walker Mother, Child, Harold F Walker	Nov 25, 1912	M	24	Sac & Fox White Sac & Fox	(Verified by Gayle) Reported by father
559[sic]		Father, John W Foote Mother, Fannie K Foote nee Keokuk Child, John Foote, Jr	Sept 10, 1912	M		White Sac & Fox	Reported by mother
560		Father, Talbert White Mother, Child, Milton Barb White	Dec 5, 1912	M		Sac & Fox White Sac & Fox	Reported by father (Verified by Gayle)
561		Father, Henry Appletree Mother, Susan Appletree Child, Robert Appletree	Jan 9, 1913	M		Sac & Fox " " " " " "	Reported by Collins
562		Father, Elmer Manatowa Mother, Grace " Child, Lorena Louisa Manatowa	Feb 7, 1913	F		Sac & Fox White	Reported by Collins
563		Father, Blaine Nawanoway Mother, Rosa " Child, Ruth Madeline Nawanoway	Nov 29-12	F		Iowa Shawnee	Reported by Collins
564		Father, Ben Walker Mother, Dora Walker Child, Harry Benson Walker	Jan 2-13	M		Sac & Fox " " " " " "	Reported by Gayle
565		Father, Jackson Ellis Mother, Ruth Ellis Child, Flora Ellis	Mar 9-13	F		Sac & Fox " " " " " "	Reported by Collins
566		Father, Mother, Hazel Furrow Child, Maxine "	Dec 11-12	F		White Sac & Fox " " "	Reported by Collins

Sac & Fox – Shawnee
1846-1924 Volume XI

Record of Births among Indians of _____ Agency

Child's Number on this Record	Parents' Numbers on Family Register	Name	Date of Child's Birth	Sex of Child	Ages of Parents	Blood or Nationality of Parents	Tribe, or Allegiance by Citizenship, of Parents
		Father,					
		Mother, Hazel Furrow				Sac & Fox	
567		Child, Momie "	Dec 11, 1912	F		" " "	Rep by Collins
		Father, Eveline Givens				Sac & Fox	
		Mother, Matilda "				" " "	
568		Child, Wa-the-no-tha	Dec 28, 1912	M		" " "	Rep by Collins
		Father, Paul Gokey				Sac & Fox	
		Mother, Lilly Gokey					
569		Child, Catherine Gokey	Apr 4, 1913	F			Rep by T P Myers
		Father, Walter M Hodsdon				White	
		Mother, Bertha Hodsdon				Sac & Fox	
570		Child, Harriet Proctor Hodsdon	Feb 22, 1913	F		" " "	Rep by father
		Father, Elbert Mack				Sac & Fox	
		Mother, Laura Mack				" " "	(verified by Gayle)
571		Child, Kaw-waw-so Mack	May 15, 1913	M		" " "	Rep by father
		Father, George Masquat					
		Mother, Juliet Masquat				Sac & Fox	
572		Child, Chuck'e'quah Hilda Masquat	May 18, 1913	F		" " "	Rep by Collins
		Father, Walter Nullake				Sac & Fox	
		Mother, Ida Nullake					(verified by Gayle)
573		Child, George Nullake	May 18, 1913	M		Sac & Fox	Rep by father
		Father, Samuel Falls				Sac & Fox	
		Mother, Edna Falls				" " "	
574		Child, Kishko Falls	May 23, 1913	M		" " "	Rep by Alex Connolly
		Father, Harvey Labelle					
		Mother, Linda Labelle				Sac & Fox	
575		Child, Edith Rose Labelle	Apr 18, 1913	F		" " "	Rep by Collins
		Father, George G Foster				Sac & Fox	
		Mother, Jane Foster (nee Butler)				" " "	
576		Child, Catherine Foster	Apr 18, 1913	F		" " "	verified by Gayle
		Father, ~~Harvey Labelle~~					
		Mother, ~~Linda Labelle~~					
~~577~~		Child, ~~Edith Rose Labelle~~					
		Father, Charlie Smith				Sac & Fox	
		Mother, Theresa Smith				" " "	
577		Child, Cora Smith	June 2, 1913	F		" " "	
		Father, Edward Butler				Sac & Fox	
		Mother, Ida Butler				" " "	
578		Child, Mamie Butler	May 2, 1913	F		" " "	Rep by Collins
		Father, Saginaw Grant				Sac & Fox	
		Mother, Stella Grant				" " "	
		Child, Charley Grant	July 3, 1913	M		" " "	Rep by Collins

Sac & Fox – Shawnee
1846-1924   Volume XI

28

Record of Births among Indians of   Agency

Child's Number on this Record	Parents' Numbers on Family Register	Name	Date of Child's Birth	Sex of Child	Ages of Parents	Blood or Nationality of Parents	Tribe, or Allegiance by Citizenship, of Parents
		Father, George Butler				Sac & Fox	
		Mother, Edith "				" " "	
579		Child, Pearl "	Aug 3, 1913	F		" " "	Rep by Collins
		Father, Hugh Wakolle				Sac & Fox	
		Mother, Mabel Wakolle				" " "	
580		Child, Guy Wakolle	June 20, 1913	M		" " "	
		Father, Alex Jefferson				Sac & Fox	
		Mother, Sarah Jefferson				" " "	
581		Child, Etheline Jefferson	Aug 7, 1913	F		" " "	
		Father, Jacob Wyman				Sac & Fox	
		Mother, Mary Wyman				" " "	
582		Child, Bertha Wyman	Sept 15, 1913	F		" " "	
		Father, Robert T Pate				White	
		Mother, Nellie R Pate				Sac & Fox	
583		Child, Robert Charles Pate	Aug 27, 1913	M		"	Rep by Collins
		Father, Silas Grass				Sac & Fox	
		Mother, Ada Grass				" " "	
584		Child, Ne-ta-ko-tha Grass	Oct 1, 1913	F		" " "	Rep by Collins
		Father, Joseph Carter				Sac & Fox	
		Mother, Madeline Carter				" " "	
585		Child, Florence Carter	Nov 13, 1913	F		" " "	Rep by Chandler
		Father, Jennings				White	
		Mother, Mamie Jennings				Sac & Fox	
586		Child, Edwin Cornelius Jennings	Nov 14/1913	M		" " "	Rep by Chandler
		Father, Spooner				Munsee	
		Mother, Ida Spooner				Sac & Fox	
587		Child, Burnice Henrietta Spooner	Nov 12, 1913	F		Sac & Fox	
		Father, Peyton Keokuk				Sac and Fox	
		Mother, Claudia Keokuk				White	
588		Child, Katherine Lucile Keokuk	Oct 9, 1913	F			Rep by Collins
		Father, Earnest Wright				White	
		Mother, Irene Wright				Sac and Fox	verification
589		Child, Mary Emily Wright	July 3, 1913	F			made by Mrs Annie Longshore
		Father, Benjamin Harris				Sac and Fox	
		Mother, Grace Harris				White	
590		Child, Marie Harris	Dec 17, 1913				Rep by WM Hodsdon
		Father, Willie Springer (Alley)				Iowa	
		Mother,					Reported by
591		Child, Daniel Alley	Mar 7, 1912	M			Supt Otoe Ind School
		Father, Randall Franklin					
		Mother, Sora "					Reported by
592		Child, Benjamin "	Oct 24, 1912	M			Frank Carter

Sac & Fox – Shawnee
1846-1924   Volume XI

Record of Births among Indians of   Agency

Child's Number on This Record	Parents' Numbers on Family Register	Name	Date of Child's Birth	Sex of Child	Ages of Parents	Blood or Nationality of Parents	Tribe, or Allegiance by Citizenship, of Parents
593		Father, Albert D Kenyon				White	
		Mother, Isabel Kenyon				Sac and Fox	
		Child, Ruth L Kenyon	Dec 9, 1913	F			Rep by Chandler
594		Father, Robus Roubideaux					
		Mother, Emily Roubideaux				Iowa	
		Child, May Columba Roubideaux	Aug 21, 1913	F			Rep by Collins
595		Father, David McCoy				Sac and Fox	
		Mother, Eliza McCoy				" " "	
		Child, Curtis McCoy	Aug 16, 1913	M			Rep by Chandler
596		Father, Dan McCoy				Sac and Fox	
		Mother,				(White)	
		Child, Maxine Rosella McCoy	Feb 2, 1914	F			Rep by Isaac McCoy
		Father, Weston Fritz				(White)	
		Mother, Shelah Fritz				Sac and Fox	
		Child, Ixie Weston Fritz	Jan 17, 1914	F			Rep by C.Chandler
		Father, Leo Gokey				Sac and Fox	
		Mother,				not enrolled here	
		Child, Minnie Gokey	Sept 19, 1913	F			Verified by Collins
		Father, Rhodd					
		Mother, Adaline Rhodd				Sac and Fox	
		Child, Edith Fustena Rhodd	Jan 12, 1914	F			Verified by Affidavit
		Father, John McClellan				Sac & Fox	
		Mother, Fannie McClellan				" " "	
		Child, Lorena Jane McClellan	Apr 13-14	F		" " "	Verified by Chandler
		Father, Hiram Starr				Sac and Fox	
		Mother, Mandy Starr				" " "	
		Child, Ella Starr	Mar 25, 1914	F		" " "	Rep by Collins
		Father, Guy Walker				Sac and Fox	
		Mother, Maggie Walker					
		Child, Raymond Walker	4-16-14	M			Rep by Chandler
		Father, David Harris				Sac & Fox	
		Mother, Annie G Harris				" " "	
		Child, Paul Jonathan "	4-18-14	M		" " "	Rep by Collins
		Father, Frank Kent				Iowa	
		Mother, Emma Kent				"	
		Child, Philip Kent	5-3-14	M		"	Rep by Collins
		Father, Jackson Wakole				Sac & Fox	
		Mother, Esther Wakole				" " "	
		Child, Jackson Wakole, Jr	6-1-14	M		" " "	Rep by Chandler
		Father, Kerwin Murry				Iowa	
		Mother, Alice Murry, nee FawFaw				"	
		Child, Esther Murry	6-1-14	F		"	Rep by Collins

Sac & Fox – Shawnee
1846-1924   Volume XI

30

Record of Births among Indians of   Agency

Child's Number on This Record	Parents' Numbers on Family Register	Name	Date of Child's Birth	Sex of Child	Ages of Parents	Blood or Nationality of Parents	Tribe, or Allegiance by Citizenship, of Parents
		Father, Boyd				Mexican	
		Mother, Christine Boyd				Sac & Fox	
		Child, Benjamin Boyd	June 2, 1914	M.		" " "	Verified by Affidavit see packet of Benjamin Boyd
		Father, White Unknown					
		Mother, Bigwalker, Lelia				Sac & Fox	Reported by Dr F W Wyman
		Child, " Elizabeth	Feb 8/1914	F			
		Father, Ira Walker				Sac & Fox	
		Mother, Marie Walker					Reported by Ira Walker
		Child, Ira Walker, Jr	7/10/1914	M			
		Father, John Springer				Iowa	
		Mother, Gertrude Springer				Otoe	Reported by Arza B Collins
		Child, Thoroughman Springer	7/12-14	M			
		Father, Omer D Lewis					
		Mother, Pauline Lewis				Sac & Fox	Reported by Isaac C McCoy
		Child, Mary Matilda Lewis	9/3/14	F			
		Father, Guy Whistler				Sac & Fox	
		Mother, Margaret Whistler				White	Reported by Claud Chandler
		Child, Margaret Whistler	9-9-14	F			
		Father, J W Taylor				White	
		Mother, Gertie Taylor				Sac & Fox	Reported by Claud Chandler
		Child, John Henry Taylor	4-27-14	M			
		Father, Blaine Nawanoway				Iowa	
		Mother, Rosa "				(Shawnee)	Reported by A B Collins
		Child, Isaac "	8-20-14	M			
		Father, Henry Appletree				Sac & Fox	
		Mother, Susan "				" " "	Reported by A B Collins
		Child, Charles "	9-4-14	M		" " "	
		Father, Charles Smith				Sac & Fox	
		Mother, Theresa Smith				" " "	Reported by A B Collins
		Child, Pearl Smith	10-11-14	F		" " "	
		Father, Joe Connalis					
		Mother, Martha Connalis				Sac & Fox	Reported by Claud Chandler
		Child, Clifford Connalis	4-18-14	M		" " "	
		Father, Austin Grant				Sac & Fox	
		Mother, Alice "				" " "	Reported by Arza B Collins
		Child, Caroline "	10/29/14	F		" " "	
		Father, George G Foster				Sac & Fox	
		Mother, Jane Foster				" " "	Reported by Claud Chandler
		Child, Viola May Foster	11/16/14	F		" " "	
		Father, Henry Hunter				Sac & Fox	
		Mother, Alice Hunter				" " "	Reported by A B Collins
		Child, Mamie Hunter	11/16/14	F			

Sac & Fox – Shawnee
1846-1924 Volume XI

Record of Births among Indians of _____ Agency

31

Child's Number on this Record	Parents' Numbers on Family Register	Name	Date of Child's Birth	Sex of Child	Ages of Parents	Blood or Nationality of Parents	Tribe, or Allegiance by Citizenship, of Parents
Payne		Father, Jacob Dole				Iowa	
		Mother, Amelia Dole				"	Reported by
		Child, Shermian Dole	Dec 2, 1914	M		"	Collins
Pottawatomie		Father, George W McClellan				Sac & Fox	Reported by
		Mother, Rosa McClellan				Shawnee	Claud Chandler
		Child, Lorena Margaret McClellan	Jan 6, 1915	F			Shawnee Supt reports not enrolled there
		Father, William H Jefferson				Sac & Fox	
		Mother, Esther (Bigwalker) Jefferson				" "	Reported by
		Child, Rose Homer Jefferson	Mar 2, 1915	F			A B Collins
		Father, Walker, Ben					
		Mother, " Dora					verified by
		Child, " Luther	Jan 3, 1915				Claud Chandler
		Father, Manatowa, Elmer					
		Mother, "					verified by
		Child, " Bessie	Dec 31, 1914	F			A B Collins
		Father, Thorp, Frank					
		Mother,					verified by
		Child, " Wilber	Apr 4, 1915	M			Claud Chandler
		Father, Samuel Falls					
		Mother, Edna "					verified by
		Child, Walter Samuel Falls	Apr 8, 1915	M			A B Collins
		Father, Saginaw Grant				Sac & Fox	
		Mother, Stella Grant				" "	verified by
		Child, Pearl Bessie Grant	Feb 22 1915	F		" "	A B Collins
		Father, Jacob Wyman				" "	
		Mother, Mary "				" "	Reported by
		Child, Clifford "	June 22 1915	M		" "	A B Collins
		Father, Silas Grass				" "	
		Mother, Ada Grass				" "	Reported by
		Child, John Grass	Mar 24, 1915	M			A B Collins
		Father, John Isaac Goodell				Sac & Fox	
		Mother, Bertha (McCurry) Goodell				white Indian Office refuses enrollment with S&F Indians	L-C 71695-15, 77366-15
		Child, James Isaac Goodell	March 3/1915	M			Reported by father
		Father,					
		Mother, Adaline Rhodd				Enrollment auth. 7/27/15	Reported by
		Child, Viola Esther Rhodd	5/17/15	F		L-C 66659-15, 78095-15	mother
		Father, Jim Scott					
		Mother, Martha Scott				Request for enrollment at	Reported by
		Child, Minnie Scott	4/11/15	F		Sac & Fox Iowa filed	Collins
		Father, George Oliver Morton	L-C 72062-16				
		Mother, Mary Morton	7/14/16				Reported by Father
		Child, Clifford H Morton	8/22/15	M			Verified by Collins

Sac & Fox – Shawnee
1846-1924 Volume XI

32

Record of Births among Indians of ___ Agency

Child's Number on this Record.	Parents' Numbers on Family Register	Name.	Date of Child's Birth.	Sex of Child	Ages of Parents	Blood or Nationality of Parents	Tribe, or Allegiance by Citizenship, of Parents
		Father, Robert Pate					
		Mother, Rachel Pate				Auth. for Enrollment	Reported by
		Child, Harry Samuel Pate	6/28/15	S[sic]		L-C 16315-16	Collins
		Father, Grover Wakole					Reported by Father
		Mother, Barney Curtis Wakole		S		Authority for Enrollment	Verified by Claud
		Child, Sylvia Pauline Wakole	9/21/15	D		L-C 4334-1916	Chandler
		Father, James Sine (nee				Certificate filed	
		Mother, Fulwood Sine Lincoln)				Auth for Enrollment	Reported by
		Child, Alma Leona Sine	7/15/15	D[sic]		43050-16 Iowa	Arza B Collins
		Father,				Auth to enroll	Reported by
		Mother, Fannie Tyner				38714-16	Maggie Tyner
		Child, Houston Tyner	6/12/15	S			Verified by Chandler
		Father, Guy Walker				Certificate of election to enroll with S&F filed	
		Mother, Maggie Walker				Auth. to enroll L.C. 25072-16	
		Child, Lester Walker	10/4/15	S			Verified by Chandler
		Father, Thomas Miles					
		Mother, Rhoda Miles					
		Child, Mildred E Miles	8/1/15	D			Verified by Chandler
		Father, Lee Bass				Certificate of election to enroll with S&F filed	
		Mother, Ellen Roubidoux Bass				Auth. to enroll L.C. 23965-16	Reported by Father
		Child, Cora Bass	11/10/15	D			Verified by Collins
		Father, John Thompson				Not entitled to enrollment for annuity	
		Mother, Sarah Thompson				32335-16 CCB	
		Child, Alice Thompson	12/13/15	D			Reported by Collins
		Father, Painter MᶜKosato					
		Mother, Annie MᶜKosato					Verified by Supt
		Child, Woodrow MᶜKosato	1/26/16	S			Reported by mother
		Father, Henry Appletree					
		Mother, Susan Appletree					Reported by Father
		Child, Marie Appletree	2/18/16	D			Verified by Collins
		Father, Alex Jefferson					
		Mother, Sarah Jefferson					Reported by Father
		Child, Alex Jefferson, Jr	2/8/16	S			Verified by Collins
		Father, J Harvey Labelle				Certificate of election to enroll with Sac & Fox filed	
		Mother, Linda Labelle				Auth. 56922-16	Reported by
		Child, Arthur H Labelle	9/13/15	S			Chandler
		Father, Kirwin Murray					
		Mother, Alice Murray					
		Child, Charles Murray	1/27/16	M			Reported by Collins
		Father, Carter Joseph					
		Mother, " Madeline					Reported by
		Child, " Lulu	3/31/16	F			Chandler

Sac & Fox – Shawnee
1846-1924   Volume XI

Record of Births among Indians of Agency

Child's Number on This Record	Parents' Numbers on Family Register	Name	Date of Child's Birth	Sex of Child	Ages of Parents	Blood or Nationality of Parents	Tribe, or Allegiance by Citizenship, of Parents
		Father, Walter Washington				Shawnee	Certificate of election to enroll with S & F filed 124253-16
		Mother, Minnie Washington				Sac and Fox	Enrollment refused
		Child, Vina Marie Washington	12/29/15	F			Reported by Chandler
		Father, Dave Harris					
		Mother, Annie Harris					
		Child, Irene Harris	3/27/16	F			Reported by Collins
		Father, Randall Franklin					Certificate of election to enroll with S &F filed
		Mother, Sora Franklin					Auth. to enroll 42115-16 47417-16
		Child, Gladys Franklin	3/11/16	F			Reported by Collins
		Father, Thomas Brown					
		Mother, Bertha Brown (Nah-na-we)					Reported by Father
		Child, Zilla Gertrude Brown	4/15/16	F			Verified by Chandler
		Father, Eveline Givens					
		Mother, Matilda Givens					
		Child, John Givens	4/1/16	M			Reported by Collins
		Father, William L Harris					Reported by Father
		Mother, Harris					Verified by
		Child, William Harris, Jr	1/16/15	M			Mary Johnson Clk
		Father, Benjamin Harris					
		Mother, Grace Harris (white woman)					Reported by Collins
		Child, Fannie Harris	9/27/16	F			
		Father, Ira Walker				Sac and Fox	Reported by Father
		Mother, Marie Walker				Shawnee	
		Child, George Lee Walker	10/1/16	M		auth. to enroll 8928-17	Verified by Chandler
		Father, John McClellan					
		Mother, Fannie McClellan					Reported and
		Child, Emmett McClellan	5/2/16	M			Verified by Chandler
		Father, Frank Kent					
		Mother, Emma Kent					Reported by Father
		Child, Vera Kent	11/26/16	F			Verified by Chandler
		Father, Weston Fritz					
		Mother, Shelah Fritz					Reported and
		Child, John Henry Fritz	8/17/16	M			Verified by Chandler
		Father, Jackson Wakole					
		Mother, Esther Wakole					
		Child, Walter Wakole	11/15/16	M			Reported by Chandler
		Father, Elbert Mack					
		Mother, Louisa Mack					
		Child, {Cora Mack / Carrie Mack}	Born 12/9/16 " 12/10/16 } Twins	F F			Reported by Chandler
		Father, Jackson Ellis					
		Mother, Ruth Ellis					1/21/17
		Child, Levi Ellis	12/21/16	M			Reported by Chandler

Sac & Fox – Shawnee
1846-1924   Volume XI

34

Record of Births among Indians of _____ Agency

Child's Number on this Record	Parents' Numbers on Family Register	Name	Date of Child's Birth	Sex of Child	Ages of Parents	Blood or Nationality of Parents	Tribe, or Allegiance by Citizenship, of Parents
		Father, Silas Grass					
		Mother, Ada Grass					Reported by Mother
		Child, Matilda Grass	12/12/16	F			Verified by Arza B Collins
		Father, Kirwin Murray Iowa					
		Mother, Alice Murray					
		Child, Opal Murray		F			Reported by Collins
		Father, John Springer					
		Mother, Gertrude Springer					
		Child, Joseph Springer	12/27/16	M			Reported by Collins
		Father, Omar Lewis				Pottawatomie	
		Mother, Pauline Lewis				Sac and Fox	
		Child, Oma Lucille Lewis	8/25/16	F			Reported by Mother
		Father, Jacob Wyman					
		Mother, Mary Wyman					Verified by Collins
		Child, Florine Wyman	3/16/17	F			Reported by Mother
		Father, George Butler					
		Mother, Edith Butler					
		Child, Benjamin Butler	8/7/16	M			Reported by Collins
		Father, Harding Franklin					
		Mother, Minnie Franklin					
		Child, Daniel Franklin	10/19/16	M			
		Father, Edward Butler					
		Mother, Ida Butler					
		Child, Fred Butler	1/7/17	M			Reported by Collins
		Father, Robert Roubidoux					
		Mother, Emily Roubidoux					
		Child, Aron Roubidoux	1/23/17	M			Reported by Collins
		Father, Elmer Manatowa					
		Mother, Grace Manatowa					
		Child, Joseph Manatowa	2/3/17	M			Reported by Chandler
		Father, Austin Grant					
		Mother, Alice Grant					
		Child, Grover Grant } Twins Mamie Grant	4/8/17	M F			Reported by Collins
		Father, Grover Morris					
		Mother, Clara Morris					
		Child, Samuel Morris	5/8/17	M			Reported by Collins
		Father, Benjamin Walker					
		Mother, Dora Walker					verified
		Child, Mary Walker	6/4/17	F			Reported by John Brown
		Father, Harvey Labelle					
		Mother, Linda Labelle					
		Child, Louis P Labelle	6/27/17				Reported by Collins

Sac & Fox – Shawnee
1846-1924 Volume XI

Record of Births among Indians of Agency

Child's Number on this Record	Parents' Numbers on Family Register	Name	Date of Child's Birth	Sex of Child	Ages of Parents	Blood or Nationality of Parents	Tribe, or Allegiance by Citizenship, of Parents
		Father, Spooner				Munsee	
		Mother, Ida Spooner			26	Sac and Fox	
		Child, Lena Josephine	7/11/17	F			Reported by Mother
		Father, Thomas Brown				S&F	Reported by Parents
		Mother, Bertha Carter-Brown				"	
		Child, Frank P Brown	7/13/17				
		Father, George Foster				Sac & Fox	
		Mother, Jane Foster				" "	
		Child, Fred Foster	10/25/17				Reported by Mother
		Father, Frank Thorp				Sac & Fox	
		Mother, Angeline Thorp (Shawnee)				Shawnee	
		Child, Lucile Thorp	48/7/17				Reported by Parents
		Father, Saginaw Grant				Sac & Fox	
		Mother, Fannie Grant				" "	Reported by Mother
		Child, Alma Adaline "	11/9/17				Verified
		Child, Elmer Harold "	11/9/17				
		Father, William H Jefferson				Sac & Fox	
		Mother, Esther Jefferson				" "	Reported by Mother
		Child, Frances Irene "	1/18/18				Verified by Dr Wyman
		Father, Frank Gokey					
		Mother, Dollie Gokey					Reported by Dr Wyman
		Child, Augustina	1/17	F			
		Father, Lee Bass				Sac & Fox	Reported by Collins
		Mother, Helen Bass				Pottawatomie	Verified
		Child, Florine Bass	1/9/18			L.C. 48524-18 W M W 6/28/18 entitled to enrollment	
		Father, Paul Gokey					
		Mother, Lilly Neal Gokey					Reported by Mr Chandler
		Child, General Pershing Gokey	5/11/18				Verified
		Father, Willie Washington				Shawnee	Reported by Mr Chandler
		Mother, Mary E Brown Washington				S F children not entitled to enrollment	L.C. 48606-18 W M W 6/28/18
		Child, Berta Zilla " " "	April 30.1918				
		Father, Fred DeLansanne				White	Reported by Collins
		Mother, Pearl Conger DeLansanne				Sac & Fox full	
		Child, Pearl May Juliet	7/3/18			Half Blood	
		Father, Grover Morris				Sac & Fox full	Reported by Collins
		Mother, Clara Falls Morris				" " "	
		Child, Alice Morris	8/29/18			" " "	
		Father, Jacob Wyman					
		Mother, Mary Wyman					Reported by Parents
		Child, Frank P Wyman	10/26/18				
		Father, Edward Butler				Full S & Fox	
		Mother, Ida Butler				" "	Reported by Jane Foster
		Child, Harry Francis Butler	10/18/18			" "	

Sac & Fox – Shawnee
1846-1924 Volume XI

36

Record of Births among Indians of ___ Agency

Child's Number on this Record	Parents' Numbers on Family Register	Name	Date of Child's Birth	Sex of Child	Ages of Parents	Blood or Nationality of Parents	Tribe, or Allegiance by Citizenship, of Parents
		Father, Joe Carter			1872	Sac & Fox Full	
		Mother, Madeline Houston Carter			1881		
		Child, James Carter II	1/23/19	M			
		Father, Fryor Franklin Brown				Sac & Fox	
		Mother, Margaret ChristJohn "				Oneida	
		Child, Melinda Delphine "	9/14/17				
	478	Father, John McClellan				Sac & Fox Full	
	111	Mother, Fannie Groinhorn "					
	Census Reg #2 I.O.	Child, Harriet McClellan	2/21/19			" " "	
		Father, Jesse				White	
		Mother, Nellie B Jesse			19	Less than 1/2	
		Child, Joy Dell Jesse	11/25/18	F		Not entitled to enrollment L-C13991-19 WMW	
		Father, Blaine Kent				Iowa	Not reported for enrollment until March 13, 1919 by father
		Mother, Rosa Hurr (Wolf) Kent				Ottawa	
		Child, Louise "	6/11/16	F			
		Father, Blaine Kent				Iowa	Reported by father for enrollment March 13, 1919
		Mother, Rosa Hurr (Wolf) Kent				Ottawa	
		Child, Emma "	4/24/18				
		Father, Elmer Manatowa				Full Sac & Fox	Born on Reservation Laura Carter allottment Reported by Mr Collir
	I.O. Reg #2	Mother, Grace "				White	
		Child, Grace Margaret "	Feb 6/19	F		1/2	
		Father, McHanon Keahna				Sac & Fox Iowa	Reported by Parents Elect to enroll in Okla Waiver signed
		Mother, Jennie Thurman				Sac & Fox Okla	
		Child, Marie Keahna	12/21/18				
		Father, Silas Grass				Sac & Fox Full	
		Mother, Ada Struble Grass				" " "	
		Child, Charles Grass	4/18/19	M		" " "	Reported by Collins
		Father, Walter M Hodsdon(?)					Reported by Chandler Not known whether entitled to share in tribal benefits
		Mother, Bertha L Hodsdon				Sac & Fox full	
		Child, George Maxwell Hodsdon	2/24/19			Not known	
		Father, Benjamin Harris				S & F Full	Reported by Mr Collir Question right to share Tribal Benefits See Amendment #6 Paragr
		Mother, Grace Harris				White	
		Child, Patsy Harris	3/17/19			1/2 Blood	
		Father, Allen G Thurman			S&F	Full Blood	Section 324 April, 19, Indian Service Regulat
		Mother, Bessie Wakole				" "	Reported by Mabel Wakolle Gr Mo.
		Child, Lucinda Thurman	4/28/19			" "	
		Father, John Thompson				Iowa Sac & Fox Full	Reported by Collins Illigitimate[sic]
		Mother, Carrie H Hunter				Okla Sac & Fox Full full	
		Child, Harrison Hunter, Jr	5/2/19				
		Father, Lester Weston Fritz				White	Reported by Chandler Child not entitled to share in tribal benefits see amendment #6 & Paragraph 4 of sec 32 April 1, 1905
		Mother, Shela Guthrie Brown				Sac & Fox full	
		Child, Lulah H Fritz	5/27/19				

Sac & Fox – Shawnee
1846-1924 Volume XI

37

Record of Births among Indians of   Agency

Child's Number on this Record	Parents' Numbers on Family Register	Name	Date of Child's Birth	Sex of Child	Ages of Parents	Blood or Nationality of Parents	Tribe, or Allegiance by Citizenship, of Parents
		Father, Supposed to be Fred Grant			23	Sac & Fox Full	
		Mother, Susie Rice				Sac & Fox Full	
		Child, Clarence Grant Rice	6/12/19	M	19		Reported by Collins
		Father, Peyton Keokuk				not entitled to enrollment & share in tribal benefits see amendment April 3, 1905 to I.S. Regulations	
		Mother, White					
		Child, Laura Lorena "	7/6/18				Reported by Collins
		Father, John Thompson					
		Mother, Sarah Mansur Thompson					
		Child, Ellen Thompson	8/8/18			Died 8/9/18	"
		Father, Randall Franklin					
		Mother, Sora Franklin					
		Child, Lorena May	12/7/18				Reported by Collins
		Father, Dan McCoy				Sac and Fox	
		Mother, Mary Rosengrant McCoy				White	
		Child, John Barry McCoy	7/8/19	M			Reported by Father

283

Sac and Fox-Shawnee –

LOG BOOK RECORDS OF DEATHS

1902-1919

Sac & Fox – Shawnee
1846-1924   Volume XI

101

Record of Deaths among Indians of   Sac & Fox   Agency

NUMBER ON THIS RECORD	NUMBER ON RECORD OF BIRTHS	NUMBER ON FAMILY REGISTER	NAME	AGE	SEX	DATE OF DEATH	MARRIED SINGLE, WIDOW WIDOWER, OR DIVORCED	NAME OF A LIVING RELATIVE	RELATION	NUMBER OF RELATIVE ON FAMILY REGISTER
1	----	39	James Black	21d	M	April 18-2	single	Carl Black	brother	
								Amos & Mary Black	father & mother	------
2		57	Benjamin Butler	55	M	June 30-2	widower	Edward, George and Jane Butler	sons & dau	------
3			Dennis Coon	43	"	June 5-2	widower	Ella Carter	sister	
4			May Duncan	11	F	April 28-2	single	Dickson Duncan	brothers	126
								Allen G Thurman		
5	Law-Heirship 124973-14		Alex Ellis	5/12	M	June 26-2	single	Jackson & Ruth Ellis	father & mother	132
6		159	Charlotte Givens	18	F	May 31-2	single	Gertrude Givens	mother	
7		171	Isaac Goodell	53	M	Aug 1-2	married	Fannie & John I Goodell	dau & son	
8		202	Rufus Hall	10	M	May 31-2	single	Harry Hall Sadie, Henry,& [Illegible]	father sister & bro	
9		233	William Ingalls	14	M	Aug 18-2	single	Mattie Ingalls	mother	
10		241	Irene Jefferson	27	F	Aug 10-2	Divorced	William H Jefferson	son	
11	12		Horace M<u>c</u>Kosato	1d	M	July 7-2	single	Painter & Annie M<u>c</u>Kosito[sic]	father & mother	
12		380	Roger Parkinson	19	M	Oct 27-2	single	William Parkinson	father	
13		418	Thomas Smith	5/12	M	June 1-2	single	Frank and Annie Smith	father & mother	
14		447	Eugene E Tyner	4	M	Oct 5-2	single	Maggie & Claude Tyner	father & mother	
~~15~~		380	Roger Parkinson	19	M	Oct 27-2	single			
16		62	John G Carlisle	35	M	Aug 31-1903	Single	Dah-tup-puck-e	1/2 brother	
17		120	Flora Davis	31	F	Dec 2-1903	married	Frank Davis	husband	
18		108	Charley Crane	38	M	Sept 16-1903	married	Mary L Crane	Wife	
19	35		Mary Davis	1d	F	Dec 2-1903	single	Frank Davis	father	
20	36		Herbert Falls	3/12	M	Oct 20-1903	single	Samuel Falls	father	
21	22		Ross Franklin	1	M	Aug 2-1903	single	Benj Franklin	father	
22		178	Maxey Grant	1	M	Oct 20-1903	single	Austin Grant	father	
23		201	Harry Hall	38	M	Oct 25-1903	married	Jennie Hall	wife	
24	19		Carrie Hall	1	F	Sept 15-1903	single	Jennie Hall	mother	
25		266	Moses Keokuk	81	M	Oct 27-1903	married	Mary A Keokuk	wife	
26		297	May Mansur	10	F	Aug 10-1903	single	Maggie Hawk	mother	
27	49		Ernest Thorp	4/12	M	Aug 2-1903	single	Hiram Thorp	Father	
28	50		Rosetta Thorp	4 da	F	July 24-1903	single	Frank Thorp	father	
29	41		Sadie Logan	7mo	F	April 18-1904	single	Clarence Logan	father	279
30	25		George Jefferson	1	M	April 18-1904	single	Alex Jefferson	father	240
31		30	Jennie Bigwalker Hall	24	F	April 19-04	married	Harry Hall	husband	201
32	Law-Heirship 48940-12 33771-15	432	Hiram Thorp	52	M	April 22-04	married	George Thorp	brother	

Sac & Fox – Shawnee
1846-1924 Volume XI

102

Record of Deaths among Indians of Sac & Fox Agency Okla

Number on this Record	Number on Record of Births	Number on Family Register	Name	Age	Sex	Date of Death	Married Single, Widow Widower, or Divorced	Name Of A Living Relative	Relation	Number of Relative on Family Register
33		262	Charles H Keokuk	49		June 7-04	Divorced	John Earl Keokuk	Son	
34		226	Robert Hunter	47		June 10-1904	Widow	Harrison Hunter	Son	
35		Lak10	Carrie Crane	3	F	June 13-1904	Single	Mary L Crane	Mother	
36	62	Heirship	Harry Thurman	10da	M	June 27-04	Single	Lucy Thurman	Mother	
37			Mary Ingalls	7da	F	June 2-04	Single	Mattie Ingalls	Mother	
38			Leah Tohee	24	F	June 4-04	Married	Dave Tohee Jr	Husband	
39			Daniel Tohee	40da	M	July 7-04	Married	Dave Tohee Jr	Father	
40			Ida White	50	F	Aug 21-04	Married	Tom Penashe	Husband	
41	913867-13		Jane Tohee	5da	F	Nov 23-1894	Single	William Tohee	Father	
42	92350-13		Lee Patrick	1/6m	M	June 20-91	Single	David Tohee	Father	
43 49			Big Ear	73	M	Oct 27-1891	Married	Theresa Bigear	Wife	
44 50			No-ah-tom	69	F	Sept 4-1891	Married	Robert Small	Gr son	
45			Maggie Dupee	1da	F	July 11-1891	Single	Victor Dupee	Father	
46 52			Naw-a no-way	59	M	Aug 25-1891	Married	Susan Nawanoway	Wife	
47			Willie Dole	28	M	Mar 7-1891	Married	Josie Dole	Wife	
48 54			Lucinda	48	F	Dec 4-1890	Married	Moses	Husband	
49 43			Big Ear	73	M	Oct 27-1891	Married	Theresa Bigear	Wife	
50 44			No-ah-tom	69	F	Sept 4-1891	Married	Robert Small	Gr Son	
51			Lah-ton shis-me	16	F	Mar 25-1891	Single	Eliza White	Dau	
52 46			Naw-a-no-way	59	M	Aug 25-1891	Married	Susan Naw-a-no-way	Wife	
53 47			Willie Dole	28	M	Mar 7-1891	Married	Josie Dole	Wife	
54 48			Lucinda	48	F	Dec 4-1890	Married	Moses	Husband	
55			William Tohee	44	M	Feb 2-1892	Married	Ethu-qui-je	Wife	
56			Lucy Vetter	14	F	June 26-1892	Single	Joe Vetter	Father	
57			Samuel L Ely	2	M	July 2-1892	Single	Jane Ely	Mother	
58			Sallie Vetter	3/12	F	July 4-1892	Single	Sam Vetter	Father	
59			Emma Kirk	5/12	F	July 5-1892	Single	Joe Vetter	Father	
60	9097-14		Lina B Lunt	1	F	July 3-1892	Single	Au-gre	Mother	
61			Harry Task	4	M	June 17-1892	Single	Benj Hallowell	Father	
62	10265-13		Irene Hallowell	3	F	June 15-1892	Single	Benj Hallowell	Father	
63			Jane Hallowell	2/12	F	June 6-1892	Single	Benj Hallowell	Father	
64	57991-14		Lizzie Whitecloud	3	F	Aug 22-1892	Single	Jefferson Whitecloud	Father	

Sac & Fox – Shawnee
1846-1924   Volume XI

Record of Deaths among Indians of Sac & Fox Agency Okla

Number on This Record	Number on Record of Births Law	Number on Family Register Heirship	Name	Age	Sex	Date of Death	Married Single, Widow Widower, or Divorced	Name of a Living Relative	Relation	Number of Relative on Family Register
65			Robert Whitecloud	1da	M	May 7-1892	Single	Jefferson Whitecloud	Father	
66			Louisa Dupee	5	F	May 16-1892	Single	Victor Dupee	Father	
67			Frederick Dupee	2	M	May 13-1892	Single	Victor Dupee	Father	
68			Mary Naw-a no-way	2	M	May 11-1892	Single	Nellie Nawanoway	Mother	
69			John Naw-a no-way	6da	M	Jany 18-1892	Single	Frank Kent	Father	
70			Billie Lincoln	4	M	Nov 6-1892	Single	Abraham Lincoln	Father	
71			Abraham Lincoln, Jr	1/12	M	Mar 29-1892	Single	Abraham Lincoln	Father	
72			John Mohee	2	M	May 31-1892	Single	Maggie Mohee	Mother	
73			~~Sha-tah-cher~~	39	F	Error still living				
74	144062-13		Ed Townsend	14	M	June 1894	Single	Sha-tah-cher	Mother	
75			Kerwin Murry	54	M	July 6/1894 June 1894	Married	May Murray[sic]	Wife	
76			Richard Mohee	1	M	Apr 1894	Single	Maggie Mohee	Mother	
77			Mary Neal Tohee	7	F	Dec 1-1895	Single	David Tohee	Father	
78			Pauline Tohee	2	F	Sept 1895	Single	David Tohee	Father	
79			Wah-to-gra-me	9	F	Dec 31-1895	Single	David Faulk	Father	
80			Annie Vetter	1	F	Jan 20-1896	Single	Sam Vetter	Father	
81			Isaac Perry	43	M	Dec 1-1896	Married	Annie Perry	Wife	
82			Joe Lawrence Dupee	1½	M	Feb 21-1896	Single	Victor Dupee	Father	
83			Margaret Tohee	8	F	July 15-1896	Single	David Tohee	Father	
84			Muc-cum-pem-e	64	F	Sept 1-1896	Married	Hot chi see	Husband	
85			Susan Naw-a no-way	69	F	Aug 7-1896	Married	Naw-a-no-way	Husband	
86			Wa-ho-nee-mie	50	F	Sept 1-1896	Married	Thos Doran	Husband	
87			Ida Vetter	2/12	F	Nov 1-1897	Married	Sam Vetter	Husband	
88			Louis Murray	1/12	M	Feb 1-1897	Single	Emily Murray	Mother	
89			Don Naw-a no-way	1/12	M	Feb 12-1897	Single	Frank Kent	Father	
90			Hot-chi-see	64	M	July 20-1897	Married	Frank Kent	Father	
91			Horace Crane	5/12	M	Feb 23-04	Single	Mary Crane	Mother	
91			Sadie Grass	12d	F	June 8-04	Single	May Grass	Mother	
93			Lulu Wyman	22	F	April 3-04	Single	Jacob Wyman	Father	
94			Henry H Mansur	7	M	Oct 10-04	Single	Benjamin Hull	Brother	
95			James Wolf	20	M	Sept 16-04	Single	George Paddock	Cousin	
96			Jennie Buffalohorn	53	F	Sept 22-04	Married	Thos J Buffalohorn	Brother	

Sac & Fox – Shawnee
1846-1924 Volume XI

104
Record of Deaths among Indians of   Agency

Number on this Record	Number on Record of Births	Number on Family Register Law Heirship	Name	Age	Sex	Date of Death	Married Single, Widow Widower, or Divorced	Name Of A Living Relative	Relation	Number of Relative on Family Register
97		60628-14	Jay Conger	59	M	July 26-04	Widower	Andrew Conger	Son	
98			William Kehega[sic]	2	M	Mar 27-04	Single	Charley Kihega	Father	
99			Amos Grant	3	M	Oct 24-04	Single	Ulyses S Grant	Father	
100			Iva Neal	2/12	F	Aug 31-04	Single	Victor Neal	Father	
101			Sadie Thurman	20d	F	July 6-04	Single	Lucy Thurman	Mother	
102			Ceceal McKinney	32d	F	Oct 1-1904[sic]	Single	Aron[sic] McKinney	Father	
103			Helen Crane		F	Dec 2-1904	Married	Webster Smith	Husband	
104			Wilson McKinney	60	M	Dec 24-1904	Widower	Arron McKinney	son	
105			May Grass	29	F	Dec 29-04	Married	Andrew Conger	Husband	
106			Mary Grass	1d	F	Dec 29-04	Single	Andrew Conger	Father	
107			Daniel Tohee	41d	M	July 7-04	Single	Dave Tohee, Jr	Father	
108			Leah Tohee	24	F	June 4-04	Married	Dave Tohee, Jr	Husband	
109			Gra-tah-ha-ma	87	F	Dec 6-04	Widow	Lizzie Hallowell	Gr dau	
110		36508-14 13134-14	Lizzie Rice		F	Feb 4-05	Widower	Edward Rice	Son	
111		149437-13	Clifford H Morton		M	Feb 1-05	Single	Geo Oliver Morton	Brother	
112			Ollie Logan	5d	F	Feb 11-05	Single	Clarence Logan	Father	
113			Grover Fall		M	Mar 14-05	Divorced	Samuel Fall[sic]	Brother	
114			Joshua Tyner	1/2	M	Dec 20-04	Single	Maggie Tyner	Mother	
115			Luke Conley		M	Apr 25-05	Single?			
116			William Falls	1/4	M	Apr 30-05	Single	Sam. Falls	Father	
117			Lizzie Springer		F	May 10-05	Married			
118			William Mason	2/12	M	June 20-05	Single	Edith Mason	Aunt	
119			Walt Grayson			June 24-05	Single	Edith Mason	Niece	
120			Grace Mason			June 24-05	Married	Edith Mason	sister	
121			Benj Wyman	1½	M	Sept 18-05	Single	Jacob Wyman	Father	
122			Thomas Grant	3/12	M	Sept 28-05	Single	Austin Grant	Father	
123			Peah-twa-tah	1d	F	Oct 2-05	Single	Frank Smith	Father	
124			Annie Smith	23	F	Sept 23-05	Married	"	"	husband
125			Whitecloud Kihega		M	Sept 23-05	Single	Charles Kihega	Father	
126			Smith	1	M		"	Frank Smith	Father	
127			Jefferson Carter		M	Oct 19-05	"	Joe Carter	Father	

Sac & Fox – Shawnee
1846-1924 Volume XI

Record of Deaths among Indians of _____ Agency

Number on this Record	Number on Record of Births	Number on Family Register Law Heirship	Name	Age	Sex	Date of Death	Married Single, Widow Widower, or Divorced	Name of a Living Relative	Relation	Number of Relative on Family Register
128	64670-14		Cami J Littlebear		F	Nov 5-05	Married	George Littlebear	Husband	
129			Bass	1d	M	Oct 10-05	Single	Inez Bass	Mother	
130			Myrtle Marie O'Brien		F	Dec 10-05	Single	Lucy O'Brien	Mother	
131	124456-14		Gertrude Givens		F	Dec 10-05	Married	Jno Brown	Husband	
132	72149=14		Judith Houston		F	Dec 31-05	Married	Samuel Huston[sic]	Husband	
133			Roger Mathews		M	Jan 17-06	Married	Edward Mathews	Father	
134	64963-15		Ange Ford	36	F	Nov 17-05	"	Tom Hartico	Husband	
135			Tom Ford	70	M	June 3-05	Married			
136			Jane Ely		F	July 25-05	Single			
137			William Shaw		M	Feb 5-05	Married	Jane Shaw	Wife	
138			Emma Logan	1d	F	Mar 10-05	Single	Clarence Logan	Father	
140[sic]			Theodore R Longshore	1½	M	Mar 14-04	Single	Annie Longshore	Mother	
141			Anna Butler	1/2	F	Mar 16-06	Single	Ida Butler	Mother	
142			Julia Clay		F	Mar 11-06	Widow	Inz[sic] Bass	Daughter	
143	65845-13		Naomi Sullivan		F	Mar 19-06	Married	William Parkinson	Father	
144	63260-14		John A Logan		M	Apr 9-06	"	Mollie Logan	Wife	
145			Margaret Bigwalker		F	June 18-06	Single	Geo Appletree	½ bro	
146	123575-14		Lucy Thurman		F	June 27-06	Married	Lydia Grant	sis	
147			Emma Logan	8d	F	Mar 10-06	Single	Clarence Logan	Father	
148			John Nullake	6d	M	Mar 28-06	Single	Walter Nullake	Father	
149			James Springer		M	July 17/06	Single	Joe Springer	Father	
150			Mary Neal		F	Sept 28/06	Single	Victor Neal	Father	
151			Charley Wyman		M	Oct 6/06	Single	Jacob Wyman	Father	
152			Mary Givens		F	Oct 18/06	Single	Matilda Barker	Mother	
153	126324-12		Lewis Carter		M	Oct 12/06	Single	Milton Carter	Father	
154			Anne Nellie Grant		F	Oct 8/06	Married	William Atkins	husband	
155			Ellen McKosito		F	Oct 24/06		Chief McKosito	Husband	
156			George Starr	1/12	M	Oct 25/06		Hiram Starr	Father	
157	65540-13		Charles Murray	28	M	Oct 18/06		Emily Murray		
158			Pauline Gokey	1	F	Nov 2/06		Mary Gokey	Mother	
159			William Parkinson		M	Nov 9/06		Maggie Parkinson	Wife	
160			Joe Northfork	56	M	Nov 15/06	Single	Logan Kakaque	Bro	

Sac & Fox – Shawnee
1846-1924   Volume XI

106
Record of Deaths among Indians of Sac & Fox Agency

Number on this Record	Number on Record of Births	Number on Family Register Law Heirship	Name	Age	Sex	Date of Death	Married Single, Widow Widower, or Divorced	Name of a Living Relative	Relation	Number of Relative on Family Register
161		144638-13	Eliza White Kebolte		F	Jan 26/07	M	Charley Kebolte	son	
162			Mary Gokey		F	Feb 17/07	M	Paul Gokey	husband	
163		84626-13 90585-13	Mary Roubidoux[sic]		F	Dec 20/06	M	Robt Roubideaux	husband	
164			William Dole		M	Mar 30/07	Wdr	Jake Dole	son	
165		17698-10	Lena Seaborn	27	F	May 23/07		Isabel Barney	dau	age 13
166			Ozettie Kihega	9mo	F	June 10/07	S	Julia Kihega	Mother	
167			Rufus Roubideaux	2mo	M	Jan 21/07	S	Bessie Roubideaux	Sister	
168		117752-13	Maggie Burgess	34	F	July 23/07	Single			
169			Tecumseh Sherman	37	M	June (?)	Married	Dolly Sherman	wife	
170		111467-11	Paul Randall	19	M	Aug 19/07	Single	Tom Penashe	Father	
171		115462-14 131036-14	Cora Smith	30	F	Aug 19/07	Married	Frank Smith	Husband	
172		61517-12 5225-13	Nancy Curtis	73	F	Aug 17/07	Single			
173		48326-14	Walter Mathews	19	M	Aug 22/07	Married	Cornelia Mathews	dau	
174			Henrietta Mack	15da	F	Sept 15/07	Single	Laura Mack	Mother	
175			John Gokey	6mo	M	Sept 16/07	"	Paul Gokey	Father	
176			Emma Foster	6mo	F	Oct 9/07	"	W^m G Foster	"	
177			Maude Franklin	20	F	Nov 1/07	Married	Osmond Franklin	husband	
178			George Sullivan	5	M	Nov 2/07	Single			
179			D Dennis Keokuk	2mo	M	Nov 21/07	Single	John Earle Keokuk	Father	
180			Charles Starr	1 yr	M	Dec 1/07	Single	Mandy Starr	Mother	
181		72201-14	Frank Davis	34	M	Dec 3/07	Single	Frank B son age 10 Harry " " 7		
182			Mary Franklin	1	F	Nov 20/07	Single	Osmond Franklin	Father	
183			Lydia Falls	53	F	Dec 14/07	Married	Albert Wilson	Husband	
184			Addie Pattequa	14	F	Dec 31/07	Single	Wm Pattequa	Father	
185			Sadie Grant	1	F	Feb 19/08	Single	Austin Grant	Father	
186			Dewey Dupee	8	M	Feb 24/08	Single	Victor Dupee	Father	
187			Shelah Grant	1	F	Dec 19/07	Single	Saginaw Charley Grant	Father	
188			Belle Strubble	1mo	F	Jan 29/08	Single	Ada Strubble	Mother	
189			Beulah Brown	12	F	March 3/08	Single	John Brown	Father	
190			Orilla Davis	23	M	Apr 27, 1908	"	Mary Hurr	Mother	
191			Thos Buffalohorn	54	"	Apr 13 1908	Married	Grace Buffalohorn	wife	
192		76153-11 108749-12	Webster Smith	58	"	May 17-08	Married?			

Sac & Fox – Shawnee
1846-1924   Volume XI

Record of Deaths among Indians of Sac & Fox Agency

Number on This Record	Number on Record of Births	Number on Family Register Law Heirship	Name	Age	Sex	Date of Death	Married Single, Widow Widower, or Divorced	Name of a Living Relative	Relation	Number of Relative on Family Register
193			Mary E Givens	6mo	F	June 14	Single	Isaac Givens	dau	
194			Samuel F Rice	1da	M	May 8th	"	Edith Appletree	father	
195			Eva Baker		F	May 28-08	"	Jacob Wyman	son	
196			Ben Wakolle	6da	M	April 6-08	"	Hugh Wakolle	father	
196½		1909	Crain[sic] Mamie Lorena			July 2, 1908				
197			Sadie Nullake		F		"	Walter Nullake	"	
198			Ethel McClellen[sic]	1/4	F		"	Fannie McClellan	Mother	
199			Josie Harrison	10	F	Dec 13 '08	"	Amanda Starr	"	
200		79698-15	Theresa Bigear	86	F	Dec 30-08	"	Farrah Roubidoux	Gr-son	
201		119800-13	Cora Smith nee Bass	19	F	Jan 11-09	Married	Charles Smith	husband	
202		6698-15	Charley Mohee	19	M	March 6	Single	Osmond Franklin	half-bro	
203		71910-13	Walter Kakaque	25	M	March 10	Married	Wife - Father		
204			William Jones	38	M	Mar 28-09		Father brother		
205			Cornelia Mathews	3	F	Apr 4-09		Mamie Mathews	mother	
205			Lizzie Boyd	18da	F	March 23'09		Christine Boyd	mother	
206			Emily Lucinda O'Brien	3mo	F	" 11/09		Fa. M. B. S. [sic]		
207			Guy Preston House	10	M	May 23-09	Single	Pauline House	mother	
208			Ione C Strubble	47	M	May 23-09		Isaac Strubble	Husband	
209		34323-13	Susie Grant	21	F	April 20-09		Saginaw Grant	"	
210			Emma Black		F	June 27-09	Single	Phoebe Black	mother	Iowa
211			Francis Kihega		M			Julia Kihega	mother	
212			Bessie Robedeaux[sic]	7	F	May 10-09	Single	Robert Roubidoux	Father	
213		21769-13	Dosh Gibb Kakaque	66	F	Oct 9-09	Married	Logan Kakaque	Husband	
214		77370-15	Jessie Sampson	70	F	Oct 21-09	Single			
215			Della Ingalls	2	F	July 10-09	"	Mattie Ingalls	Mother	
216			Stella Ingalls	3mo	F	June 25-09	"	" "	"	
217			Robert Duncan	2	M	July 26-09				
218			Marion McKosito	1	M	July 30-09		Painter McKosito	Father	357
219		79698-15	Samuel W Peel	73	M	Jan 8-10	Single	Edith Butler	gr-niece	
220	228		Gertie Mansur	1	F	Jan 17-10	"	Ed Butler	father	
221	264		Ida Longshore	9m	F	Aug 14-09	"	Annie Longshore	mother	
222			Theresa Wood	23	F	Mar 1-10	married	Jim Wood	husband	
223			Joseph Dole	4	M	Mar 14-10	Single	Jake Dole	father	

Sac & Fox – Shawnee
1846-1924 Volume XI

108

Record of Deaths among Indians of Sac & Fox Agency

Number On This Record	Number On Record of Births	Number On Family Register Heirship Law	Name	Age	Sex	Date of Death	Married Single, Widow Widower, or Divorced	Name Of A Living Relative	Relation	Number Of Relative On Family Register
224	82681-12		(Harry M Fox) Harvey Madison	22	M	Mar 22-10	single			
225	270		Theodore Kent	10da	M	Feb 13-10	"	Blaine Kent	father	
226	123590-14		Lizzie Gokey	31	F	April 20-10	married	Paul Gokey	Husband	
227	126329-12		Benj Franklin	50	M	April 30-10	married	Leona Franklin	wife	
228	cl 209483		Silas Hawk	23	M	May 12, 1910	single	Unice Pattock	grand mother	421
229			---------- McKosito	1da	M	May 15 1910	single	Painter McKosito	Father	
230			Mary Frances Whistler	1	F	June 29, 1910	"	Guy Whistler	"	
231			Scott Barker	13	M	June 5-10	"	Matilda Givens	mother	
232			--------- McKosito	10da	M	May 24-10	"	Painter McKosito	father	
233	193		Juanita Connalis	3	F	July 7, 1910	"	Martha Connalis	mother	
234	247		Joseph Connalis	1	M	July 7, 1910	"	Martha Connalis	mother	
235	121		Pearl Connalis	6	F	June 13, 1910	"	Mary Connalis	mother	
236	143573-13		Shar-tar-cher	55	F	Mar 11, 1910	married	Sam Ellis	husband	
237	110629-11		Laura (Ellis) Benson	19	F	July 31, 1910	married	Harry Benson	husband	
238	109166-11		Artemus Ward	47	M	Aug 30, 1910	single	Nora Barker	mother	
239			Cora Franklin	5m	F	Sep 20, 1910	single	Osmond Franklin	father	
240	109167-		Julia Brown	32	F	Oct 20, 1910	married	George T Brown	husband	
241	110539-11		Nancy Coon	60	F	Nov 23-10		Paul Gokey	son	
242			Daniel McKinney	3	M	Dec 24-10	single	Aaron McKinney	father	
243	18116-12		Samuel Johnson	63	M	Feb 2-11	married	Emily Johnson	wife	
244	140204-13		Benjamin Hallowell	58	M	Feb 7-11	"	Lizzie Hallowell	wife	
245			Carl Ward	16	M	Dec 31, 1910	single	Cora Ward	mother	
246	18311-12		Mary Black	34	F	Feb 24, 1911	married	Amos Black	husband	
247	248		Clifford E Labelle	2	M	Mar 2, 1911	single	Linda Labelle	mother	
248	2394-15		Bion Sullivan	6	M	Apr 18, 1911	single	Maggie Parkinson Harris	gm mother	
249	301		Guy Garfield Hensley	7d	M	Jan 4, 1911	single	Minnie Rider Hensley	mother	
250			Charley Howard Small Kent	20	M	May 24, 1911	single	Jack Small [Illegible] Kent	Half-bro	
251	288		Samuel Nawanoway	2mo	M	June 28, 1911	"	Frank Nawanoway	Father	
252			Scott, William Jr	8da	M	Feb 15-11	single	William Scott	father	
253	106208-11		Bertha Pattequa	20	F	June 16-11	"	William Pattequa	Father	
254			Herbert Longshore	4	M	Apr 22-1911	"	Annie Longshore	mother	
255	18364-12		Victor Neal	32	M	Sept 17-1911	married	Pearl Neal	Daughter	

294

Sac & Fox – Shawnee
1846-1924   Volume XI

Record of Deaths among Indians of Agency

Number on this Record	Number on Record of Births	Number on Family Register Law Heirship	Name	Age	Sex	Date of Death	Married Single, Widow Widower, or Divorced	Name of a Living Relative	Relation	Number of Relative on Family Register
256	18140-12		Caroline Morris	21	F	Sept 20, 1911	married	Thomas Shaw Morris	husband	
257	68709-13		Eugenia Appletree	4m	F	" 30, "	single	Henry Appletree	father	
258			Evelyn Morris	36d	F	Oct 5- "	"	Thomas Shaw Morris	father	
259	68708-13		Carl Black	11	M	Oct 17-11	"	Amos Black	"	
260	71403-15		Jerome Wolf	46	M	Dec 4, 1911	"	Eunice Hawk	To be determined	
261			Tyner, Ralph B	3	M	Mar 15, 1911	"	Maggie Tyner	Mother	
262			Spooner, Beatrice	1	F	Jan 5, 1912	"	Ida Spooner	"	
263	60508-14		Vetter, Joe	75	M	Jan 13, 1912	"	Fred Vetter	Gr Son	
264			Walker, Andrew	7d	M	Jan 31, 1912	"	Elmer Walker	Father	
265	153587-13		Embler, Joseph	48	M	Feb 8, 1912	married	Kish-tah-che-um	Wife	
266			Jones, Henry C	67	M	Feb 20, 1912	"	Melissa Jones	Wife	
267	6962-15		Pickering, Julia	43	F	Feb 18, 1912	"	James Pickering	Husband	
268	80312-12		Washington, Juanita (Davis)	17	F	Apr 2, 1912	single	Deborah Kakaque	Mother	
269	65912-14		Crane, Lizzie	79	F	Mar 23, 1912		Sarah Ellis	Daughter	
270	80310-12		Kakaque, Deborah	33	F	Apr 18, 1912	single	Mary Hurr	Mother	
~~271~~	18140-12		~~Crane, Lizzie~~	~~79~~	~~F~~	~~Mar 21, 1912~~	~~"~~	~~John Crane~~	~~Gr Son~~	
271			Keokuk, John Earle Jr	3	M	May 23-12	single	John Earle Keokuk	Father	
272	82651-13		Mack, Edgar	58	M	June 26-12	married	Sarah Mack	Wife	
273	84292-12		Logan, Mattie	71	F	July 5-12	single	Clarence Logan	Son	
274			Hunter, Mary	1	F	Aug 7-12	single	Harry Hunter	Father	
275	92052-13		Thurman, Mary (Killed by R.R.)	15	F	Aug 15-12		Jim Scott	Father	reported by Collins
276	57310-17 76801-17		Jones Thomas	29	M	Sept 20-12		Melissa Jones	Mother	reported by Supt Green
277	110055-14		Moore, Samuel L	31	M	Oct 16, 1912	single	Ellen Mason	Daughter	Hospital Norman Okla
278			Peter Dole	1m	M	Oct 21, 1912	"	Jacob Dole	Father	Reported by Collins
279			Waw-sah-kal	4m	F	Dec 18-1912	"	Martha Baker nee Givens	Mother	Reported by Collins
280	41505-13 144521-13		Benson, Harry	27	M	Mar 11, 1913	married	Clara Benson nee Ellis	Wife	Reported by Gayla
281			Helen Scott	20	F	Mar 20, 1913	"	Bill Scott	Husband	
282			Maxine Furrow	35d	F	Jan 15, 1913		Hazel Furrow	Mother	Rep by Collins
283			Morine "	39d	F	" 19 "		" "	"	
284	147044-13		Jack Bear	71	M	Apr 21, "	married	Sarah Bear	Wife	Rep by Alex Connolly
285			Cora Smith	7d	F	June 9, 1913		Charlie Smith	Father	Rep by Collins
286	9840-15		Edith Rice	34	F	July 25, 1913		Edward Rice	Husband	reported by Robt Davis

Sac & Fox – Shawnee
1846-1924 Volume XI

110
Record of Deaths among Indians of   Agency

Number on This Record	Number on Record of Births	Number on Family Register Law Heirship	Name	Age	Sex	Date of Death	Married Single, Widow Widower, or Divorced	Name Of A Living Relative	Relation	Number of Relative on Family Register Reported
287	94292-14		Eunice Pattock	74	F	Aug 5, 1913	M	George Pattock	Husband	by Collins
288	29608-14		Amos Black	32	M	Sept 23, 1913	M	Julia Black	Wife	
289			Harold Frances Walker	10m	M	Sept 29-13	S	Ira Walker	Father	Reported by father
290			Robert Appletree	9m	M	Oct 21-13	S	Henry Appletree	Father	Reported by Robt Davis
291	100915-1914 95834-14 77368-15		Andrew Barker	78	M	Dec 11, 1913	M	Nora Barker	Wife	Reported by Supt Toledo
292			Frank Wyman	4	M	Feb 14, 1914	S	Jacob Wyman	Father	Reported by Collins
293			Wa-the-no-tha Givens	2	"	Mar 17, 1914	S	Eveline Givens	"	"
294			Cuppawhe, Henry	2	"	March, 1912				
295	110057-14		Pearl Neal	6	"	May 26, 1914	S	Lilly Neal	Mother	Reported by Chandler
296	84869-15		Emma Barker	9	"	May 6, 1914	S	Stella Barker	Mother	Reported by Supt Toledo
297			Thoroughman Springer	14da	M	July 26, 1914	S	Gertrude Springer John Springer	Mother Father	Reported by Collins Reported by Chandler
298	27222-17		Catherine Gokey	1	F	Aug 10, 1914	S	Paul Gokey	Father	
299			Bertha Wyman	1	F	July 19, 1914	S	Jacob Wyman	Father	Reported by Collins
300	5436-15 41019-15		Linda Rogers	44	F	Oct 24, 1914	M	Samuel L Brown	Husband	Reported by Collins
301	27222-17		Frank Carter	46	M	Jan 8, 1915	M	Laura Carter	Wife	Reported by Collins
302			Charles Appletree	5mo	M	Feb 2, 1915	S	Henry Appletree	Father	Reported nurse at hospital
303			Benjamin Boyd	8mo	M	Jan 22, 1915	S	Christine F Boyd	Mother	Christine Boyd Reported by
304	74639-15		Flora Foster	29	F	Apr 28, 1915	M	William G Foster	Husband	Rep by A B Collins
305			John E Connalis	18	M	Apr 16, 1915	S	Mary Connalis	Mother	Rep by Claud
306	55371-15		Lola Carter	8	F	Apr 30, 1915	S	Joseph Carter	Father	Rep by Supt
307			Ne-ta-ko-tha	2	F	June 1915	S	Silas Grass	Father	Rep by Collins
308			Gertrude Kirtley		F	" 1915				Rep by Collins
309	9005-15		Henry C Jones, Jr	22	M	Nov 27, 1897	Married	Helen Jones	Daughter	
310	64964-15		Hog-gra-ah-chey	68	M	June 3, 1905		Joseph Embler	Son	
311	5700-15 41408-15		Hester Pennock	39	F	Sept 5, 1900	Married	William Pennock	Husband	
312	11060-15 116014-14		Mollie Guthrie		F	Jan 1, 1893	Married	Guthrie	Husband	
313	Land Sales 79600-11 Law-Heirship		Charles Lightfoot		M			Jack Lincoln	½ Bro	
314	5699-15		William Pennock	35	M	Feb 5, 1902	Married	Inez Bass	Wife	
315	43499-15 41410-15		Florence Bigwalker	21	F	Feb 26, 1894	Single	William Pennock	½ Bro	
316	124973-14		Charlotte Pattequa		F	May 31, 1902	Single			
317	77369-15		Abby Red Rock	54	F	Dec 10, 1898	Single			
318	2392-15		George Grass	36	M	Apr 13, 1899	Married	Mary Grass Silas Grass	Wife son	

Sac & Fox – Shawnee
1846-1924 Volume XI

Record of Deaths among Indians of _____ Agency

111

Number on this Record	Number on Record of Births	Number on Family Register / Heirship Law	Name	Age	Sex	Date of Death	Married, Single, Widow, Widower or Divorced	Name of a Living Relative	Relation	Number of Relative on Family Register
319	793206-15		John McKuk		M	Mar 28, 1894	Single	Nancy Davenport	1st Cousin	
320	76777-15	109156-15	Bessie Davis	15	F	Dec 15-1897	Single	Mary Hurr Davis	Mother	
321			Hiram Starr		M	Oct 17-1915		Maude Starr	Wife	Reported by Collins
322			Alice Thompson	8da	F	Dec 21-1915	"	Sarah Thompson	Mother	Reported by Collins
323			John Moses	65	M					
324			Liza Connolly	50	F	1-3-16	Married	Alex Connolly	Husband	Reported by Supt
325			Ella Wakole	78	F	1-28-16	Married	David Wakole	Husband	Reported by John Brown
326			Leona Wyman	46	F	2/9/16	Married	Clarence Logan	Husband	Verified by Claud Chandler
327			Grace Lee	53	F	3/22/16	Married	Philip Lee	Husband	Reported by Randall Franklin
328			Samuel Falls	35	M	2/28/16	Married	Edna Falls	wife	Reported by Husband
~~329~~			~~Stella Grant~~	~~27~~	~~F~~	3/25 ~~5/22/16~~ Collins reports that Stella Grant is still alive ~~Married~~		~~Charles Grant~~	~~Husband~~	Reported by Alex Connolly
330			Charles Murray	2mo	M	3/21/16	Single	Kirwin Murray	Father	Reported by Collins
331			Caroline Pickett	53	F	3/28/16	Married	Jesse Pickett	Husband	Reported by Collins
332			Olive Givens	12	F	4/13/16	Single	Eveline Givens	Father	Reported by Collins
329			Stella Grant	27	F	4/24/16	Married	Charles Grant	Husband	Reported by Chandler
333			Clarence Logan	38	M	4/26/16	Widower	Lucy Logan	Daughter	Pox Camp
334			Ulyses S Grant	60	M	4/25/16	Married	Lydia Grant	Wife	Reported by Collins
335			Cora Ward	55	F	4/26/16	Single	Nora Barker	Mother	Died in Kickapoo Country
336			Henry Appletree	44	M	4/29/16	Married	Susan Appletree	Wife	Reported by Collins
337			John Givens	27da	M	4/28/16	Single	Eveline Givens	Father	Reported by Collins
338	53754-14		Marie Appletree	2mo 14da	F	5/3/16	"	Susan Appletree	Mother	Reported by Collins
339	133942-15 21408-16		Waw-ko-pah-she-toe		M	6/20/1890	"	Henry Shaquequot	Father	
340	2393-15		Rhoda Mansur		F	12/18/1899	Married	Chas H Mansur	Husband	
341			Philip Nawanoway	2	M	4/27/16	Single	Frank Nawanoway	Father	Reported by Father
342			Woodrow McKosato	3mo 17da	M	5/11/16	Single	Painter McKosito	Father	Reported by Chandler
343	73311-16		Nona Grant	5	F	4/7/16	Single	Austin Grant	Father	Reported by Collins
344	73310-16		Caroline Grant	2	F	4/17/16	"	"	"	Reported by Collins
345	73313-16		Pearl Smith	2	F	4/18/16	"	Charley Smith	Father	Reported by Collins
346	73312-16		Walter Samuel Falls	1	M	4/26/16	"	Edna Falls	Mother	Reported by Collins
347			Sarah Bigwalker	60	F	5/12/16	Widow	Lelia Bigwalker	Dau	Reported
348	Probate 86942-17		Jackson Wakole, Jr	2	M	6/2/16	Single	Jackson Wakole	Father	by Supt
349			Isaac Givens	35	M	4/7/16	Divorced			
350			Clifford Wyman	1	M		Single	Jacob Wyman	Father	

Sac & Fox – Shawnee
1846-1924   Volume XI

112
Record of Deaths among Indians of   Agency

Number On This Record	Number On Record Of Births	Number On Family Register Law Heirship	Name	Age	Sex	Date of Death	Married Single, Widow Widower, or Divorced	Name Of A Living Relative	Relation	Number Of Relative On Family Register
351			Jesse Smith	41	M	4/9/16	Married	Frank Smith	Husband	Reported by Collins
352			Rachel Pate	23	F	7/3/16	Married	Robert Pate	Husband	Reported by Collins
353		Probate 86945-17	Matilda McKosato	4yr	F	6/17/16	Single	Painter McKosato	Father	Reported by Chandler
354		Probate 67789-17	Logan Kakaque	76	M	6/20/16	Widower	Jesse Kakaque	Son	Reported by Chandler
355		Probate 96446-17	Zella Brown	3mo 12das	F	7/27/16	Single	Thomas Brown	Father	Reported by Chandler
356			Amanda McKosato	67	F	7/24/16	Married	Chief McKosato	Husband	Reported by Chandler
357		39909-15	Della Matthews	34	F	11-20-93	Married	Edward Matthews Rosa Appletree	Husband Dau	
358		Probate 67548-17	Chief McKosato	83	M	11/8/16	widower			Reported by Chandler
359			Walter Nullake	36	M	7/31/16	Married	Ida Nullake	Wife	Reported by Chandler
360			Ulyses S Grant, Jr	6	M	10/24/16	Single	Saginaw Grant	Father	Reported by Father
361			Pearl Bessie Grant	1yr	F	2/21/17	"	Saginaw Grant	Father	Reported by Father
362			Benjamin Butler	1	M	9/27/16	Single	George Butler	Father	Reported by Collins
363			Daniel Franklin	2mo	M	12/27/16	"	Harding Franklin	"	" "
364			Fred Butler	7mo	M	1/21/17	"	Edward Butler	"	" "
365		Probate 86943-17	Viola May Foster	2	F	10/30/16	"	Jane Butler nee Foster	Mother	Reported by Chandler
366			Ople[sic] Murray		F	4/1/17	"	Kerwin Murray	Father	Reported by Collins
367			Grover Grant	21da	M	4/29/17	"	Austin Grant	Father	Reported by Collins
368			Florine Wyman	3mo	F	5/24/17	Single	Mary Wyman	Mother	Reported by Mother
369			Louis P LaBelle	9da	M	7/5/17	Single	Linda LaBelle	Mother	Reported by Chandler
370			Francis Martin	47	M	10/9/17	Married	Liza Martin	Wife	Pneumonia complications
371			Alex Jefferson Jr		M	1/23/18	Single	Alex Jefferson	Father	F.W. Wyman Tuberculosis
372			James Carter	1897	M	3/2/18	"	Joseph Carter	Father	Reported by Supt
373			Sarah Bear	1846	F	3/11/18	Widow	George O Morton	grandson	Old Age Reported by W.G. Foster
374			Carrie Rice	1903	F	3/28/18	Single	Edward Rice	Father	Pneumonia Supt Haskell Institute
375			Frank Falk Springer (Robert)	25	M	/18				
376			Mary E Brown Washington	20	F	5/28/18	Married	John Brown	Father	Reported by Chandler
377			Maggie Tohee	68	F	7/13/18	Single	Joseph Springer	Aunt	Reported by Robert Small
378			David Wakole		M	7/9/18 Demented	"	Hugh Wakole	Son	Reported by Chandler Reported by
379			Isaac Longshore	20	M	6/24/18	"	Anna Satterlee	Son	Supt Carlisle Institute Pa
380			Alma Grant	9mo	F	suicide (shot himself) 8/8/18		Saginaw Grant	Father	Reported by Chandler
381			Oliver Jackson	54 (1864) (1889)	M	Oct 3 1918	Widower			Reported by Collins
382			Randall Franklin	29	M	Oct 3 1918	Married	Sora Franklin	Wife	Reported by Collins

Sac & Fox – Shawnee
1846-1924   Volume XI

Record of Deaths among Indians of Agency

NUMBER ON THIS RECORD	NUMBER ON RECORD OF BIRTHS	NUMBER ON FAMILY REGISTER Law Heirship	NAME	AGE	SEX	DATE OF DEATH	MARRIED SINGLE, WIDOW WIDOWER OR DIVORCED	NAME OF A LIVING RELATIVE	RELATION	NUMBER OF RELATIVE ON FAMILY REGISTER
383			Gladys Franklin	2yr (1916)	F	10/9/18	S	Sora Franklin	Mother	Reported by George R Franklin
384			Harry Brown	25 (1893)	M	8/30/18	S	John Brown	Father	Reported killed in action France
385			Hoke Smith McKosato	23 (1915)	M	10/15/18	S	Anna McKosato	Mother	Reported by Chandler
386			Sylvia Pauline Wakole	3yr	F	10/17/18	S	Grover Wakole	Father	Reported by Chandler
387			Allen G Thurman	31 (1887) (1863)	M	10/12/18	M	Bessie Thurman	Wife	Collins
388			Samuel L Brown	35	M	10/13/18	Widower	Stella Barker	Sister	"
389			Grace Butler	12 (1906)	F	10/ /18	S	George Butler	Father	Reported by Supt Haskell
400			Charles Smith	34 (1884)	M	10/13/18	M	Theresa Smith	Wife	
401			Frank Gokey (Louisa)	Died in Camp Logan, Texas 1890 28	M	10/28/18	M	Dolly Gokey	"	Reported by Collins
402			Laura Mack	1882	F	Nov/15/18	M	Elbert Mack	Hus	Reported by Agent Avery
403			Phoebe Whitecloud Black	1887	F	Nov 4/1918	M			Rep by Chandler
404			Edward L Crane (Morris)	1893	M	2/18/19	M	Viola May Crane (Morris)	wife	Reported by William G Foster
405			Zella Washington } Twins	1918	F	10/1/18	------	Willie Washington Shawnee	Father	Rep by Chandler
406			Berta " }	1918	M	6/22/18	(seperated)[sic]	"	"	"
407	Census Bureau Reg #1		Inez Bass	1871	F	3/17/19	Married	Lee Bass	son	Reported by Collins
408	Reg 1 May 1919		Mary A Keokuk	1828	F	5/1/19	Widow	Leo Whistler	nephew	occurred at Agency
409			Sophie Embler Lincoln	1881	F	4/23/19	Married	Thomas Lincoln	Hus	Reported by Collins
410			Charles Grass	8da	M	4/26/19	S	Silas Grass	Father	"
411			Pearl Conger DeLansanne		F	5/28/19	Married	Andrew Conger	Father	
412			Thompson, Ellen	1da	F	8/9/18	S	Sarah Thompson	Mother	"
413			Struble, Isaac	80	M	4/6/19	Widower	Ada Grass	dau	"

299

Index

[ILLEGIBLE]
  Eunice 127
  G G 23
  J P 15
  Julia....................................... 23
  Laura 96
AARON 27
ACTON, James 41
AH-KE-NA-NAH-THO 265
AH-NAH-ME 91
AH-NAH-ME-NE-QUAH 100
AHNAKWENGUAH 13
AH-PAH-CHE-KAH-TAW-QUAW .
.... 95
AH-PAW-HAH-MO-QUE 92
AH-QUAW-SAW 67,97
AH-SHE-KAW 98
AH-SHE-TAH 72
AH-SKE-PUCK-KA 99
AH-SQUAH-SUP-PIT 79
AH-SQUAH-TUP-PIT 104
ALFORD, Thomas W 175
ALLEN 10
  Mr 35
ALLEY
  Daniel 274
  Enos 241,261
  William 261
  Willie 274
ANGELINE 41
ANIGRE 115,146,147
ANNIE 32
ANNIS, O W 23
ANTOINE, Mary 20,21,22
APPLETREE
  Carrie 241,248
  Charles 276,296
  Edith 116,210,248,263,293
  Eugenia 269,295
  Geo 291
  George 186,187,236
  Henry 81,115,226,269,272,276, 278,295,296,297
  Marie 278,297
  Robert 272,296
  Rosa 186,236,298
  Rosa Battice 226,229
  Susan 197,198,226,269,272, 276,278,297
ASMIDT, Joseph 15
ATHATWESKNINO 13
ATKINS
  Baxter 159,160
  Harvey 158
  Harvey Reed 159,160
  J D C 10
  William 291
  William, Jr 159,160
  Wm, Jr 158
AT-TON-NO-TO 83
AU-GRE 251,288
AUGRE 108,115,146,253
AVERY, Agent 299
AW-PAW-SHE 72
AW-SAW-WAW-SE 74
AW-YAW-CHE 85,99
BAKER
  Eva 82,102,241,293
  Martha 50,82,272,295
  Timothy 67,82,102
BARADA
  Fred 262
  Lizzie 220
  Minnie 141,142,165,262
  Newlyn 241,262
BARKER
  Andrew 13,74,115,119,154,155, 214,215,296
  Emma 296
  Levi 115,154
  Matilda 250,291
  Minnie 214
  Nora 13,119,149,154,214,230, 231,294,296,297
  Olive 250
  Oliver 241
  Scott 294
  Stella 214,256,296,299
BARNEY, Isabel 272,292
BASEL, R J 23
BASS 241
  Carrie 67,98
  Cora ... 98,99,115,179,236,278,293
  Ellen Roubidoux 278
  Florine 281
  Helen 281

Index

Inez 71,98,99,167,171,179,200, 201,257,291,296,299
Inz 291
Ione C 98,99,179
Lee 98,99,179,278,281,299
Samuel 67,98
BASSETT
    Frank 241,261
    Margaret 219,261
    Sam 261
BATTICE, Walter 11
BEAR
    Cora 84,116,201,202,206
    Jack ... 13,77,115,119,127,128,133, 173,231,234,295
    James 67,97,115,177,236
    Mollie 67,97,99
    Sarah ... 13,85,98,133,173,174,177, 178,180,181,213,236,295,298
    William 83,100,173,201,213
BENNETT
    Joseph 31
    Marry 31
    Mary 31
BENSON
    Clara 165,168,170,182,189,295
    Edith 165,168,182
    Harry 115,121,122,128,170,231, 232,294,295
    Laura (Ellis) 241,294
    Laura Ellis 115,128,231
BENTLEY, Jane 186
BEULAH 96
BIG EAR 241,288
    Theresa 115,220
BIGEAR 241
    Theresa 241,252,288,293
BIGWALKER
    Elizabeth 276
    Esther 82,169,188,227
    Florence 67,83,115,196,200,296
    Jennie 20,21,82,115,168
    John N 20
    John W 67,82
    Lelia 168,169,188,227,276,297
    Lillie 82
    Margaret 83,291
    Maud 82
    Sarah ... 20,82,92,115,168,169,187, 188,227,297
BIGWALKER HULL, Jennie 241
BLACK
    Amar 74
    Amos 81,104,115,130,137,150, 187,232,248,255,287,294,295,296
    Amos, Jr 129,130,137,150,187, 218,232,241,248
    Bertha 129,130,137,150,151, 187,218,232,241,255
    Carl 129,232,287,295
    Emma 241,259,293
    Fannie 241,262
    Henry 262
    James 67,78,79,104,241,287
    Julia 187,296
    Lucy 67,78
    Mary 115,129,232,241,248, 287,294
    Nancy 67,78
    Pheobe Whitecloud 259
    Phoebe 162,262,293
    Phoebe Whitecloud 299
BLACKHAWK, Jacob 220,221
BOB, Charley 175
BOHNER, Lillie L 61
BOYD
    Benjamin 276,296
    Christine 150,230,276,293,296
    Christine F 264,267,271,296
    Cora 271
    Joe 264,271
    Joe A 267
    Lizzie 241,264,293
    Rosie 241,267
BRADLEY, C W 31
BRADY, Peter 175
BRAIN, Edith 165
BRIEN
    Josie 159,160
    Louise 159,160
    Mary 159,160
    Thaddeus 159,160
BROWN
    Bertha 279
    Bertha Carter 281
    Beulah 79,292

Index

Edith............. 168,170,182,189,210
Ella..220
Elsie F 130,241,262
Eva..................................67,81
Frank P..................................281
Fred..262
Fryor Franklin............150,213,282
G T... 29
Geo T....................................130
George..................................254
George T 130,267,294
Gertrude 86,92,96,193
Harry 79,125,207,234,235,299
Jno..291
John.......... 79,96,119,120,121,122,
125,126,128,129,133,134,174,182,
187,188,193,194,205,207,223,231,
232,233,234,235,236,280,292,297,
298,299
Josephine...........67,79,96,115,193,
205,207
Julia............. 115,130,241,254,262,
267,294
Linda......................................137
Lindy......................................150
Lorena J 130
Lorena Julia......................241,267
Margaret ChristJohn.................282
Mary...........................125,234,235
Mary E 79,207
Melinda Delphine....................282
Mjishke..................................125
Noble H.................................130
Pearl.......................................130
Sam 81,150,151,189
Samuel 13
Samuel L 205,218,296,299
Samuel Lo..............................208
Shela Guthrie 282
Sissie....................................... 13
Thomas 79,125,207,234,235,
279,281,298
William T..............................130
William Theodore 241,254
Zella......................................298
Zilla Gertrude..........................279
BROWN-GIVENS...................... 44
BUFFALOHORN

Clara .. 67,79,115,189,190,210,211
Grace 292
Jennie................................241,289
Mama.. 79
Mamie................. 67,190,211,228
Thomas J 79,93
Thomas Jefferson............ 115,189,
190,210
Thos............................... 292
Thos J 289
BUNTIN
Hon J A......................................30
John A 3
Mr..42
Mr J A............................36,37,38
BURGESS
Carl N 261
Earl N 241
Frank 184,218
Mack................................... 218
Maggie......... 115,183,237,261,292
Mark 184
Roy 184,218
William.......................... 184,261
BUTLER
Anna..291
Benj 67,77,80
Benjamin 115,176,236,241,
280,287,298
Carl.................................. 241,267
Dewey.............................. 241,262
Ed................................ 260,293
Edith 262,267,274,280,293
Edward 80,81,99,130,133,177,
255,263,273,280,281,287,298
Fred 280,298
George 55,80,81,99,177,262,
263,267,274,280,287,298,299
Grace 299
Harry Francis........................281
Ida........ 132,133,180,184,203,204,
232,273,280,281,291
Jane...... 80,81,99,177,273,287,298
Lizzie.................................. 67,77
Mamie................................. 273
Mollie................................ 67,81
Pearl....................................274
CAMERON, C W..........................38

303

Index

CAMPBELL, Supt 35
CAPPER
   Alfred Rodell 241,266
   John T 266
   Mabel 266
CARLISLE, John G 241,287
CARSON
   Frank, Jr 220
   George 220
   Joe 220
CARTER 241
   Andrew 241,265
   Bertha 77,148,223
   Della 270
   Dennis 241,258
   Ella 13,99,144,186,187,258,287
   Ellen 248
   Etheline 241
   Ethline 188,189,248
   Florence 274
   Frank 13,77,130,142,144,148,
   206,222,223,274,296
   James 298
   James II 282
   Jefferson 241,248,290
   Jesse 50,85,88
   Joe 187,188,248,257,260,
   270,282,290
   Joseph 265,274,278,296,298
   Laura 124,126,186,188,191,
   192,213,223,235,282,296
   Lewis 115,144,148,291
   Lillie 23
   Lilly 213
   Lola 241,260,296
   Louise 13,67,77,115,144,148
   Lucy 241,248
   Lulu 278
   Madaline 257,265,270
   Madeline 215,248,260,274,278
   Madeline Houston 282
   Martha 67,77
   Milton 13,130,144,145,148,187,
   248,258,291
   Mrs 35
   Mrs Lillie G 33
   Sadie 115,144
   Sarah 17

CASTEEL
   Clarence 270
   Edith Clarence 241,268
   Elizabeth 263
   Elizabeth McKinney 268
   James Clarence 268
   Lizzie 263,270
   Reba 270
CEGAR, Jennie 175
CHACAKLAHTOKEHAL 13
CHAH-KAH-QUAH 230
CHAH-YAH-KAW-SE 72
CHANDLER ... 274,278,279,280,282,
296,298,299
   Claud 221,272,276,277,
   278,296,297
   Claudia Elizabeth 272
   Leona 212,213,272
   Mr 281
CHAW-KAH-NE-MAH 89
CHAW-KAW-PE 73
CHECK-E-QUA 95
CHEEKOS-KUK 67
   Mary 91
CHEEKOS-KUK-KAH-TAH-KO-WA
H 91
CHE-KAW-MAH-QUAH 98
CHE-KO-SKUK 269
CHE-NAW-QUE-NAW 241,252
CHE-QUAM-ME-GO-CO 87
CHIP KO QUAH, Sacto 54
CHUCH-E-QUAH 102
CHUCK E QUA 96
CHUCK-E-MAW-E-SAY 92
CLARK
   Geo F 34,42,43,49
   Geo T 38
CLAY
   Henry 88
   Julia 291
CLOUD, T J 25
CLUTE 241,255
COFER, Jennie 145
COLLINS 273,274,277,278,279,
281,283,295,296,297,298,299
   Arza B 38,52,173,276,278,280
   A B 276,277,296
   Mr 60,282

Index

Mr A B 51
CONALIS
  Bud 265
  Joe 265
  Joseph 265
  Martha 265
CONALLIS
  James 241,268
  Martha 268
CONALLY, Alex 13
CONGER
  Andrew 78,120,121,167,190,
  191,202,203,215,216,217,231,255,
  257,290,299
  Hattie 67,85,99,115,190,202
  Jasper 67,77,115,190,191,202
  Jay 77,78,85,86,90,99,101,
  115,190,241,290
  Julia 67,81
  Julia Black 67,78
  Martha 67,85
  May 67,99
  Pearl 78
  Silas 67,77,115,120,231
  William 67,78,115,190,191
CONKLIN, E L 174
CONLEY, Luke 115,119,290
CONNALIS
  Bud 255
  Bull 258
  Clifford 276
  Elizabeth 241,250
  Joe 248,276
  John E 296
  Joseph 241,255,294
  Juanita 241,260,294
  Katharine 248
  Leona 241,258
  Martha 260,271,276,294
  Martha M 248,250,255
  Mary 255,258,294,296
  Pearl 241,255,294
  Remona 241,255
  Viola Marie 271
CONNALLY, Liza 13
CONNELLY
  Alex 249
  Edgar 249

Liza 249
CONNOLIS
  Elisabeth 250
  Joe 250
  Katharine 241
  Martha 250
CONNOLLY
  Alex 124,125,127,132,133,134,
  136,137,138,139,140,141,142,143,
  144,145,148,149,150,151,152,153,
  154,155,165,166,167,168,169,170,
  171,172,173,174,177,178,179,182,
  184,186,187,188,189,204,212,213,
  222,223,224,232,234,236,273,295,
  297
  Alexander 151,152,154,172,
  189,190,191,192,193,194,195,196,
  197,198,199,200,201,202,203,204,
  205,206,207,208,209,210,211,212,
  213,215,216,217,224
  Alvira 224
  Charles 224
  Edgar 224,241
  Grace 224
  Liza 115,224,297
COON
  Dennis 67,99,241,287
  Mancy 231
  Nancy 115,128,241,294
COONSKIN 105
CORDELL
  Judge S A 21,47
  S A 17,20
COUTEAU
  Carl 241,249
  Ernest Antoinne 241,255
  John 249,255
  Lettie 249,255
CRAIN
  Alice M 258,262
  Allen 258
  Allen Lenard 262
  Mamie Lorena 241,293
  Mayme Lorea 258
CRANE
  Carrie 241,288
  Charles 99,115,195,196,197
  Charley 249,287

Charlie	241
Edward L	299
Harry	141,196,197,198,241,249
Helen	290
Horace	241,249,289
John	141,196,197,198,295
Lizzie	115,127,196,197,295
Mary	249,289
Mary L	287,288
Viola May	299

CROSSAN, W B 31
CROSSAN & REPLOGLE 31
CUP PAHE, Lee 225
CUP PAW HE, Mary 78
CUPPAHA
- Lee 258
- Louis 241,258

CUPPAHE
- Chief 67,103
- Edwina 241
- Mary 67,103

CUP-PAW-HE 103
CUPPAWHE
- Edwina 249
- Henry 241,265,296
- Lee 249,265,269
- Lee, Jr 269
- Mary 78

CURTIS
- Fannie 262
- J M 262
- Juanita Evalena 241,262
- Nancy 115,222,292

DAH-TUP-PUCK-E 287
DAVENPORT
- ------ 89
- Nancy 89,297
- Seba 89
- William 213
- Wm 89

DAVID
- Frank 75
- Robert 166

DAVIS
- Bessie 67,101,115,215,216,297
- Flora 89,90,241,249,287
- Frank 115,210,211,249,287,292
- Frank B 211,292

Harry	211,292
Jefferson	13,67,101
Junetta	71
Lizzie	295
Marie	67,101,115,138,165
Mary	241,249,287
Mary Hurr	216,297
Orilla	292
Osville	101
Rachael	13
Rachel	67,90,101,115,215,216
Robert	216
Robt	101,295,296

DEAVER, Ira C 3,4,54,55
DEAVERS, Ira C 4
DEK, Emma 33
DELANSANNE
- Fred 281
- Pearl Conger 281,299
- Pearl May Juliet 281

DERAN, Alice 108
DEROIN
- Birdie 109
- Eliza F 162
- Frank 108
- James 220
- John 220
- Joseph 185
- Josephine 146,159
- Kah In Go Hah 108
- Lizzie 131,185,186
- Mitchell 185,218,219,220,221
- Sallie 218,221
- Susie 159
- Susie Grant 160
- William 185

DICKENS, Mrs 35
DOLE
- Amelia 272,277
- Jacob 175,176,237,272,277,295
- Jake 24,256,292,293
- Joseph 241,293
- Josie 288
- Peter 272,295
- Shermain 277
- William 292
- Willie 241,288

DORAN, Thos 289

Index

DORIAN, Thomas 108
DUNCAN
    Ada 67,85,95
    Alice 67,100,101,270
    Alice Fox 268
    Allie 256
    Allie F 247
    Allie Fox 261
    David 13,67,88,100,115,198
    Dickson 88,100,215,270,287
    Lettie 13
    Lottie 67,100,115,198,199
    Lulu 241,247
    May 67,100,115,198, 199,241,287
    McKinley 95
    Morcealus 241,256
    Richard 95,100,101,155, 204,241,247,256,261,268
    Richard, Jr 241,268
    Robert 241,261,293
    Robt 67,101
DUNN
    Albert 67,95,100
    Caroline 78,85,100
    Lewis 67,85
    Ralph 67,85,100
DUPEE
    Dewey 292
    Frederick 241,289
    Joe Lawrence 241,289
    Louis 266
    Louisa 241,289
    Louise 241
    Mabel 241,253
    Maggie 241,251,288
    Mary 14,115,119,251,252,253
    Mary M 241,252
    Victor 14,251,252,253,266, 288,289,292
DUPRES, Ella 90
EAHEART, Mr W A 3
EATON, Cassie 67,80
EAVES, Carl 23,32,33,35
EDMISTER, Chas W 52,54
ELLIS
    Alex 241,287
    Anna 182
    Clara .. 82,86,165,168,182,189,295
    Dick 86
    Edgar 241,250
    Flora 272
    Frank 175,241,260
    Jackson 17,82,86,182,260,264, 268,272,279,287
    Kate 86
    Katie 67,80,86,87,115,174, 175,241,264
    Laura 82,86
    Levi 279
    Mabel 67,82
    Minnie 241,268
    Ruth 250,260,268,272,279,287
    Ruth Grayeyes 264
    Sallie 175
    Sam 173,183,294
    Sarah 78,82,86,128,167,169, 182,184,197,198,199,205,206,208, 231,236,295
    Sargeant 175
    Stella 82,86,182
ELY
    Albert 107
    George W 241,252
    Jane 107,109,115,160,288,291
    John 252
    Mary 252
    Samuel 67,107
    Samuel L 241,288
EMBLER
    Joseph 115,146,147,295,296
    Sophie 146,147
EMERSON 241,255
    Ed 259
    Edward Henry 241,259
    Lena 259
EMMERSON
    Alice Gertrude 264
    E H 264
    Frederick William 241,264
ENGLISH
    Frank 156,158
    Frank O 156,158
    Katie Roubidoux 225
ETHU-QUI-JE 288
FALK

Amelia ... 24
Daniel ... 252
John C ... 219
Julia ... 116,219,252,253
Lawrence Dupee ... 241,253
FALL ... 290
Grover ... 290
FALLS
Addie ... 228,269
Annie ... 85,115,166,228,241,258
Clara ... 52
Edna ... 112,228,249,254,258, 264,269,273,277,297
Emily ... 67,85
Emma ... 13
Grover ... 85
Herbert ... 241,249,287
Kishko ... 228,273
Lydia ... 292
Robert ... 13,228
Sam ... 85,254,290
Samuel ... 115,228,249,258,264, 269,273,277,287,297
Walter Samuel ... 277,297
William ... 228,241,254,264,290
FA-MO-THAW-HAW ... 263
FAULK, David ... 289
FAWFAW
Alice ... 275
Emma ... 162
Jennie ... 182
William ... 184,237
Wm ... 182,183
FEAR, Marie A ... 104,163
FILTICH, Darwin ... 45,49
FILTSCH, Darwin ... 14,44
FOLK, Frank ... 241,252
FOOT, Fannie K ... 164
FOOTE
Fannie ... 163,164
Fannie K ... 163,164,272
John W ... 272
John, Jr ... 272
FORD
Ange ... 291
Angeline ... 241,253
Augie ... 147
John ... 108

Tom ... 291
FORTIER, Teresa ... 15
FOSTER
Catherine ... 273
Edna ... 222
Emery A ... 43
Emma ... 241,258,292
Flora ... 115,222,258,296
Fred ... 281
George ... 281
George G ... 273,276
Green ... 222
Jane ... 177,273,276,281,298
Roy ... 222
Viola May ... 276,298
W G ... 298
William ... 50
William G ... 130,135,168,171,179, 180,181,222,236,296,299
Wm G ... 120,121,122,123,124, 126,127,132,133,231,232,233,234, 258,292
FOX
Bettie ... 72,86,102,175
Harry M ... 241,294
Joseph ... 67,86,115,174
FRANKLIN
Alex ... 150,230,241,254
Benj ... 93,94,287,294
Benjamin ... 115,149,241,248, 254,274
Christine ... 150
Cora ... 241,266,294
Daniel ... 280,298
Doris ... 269
Fryor ... 90
Geo R ... 150
George R ... 150,230,299
Gladys ... 279,299
Harding ... 51,150,230,268,280,298
Kate ... 157
Leona ... 74,104,127,248,254,294
Leona Wyman ... 150
Lorena May ... 283
Mary ... 241,259,261,292
Maude ... 259,261,292
Minnie ... 280
Osmond ... 111,149,150,168,169,

188,218,259,261,266,292,293,294
Pearl 157
Rachel 121,122,165,168,189,
232,266
Randal 264
Randall 150,230,269,274,279,
283,297,298
Randall, Jr 269
Ross 241,248,287
Sora 274,279,283,298,299
Sora Ellis 264
Susan 67,90
Velinda 157
Vestina 157
William, Jr 157
FRITZ
   Chela 212
   Ixie Weston 275
   John Henry 279
   Lester Weston 282
   Lulah H 282
   Shelah 213,275,279
   Weston 275,279
FURROW
   Hazel 272,295
   Maxine 272,295
   Momie 273
   Morine 295
GAILLAND, M 15
GATES, Merrill E 19
GAWHEGS, Raymond 52
GAYLA 295
GAYLE 273
GEORGE 97
GERTRUDE 27
GIBBS
   Alice 249
   Augusta 241,249
   Gilbert 137,150,218,247
   Hiram 115,137
GIVENS
   Charlotte 241,287
   Eveline 86,96,188,194,227,
257,273,279,296,297
   Gertrude 13,115,193,194,
195,287,291
   Isaac 96,115,193,194,227,
261,293,297
   John 279,297
   Joshua 13,67,96,97
   Lizzie 188,248
   Martha 261,272,295
   Mary 242,257,291
   Mary E 242,261,293
   Matilda 119,127,273,279,294
   Matillda 257
   Olive 297
   Oscar 86
   Wa-the-no-tha 296
GIVES WATER NOW, Mary 220
GOKEY
   Agnes 188,242,262
   Agnus 189
   Amelia 241,247
   Augustina 281
   Catherine 273,296
   Dollie 227,281
   Dolly 299
   Elmer 242,268
   Emma K 11,12
   Francis Martin 254
   Frank 224,281,299
   General Pershing 281
   George 13
   James 242,257
   John 11,12,242,260,292
   Lee 247,257
   Leo 241,255,264,268,275
   Leona 188,189
   Lilly 222,273
   Lilly Neal 281
   Lizzie 13,115,188,242,247,
255,257,262,264,294
   Louis 224
   Mary 257,260,291,292
   Mary M 247
   Minnie 275
   Paul 78,123,128,129,134,188,
189,231,233,241,257,260,262,273,
281,292,294,296
   Pauley 247
   Pauline 242,257,291
   Rosetta 241,264
   Ross 241,247
   Unice 242,255
GOODELL

Index

Bertha (McCurry) 277
Fannie 287
Isaac 13,241,287
James Isaac 277
John I 287
John Isaac 265,277
Larona Modesta 241,265
Mary 13
GOODMAN, Emma 212
GRAEYES
   Leona 212,213
   Lizzie 115,188
GRA-LAW-THA-WA-ME 67
GRANT
   Ah Ne Ko Wa 271
   Ah-ne-kowa 226
   Alice 83,197,198,247,251,
   259,264,270,276,280
   Alma 298
   Alma Adaline 281
   Amos 241,290
   Anna 107,156,159,160
   Anne Nellie 109,291
   Annie Nellie 107,115,159
   Austin 225,241,247,251,259,
   264,270,276,280,287,290,292,297,
   298
   Bessie 225
   Caroline 276,297
   Char S 266
   Charles 297
   Charley 226,273
   Elmer Harold 281
   Eveline 193
   Fannie 281
   Frank 107,158,159,160
   Fred 225,283
   Grover 280,298
   Isaac 193
   John 14,67,107,108,109,115,
   157,158
   Lydia ... 13,86,96,143,193,194,195,
   204,225,227,266,291,297
   Mamie 280
   Mary 14,107,109,156,157,158,
   159,160
   Mary Green 107,109,156
   Mary McGlaslin 107,109,159
   Maxey 241,247,287
   Myrtle 241,264
   Nona 270,297
   Pearl Bessie 277,298
   Sadie 259,292
   Saginaw ... 51,52,167,168,225,259,
   271,273,277,281,293,298
   Saginaw Charley 292
   Shelah 242,259,292
   Stella 115,180,184,204,225,
   266,271,273,277,297
   Susie 115,167,242,259,293
   Thelma 107,158,159,160
   Thomas 67,290
   Thomas Judge 242,251
   Thomas Stanley 107,109
   U S 123,124,126,127,128,129,
   130,135,141,165,204,213,231,232,
   233,234,235
   Ulyses S 266,290,297
   Ulyses S, Jr 242,266,298
   Ulysis S 13
   Ulysses S 115,172,225
   Vestina 107,109,158,159,160
   William 107
   William Green 109
   Zolo 156,157,158,159
GRASS
   Ada 269,271,274,277,280,299
   Ada Struble 282
   Charles 282,299
   Emery 271
   Flora 222,249
   Florance 167
   Florence 167,171,214,215
   Geo 67
   George 73,115,214,296
   John 67,92,277
   Mary 73,242,255,290,296
   Matilda 280
   May 71,249,255,289,290
   Ne-ta-ko-tha 274
   Sadie 241,249,289
   Silas 51,73,214,215,222,269,
   271,274,277,280,282,296,299
   Silas, Jr 269
   TiCora 73
   Walter 241,249

Index

GRA-TAH-HA-MA 290
GRA-TAW-THA-WA-ME 107
GRAYEYES
   Leona 242
   Ruth 17
GRAYSON
   Fannie 154
   Walt 290
   Watt 115,171,203,204
GREEN
   Jefferson 107
   R C 28
   Ralph 107,159,160
   Supt O J 53
   William 107
GREY EYES
   Lillie 32
   Lily 33
GREYEYES
   Leone 257
   Lillie 23,33
   Lizzie 257
GRIFFIN, Ross 19
GROINHORN
   Bettie 136,139,140,141,165,
   174,179,236
   Charley 86
   Charlie 67
   Milford 86
GULICK
   W R 18,20,21,22
   Wm R 17
GUTHRIE 296
   Chela 212
   Mollie 115,212,296
   Shelah 213
HALE
   Bessie 54,55
   John S 23
HALL
   Carrie 242,248,287
   Eudora 67,82
   Eudore 81
   Harry 20,21,28,29,82,91,115,
   187,242,248,287
   Henry 28,287
   Jennie 248,287
   Jennie Bigwalker 242,287

Nellie R 38
Rachel 81,188
Rufus 67,91,242,287
Sadie 287
HALLOWELL
   Ben 108,110
   Benj 252,288
   Benjamin 131,242,294
   Harry Falk 67,110
   Irene 242,288
   Jane 242,252,288
   Lizzie 108,290,294
   Nannie 67,108,131,252
HAMBLEN
   Ada 242
   Frank W 268
   Lydia 268
   Pauline 242,268
HAMBLIN
   Ada 248
   Grace 242,256
   Lydia 248,256
HAMES 259
   Mamie Ruby 259
   Sarah M 259
HAMILTON, William 67,111
HANA QUE, Mary 156
HARDIN, Davis 36
HARNES
   Avis Eleanor 242,267
   Lulu 242,247
   Sarah 242,247
   Sarah M 267
   William 247,267
HARRAGARA, Mary 159,220
HARRIS
   Anna 267
   Annie 279
   Annie G 271,275
   Battice 242,267
   Benjamin 274,279,282
   Dave 279
   David 267,271,275
   Fannie 279
   Frances 115
   Francis 67,103,172
   George William 271
   Grace 274,279,282

Index

Henry 28
Irene 115,205,208,279
Joseph 103,115,208,209
Liza 209
Maggie 134
Maggie Parkinson 123,124,233, 294
Mamie Ruby 242
Marie 274
Mary 104,173,209
Moses 104,172,173,209
Patsy 282
Paul Jonathan 275
Sarah 28,29
William 124,188
William L 130,279
William, Jr 279
Wm L 130
HARRISON
   Ben 104
   Benj 73,75,132
   Benjamin 103
   Jane 142,170,172,190,191, 192,202,203,204
   Josie 242,293
   Martha 67,73
   Rufus 67,103
   Sarah 17,18
   Stephen 74,230
   Steven 104
HARRY 96
HARTICO, Tom 146,147,291
HARVEY, W L 17
HAUKE, C F 9
HAWK
   Eunice 21,22,81,143,295
   James 67,73,81,115,185
   John 67,73
   Maggie 67,73,287
   Richard 67,73,115,180
   Samuel 67,73,81,115,185
   Silas 73,115,132,232,242,294
   Stella 81,180,184,204
   Unice 184,236
HAYES, Sallie 103,188
HENSLEY
   Fletcher 268
   Guy Garfield 242,268,294

Minnie Rider 268,294
HE-NU-KAW 9
HE-NU-NIC-KAW 9
HERDFORD, Martha 67,92
HERR, Wm 31
HERRON, Joshua 18
HITCHCOCK, E A 8
HOAG
   Enoch 67,84,92
   Lucy 67,92
HODGE
   Julia 71,115,171
   Mary 166
HODSDON 125
   Bertha 124,125,192,273
   Bertha L 282
   George Maxwell 282
   Harriet Proctor 273
   W M 124,125,173,174,175, 176,182,183,184,189,195,196,197, 198,199,201,203,205,206,207,208, 209,212,214,274
   Walter J 181
   Walter M 136,138,139,141,143, 144,146,147,148,150,151,152,153, 154,155,156,157,158,159,161,162, 163,164,166,167,168,169,170,171, 172,173,177,179,180,181,187,188, 189,190,191,192,193,194,195,199, 200,201,202,203,204,207,210,211, 215,216,217,218,219,221,273,282
HODSON 125
   Walter M 188
HOFFMAN, Roy 43,44
HOFFMAN & FOSTER 43
HOG-GRA-AH-CHEY 107,115, 146,147,148,296
HOLLOWELL
   Benjamin 14,115,185
   Irene 115,185,186
   Lizzie 185,186
   Nannie 14,115,185,186
HOMORATHA, Lizzie Roubidoux 225
HOOGRADORA, Eva 159,160
HOT CHI SEE 289
HOT-CHE-SEE 242
HOT-CHI-SEE 289

Index

HOUSE
   Guy Preston 242,293
   Pauline 293
HOUSTON
   Judith 92,291
   Judity 115,214,215
   Samuel 187,215
HOWARD, Charley 242
HOYLE 42
HOYO, Geo A 225
HUDSON, Dora E 161,162
HULL
   Ben 71,72,172,192,193,203
   Benjamin 289
   Harry 242
   Henry 71,72,203
   John 115,192
   Lucy 67,71,72,115,192
   William 67,71,115,172,192
HUNTER
   Alice 137,150,217,218, 261,270,276
   Carrie H 282
   Daniel S 149
   Emma 149,242,247,248
   Geo 67
   George 80,242,247,248,261
   Gertrude 149
   Harrison 149,288
   Harrison, Jr 282
   Harry 149,270,295
   Henry 102,127,137,149,188, 217,261,276
   John 67,72
   Lillie G 80
   Mamie 276
   Mary 242,270,295
   Mary W 102
   Robert 115,149,242,288
   Robt 72,80
HURR
   Mary 96,101,127,136,137,138, 139,140,165,166,216,292,295
   Rev Wm 11,21
   William 18,20,22
HUSTON, Samuel 291
HUTCHINSON, John 30
I-CHA-NE 220
INDUS
   Ed 145,149,150,153,155, 157,158,161,162,167,169,170,172, 182,183,184,185,186
   Edw 152,159,177
   Edwd 141,146
INGALLS
   Bessie 67,93,94
   Della 242,260,293
   Frank 242,247
   Henry 93,169
   Horace 67,94
   John J 67,94
   Leila 242,256
   Lucile 94
   Lucy 67
   Mary 242,251,254,288
   Mattie 86,93,94,169,182,242, 247,251,254,256,260,264,287,288, 293
   Sadie 93,94,169
   Stella 242,264,293
   William 93,94,115,169,242,287
   Wm 67
JACKSON
   Olive 171
   Oliver 132,143,298
JAH-MO-WAS 262
JAMES 27,55
   Dora 109
   Jesse 92,101,216
   Mary 175
JANES
   Lillie L 61
   Mr W W 61
JARRETT
   H M 34,42,47,48,49
   I M 50
JEANS
   Edmore 220
   Eliza 220
   Joseph 220
JEFFERSON
   Alex 13,18,93,94,208,222,223, 248,253,254,259,263,266,270,274, 278,287,298
   Alex, Jr 278,298
   Benjamin Franklin 270

Index

Carrie 115,209
Emanuel 242,259
Esther 281
Esther (Bigwalker) 277
Etheline 274
Frances Irene 281
George 242,248,287
Irene 13,208,242,287
James Thurman 266
Katharine 253,254
Katherine 242
Omer 242,263
Rose Homer 277
Sarah 248,253,254,259,263,
270,274,278
Savola 266
William H 208,277,281,287
JENNINGS 274
Cecelia Maybell 270
Edgar 265,270
Edwin Cornelius 274
Mamie 120,168,173,180,
181,270,274
Mamie F 169,174,180,181,182,
188,227,265
Pearl Elizabeth 242,265
JESSE
Joy Dell 282
Nellie B 282
JIMMY 41
JOHNSON
Arthur 90
Bill 52,53,54
David 90
Emily 13,129,207,232,294
Harry 115,137,138,139
Horace J 38,42,43,45,47,48,49,
50,52,60,124,125,136,138,139,141,
143,144,145,146,147,148,150,151,
152,153,154,156,157,158,159,161,
162,163,164,166,167,168,169,170,
171,172,173,174,175,176,177,179,
180,181,182,183,184,187,188,189,
190,191,192,193,194,195,196,197,
198,199,200,201,202,203,204,205,
206,207,208,209,210,211,212,214,
215,216,217,218,219,221,222,224,
225

Horace J 215
Jane 101,115,138,139
Mary 279
Mercie 115,138,139
Mr 44
Orlando 101,137,138,139,165,
166,216
Samuel 13,115,129,232,294
JONES
Artemus 264,267
Arthur 264
Arthur Clarke 26
A B 42
Emily 67,103
Emma 13
Frances Orales 242
Harry C, Jr 212
Helen 212,296
Henry 224
Henry C 103,295
Henry C, Jr 115,242,296
Henry Lee 242,267
Henry, Jr 13
Henry, Sr 13
Leona Mildred 242,264
Leroy 260,263
Leroy, Jr 242,260
Levi M 271
Levi W 266
Melissa 13,295
Mrs Levi W 266
Mrs Pansy 27
Mrs Pansy V 61
Naoma Mildred 26
Pansy 26,264
Robert Dwight 271
Thomas 295
W A 8,16
William 242,293
William Woodward 242,266
KAH-COM-MO-SAQUE 87
KAHLKAYYAH 13
KAH-NO-SE 72
KAHTEYWAH 13
KAH-US-SEN-WE
Guthrie 212
Henry 212
KAKAQUE

314

Index

Deborah.............. 115,127,136,295
Dosh......................115,150,151
Dosh Gibb............................293
Jesse........ 80,174,182,226,258,298
John A......................................197
Logan... 115,120,121,122,123,124,
126,127,128,129,130,133,134,137,
150,151,186,189,195,196,197,199,
200,201,202,203,204,205,206,207,
208,209,210,211,212,214,215,216,
226,231,232,233,234,235,291,293,
298
   Maud.............................80,82,182
   Maude 174,182
   Walter 115,242,293
KAN PAWK....................................119
KAP-POL-LAW 100
KASHWAY, Vina 111
KATHEMENAW 14
KAWHUCK..................................... 13
KAW-KAW-KEESE 242,263
KAW-KE-KA-TOE 96
KE WAH KA ME..........................123
KEAHNA
   Marie..............................282
   McHanon 282
KEBOLT
   Charles 14
   Eliza White 14
KEBOLTE
   Charles 173
   Charley....................................292
   Eliza White 115,173,292
KECHKOKA 13
KEESIS, Frank..............................126
KEHEGA, William 290
KE-KAW-SAQUE....................101
KE-KE-TAH-KAH 78
KE-KE-TAH-WAS 78
KE-NAH-NUM-MO-QUAH 76
KE-NAH-PO................................. 92
KEN-NE-SUE............................... 80
KENNOTIPPE.............................. 13
KEN-NO-TUP-PE 100
KENT
   Bessie.....................................263
   Bessie Naw-a-no-way 242
   Blaine......................266,282,294

Edmund 218
Edward L 242,253
Emma 14,131,185,186,252,253,
263,275,279,282
Frank 14,111,112,131,146,147,
148,155,156,157,158,159,182,183,
184,185,186,218,219,221,237,252,
253,267,275,279,289,294
Frank Nawanoway 263
Gertie.. 106
John 242,252
Philip 275
Rosa Hurr 282
Samuel..................... 242,267,294
Theodore................... 242,266,294
Vera..279
KENYON
   Albert D................... 145,272,275
   Isabel 145,272,275
   Jewel Virginia............................272
   Ruth L 275
KEOKUK
   Alice 104
   Charle 164
   Charles.................... 115,163,164
   Charles H....................... 242,288
   Claudia 274
   D Dennis................... 242,261,292
   Dorothy Luella 242,268
   Dosh 242
   Emma 11,12
   Fannie....................... 163,164,272
   Frank 163
   J E..264
   J Earle 242,264
   John 268
   John E........................ 163,164,261
   John Earl................................. 288
   John Earle 163,292,295
   John Earle, Jr 295
   Katherine Lucile 274
   Laura 115,163,164
   Laura Lorena 283
   Mabel..................... 261,264,268
   Marie A 104
   Mary A 13,163,287,299
   Moses 13,104,242,287
   Peyton............................ 274,283

Phoebe............67,104,115,163,164
Robert (Peyton).........................163
Robert Peyton............163,164,216
KE-OM-MO-WHAT.....................102
KE-SHA-SAH...............................213
KETCHE SHAWNO, Albert.........134
KETCH-SHOW-NO, Albert..........217
KETCH-SNOW-NO, Albert..........134
KET-TO-NE-QUAH....................... 90
KE-WACO-TO-QUAH.................101
KE-WAH-AW-KOQUE................. 80
KEWAHAWKOQUE..................... 13
KE-WA-SA-NO-QUA....................213
KE-WAS-HAW.............................. 71
KE-WAW-HAW............................. 67
KE-WAW-HO-QUE...................... 97
KEWAWTUK................................. 13
KE-WY-KAH-ME........................261
KHOLENBERG, Mr W O............. 28
KIHEGA
    Charles................146,147,148,290
    Charley................253,263,269,290
    Francis........................242,263,293
    George..............................242,253
    Julia............160,161,162,253,260,
    263,269,292,293
    Lillian L.....................................269
    Lina.....................................242,252
    Ozetta.................................242,260
    Ozettie...292
    Whitecloud.................................290
KIHIGA, Julia.................................109
KIRK, Emma...................106,242,288
KIRTLEY, Gertrude......................296
KISH-CUT-SHE.............................. 82
KISH-KO... 86
KISHKO.. 13
KISH-KUT-TUP-PE-WA................ 92
KISHOLONKAK............................. 13
KISH-SAH-SAW............................ 73
KISH-TAH-CHE-UM............147,295
KIT TOE....................................74,104
KOHLANBERG, Mr W C............. 29
KOHLENBERG
    Mr.. 35
    Mr W C.................................23,28
    W C...........24,27,29,31,34,134,235
KO-PE-WAH................................... 87

KOPEWEQUA................................. 13
KUAHQUAQUAH........................ 14
KUP-PASH-KA.............................. 89
LABELL
    Clifford E..................................265
    H M..265
    Linda..265
LABELLE
    Arthur H....................................278
    Clifford E............................242,294
    Edith Rose................................273
    Harvey................................273,280
    J Harvey....................................278
    Linda..........169,170,273,278,280,
    294,298
    Louis P.................................280,298
LAH-TON SHIS-ME....................288
LANE, John..................................... 15
LASLEY
    Fannie...................................86,248
    Florence..............................242,248
LA-TON-SHISH-ME....................242
LEE
    Alice...................................104,163
    Bessie......................................67,97
    Grace....115,140,141,165,189,190,
    211,228,297
    Jesse..97
    Philip.............97,140,228,230,297
LEECH, A W.................................. 63
LEVERGOOD, John T................... 62
LEWIS
    Cecil Day...........................242,249
    Glen Wyman......................242,257
    Mary Matilda............................276
    Oma Lucille...............................280
    Omar..280
    Omer D.......................257,265,276
    Paulena Montana...............242,265
    Pauline.........249,257,265,276,280
LIGHTFOOT
    Charles.......................................296
    Charley Howard................116,221
    Martha.......................................225
    Thomas......................................111
LILLIE......................................35,36
LINCOLN
    Abe.. 14

Index

Abraham 242,252,253,289
Abraham, Jr 242,289
Billie 242,289
Fullwood 242,253
Fulwood 278
Jack 29,221,296
Jack Small 219
Jennie 104,110,111
Maggie 14,111,112,157,252,253
Sophie 225
Sophie Embler 299
Thomas 29,219,299
Tom 27
LITTLE, Garland D 49,50
LITTLE AX, Stella 84
LITTLE JIM 175
LITTLEBEAR
Cami J 291
Carrie 93
Eliza 84
Florien 181,210
George 84,181,209,210,291
James 84
Lillie 84
Lucy 84
Shoney 84
LOGAN
Charlie 62
Clarence 115,141,195,196,197,
227,242,247,249,255,257,258,287,
290,291,295,297
Emma 242,257,258,291
Hattie 13,115,132,141
John A 13,115,195,197,200,
201,291
Leona 115,230
Lucy 227,230,242,247,297
Martha 62
Mary E 115,195,196,197
Mattie 247,255,257,258,295
Mollie 291
Ollie 242,255,290
Sadie 242,249,287
Theresa 141,196,197
LONG
Agnes ... 67,95,96,115,125,235,236
Bertha 124,125
Thomas 67,95,96,97,115,124,
125,126,234,236
LONGSHORE
[Illegible] 271
Annie 242,247,250,258,260,
264,266,291,293,294
Charles 258
Charley 247,250,264
Charlie 266
Edwrd 271
Harriet 242,258
Herbert 242,260,294
Ida 242,266,293
Iola E 242,264
Isaac 298
Mrs Annie 274
Stella E 242
Stella Elizabeth 247
Theodore R 242,291
Theodore Rosswell 247
Wilson 242,250
LUCINDA 242,288
LUNT
Lina 108
Lina B 67,115,146,148,
242,251,288
M JISH KE 96,126,234,235
MACK
Carrie 279
Charley 170,171,205
Clara 243,251
Cora 279
Edgar 92,116,126,133,170,
232,234,295
Elbert 170,171,205,251,261,
264,273,279,299
Henrietta 243,261,292
Kaw-waw-so 273
Laura 251,261,264,273,292,299
Lorena 242,264
Louisa 88,215,279,299
Sarah 170,171,205,295
MADISON
Harry 102
Harvey 115,139,243,294
Henry 72
Richard 67,72
Susan 67,72
MAH KO CHE 122

Index

MAHENAHKAH 13
MAH-KAH-KAT 101
MAH-KE-KIAH 272
MAH-KE-KOY-NAH-WAH 91
MAH-KUK 89
MAH-LAH-KO-WAH 84
MAH-NE-ASH-KO-TAH 78
MAH-TAH-WAH-QUAH 79
MAH-TAW-WAW-KAW-PE 102
MAH-TECK-CO 84
MAH-THA-PWA 115
MAKCHEPUKQUA 13
MAKE SO PEAH 233
MA-KE-SO-PE-AT 123
MAL-LO-CHAH 75
MA-ME-CHE 213
MAN-A-TAW-A 97
MANATOWA
   Bertha 235
   Bessie 277
   Elmer 124,192,235,272,277, 280,282
   George 116,172,191,192,193
   Grace 272,280,282
   Grace Margaret 282
   Joseph 280
   Laura 192,223
   Lorena 192
   Lorena Louisa 272
   Lorene 235
MANSON
   Ellen 204
   Hattie 204
MANSUR
   Anna 243,255
   Ben Hull 172,192,193,203
   Charles H 203
   Chas H 297
   Ella 243,260
   Gertie 242,263,293
   Hannah 116,203
   Henny H 242
   Henry 289
   Ida 73,132,133,255,260,263
   Mary 73,116,185
   May 243,287
   Rhoda 116,203,204,297
   Sarah 203,204

MARSHAL, Gabriel 67
MARSHALL, Gabriel 68,90
MARTIN
   Betsy 67,83
   Frances 83
   Francis 298
   Liza 172,186,209,210,236,298
   Liza Harris 226,229
MA-SHE-NA 79
MASON
   Edith 81,82,254,290
   Ellen 172,179,295
   Grace 81,82,116,171,179, 236,249,290
   Hattie 171,172,179
   Miss Hattie 55
   Nellie 67,81
   Olive 242,249
   Rachel 82
   William 243,254,290
MASQUAT
   Chuck E Quah 273
   George 267,273
   Hilda 273
   Juliet 267,273
   Narcissus 243,267
MASQUOT
   Julia 263
   Norwood 243,263
MA-TAH-SHE-QUA 261
MATHEW-PICKETT 60
MATHEWS
   Annie 243,262
   Cornelia 242,256,292,293
   Della 115,151,215
   Edward .. 74,128,129,130,132,165, 232,234,291
   Maggie 60
   Mamie 293
   Martha 102
   Nannie 256,262,268
   Ray 243,268
   Roger 291
   Walter 63,115,256,262,292
MA-TIN-A-YA 37
MATTHEWS
   Anna 127
   Annie 152

Index

Della 298
Edward 142,143,173,298
Nannie 152
Walter 152
MAW-KO-SHAH-POL-LAH-SHAW
.... 86
MAW-LA-LO-WAH-WUSH 85
MAW-MAW-KAW-SHE 95
MAW-MEL-LO-HAN 67,86
MAW-MEL-LO-HAW ... 116,182,236
MAWNAWQUAY 13
MAW-SHE-KAH 76
MAW-TAH-PWA 120,231
MAW-TAW-CHE 96,125
MAW-TAW-KO-LA-QUE 103
MCCLELLAN 90
   Benston 242,249
   Dollie 168,169,187,188
   Dolly 82,249,266
   Dolly M 258
   Edward 89,90,126,127,184,234, 236,247,251,256,264
   Edwd 260
   Emmett 279
   Ernest 242,266
   Ethel 243,262
   Fannie ... 262,266,270,275,279,293
   Fannie Groinhorn 282
   Fanny 257
   Geo B 67,68,89
   George W 277
   Harriet 282
   John 89,90,201,257,262,266, 270,275,279,282
   John B 243,257
   Lorena Jane 275
   Lorena Margaret 277
   Mamie 270
   Oscar 67,68,89
   Pauline 242,266
   Rebecca 67,68,90
   Rosa 277
   Thom 67
   Thomas 68,89,90
   Wallace 243,258
MCCLELLEN, Ethel 293
MCCOY
   Curtis 275
   Dan 250,257,262,270,275,283
   Daniel 223
   David 271,275
   David, Jr 271
   Elburne 270
   Eliza 275
   Isaac 13,223,224
   Isaac C 276
   John Barry 283
   Lizzie 271
   Loreen 242,250
   Mary 13,132,145,152,154, 186,223,257,262,270
   Mary Rosengrant 283
   Maxine Rosella 275
   Oran I 243,257
   Timothy 243,262
MCGLASLIN
   Alice B 220
   Ida 220
   John 220
   Mary 173,220
   Mary Murdock 175,176
   Robert 220,221
   Walter 220
MCKARDO, Anna 82
MCKINNEY
   Aaron 256,261,267,294
   Aron 290
   Arron 254,290
   Beatrice 243,260
   Ceceal 243,254,290
   Daniel 243,261,294
   Fred Lossen 243,254
   Lizzie 260
   Lossen Fred 243,256
   Myrtle May 243,267
   Wilson 290
MCKOSATO
   Amanda 116,166,229,298
   Anna 182,209,299
   Annie 247,278
   Chief 116,124,155,165,174, 187,204,205,207,208,209,226,298
   Flossie 247
   Hoke Smith 299
   Horace 247,287
   Matilda 298

Index

Painter 226,229,247,278,298
   Woodrow 278,297
MCKOSITO 243
------ 294
-------- 267
   (Painter) 243
   Abe 259
   Abi 243
   Alma 67,84
   Annie 86,256,259,263,267, 270,287
   Barbara 67,83,87
   Charles Wakolle 243,256
   Chief 92,119,120,121,122,123, 126,127,128,130,132,133,231,232, 233,234,291
   Ellen 291
   Flossie 242
   Horace 242
   Marion 242,293
   Matilda 270
   Moses 67,87
   Painter 242,256,259,263,267, 270,287,293,294,297
MCKUK, John 67,89,116,213,297
MCLAUGHLIN
   Claud 38
   Claude 34,42
ME KAH TAW 90
ME-AH-ME-SAH 76
ME-AH-SHE-NAH-NE 72
MEEK 271
   Annie 271
   D N 265
   Ella Beatrice 243,260
   Etta May 243,254
   Frances Cecelia 242,265
   Jennie 254,260,265
   Marie Fern 271
MEEK-E-NAW 68
MELOT
   Joe 59
   Joseph 59
   Louise 59
MEN A QUOT 95
MEN O QUOT 95,96
MEN-NA-QUOT 95
ME-OUGH-KAW 140

MESAWAT
   Julia 115,169
   Linda 170
MESH-KE-AH-KO-QUAH 87
MESH-SHAW-CHE 99
MESSAWAT, Julia 115,169
MESSAWOT
   Alma 67,87
   Julia 67,87
   Linda 87
MEU-WA-QUOT 95
MEYERS, Thomas P 136,137
MILES
   Charles 242
   Charlie 249
   Harold Isaac 242,247
   Howard Taft 242,264
   Mildred E 278
   Rhoda 13,247,249,264,278
   Thomas 264,278
   Thomas J 242,247
   Thomas, MD 13
MILLER
   F W 23,24
   Henry 13
   Ida 123
   Mackkohequah 13
   Ruth 115,123,233
MISHEWALK 13
MITCHELL
   Egbert 67,72,115,141,142,165
   James 67,91
   P D 28
MIXON, Julia 154
M-JISH-KE 95
   Leo 126
MJISHKE 96,126
MOCK-E-NAW 67,91
MOCK-KUT-TAHO-SOQUE 81
MOE-LAH-KO-WAH 92
MOHEE
   Charley 116,218,219,293
   Charlie 111,242
   Christian 111
   John 110,243,289
   Maggie 110,183,237,252,289
   Mshhir 289
   Richard 243,252,289

Index

MO-KE-TAH-HOT 93
MOKOHOKO 67
    Dickson 198,199,215
    Flora 88,100,116,152, 215,216,217
MO-LAW-KAW 92
MON YOU A ME 106
MO-NA-CHE-QUA 213
MONES-SE-MO-KE-MAGREE ..261
MON-MOL-WAH 82
MOORE
    Albert 60,204
    Christian 68
    Claudia 265
    Edwin L 265
    John 68
    Mildred Elizabeth 242,265
    Ruth 204
    Samuel L 171,295
    Samuel S 116
MOOSE, Joe 42
MORAN, Aurelia 222,224,225
MORRIS
    Alice 88,198,281
    Caroline 115,270,295
    Charles H 162
    Clara 280
    Clara Falls 228,281
    Edward 88
    Edward L 198,299
    Eliza 109
    Eva 107
    Evelyn 270,295
    George L 162,163
    Grover 51,52,88,198,280,281
    Harriet 67,88
    Herman 162,163
    James A 162,163
    James H 162
    Martha 67,93,94
    Samuel 280
    Samuel R 162,163
    Susan 88,198
    Thomas 88,135,198,270
    Thomas Shaw 135,295
    Viola May 224,299
MORTEN
    Clifford H 82

    George Oliver 82
MORTON
    Carrie J 96
    Celester 242,265
    Clifford H 96,98,180,181, 236,277,290
    Geo O 121
    Geo Oliver 96,98,290
    George 265
    George O 120,173,180,181, 213,231,298
    George Oliver 174,180,181,190, 191,203,216,217,277
    Mamie 96,98
    Mamie F 174,180,181,182
    Mary 277
    Melissa 116
    Mellisa 180,181,236
    Oliver P 67,85,96,98,116, 180,181,236
MOSES 111,288
    (John) 225
    John 116,175,237,297
MO-SO-QUA 243,256
MUC-CUM-PEM-E 243,289
MUC-CUT-TAH-O-SOQU 84
MUCH A HO 119
MUCH-E-SE-A-PO 98
MUCH-E-SE-A-TO 85
MUCK KOSE 76
MUCK-GA-HE 111
MUCK-KO-TAH-NAH-NEM-ME-KE-WAH 94
MUCK-KO-TAH-NEW-ME-KE-WAH 93
MURDOCK
    Edison 269
    Etta 269
    William 269
MURRAY
    Alice 278,280
    Charles 254,278,291,297
    Charles C 108,115,155,157
    Charley 258
    Emily 156,254,258,289,291
    Franklin 155,156,158
    Kate 155,156,157,158,243,254
    Kerwin 108,156,243,298

Index

Kirwin 67,115,155,156,157, 158,159,219,278,280,297
    Louis 243,253,289
    May 67,108,115,157,158,289
    Opal 280
    Ople 298
    Orlando 258
    Pearl 155,156,158
    Velinda 155,156,157,158,243
    Vestina 155,156,157,158
MURRY
    Alice 275
    Charley 253
    Emily 253
    Esther 275
    Kerwin 243,253,275,289
    May 108
    Pearl 52,157
MUS-QUAW-KE-A-QUAH 89
MY-AH-CHE 268
MY-AH-PE-ME-GRE-ME 67,106
MYAP-PE-ME-GRA-ME 252
MY-AW-CHE 92
MY-CH-CHE 243
MYERS
    T P 273
    Thomas P 124,125,135,150,151, 152,153,154,168,171,172,174,179, 182,187,189,192,193,194,195,196, 197,199,200,203,204,205,207,208, 209,210,211,212,214,216,217,218
    Thos P 148,165,167
MY-YAH-WAH-QUAH 88
MY-YOU-WAW-QUE 102
NA KO TWY TOCK 96
NADEAU, Fannie 163,164
NAH KUS KE 119
NAHASHE
    Emma 178
    John 116,178,236
    Susan 116,178,236
    William 178
NAH-AW-KE-KE 90
NAH-AW-TAW-WAW-PAH-MAH. 85
NAH-AW-TAW-WAW-PAH-NAH 100
NAH-CUT-TO-SHAH 87

NAH-KAH-PE-AH 92
NAH-KAH-PIQUE 81
NAHKO 106
NAH-KO-TE-IT 102
NAH-KO-TWY-TUCKS 83
NAHMOSWE, William 116,205, 206
NAH-NAW-AH-KAH 268
NAH-NAW-AU-PE 77
NAH-NA-WE 279
NAH-NE-ASH-KO-LAH 81
NAH-SAW-WAW-CHE-LAH 72
NAH-SHE-PE-OTH 38
NAH-WAW-TO-NAH 81
NA-THER-ME-NA 107
NAT-KO-TWY-TUK 95
NAW KO TWY 95
NAW-A NO-WAH, John 289
NAW-A NO-WAY 288
    Don 289
    Mary 289
    Susan 289
NA-WA-KE-KE 155
NAW-A-NO-WAY 111
    Nellie 253
    Susan 68,111,288
NAWANOWAY 14,243
    Ben 269
    Blaine 269,272,276
    Dan 243
    Emma 269
    Emma L 256
    Frank 256,267,269,294,297
    Isaac 276
    John 243
    Mary 243
    Nellie 289
    Philip 297
    Rachel 269
    Rosa 269,272,276
    Ruth Madeline 272
    Samuel 243,267,294
    Susan 243,288
    Theodore 243,256
NAW-AW-TEN-O-KAQUE 94
NAWCAWES 13
NAW-HAW-SHE-TAW 122
NAW-KO-SE-QUAH 71

Index

NAW-PAW-KE-HUCK 256
NAW-PE-SE-SAW 78
NAW-SAW-PAW-MEQUE 93
NE PAU SA QUA 233
NEAL
    Iva 243,251,290
    Kishko 68,88
    Libby 262
    Lilly 135,136,222,251,258,
    270,296
    Mary 68,88,105,243,258,291
    Moses 9,68,88
    Osidore 88
    Pearl 116,135,136,221,222,
    243,262,294,296
    Victor 88,116,135,251,258,
    262,290,291,294
NEAW-A-NO-WAY 289
NE-KOT-LO-KO-HACH 91
NELLIE 27
NE-MA-KO-WHAH 101
NE-PA-SO-QUA 265
NE-PAU-SA-QUA 123
NE-PAW-KO-NAH-WHAH 28
NE-PAW-SAQUE 90
NE-PO-PE 68,71
NESOJAME, Miss 176
NE-TA-KO-THA 296
NISHKAHAT 13
NO AH TOM 243
NO HEART, Joseph 68
NO-AH-CHE-ME 110
NO-AH-TOM 68,110,288
NOHEART, Joseph 110
NORTHFORK, Joe 291
NO-TAH-NAW 73
NO-TAH-SAGNE 75
NO-TAW-KO-SE-QUAH 100
NO-TEM-O-SHUK 78
NOTEN 14
NULLAKE
    Ada 100
    Alice 229,243,263
    Annie 100
    George 273
    Ida 229,230,268,273,298
    John 243,258,291
    Sadid 293

    Sadie 243,250
    Walter 116,229,250,258,263,
    268,273,291,293,298
    Watt 229,243,268
O'BRIEN
    Dan 259,264
    Daniel 256,266
    Edward 243,259
    Emily Lucinda 243,264,293
    Lucille 243,266
    Lucy 250,256,259,264,266,291
    Myrtle Myree 243,256,291
    Ruth 243,250
OCEAN, Bettie 68,93
O-HI-YE-SA 9
OK-O-MAW-QUAH 75
OPY-O-SAH 93
ORALES, Frances 263
O-SHA-KE 74
OSMIT 41
OUTCELT, G A 59
OZHE-OCK-PENSE 75
PA JOHIA NA 233
PADDOCK
    George 289
    George W 184,204
    Unice 180,184,236
PAH-NE-MA 68
PAH-NE-ME 105
PAH-SHA-SHAH-SHE 11
PAHTHEHUOAHEME 14
PA-MO-THAW-HAW 243
PANASHE, Tom 122
PA-PAW, Mary 86
PA-PHIA-NA 123
PARKER, Quannah 41
PARKINSON
    James 104
    Maggie 234,291
    Roger 243,287
    William 287,291
    Wm 79
PATE
    Harry Samuel 227,278
    Nellie R 274
    Rachel 116,188,227,278,298
    Robert 278,298
    Robert Charles 227,274

Index

Robert T 38,227,274
PATRICK
   Agent..59
   Lee 15,59,68,105,127,
234,243,288
PATTAQUA
   Addie..76
   Bertha..76
   Charlotte 68,86
   Mamie 68,76
   William 76,126
PATTAQUE, Mamie 98
PATTEQUA
   Addie..................................98,292
   Bertha....................98,116,133,294
   Charlotte 116,193,194,296
   Mamie 98,116,134
   Mammie......................................85
   William 127,128,132,133,135,
172,188,294
   William G 135
   Wm 88,123,124,126,128,130,
133,231,232,233,234,235,292
PATTEQUAW, William................194
PATTOCK
   Eunice 116,143,296
   Geo W 132
   George.......................................296
   George W 21,22
   Unice...294
PAW-HAW-CHE-QUAH 77
PAW-KE..83
PAW-PAS-KO-KUCK 73
PAW-SHE-PAW-HO.....................127
PAW-SHE-SAW-HA.......................71
PE AH MAW SKE 134
PE AH NU SQUET........................263
PE PE QUA 142
PEACORE, Mary...........................209
PE-AH-CHEA-WAH....................120
PE-AH-CHEW-WAH 77
PE-AH-MA-SHE 134
PEAHMASKE 134
PE-AH-ME-SQUET 243
PEAH-TWA-TAH 243,256,290
PE-AP-PAW-HAW 82
PEEL, Samuel W 116,204,205,206,
207,208,209,243,293

PEELTHEW 13
PE-KE-HAW...................................92
PEMAMI, Joanna 15
PEM-MAH-COM-SE 175
PEM-O-TOE 267
PENASHE 74
   Tom 104,122,233,288,292
PEN-E-TAL-LO-KUT....................73
PEN-NAH-HE-SE 80
PENNOCK
   David 76,95,96,125,199,200,
201,234,235
   Hester 68,76,116,196,200,296
   William 76,83,95,96,116,
196,199,296
   Wm 68,76
PEN-WAY-TAH 92
PE-PIQUE 141,165
PERKINS, Bishop W 68,76
PERRY
   Annie.................110,183,253,289
   Che-naw-que-naw....................253
   Emma 104,111
   Isaac.........................243,253,289
   Sam..104
PE-SHAW-KAW 94
PE-SHE-KE-SHE-QUAH 86
PETERS, Jim.................................143
PE-THAN.......................................77
PE-TO-PE..................................93,94
PETTIT, Sarah...............................189
PE-WAH-TAH 74
PHIA-TAW-NA-HA 214
PICKERING
   George...............................243,261
   Isaa 219
   Jeames 295
   Jennie...28
   Jim 261
   Julia 116,219,261,295
   Nellie 219
   Nora..219
PICKETT
   Caroline 116,127,186,224,297
   Caroline Dunn 103
   Clarence............................68,89,91
   Jesse..................60,77,89,91,165,
224,225,297

Jessie 84
Mary 68,77
Mrs 127
PLEAS
   M J 35
   Mrs 32
   Mrs M J 32,33
PLUM, Minnie 165
PLUMB
   Mary 68,72,74,87,116,142
   Minnie 72,74,87,142
PO-KA-TAH-KUM 37
PONE WYA TAH 233
PONE-WYA-TAH 123
PO-PO 93
POWERS
   Fannie B 74
   Fannie V 68
PUCH-E-SHIN 90
PUCKPOUNAH 13
PUH-PAH-SKO-SE-TAW 91
QUA QUAW TAH 266
QUAH-QUAH-CHE 79
QUAHQUAKCHEOTH 13
QUE-QUAH-LAH-KE-KUK 89
RANDALL
   Fannie 68,74,75
   Paul 74,104,116,122,233,292
REASOR, E D 28
RED ROCK 68
   Abby 74,296
   J Jenson L G 108
REDROCK, Abby 116,155
REGNIER, Lulu M 28
REPLOGLE, D 31
RHODD 275
   Adaline 153,154,275,277
   Edith Fustena 275
   Viola Esther 277
RHODES
   Deborah 71,250
   Sadie 136,137,151,165,166,
   168,216,243,250
RICE
   Albert 250
   Bion 243,250
   Carrie 210,298
   Clarence Grant 283

Edith 116,190,210,211,295
Edith Appletree 256
Edward 63,84,201,202,206,210,
256,263,290,295,298
Jack O 68,84
Jess 63
Lizzie 84,116,201,202,290
Lucian 243,256
Lucien 210
Naoma Sullivan 250
Samuel F 243,263,293
Susie 210,283
RIDER
   Claud Eldridge 243,260
   Ed 260
   Ellen 243,247
   Jody Sylvester 243,250
   Minnie .. 153,154,243,247,250,260
RIDGE, Jesse 68,74
ROBEDEAUX, Bessie 293
ROBERTS
   Bill 32
   Ida 32
ROBITAILLE, E 125
ROGERS
   Cassie 80
   Linda 116,217,296
   Lindy 91,137
ROUBIDEAUX
   Bessie 243,292
   Emily 275
   Farra 111
   Farrah 104
   George 243
   Jada 263
   Jennie 27
   May Columba 275
   Robt 292
   Robus 275
   Rufus 292
ROUBIDOUX
   Annie 220
   Aron 280
   Charles 220
   Emily 155,156,157,158,269,280
   Farrah 293
   Felix 220
   John 131,165,220

Index

Joseph 220
Kate 220
Lizzie 220
Louis 220
Magdalene 269
Mary 116,160,161,162,260,292
Richard 185,220
Robert 160,161,162,163,221,
269,280,293
Rufus 243
Sevinah 161,162,163
Sophie 161,162,163,220
RUBEDEAUX
Ida 97
Mary 108,109
RUBIDEAU
Annie 183
Fannie 68,110
Farrah 110
George 110
RUBIDEAUX
George 253
Ida 258
Jennie 253
RUBIDOUX, Rufus 260
RUBY 53
RUSSELL, R S 213
SACQUOT, Theodore 55
SA-KE-NA-WA-QUE 143
SAMPSON
Jennie 116,205,207
Jessie 243,293
SATTERLEE, Anna 298
SAU-E-QUAH 103
SAWPEQUAW 13
SAW-SWAH-WAH 71
SAXON, Felix J 28
SCOTT
Bill 265,295
Helen 265,269,295
James 50
Jim ... 91,193,194,195,223,277,295
Jim, Jr. 272
John 167,256
Joseph 68,91
Manda 257
Martha 277
Minnie 277

Mr A C 42
William 269,294
William, Jr 294
Winfield 243,265
SEABORN
Lena 116,145,292
William 145
William M 145
Wm 145
SEARS, H B 36,37,38
SENACHE
Alma 98
Anna 68,85,98
Fred 68,85,98
SE-PO-AH-S[??] 75
SE-SA-HO 243,264
SE-TAW-ME 93
SHA QUE QUOT, Cora 122
SHAQUEAUOT, Cora 116
SHAQUEQUET, Cora 233
SHA-QUE-QUOT
Jerome 68,99
Mary 97
SHAQUEQUOT
Grace Lee 142
Henry 116,140,297
Kate 140,228
Katie 140,142
SHAR-TAR-CHER 104,243,294
SHA-TAH-CHER 110,111,289
SHA-TH-CHER 116,183,237
SHAW
Edward 68,79
Jane 86,178,236,291
William 291
Wm 79
SHA-WAS-KA-KUK 79
SHEQUEME 13
SHERMAN
Anne Anderson 68
Annie Anderson 83
Dollie 26
Dolly 292
James 243
Lucy Anderson 68,75
Tecumseh 26,83,97,99,292
SHIH SHE WAHN O 235
SHIH SHE WAHNO 234

Index

SHO-JO MON 106
SHOQUE 141
SHU-TAH-CHAR 106
SINE
    Alma Leona 278
    Fulwood 278
    James 278
SLAUGHTER, John 222
SLUTH
    Emma Dek 32
    Mrs 32
SMALL
    Charley Howard 116,221,294
    Edward 29,221,243,253
    Elwood 219
    Jack 294
    Mary 29,105,146,147,148,219
    Mary Ford 146,147
    Robert 29,110,131,146,147,148, 155,156,157,158,159,160,161,162, 185,186,218,219,253,288
    Robt 105
SMITH
    Alex 68,83
    Annie 256,287,290
    Ben 51,121
    Benj 80,232
    Benjamin 121,122,165,168, 189,255
    Charles 165,168,276,293,299
    Charley ... 80,121,122,179,189,232, 269,297
    Charlie 273,295
    Cora 116,201,202,206,214, 255,273,292,293,295
    Cora (nee Bass) 243
    Ella 220
    Frank 80,121,122,165,166,168, 189,201,202,206,230,232,256,287, 290,292,298
    Geo E 28
    Grace 269
    Hon Sam 24
    Ida 71
    Jennie 194
    Jesse 298
    Jessie 51,230
    Martha 68,80
    Mattie 243,255
    Oda 68,75
    Pearl 276,297
    Rachel 80,165,189
    Samuel 24
    Theresa
    193,194,195,269,273,276,299
    Thomas 243,287
    Webster 71,75,80,83,116,121, 232,290,292
SNAKE, John 175
SNOWDEN, J O 43
SNYDER
    Mr A R 55
    A R 54
SPONER
    Ida 271
    Irwin 271
    Mary Elizabeth 271
SPOONER 274
    Beatrice 243,268,295
    Burnice Henrietta 274
    Ida ... 123,233,268,271,274,281,295
    Irwin 268,271
    Lena Josephine 281
    Mary Elizabeth 271
SPRINGER
    Frank Falk 298
    Gertrude 276,280,296
    Grace 271
    James 243,257,291
    Joe 291
    John 276,280,296
    Joseph 146,147,148,156,157, 158,159,160,161,162,173,175,182, 183,218,219,221,237,257,271,280, 298
    Josie 257,271
    Lizzie 290
    Robert 298
    Thoroughman 276,296
    Willie 274
SQUIRREL 105
    Carrie 68,106
    Charley Howard 243,251
    Garrie 243,253
    Gerry 105
    Jane 243,252

Index

Julia 253
Mary 29,105,116,251,252,253
SQUIRRELL, Mary ... 29,218,219,221
STANION
    Ralph P 27,29
    Supt 35
STANLEY
    Mattie 68,84,93
    Popo 68,93
STAR
    Hiram 263
    Leona 243,263
    Manda 263
STARR
    Amanda 137,150,217,218,293
    Charles 243,259,292
    Cora 175
    Ella 224,275
    George 243,257,291
    Helen 189
    Hellen 116,189
    Hiram 116,223,257,259,271,
    275,291,297
    Hiram P 189
    Leona 224
    Mabel 224,271
    Manda 137,223,224
    Mandy 259,271,275,292
    Maude 297
STINCHECUM, Mr 53
STOUCH, Geo W H 5
STRUBBLE
    Ada 261,292
    Belle 261,292
    Geo 68
    George 75
    Ione C 243,293
    Isaac 75,76,122,123,126,127,
    132,133,141,165,171,179,180,181,
    232,233,234,236,293
STRUBLE, Isaac 142,143,149,151,
152,172,189,190,191,192,193,194,195,
196,197,198,199,200,201,202,203,204,
205,206,207,208,209,210,211,212,214,
215,216,222,224,299
STUDER
    Alice 256
    Edward 256

Ollie 243,256
SUCK-KO-PE-AH, Annie 220
SUFFECOOL, J L 56,61,62
SULLIVAN
    Bion 116,217,243,294
    George 292
    John L 68,75
    Julia 83,187
    Lewis 75
    Louis 134
    Maggie 75
    Naomi 75,291
    Neoma 116,134
TAGGART, Special Agent 15
TAN-NO-SAQUE 84
TAP-PE-NO-WA 103
TASK
    Harry 243,288
TAYLOR 271
    Eugene Lewis 244,267
    Gertie 265,267,271,276
    J W 267,276
    John Henry 276
    Sarah Harriet 271
    Susan 68,75
    Willis 265
    Willis Lee 243,265
TERRY, Miss Beulah 30
THACKERY 42
    Frank 27
    Frank A 25
THOMAS 96
    Lena 52,53
THOMPSON
    Alice 278,297
    Ellen 283,299
    John 278,282,283
    Sarah 203,204,278,297,299
    Sarah Mansur 283
THORP
    Adaline 153,154
    Angeline 255,259,266,281
    Angie 266
    Bernice 243,266
    Charlotte 116,152,153,154
    Edward 153,154
    Ernest 243,250,287
    Frank 153,154,250,255,

259,266,270,277,281,287
  Geo 153
  George 153,154,287
  Hiram 116,152,153,154,243,
  250,251,287
  Hiram P 152,153,154
  James 153,154
  Julia 154,251
  Lucile 281
  Mary 153,154
  Minnie 153,154,270
  Myrtle Agnes 243,255
  Roscoe 154,243,251
  Rosetta 250,287
  Rossetta 243
  Walter 243,259
  Wilber 277
  William Lasley 154
THRIFT
  William 112
  Wm 68
THURMAN
  Allen G 100,193,194,195,198,
  199,227,282,287,299
  Bessie 299
  Harry 243,251,288
  Jennie 193,194,195,228,282
  Lucinda 282
  Lucy 86,96,100,116,193,195,
  251,288,290,291
  Mary 116,223,295
  Roy V 194,195,228
  Sadie 243,251,290
  Theresa 194,195,228
TOHEE 243
  "Little" Dave, Jr 176
  (Little) Dave, Jr 237
  Amelia 24,256
  Annie Perry 175,176,237
  Charley 105,184
  Dan, Jr 259
  Daniel 243,251,255,288,290
  Dave, Jr 105,251,255,288,290
  David 14,105,106,131,146,147,
  148,155,156,157,158,159,160,161,
  162,173,175,176,185,186,218,219,
  221,237,251,288,289
  Ed 268

  Edward 106
  Jane 243,288
  Julia 105,106
  Julie 105
  Leah 243,251,255,288,290
  Lee 68,105
  Lee Patrick 116,175,176,
  237,243,251
  Maggie 298
  Margaret 244,289
  Mary 14,68,105,106,251
  Mary Neal 243,289
  Millie 24
  Nellie 111,112
  Noah 244,268
  Pauline 243,289
  William 68,105,243,259,288
TOWNSEND 104,116,182,183,237
  Ed 68,111,243,289
TURNER
  Clarence 68,75,76
  Fannie 68,76
  Thomas 68,75,76
TUTWILER, S Y 225,226
TYNER
  Alice 244,267
  Claude 243,247,251,258,287
  Eugene 287
  Eugene E 243
  Fannie 52,278
  Houston 278
  Johnson 243,251
  Joshua 290
  Maggie 84,93,247,251,258,262,
  267,270,278,287,290,295
  Mattie 94
  Ralph B 295
  Ralph Benjamin 243,262
  Raymond 270
  Stella 243,247
  William B 243,258
UPTON, E A 222
URIBES, Wiley 98
UT TAH QUOS 132
VAN VALKENBURG, Sylvynia ....
  220
VETTER
  Annie 244,289

Emma Kirk 252
Fred 173,183,244,252,295
Ida 244,253,289
Joe 106,252,288,295
Joseph 176
Lucy 183,244,254,288
Mary 252,253,254
Sallie 244,252,288
Sam 106,252,254,288,289
Saml 253
VETTERS
   Fred 176,182
   Joe 116,175,176,237
   Lucy 68,106,183
   Lucy Ruth 176
   Nesojame 176
WAH-MAW-NAH-TO-MAH 80
WAH-NAW-KE 92
WAH-NECK-KO-WAH 97
WA-HO-NEE-MIE 244,289
WAH-SHAW-NAH 91
WAH-TAW-SAH 68,78,116,205
WAH-TO-GRA-ME 244,289
WAH-TO-GRAM-ME...........105,106
WAH-TO-GRAMME 68,106
WAH-WAW-KE........................... 92
WAH-WAW-TO-SAH 89
WAKHENLAW............................ 13
WAKOLE
   Barney Curtis 278
   Bessie..282
   David....................229,297,298
   Ella 116,229,297
   Esther 226,275,279
   Grover 209,229,278,299
   Hugh 120,229,298
   Jackson.................229,275,279,297
   Jackson, Jr...........................275,297
   Lucien 229
   Mabel..174
   Rufus............................116,208,209
   Sylvia Pauline 278,299
   Walter 279
WAKOLLE
   Allie 244,251
   Ben................................244,263,293
   Cora 244,267
   David....................92,120,121,122,
123,127,128,130,133,134,135,231,
232,233,234
   Edgar 244,254
   Ella 123,233,234
   Ester................................... 254,267
   Esther................ 248,257,262,272
   Glade 244,262
   Grace 272
   Guy..274
   Hugh 120,170,231,244,247,
251,263,266,274,293
   Jackson 244,248,254,257,
262,267,272
   Leo..234
   Mabel................ 247,266,274,282
   Mabell......................................263
   Mable..251
   Mrs 120
   Richard 244,257
   Ruth 248
   William 244,247
WALKER...................................244
   Andrew 116,142,143,271,295
   Ben ...87,250,257,263,268,272,277
   Benjamin 186,187,226,229,280
   Dora.................. 250,257,263,268,
272,277,280
   Edith 143
   Elma 89
   Elmer............. 68,87,143,186,187,
210,226,229,259,271,295
   Evans 244,250
   Frances 244,268
   George Lee 279
   Guy ...87,186,187,226,229,275,278
   Harold F....................................272
   Harold Frances 296
   Harry Benson..........................272
   Ira 87,186,187,214,215,
226,229,272,276,279,296
   Ira, Jr 276
   Leo............... 87,119,120,121,122,
126,127,128,129,130,132,165,186,
187,226,229,231,232,233,234,235
   Lester.......................................278
   Lidia 116,186,236
   Luther 277
   Lydia 87

Index

Mabel 244,257
Maggie 275,278
Marie 276,279
Mary 280
Raymond 275
Willard 244,263
WALTERS, Mrs John 220
WAN-SAW-KO-HUK 124
WANTLAND, Lewis 31
WA-PAL-AH-WAH-NAH 92
WA-PE-KO-HOL 68,97
WARD
   Artemus 116,119,231,244,294
   Carl 244,294
   Cora 91,119,154,230,294,297
WASHINGTON
   Albert 68,71,168
   Berta 299
   Bertha 281
   Geo 68
   George 71,116,127,231
   Juanita 127,128,231
   Juanitta 116,136,139,295
   Junita 127
   Mary 68,71,116,127,231
   Mary E Brown 281,298
   Minnie 279
   Vina Marie 279
   Walter 279
   Willie 281,299
   Zella 299
   Zilla 281
WAS-KO-PAH-SHE-TOE 68
WAS-KO-SE-MON 261
WA-SO-SAH 216
WAS-WAW-KO 76
WA-THE-NO-THA 273
WATSON
   Charles 156,158,221
   Charlie 156,221
WAW PAW 95
WAW SAW KO 95
WAW WA SUM MO QUA 95
WAW WAW SOM O QUA 96
WAW WAW SOM O QUAH 96
WAW WAW SUM O QUAH 96
WAWASICA 13
WAW-HO-PAH-SHE-TOE 116
WAW-KAW-PE 85
WAWKAWPE 13
WAW-KO-DAH-SHE-TOE 87
WAW-KO-MO 94
WAW-KO-PAH-SHE-TOE 142, 165,297
WAW-KO-PAH-SHE-TOW 141
WAW-KO-SE-QUAH 127
WAW-MAW CO 11
WAW-NAW-SOM-O-QUZA 83
WAW-P[?]-MO[?] 260
WAW-PAS-SHE-TE-PAH 99
WAW-PAW-KO-HUCK 95,244
WAW-PAW-KO-LAS-[??] 102
WAW-PAW-NO-QUAH 79
WAW-PE-KO-HAL 121
WAW-PE-SE-TAW 78
WAW-PUSH-SHAW-KOL 89
WAW-SAH-KAL 295
WAW-SAH-KO 272
WAW-SAH-QUE 82
WAW-SAW-HOL-LO-QUAH 83
WAW-SE-NAH-A-TAH 96
WAW-SE-TAL-O-QUAH 81,99
WAW-SHA-LAW 244,266
WAW-SO-SAH 101
WAW-SUCH-CHE 98
WAW-WAW SON O QUAH 96
WAW-WAW-KO 78
WAW-WAW-SAM-O-QUAH 79
WAW-WAW-SHE 90
WAW-WAW-TAW-QUAH-SHE .. 88
WE-KE-AW 88
WE-SHE-KAW-MAH-E-QUE 88
WE-WE-NES 75
WHEELER
   Eva 68,84
   Robert 26
WHISTLER
   Guy 263,269,276,294
   John 269
   Leo 13,126,133,137,138, 139,163,164,165,166,167,169,212, 222,234,299
   Maggie 269
   Margaret 263,276
   Mary Frances 244,263,294

Index

Maude 13
WHITE
  Ada 261
  Eliza 110,288
  Ida 244,288
  James Tyner 261,265
  Lahoma Edith 244,265
  Leonard 244,261
  Maggie 104
  Milton Barb 272
  Myrtle Amanda 244,248
  Roxie 13
  Talbert 248,255,272
  Talbert Glenore 244,255
  Thomas 110
  Tolbert 13
  Tom 111
WHITE HORSE, Maggie 105
WHITECLOUD
  Albert 116
  Dan 225
  Eliza 109
  Emma 109
  James 220
  Jefferson 68,109,116,161,162, 252,288,289
  Lizzie 116,161,162,244,288
  Louise 225
  Phoebe 109
  Robert 244,252,289
  Sarah 225
  Susan 109,161,162,252
WHITEHORSE, Clem 106
WHITEWATER
  Bessie 109
  James 68,109
  Nellie 108
  Nettie 148
  Susan 108,148
WICH TO AH 235
WIGGINS
  E A 10
  Mr 10
WILCOX, W H 43
WILLIAM 95
WILLIAM & FOSTER 124
WILLIAMS 262
  Cassie 254,258,262
  Elsie Marie 244,262
  Francis Martin 244
  Frank 254
  Geo E 42
  Hazel Faye 244,258
WILLIE 32
WILMETH, Warner L 223
WILSON
  Aaron 27
  Albert 265,292
  Bettie 72
  Israel 244,265
  James 68,102
  Mary 153,154,265
WIND, Mrs 32,33
WINONA 9
WINSOR, Frank A 223
WISH TA AH 234
WITONOSEE, John 213
WOLCOTT, Mr 41
WOLF
  James 102,103,116,131,132, 232,244,289
  Jane 68,103,116,132,232
  Jerome 116,143,295
  John 68,102,103,116,131, 132,232
  Rosa 282
WOOD
  Ethelyn Gladys 244,266
  Jim 260,266,293
  Stella 244,260
  Theresa 244,260,266,293
WOODARD, Levi 12
WRIGHT
  Cedro 270
  Earnest 30,274
  Ernest 270
  Irene 270,274
  James H 174
  Mary Emily 274
  Mrs Irene 30
WYMAN
  Belle 244,261
  Benj 290
  Benjamin 244,254
  Bertha 68,102,274,296
  Charley 244,259,291

Clifford 277,297
Dr...281
Dr F W 276
Esau 68,102
F W 298
Florine...............................280,298
Frank..................................268,296
Frank P.....................................281
Jacob 102,127,254,259,261,
268,274,277,280,281,289,290,291,
293,296,297
Leona 149,297
Lulu....................................244,289
Mary............ 140,228,254,259,261,
268,274,277,280,281,298
Peter 68,102
Reuben 102,261
Rosa 244,261
WY-YOU-WA-JUA 72
YOUNG
   Josephine................................159
   Josephine Deroin...............159,160
   Thomas 146
ZANE
   I P.. 4
   Irven P.. 3
   Irvin P 3,4
   Jennie M..................................... 4
   Mary S 3,4
   Maud B 4

www.ingramcontent.com/pod-product-compliance
Lightning Source LLC
Chambersburg PA
CBHW020242030426
42336CB00010B/580